D1672486

RADICAL INTERACTIONISM AND CRITIQUES OF CONTEMPORARY CULTURE

STUDIES IN SYMBOLIC INTERACTION

Series Editor: Norman K. Denzin

Recent Volumes:

STUDIES IN SYMBOLIC INTERACTION, VOLUME 52

RADICAL INTERACTIONISM AND CRITIQUES OF CONTEMPORARY CULTURE

EDITED BY

NORMAN K. DENZIN

University of Illinois at Urbana Champaign, United States

MANAGING EDITORS

JAMES SALVO

University of Illinois at Urbana Champaign, United States

SHING-LING SARINA CHEN

University of Northern Iowa, United States

United Kingdom – North America – Japan
India – Malaysia – China

Howard House, Wagon Lane, Bingley BD16 1WA, UK

First edition 2021

Copyright © 2021 Emerald Publishing Limited

Reprints and permissions service
Contact: permissions@emeraldinsight.com

No part of this book may be reproduced, stored in a retrieval system, transmitted in any form or by any means electronic, mechanical, photocopying, recording or otherwise without either the prior written permission of the publisher or a licence permitting restricted copying issued in the UK by The Copyright Licensing Agency and in the USA by The Copyright Clearance Center. Any opinions expressed in the chapters are those of the authors. Whilst Emerald makes every effort to ensure the quality and accuracy of its content, Emerald makes no representation implied or otherwise, as to the chapters' suitability and application and disclaims any warranties, express or implied, to their use.

British Library Cataloguing in Publication Data
A catalogue record for this book is available from the British Library

ISBN: 978-1-83982-029-8 (Print)
ISBN: 978-1-83982-028-1 (Online)
ISBN: 978-1-83982-030-4 (Epub)

ISSN: 0163-2396 (Series)

Printed and bound by CPI Group (UK) Ltd, Croydon, CR0 4YY

ISOQAR certified
Management System,
awarded to Emerald
for adherence to
Environmental
standard
ISO 14001:2004.

Certificate Number 1985
ISO 14001

INVESTOR IN PEOPLE

CONTENTS

ABOUT THE CONTRIBUTORS

Norman Conti is a Professor of Sociology at Duquesne University of the Holy Spirit and a founding member of the Elsinore Bennu Think Tank for Restorative Justice. He has published widely on police socialization and coauthored research on destigmatization and humility among activists.

Christopher Ferree: Whether as a salesman in mass-market fashion or luxury retail, or as a Coordinator of Visitor Experience at the Metropolitan Museum of Art in New York, impeccability, graciousness, and thoughtfulness have been the guiding principles of Ferree's career.

Stacey Hannem is Associate Professor and Chair of the Department of Criminology at Wilfrid Laurier University in Brantford (Ontario), Canada, and past Vice-President (2019) of the Society for the Study of Symbolic Interaction. Her research considers how marginalized people experience the effects of legal and regulatory structures in their everyday lives.

Michael A. Katovich is a Professor of Sociology and Chair of the Department of Sociology and Anthropology at Texas Christian University. He received his PhD from the University of Iowa, where he studied symbolic interactionism and social processes under the tutelage of Carl Couch. His research and teaching emphasizes symbolic interactionist approach advocated by Couch.

Krzysztof T. Konecki is a Professor of Sociology and works at the Institute of Sociology, Faculty of Economics and Sociology, University of Lodz. He is the editor-in-chief of Qualitative Sociology Review and holds the position of President of Polish Sociological Association and is the member of the Committee of Sociology of the Polish Academy of Science.

Joseph A. Kotarba is Professor of Sociology and Director of the Music Across the Life Course Project at Texas State University. He also serves as Medical Sociologist at the Institute for Translational Sciences at the University of Texas Medical Branch, Galveston. He is currently writing on interactionist features of team science; music experiences among senior citizens; and the persistence of existential ideas in contemporary intellectual life.

Erick Laming is a PhD candidate in criminology at the University of Toronto. He is a member of the Shabot Obaadjiwan First Nation and his research largely focuses on police use of force, police oversight and accountability, and Indigenous community members' perceptions of and experiences with the criminal justice system.

Veronica Manlow is a Sociologist Teacher in the Department of Management in Brooklyn College's Koppelman School of Business. Recent research focuses on those who work within the luxury fashion sector in various roles, specifically as salespersons and as designers and artisans who work for global brands and smaller independent firms.

Marco Marzano is Professor of Sociology at the University of Bergamo, Italy. His research focuses on Catholicism, cancer, illness narratives, and organization theory. He is also interested in ethical issues and autoethnography.

Gil Richard Musolf is Professor Emeritus from the Department of Sociology, Anthropology, and Social Work at Central Michigan University. He has published on symbolic interactionism in a variety of journals, including: *The Sociological Quarterly*, *Symbolic Interaction*, *Studies in Symbolic Interaction*, *Michigan Sociological Review*, *Sociological Focus*, and *Journal of Contemporary Ethnography*.

Robert Perinbanayagam is a Professor Emeritus of Sociology at Hunter College of the City University of New York. He is the author of *Signifying Acts*, *Discursive Acts*, *The Rhetoric of Emotions*, and *Rhetoric of Signs*. He has won the Charles Horton Cooley Award and the G.H. Mead Award from the Society for the Study of Symbolic Interaction.

Alina Pop is a Senior Lecturer of Communication Psychology at the Dimitrie Cantemir Christian University in Bucharest, Romania. Her main research interests focuses on social representations in conflict situation, environmental risks, sense of place, and autobiographical memory.

John C. Pruit is Assistant Professor of Sociology at Stephen F. Austin State University. His current research program analyzes people's talk and interaction in education contexts. His book, *Between Teaching and Caring in the Preschool*, considers preschool teachers' identity work in relation to early childhood education.

Amanda G. Pruit is a Doctoral Student at Adams State University. Her current research focuses on graduate student experiences and academic environments. Her work has appeared in the *Journal of Human Services: Training, Research, and Practice*.

Carol Rambo is Professor of Sociology at the University of Memphis in Memphis, TN. She edited *Symbolic Interaction* from 2007 to 2011. She has researched Mentally Disabled Parenting, Childhood Sexual Abuse, and the craft of writing Autoethnography. She has published work in *Deviant Behavior*, *Journal of Contemporary Ethnography*, and *Qualitative Inquiry*.

Laura Rosenberg has a PhD in Social Sciences (Universidad de Buenos Aires, Argentina), is a Researcher at the National Scientific and Technical Research

Council in Argentina and Assistant Professor at the National University of Avellaneda. Her main research interests focuses on Journalism, Media and Culture.

Christopher J. Schneider is Professor of Sociology at Brandon University. Schneider's research and publications have focused largely on information technologies and related changes to police work. He has written or collaborated on five books and has published dozens of scholarly articles, chapters, and essays. Schneider previously held the Endowed Chair of Criminology and Criminal Justice at St. Thomas University.

Norbert Wiley is Professor Emeritus of Sociology at University of Illinois Urbana-Champaign, Illinois, and was Visiting Scholar at the University of California, Berkeley. He is a prize-winning sociologist who has published on both the history and systematics of theory.

LIST OF CONTRIBUTORS

Norman Conti	Professor of Sociology, Duquesne University of the Holy Spirit
Christopher Ferree	Coordinator, Member and Visitor Services at The Metropolitan Museum of Art, New York, New York
Stacey Hannem	Associate Professor and Chair of the Department of Criminology, Wilfrid Laurier University, Brantford (Ontario), Canada
Michael A. Katovich	Professor of Sociology and Chair of the Department of Sociology and Anthropology, Texas Christian University
Krzysztof T. Konecki	Professor of Sociology, Institute of Sociology, Faculty of Economics and Sociology, University of Lodz
Joseph A. Kotarba	Professor of Sociology and Director of the Music Across the Life Course Project, Texas State University
Erick Laming	PhD Candidate in Criminology, University of Toronto
Veronica Manlow	Sociologist Teacher, Department of Management, Brooklyn College's Koppelman School of Business
Marco Marzano	Professor of Sociology, University of Bergamo, Italy
Gil Richard Musolf	Professor Emeritus, Department of Sociology, Anthropology, and Social Work, Central Michigan University
Robert Perinbanayagam	Professor Emeritus of Sociology, Hunter College of the City University of New York
Alina Pop	Senior Lecturer of Communication Psychology, Dimitrie Cantemir Christian University, Bucharest, Romania
John C. Pruit	Assistant Professor of Sociology, Stephen F. Austin State University

Amanda G. Pruit	Graduate student, Adams State University
Carol Rambo	Professor of Sociology, University of Memphis, Memphis, TN
Laura Rosenberg	Sociologist, Universidad de Buenos Aires, Buenos Aires, Argentina
Christopher J. Schneider	Professor of Sociology, Brandon University
Norbert Wiley	Professor Emeritus of Sociology, University of Illinois Urbana-Champaign, Illinois

POLICE BODY-WORN CAMERAS AND AXON ENTERPRISE'S CLAIMS IN MEDIA

Erick Laming and Christopher J. Schneider

ABSTRACT

Body-worn cameras (BWCs) are quickly becoming standardized police equipment. Axon Enterprise, a United States company based in Scottsdale, Arizona, is currently the worldwide purveyor of BWCs having near-complete control over the police body camera market. In 2012, the company launched their Axon Flex body camera alongside claims about the efficacy of these devices. While the research is expanding, scholarship has yet to explore the role that stakeholders like Axon may play in the implementation of body cameras across police services. This empirical chapter examines claims made by Axon in media in relation to the efficacy of their body cameras over a six-year period (2012–2018). Three themes relative to our analysis of Axon claims emerged: officer and community safety; cost and officer efficiency; *and* accountability and transparency. *A basic finding that cut across all three themes is that most of Axon's claims appear to be shaped by beliefs and assumptions. We also found that Axon's claims were mostly predicated on the market (i.e., financial considerations), rather than say scientifically or legally grounded. Some suggestions for future research are noted.*

Keywords: Police body-worn cameras; Axon; media; TASER; accountability; transparency

INTRODUCTION

First piloted in the United Kingdom in 2005, body-worn cameras (BWCs) have spread across police services worldwide. Police body cameras have received

Radical Interactionism and Critiques of Contemporary Culture
Studies in Symbolic Interaction, Volume 52, 1–18
Copyright © 2021 by Emerald Publishing Limited
All rights of reproduction in any form reserved
ISSN: 0163-2396/doi:10.1108/S0163-239620210000052001

considerably more coverage in news media and on social media platforms than in the research literature on the subject (Schneider, 2018a, 2018b). The cacophony of claims across the media landscape contribute to the ongoing debates over body cameras such as whether or not BWCs should be adopted across police services. There are numerous stakeholders worldwide invested in the implementation of police BWCs, including law enforcement agencies, politicians, civil liberties associations, and industry groups, most notably, the United States–based technology and weapons company Axon Enterprise.

Headquartered in Scottsdale, Arizona, formerly known as TASER International, the publicly traded Axon Enterprise (Axon) is the worldwide purveyor of BWCs. In early May 2018, Axon purchased its main competitor company Vievu LLC. At the time of Axon's acquisition of Vievu (the latter of which retained its name but was subsequently rebranded as "now part of the Axon Network"), BWCs and related technology services (i.e., software) accounted for approximately 30 percent of Axon's revenue; however, Axon "expects the [BWC] business to surpass Taser in the next few years" (Brustein, 2018). Following the announcement of the aforementioned merger, Axon claimed to have 43 of 54 BWC contracts with major police departments across the United States.[1] "This dynamic could raise questions about whether a single company should control such a sensitive market" (Brustein, 2018).

There is no doubt that Axon dominates the BWC market, an observation made by many others (e.g., see Gelles, 2016; Stoughton, 2018).[2] The issue of Axon's near total control of the police body camera market is certainly an important one that we suspect will be the topic of much discussion and debate. In this chapter, we present another question that we think would help provide additional insight into some of the ways this single technology and weapon company controls the BWC market: What claims does Axon make relative to their body camera products in media? Addressing this question we think might help us better understand how such claims may contribute to the role that Axon's current market share dominance has over influencing law enforcement agencies' adoption and implementation of BWC technology.

Certainly, financial considerations and other conditions contributed to Axon's ascendance in the body camera market. We do not claim here to present the entire history of Axon; rather, we suggest that Axon's rise and market dominance can be empirically tracked and better understood through the collection and analysis of claims made by Axon representatives. Investigating Axon claims about their body cameras, on the one hand, provides some insights into the process of Axon gaining a dominant share over the BWC market and, on the other hand, helps to illustrate some of the ways in which the company seeks to retain its dominance over competitors.

As a publicly traded company motivated by maximizing its sales and profits for its shareholders, Axon has an obvious interest in promoting claims to persuade others, particularly law enforcement, about the value of their devices.[3] Practically no scholarship has focused attention solely on the issue of Axon claims relative to the hawking of their body camera products. In this chapter, we contribute to this gap in the research literature by examining public claims made about BWCs by Axon representatives in media.

In what follows, we begin with an overview of BWCs and review the relevant research literature. Our purpose is not to provide an exhaustive review of the literature since this has been done elsewhere (e.g., Ariel et al., 2017, pp. 4–5). Instead, we review a few more recent and selected key studies that provide evidence for the efficacy of body cameras, the findings which are pertinent to our investigation of Axon claims. We then detail our methodology, before turning to our analysis and conclusion.

POLICE BWCS

It is estimated that at least one third of all police services in the United States have adopted BWCs (Sousa et al., 2016) and, further, that organizational characteristics of police in the United States can predict the adoption of BWCs (Koen, Willis and Mastrofski, 2018; Nowacki and Willits, 2018). The widespread adoption of BWCs is also evident in other countries such as the United Kingdom, and to a lesser extent in Australia and Canada (e.g., see Laming, 2019). Body cameras are expected to produce several benefits for the police and the public. For example, empirical research suggests that the use of BWCs reduces police use of force (Ariel et al., 2015), decreases citizen complaints against police (Ariel et al., 2017), and improves evidentiary collection and efficiency (Owens et al., 2014). Some researchers suggest that BWCs can improve police accountability and transparency (Henstock and Ariel, 2017). Scholarship has also explored the perceptions of command staff views of BWCs and how this may impact the use of force by officers wearing cameras (Smylka et al., 2016). One area that has received practically no attention in the research literature is the role that various stakeholders have in the adoption of body cameras. An analysis of claims made by Axon relative to their body cameras helps provide some needed insight into the role that the company might play in terms of the implementation of police body cameras, i.e., police decisions to adopt cameras based on Axon claims.

Axon has increased its dominance in the weapons and technology market and in doing so has created subsidiary companies in several countries to help expand its reach (e.g., Axon Public Safety Canada, Axon Public Safety UK, and Axon Public Safety Australia). Previously, Axon was exclusively an electroshock weapons company that supplied stun guns to thousands of law enforcement agencies around the globe. The company then rebranded to Axon in 2017. Axon has since added BWCs and related technologies to its product offerings that collectively fall under the umbrella of "digital evidence management systems" (DEMS). The rise of DEMS is directly attributed to the expansion of BWCs, the latter of which creates digital evidence (e.g., video) that must be securely handled and stored. For instance, Axon operates its Evidence.com – a secure cloud platform for law enforcement to manage digital evidence captured by police body cameras. According to Winston (2015), Axon's:

cloud-based evidence strategy is central to the company's plan for profitability. The company is focusing on increasing annual Evidence.com subscriptions, which range from $15 to $109 per month, or up to $1,200 per year per camera – that's up to three times the $399 price tag of the hardware itself. For large departments, this carries a hefty price tag: The Los Angeles Police Department's purchase of cameras for its patrol officers is expected to cost $7 million a year.

Research on BWCs has expanded in recent years, and the literature continues to grow as more police agencies choose to test and adopt the technology. Despite the growth in scholarship, most studies have been nonexperimental, which restricts public knowledge regarding the effectiveness of BWC technology (Ariel, 2016; Cubitt et al., 2017; White, 2014). Nevertheless, police use of force and citizen complaints against the police are the most frequent outcome measures examined in experimental research involving BWCs. The research that has tested the effects of police BWCs on these two issues has been mixed; however, of these research studies, the results of the Rialto experiment has received the most attention (Schneider, 2018a).

The so-called landmark "Rialto study" is one of the most influential BWC studies conducted thus far and has set a standard for subsequent replication experiments (Ariel at el., 2016). The study was conducted in Rialto, California, between 2012 and 2013 with all frontline officers ($n = 54$). The research team employed a comparative design of shifts in which police officers wore cameras (treatment group) and shifts where officers did not (control group).[4] Over the course of the study, a total of 988 shifts were randomly assigned with 489 treatment and 499 control conditions. The findings demonstrated that police use of force was approximately 50% lower for the treatment group ($n = 8$) when compared to control conditions ($n = 17$) and that complaints against officers dropped by 88% compared with the 12 months prior to the experiment (Ariel et al., 2015). The study design was replicated in the United Kingdom with the Birmingham South Local Policing Unit in the West Midlands Police force jurisdiction for six months in 2014 (Henstock and Ariel, 2017). A total of 430 shifts were randomly assigned with 215 treatment and 215 control conditions. The primary outcome measure was the cameras' effect on use of force. These results suggest that the treatment group exhibited a 35% reduction in use of force compared to control conditions (Henstock and Ariel, 2017).

Another experimental BWC study was conducted with the Orlando Police Department in Florida between 2014 and 2015 (Jennings et al., 2015). The researchers randomly assigned 46 officers to wear cameras (treatment group) and 43 were not assigned cameras (control group). Researchers tested the effect of body cameras against response to resistance (R2R; use of force) and serious external complaints (e.g., unnecessary or excessive use of force and/or harassment by police). The findings of this study showed that officers wearing cameras had a significantly lower prevalence of R2R incidents compared to the control group, and camera-wearing officers accumulated a significantly lesser number of serious complaints compared with the officers who did not wear the cameras (Jennings et al., 2015). Similarly, Jennings et al. (2017) conducted a similar study in Florida of the Tampa Bay Police Department and found that use of force decreased by more than 8% in the 12 months after body cameras were deployed when compared to the predeployment period.

Elsewhere the Spokane (Washington) Police Department participated in an experimental BWC study between 2015 and 2016. In this study, 149 officers were given body cameras in two phases during which the first group of officers ($n = 82$; treatment group) began using cameras six months before the second group ($n = 67$; control group). This study measured the effectiveness of cameras on use of force and complaints against the officers. The results suggest that both citizen complaints and use of force incidents decreased for both treatment and control groups after they started wearing body cameras compared to predeployment (White et al., 2017). However, use of force incidents and citizen complaints increased for the treatment group during the postrandom control trial period. White et al. (2017) explain that officers may at first be willing to adjust their behavior because of the novelty of the new technology but return to "normal" behavior after the novelty wears off (White et al., 2017).

In another study involving the Las Vegas Police Department, Braga et al. (2018) found that officers equipped with BWCs had fewer complaints and use of force reports compared to officers not wearing cameras. Officers wearing cameras conducted more arrests and issued more citations relative to officers without cameras (Braga et al., 2018). In the largest randomized controlled trial of BWCs to date, Yokum et al. (2017) found very small effects across all measured outcomes, including the use of force and complaints in their study with the Metropolitan Police Department (Washington, D.C.). Notably, the outcome measures failed to reach statistical significance, meaning there were no detectable or otherwise, meaningful effects on use of force or complaints. Similarly, Ariel et al. (2016) conducted a meta-analysis of ten BWC experiments with use of force as an outcome measure and found that the cameras had no effect on police use of force and that the use of cameras led to an increased rate of assaults against officers.

Most experimental research that has examined body cameras' effect on complaints against police show significant reductions (Ariel, 2016; Ariel et al., 2017; Braga et al., 2018; Katz et al., 2014; Mesa Police Department, 2013; Owens and Finn, 2018). Research also suggests that BWCs can civilize behavior between the police and public (Ariel et al., 2015; ODS Consulting, 2011) and improve evidence collection (Katz et al., 2014). The technology has also served useful for court purposes. Owens et al. (2014), for instance, found that officers wearing cameras had a higher proportion of intimate partner violence cases that resulted in a criminal charge and conviction compared to officers not wearing cameras. Similarly, results from other studies show that BWC videos resolve significantly more cases through guilty pleas rather than criminal trials and can increase officer efficiency (Goodall, 2007; ODS Consulting, 2011; Ready and Young, 2015).

Lastly, it is worth highlighting that the majority of research on BWCs has been conducted in the United States and the U.K. Therefore, most of our knowledge of the technology is limited to jurisdictions in these two countries. Nevertheless, some police departments around the world have completed pilot projects and are slowly rolling out BWCs. Some law enforcement agencies in countries like Canada and Australia have been testing the efficacy of BWCs for years but have been slow to adopt the technology. Despite the relatively mixed and diverse research results on police use of body cameras, what has remained constant, lurking in the background across these experiments, is the presence of Axon's cameras and technology (e.g., Axon supplied their body cameras for most of the aforementioned research studies) and the obvious financial interest that Axon has in the police adoption of their technology devices. Thus, as BWC experiments continue to expand, our research question then regarding claims made by Axon relative to their body camera products, we assert, remains paramount, for garnering insight into Axon's market dominance and illuminating the company's role in influencing the adoption and implementation of body camera technology across law enforcement agencies.

METHODOLOGY

The research topic and question informed the selection of a suitable method. Given our stated interest in claims made by Axon in media, we selected *Qualitative Media Analysis* (QMA; Altheide and Schneider, 2013). QMA is an approach that places emphasis on documenting the process through which discourse is presented to audiences. A review of the research literature indicates that scholarship has not *directly* investigated Axon claims about its body cameras and related technologies in either news reports or on social media platforms. This observation indicates there exists a concerning gap in the research literature regarding understanding the role a private enterprise corporation like Axon plays in the promotion of their body cameras and related services (e.g., software). This void in the literature attracted our attention and directed our focus upon content analysis of select news media articles featuring Axon product claims.

QMA, or ethnographic content analysis, is a specific type of content analysis that differs from conventional types of content analysis as a method in that QMA focuses on a reflexive awareness of the process, meanings, and emphases to allow for concepts to emerge throughout the entire research process. The method involves 12 steps (for a longer discussion of these steps, see Altheide and Schneider 2013, pp. 39–73). The first three steps concern the topic of investigation (i.e., BWCs). The researcher first identifies the topic (step 1), reviews the literature (step 2), and then becomes familiar with some relevant documents (e.g., news reports) (step 3). Steps 4–6 involve creating a data collection instrument or research protocol. Relevant variables or categories that emerge from the previous three steps are listed (step 4), these variables are then tested against the data (step 5), and the protocol is revised if needed (step 6). After the protocol is developed, a sampling strategy is employed (step 7). The data are then collected using preset codes (step 8) followed by analyses of these data (step 9). The categorization of differences discovered during data analysis are then identified and included in written summaries (step 10) along with some typical examples (step 11). The materials should then be compared and contrasted with differences in the data and finally integrated together into a draft that will become the final manuscript (step 12).

We directed our focus upon Axon claims as presented in two media formats (steps 1–3): news media documents (mass media) as our primary data source and Twitter (social media) as our secondary data source. These formats were selected for the following reasons. First, regarding mass media, research demonstrates that the major news media continue to retain their legitimizing function, especially for law enforcement.[5] Major news media are basic aspects of popular culture, and the logic of these media or "the process through which media present and transmit information" (Altheide and Snow, 1979, p. 10) is strategically used by companies such as Axon in order to bring more widespread awareness and legitimacy to its claims about its products. For example, Axon has regularly published press releases since 2009. A principal aim of a company press release *is to direct announcements to news media*. When journalists publish stories citing press releases, the news media facilitate, whether inadvertently or not, the legitimacy of companies such as Axon, which has published 374 press releases since 2009 (found here: http://investor.axon.com/press-releases). Given the role of news media in both disseminating and legitimizing Axon's claims about BWCs, it is vital that we consider mass media news documents where we can empirically observe and track how points of view and claims may change subtly over time and across reports.

Second, regarding our secondary data source, and following news media, social media platforms increasingly serve as significant sources of supplementary legitimation. This is especially the case with Twitter as the majority of topics are news based (Kwak et al., 2010) with the platform serving as a curated news feed for many of its users (Wang, 2018). Twitter now predicts "relevant topics and send[s] breaking-news notification *based on a person's interests*" (Wang, 2018, *our emphasis*). Research indicates that Twitter is among the most used social media platforms by police agencies (Schneider, 2016). Therefore, considering police use of Twitter, news stories featuring Axon's press releases (relevant to police), Twitter's breaking news notifications that would be sent to police, and also Axon's direct engagement with police groups to help promote its claims about its products, we surmised that Twitter would provide us with additional and relevant secondary source data. We first utilized the LexisNexis database to collect our news media data (articles), which served as our *primary documents*, or those documents that comprise of the objects of study (Altheide and Schneider, 2013).

As we developed and revised our protocol instrument (steps 4–6), we searched the LexisNexis database with the terms "taser" and "axon" and "camera." We included "taser" as a search term because the company did not change its name to Axon until April 2017. We conducted searches from January 1, 2012, to August 1, 2018.[6] Therefore, it was important that we included "taser" to capture all news articles relating to body cameras prior to 2017.[7] The search parameters returned 376 "hits" across international and local news media outlets primarily in the United States but also in other countries like Canada, Australia, and the U.K. Our initial review of these data revealed that 143 news articles were either duplicates, business briefs of Axon stock, or unrelated to Axon body cameras (e.g., articles that only discussed Tasers). Our focus per our research question was with select news media reports – those articles with a thematic emphasis on Axon body camera technology and related claims (step 8). Themes are connected to stories told by journalists who must "get specific information from sources that can be tied to" the reporting of the narrative itself about BWCs (Altheide and Schneider, 2013, p. 52). For this reason, we excluded the aforementioned 143 articles that did not meet these thematic criteria, resulting in 233 reports for analysis (step 9).

The collection of Twitter data followed a careful reading of our news media data. These Twitter data serve as our *secondary documents* or those records about primary documents that "are at least one step removed from the initial data sourced by a researcher" (Altheide and Schneider, 2013, p. 7). Our data sampling strategy (step 7) of both news reports and Twitter data involved "progressive theoretical sampling," or "the selection of materials based on emerging understanding of the topic under investigation. The idea is to select materials for conceptual or theoretically relevant reasons" (Altheide and Schneider, 2013, p. 56). Lastly, numerous discussions with Axon employees in the form of in-person meetings, phone conversations, and email and Twitter exchanges with the first listed author further informed our approach and data sampling strategy.

Our primary sample of 233 news media documents were downloaded from LexisNexis and converted into a portable document format consisting of an 879-page data set for careful reading, review, and further analysis. We identified 42 news articles that featured quotes coded as claims by Axon employees about its body camera technology (step 10). Analyses of these news media data produced three basic themes (steps 11 and 12) that we explore below: *officer and community safety*; *cost and officer efficiency*; and *accountability and transparency*. The emergence of these themes from our analysis of the primary data set informed our searches of Twitter.

At the time of our secondary data collection, Twitter only allowed public access to the most recent 3,200 tweets of user profiles. A "tweet" is a user-generated posting of 280 characters or less and can include any combination of text, photos, videos, or links to websites. Tweets can also be "retweeted" or shared with others. We gathered the most recent 3,200 tweets made to Axon's United States and Canada Twitter profiles, @Axon_US and @Axon_Canada, respectively. Through the platform users can engage or tweet at (i.e., send public messages) using the @ symbol, which serves "as a marker of addressivity (i.e., to direct a tweet to a specific user)" (Honeycutt and Herring, 2009, p. 1). Hashtags (#) can also be used to categorize tweets, so topics can easily be followed by users on the platform. We retrieved our Twitter data using allmytweets.net.

Axon Canada was very active in "retweeting" law enforcement personnel tweets that limited our data to the most recent 3,200 tweets on @Axon_Canada between July 2017 and September 2018. Whereas we were able to retrieve data from the U.S. Axon account from October 2015 to September 2018. U.S. Axon Twitter posted 1,003 tweets between October 24, 2015, and September 21, 2018, and the Canadian account posted 327 Tweets between July 9, 2017, and September 21, 2018. These tweets were downloaded from Twitter for additional reading, review, and analysis and are included below, where relevant as secondary data provided in support of our primary media data.

FINDINGS

Axon's claims identified across our data are categorized into the three themes that follow. It is important to stress that *some of Axon's claims, especially those concerning efficacy, were made prior to the publication of any empirical research on BWCs.* This important observation, and one that was consistent across the data, illustrates that Axon marketed its BWCs in absence of empirical evidence regarding efficacy, which helps set the tone for much of Axon's subsequent claims that we detail below. In line with the principles of our methodological approach, we incorporated data gathered from Twitter only when these data were theoretically and thematically relevant in support of our identified news media themes. Our findings reveal among other things how Axon made and circulated claims in news media reports and later reinforced many of these claims using Twitter. We now turn to the first of our three themes, *officer and community safety.*

Officer and Community Safety

Axon claims that emerged in 2012 were largely in relation to how BWCs could protect police officers from false accusations of misconduct. As an illustrative example, Axon's Chief Executive Officer (CEO) and cofounder Rick Smith told the *Philadelphia Daily News,* "To have your own recording is the best weapon against allegations against you" (Farr, 2012). Smith's assertion speaks directly to concerns of *individual* officers and not the policing institution as a whole. The explicit suggestion here is that people cannot be trusted, a tension that is consistent across the research literature on police occupational culture (e.g., see Manning, 1978, p. 195). An implicit assumption in CEO Rick Smith's above statement speaks to those growing concerns of police control over their public perception through media. Specifically, those recent changes to this process ushered in by the advent of social media platforms where user-generated viral videos of police can quickly spread unfavorable views of police (Schneider, 2016). Here Axon provides a technological solution to offset such concerns, as Smith noted elsewhere in a *New York Times* report: "One big reason to have these [BWCs] is defensive" (Hardy, 2012).

Our analysis of the data revealed that Axon did not make any other claim related to officer safety until three years later. In 2015, Axon claims shifted from their products protecting the individual officer (from false accusations) to community safety concerns. These concerns were largely related to protecting the community from police use of force in that Axon provides a lesser force option. For instance, consider the idea that if citizens understand that they are being recorded in their encounters with police, they are more likely to act in accordance with the interests of police, thus reducing police use of force. To help illustrate the point, consider a representative example from an *Investor's Daily Business,* a newspaper that covers finance and economic matters, and not usually police or crime issues. The report, like numerous others in our data set, featured current and former police officers as cited experts, buttressed by Axon employees who spoke on the "life-saving technology" that Axon develops for law enforcement.

A retired police chief formerly with Fort Worth Police in Texas (and paid Axon consultant), Jeff Halstead commented that

> They [Axon] are in existence to make our jobs safer and save lives. When someone like Rick [Smith, CEO of Axon] in the private sector shows that visionary service for us, we're very grateful. (Fox, 2015)

Chief Halstead's statement is then supported by Smith who provided the following anecdote: "We've changed these officers' lives, and they consequently come up and hug me on a regular basis. And they've thanked me because I prevented them from killing someone" (Fox, 2015). In other words, Axon has kept the community safe from what we can probably surmise are actions of police use of deadly force. It is important to note that the above statements by Halstead and Smith were each made when the company was Taser and, therefore, very likely refer to its entire product line (i.e., Tasers, BWCs, digital evidence). Nevertheless, each of these statements helps to thematically illustrate the usefulness of Axon's technology in regard to community safety concerns.

The news outlet from which the above claims derived is representative of the business-oriented coverage that regularly featured stories and claims made by Axon over six years of media coverage between 2012 and 2018. Coverage in business media is significant in presenting Axon's claims as market based, rather than say scientifically or legally based, and thus suggests how business media may help influence Axon's claims in regard to community safety (i.e., to market its products to law enforcement who are in the business of managing public safety). To demonstrate the point, let us consider three thematic statements made by Axon executives in *Progressive Media,* a privately held International group of companies that span media, business information services, technology, and communications. "Our body cameras and Evidence.com platform are providing new and innovative ways to maximize officer safety," suggested Axon's CEO Rick Smith (*Progressive Media*, 2015). Chief Operating Officer Jeff Kukowski asserted in a different report, "Our AXON cameras coupled with the EVIDENCE.com platform are a game-changer for law enforcement as they increase transparency, save taxpayer dollars and ultimately help make communities safer" (*Progressive Media*, 2014b). Further touting community safety issues, former Axon executive Vice President Marcus Womack claimed "We're thrilled to see that our Axon body-worn video cameras have a positive effect on police agencies and are ultimately making communities safer" (*Progressive Media*, 2014a). None of these Axon claims were supported with empirical evidence, and at the time of this writing, little research has examined the link between BWC use and officer and/or public safety. Further, it might be noted that contrary to the aforementioned claims, one study by Ariel et al. (2016) even found that officers wearing BWCs faced more assaults from the public.

Perhaps not surprisingly, as Axon's business model shifted to focus increasingly on BWCs in 2017, the frequency and duration of Axon claims relative to body cameras in news reports increased. For instance, in April 2017, Axon announced that they would provide free body cameras and related software services to all frontline police in the United States for one year, and in July 2017, this same offer was extended to officers across Canada. Following Axon's unprecedented offer to outfit all frontline police across North America with free body cameras, CEO Rick Smith asserted

> We are going 'all in' to empower police officers to more safely and effectively do their jobs and drive important social change by making body cameras available to every officer in America (Rayman, 2017)

Smith claimed elsewhere, "We believe these cameras are more than just tools to protect communities and the officers who serve them" (The Record, 2017). Smith provided no evidence in support of either of his statements; rather, the efficacy of his safety claims appears to be shaped by his personal beliefs and assumptions. Similar claims sans evidence and drawing on assumptions also appeared regularly on Twitter.

As one thematic example, consider an August 17, 2018 tweet made on Axon's U.S. account:

> Leveraging technology is more than just adapting a few new devices & putting a couple more gadgets on the belt. It's a global shift. It's a cultural shift. It's a huge undertaking...but it's making your department smarter and safer.

Such assertions pertaining to safety – let alone any global or cultural shifts – are quite difficult to make with empirical certainty. Nevertheless, when Axon did provide support of its unverified safety claims, it did so by tweeting indirect and unsubstantiated statements attributed to police departments and officers, what might otherwise be characterized as hearsay. Consider the following two representative examples.

> We [Axon Canada] are extremely proud to partner with @CalgaryPolice on their Body Worn Camera Proof of Concept. We could not agree more that this program will help "to create a safe, transparent, accountable and innovative policing environment for the City of Calgary". (July 18, 2018)

In another example directed at both a department and individual officer, Axon tweeted: "Proud 2 partner w @CityFredPolice on their #DigitalEvidenceManagement System. 100% agree w @Deputy_Gaudet 'We believe that by being equipped with cutting-edge technology, we can better serve and protect our community'" (July 16, 2018).

Cost Saving and Officer Efficiency

Axon made numerous claims across our data set concerning body cameras as cost saving devices. For example, Axon BWCs would reduce cost for police departments in relation to the more than $2 billion annually that is reportedly spent by law enforcement "paying off complaints about brutality" (Hardy, 2012). Video evidence generated by Axon body cameras would presumably help defend and subsequently corroborate police statements against allegations of abuse. Such statements seem at the very least to suggest that "brutality" payments are largely frivolous in nature and video evidence would prove such. Further, Axon's cost savings claims preceded evidence showing a link between body camera use and cost reduction. Empirical and anecdotal evidence has since emerged in support of BWCs reducing complaints against officers (e.g., see Ariel et al., 2015; Ariel et al., 2017; Braga et al., 2018; White et al., 2017). Logically, a reduction in complaints made against police may translate into cost savings. However, just one published study has found that BWCs contribute to *significant* cost savings due to complaint reductions (Braga et al., 2017).

Nevertheless, before the publication of any of the aforementioned studies, Axon continued to promote numerous and unverified claims that BWCs reduce costs for law enforcement agencies and the communities they serve. As one example, in 2014, Axon asserted that BWCs would "save taxpayers dollars" (*Progressive Media*, 2014b). A few years earlier in 2012, Axon affirmed that BWCs coupled with its software would achieve cost savings for law enforcement agencies by removing the need to have information technology employees on the payroll (Hardy, 2012). CEO Rick Smith even guaranteed certain law enforcement agencies "complete predictability of the costs of their on-officer video and TASER program" (*Progressive Media*, 2014c). In spite of Smith's bold claim, there have been several cases where law enforcement agencies reported that costs *increased* after BWC adoption and that new positions were created for personnel to deal with various information requests and data management concerns. Consider, for instance, that the Palm Beach Gardens (Florida) Police Department (Peters, 2018) and Minneapolis Police Department (Jany, 2018) (both police services use Axon BWCs) had to hire additional employees to reduce the backlog of data management issues.

Analysis of Axon activity on Twitter was consistent with our findings related to cost saving claims made in news media reports. Consider the following tweet from the @Axon_Canada Twitter account: "Contact us to see how police services across Canada & around world are reducing costs & increasing disclosure speed & security" (May 6, 2018). Not only do such claims by Axon run counter to instances like those examples above where police have experienced increased costs due to BWC adoption, there is currently no empirical evidence in Canada that supports BWCs as a cost reduction strategy for police. Nevertheless, a great deal of Axon's cost reduction claims were presented under the pretense of officer efficiency. For instance, in reference to Axon's redaction software, spokesman Steve Tuttle asserted,

> When someone requests a video of an officer's entire shift, that creates an extreme burden on an agency. Police work is a lot of walking around. It's like war. You can go for a week and have a five-minute battle. We make it very simple. (Spivack, 2016)

Axon has also claimed numerous times that the use of their BWCs will eventually make writing reports obsolete for officers.

Let us consider two thematic statements each made in 2017 by CEO Rick Smith where he claims that BWCs will end up "reducing the need for endless paperwork" (The Record, 2017), and "Police officers are now video creators, and that could eventually replace traditional written reports" (Shiffer, 2017). Presently, there is no indication that law enforcement will discontinue report writing and likely we can surmise that body camera footage will complement written reports. Nevertheless, Axon statements in support of such efficiency claims on Twitter are abound, as one example:

> Thank-you to all the attendees from across Canada at our Axon Demo Day in #Vancouver today. We hope we have been able to showcase how our solutions can help save time and improve efficiency. (February 28, 2018)

Accountability and Transparency

Police body cameras are expected to enhance both accountability and transparency (Henstock and Ariel, 2017). These are among the two oft-cited claims of BWC technology in the research literature (Ariel et al., 2017; White, 2014; White et al., 2017). Axon also regularly heralded these claims. For instance, in a 2012 *Salt Lake Tribune* article, CEO Rick Smith asserted that BWC technology "holds everybody accountable" (Stecklein, 2012). Axon representatives have also claimed that their BWCs are an asset for law enforcement "as they increase transparency" (*Progressive Media*, 2014b) and that the technology "assists police in capturing, managing, and sharing their digital facts without the complexity as well offering greater transparency" (*Progressive Media*, 2014a). In relation to accountability and transparency claims, analysis of these data revealed that most of Axon's claims in this regard were directed at specifically named (identified) police agencies.

As one illustrative example, Smith identified the Louisiana State Police (LPD) specifically by name and the LPD's decision to adopt BWCs by stating: "Fully deploying HD body cameras, let alone taking the innovative step of purchasing two per officer, is undoubtedly a bold move in the direction of improved accountability," further continuing that the LPD's BWC adoption

> ...virtually ensures that important interactions don't go unrecorded, and you're looking at an agency whose technology can help them go above and beyond. We commend them on being the first major, statewide agency to take these steps. (Plus Media Solutions, 2016)

As evidenced across the research literature on police body cameras, accountability and transparency are identified as two critical areas of concern with respect to implementation. We might surmise that Axon would identify individual departments who have adopted their cameras in order to draw the attention of law enforcement agencies considering BWCs but opting for a "wait-and-see" approach in relation to what police services testing the devices on a trial period decide regarding their own BWC adoption (e.g., see Bellano, 2017; Wakefield, 2017 as a few examples). It is perhaps understandable then that Axon would link accountability and transparency issues with individual departments given that law enforcement have been under public scrutiny to be more accountable and transparent in their actions with the public and that BWCs are sometimes lauded as a panacea, a perspective supported by Axon claims. When viewed strategically, Axon's accountability and transparency claims then might attract police departments to adopt its products while appeasing the public.

CONCLUSION

A key finding of this empirically driven chapter is how many of Axon's very own and often frivolous claims is somewhat consistent with the research literature that suggests that the current debates over body cameras are informed by "beliefs and assumptions rather than empirical evidence" (Mateescu et al., 2016, p. 122). Our finding is especially salient given the dubious interest Axon has in promoting its claims in hopes that police agencies will continue to adopt their body cameras and related services. This chapter also reveals how many of Axon's claims occurred in the absence of evidence. While many of Axon's claims continue to remain suspect, some of their early claims (especially those related to reduced use of force) would be later supported ex post facto in the research literature as noted herein. Frivolous or not, it is likely that Axon's claims about its body cameras will remain influential in the ongoing debates over the implementation of these devices. Let us now briefly return to the question we posted at the outset of this chapter: What claims does Axon make relative to their body camera products in media?

Our data demonstrate that Axon made numerous claims about its products including some that heavily favored pro-police sentiments such as literally weaponizing video evidence as a combative measure against public accusations of misconduct. Our analysis illustrates that Axon mostly, although not entirely, made unverified statements absent any empirical evidence in support of their claims in news media reports and on Twitter. Axon claims that begin with "we believe" as evidenced in this chapter are certainly indicative of this finding. When support of claims was provided by Axon, it most usually occurred in the form of statements made by either paid consultants who are (or were) law enforcement officers or by reaffirming unconfirmed statements made by police not working as Axon representatives, which was more typical on Twitter. Some of Axon's own claims about the efficacy of their body cameras were made far in advance of the publication of any reviewed studies that could confirm or refute Axon claims. Even in more recent circumstances where body cameras have been the subject of academic evaluation, Axon has solicited and publicized the endorsements of scholars prior to peer review and publication of research results. For example, on May 8 2019, Axon Canada shared a link to a short promotional "case study video" on Twitter highlighting "preliminary research" findings about the impact of body cameras on public perceptions. In the video, the findings were described by the researcher, Lakehead University Assistant Professor Alana Saulnier, alongside Vishal Dhir, the Managing Director of Axon Canada, giving the weight of academic evidence to Axon marketing claims. In other circumstances, as outlined earlier in this chapter, Axon made claims contrary to evidence, which lends support to our finding that some of Axon's statements were based on company beliefs rather than evidence.

Another point for additional consideration only touched on briefly herein is how endorsements about body cameras from police help support Axon's claims in business-related media as a strategy for raising interest among investors. Police and academic endorsements provide much needed legitimacy to Axon's products and suggest their products are successful, attracting would-be investors to purchase shares in the company, which subsequently raises the share price. What Axon claims police say about the success of their products helps Axon attract investors and also expand into new markets. A point illustrated by Hoium (2018) in "Why Axon Enterprise's Growth Is Just the Beginning,"

> Axon Enterprise Inc.'s revenue has nearly tripled over the past five years as body camera and taser use has increased in law enforcement agencies around the world [...] *Axon could conceivably grow its customer base more than six times without any new products* just by expanding into new markets and getting more penetration in existing markets (*emphasis added*).

This chapter contributes to the limited amount of research on Axon efficacy claims in relation to their body cameras, provides some empirical insight into Axon claims over a six-year growth period of rapid deployment of police body cameras, contributes to the burgeoning body camera literature, and is the first study to conduct QMA on Axon claims in media. The goal of this methodology is not to generalize findings but rather to gain understanding by studying documents (i.e., news reports and social media posts) as representations of social meanings and institutional relations. Future research could incorporate additional sampling procedures such as random sampling to accommodate those scholars interested in generalization or use Twitter as a primary data source (web scraping and mining tools could help with this process).

Axon will likely continue making claims about its products and at the very least will engage in efforts to retain its dominance in the body camera market. Independent academic studies that are not funded or connected to Axon are necessary to continue to learn more about Axon's role in the body camera market including the promotion of other Axon products such as drones. Future studies could also examine Axon press releases, the claims that are made in these documents, and which of these press releases and claims gain attention in news media or on social media. Lastly, our research was limited to North America. Future studies might examine Axon claims in other countries and markets and on other social media platforms. We feel that understanding these developments in relation to the expansion of body cameras among law enforcement remains crucial. We look forward to such endeavors.

NOTES

1. There are 69 major police departments in the United States, but not all have adopted BWCs.

2. Axon's dominance is often discussed in news media articles and usually is only noted in passing reference in the academic research literature. These two citations serve as thematic examples of this dichotomy.

3. Some evidence suggests that police agencies are aware of body camera maker's interests and the profits that companies will make from the adoption of body-worn camera devices by police (del Pozo, 2017).

4. Axon supplied body cameras for the Rialto study and has supplied cameras for nearly every single one of the replication studies that have followed.

5. For example, when police conduct is questioned or scrutinized by the public, law enforcement continues to issue press releases through traditional news media outlets rather

than utilizing their social media for direct communication of such matters with publics (e.g., see Schneider, 2015, 2016).

6. In 2010 and 2011, Axon (then Taser) published just two press releases each year. In 2012, the company began to publish press releases more frequently (at 37), and since 2013, Axon has published about 50 press releases each year. This observation informed the years of our search parameters in LexisNexis.

7. Note: Axon was the name of the camera model since its creation in 2012.

REFERENCES

Altheide, D. L. and Schneider, C. J. 2013. *Qualitative Media Analysis*, 2nd ed., Thousand Oaks, CA, SAGE Publications.

Altheide, D. L. and Snow, R. 1979. *Media Logic*, Thousand Oaks, CA, SAGE Publications.

Ariel, B. 2016. Increasing cooperation with the police using body worn cameras, *Police Quarterly*, 19(3), 326–362.

Ariel, B., Farrar, W. A. and Sutherland, A. 2015. The effect of police body-worn cameras on use of force and citizens' complaints against the police: a randomized controlled trial, *Journal of Quantitative Criminology*, 31(3), 509–535.

Ariel, B., Sutherland, A., Henstock, D., Young, J., Drover, P., Sykes, J., … Henderson, R. 2016. Wearing body cameras increases assaults against officers and does not reduce police use of force: results from a global multi-site experiment, *European Journal of Criminology*, 13(6), 744–755.

Ariel, B., Sutherland, A., Henstock, D., Young, J., Drover, P., Sykes, J., … Henderson, R. 2017. "Contagious accountability" A global multisite randomized controlled trial on the effect of police body-worn cameras on citizens' complaints against the police, *Criminal Justice and Behavior*, 44(2), 293–316.

Bellano, A. 2017, August 15. Princeton officials take wait and see on police body cameras, *Princeton Patch*. Available at: https://patch.com/new-jersey/princeton/amp/27220221/princeton-officials-take-wait-and-see-approach-on-police-body-cameras

Braga, A. A., Coldren, J. R., Sousa, W. H., Rodriguez, D. and Alper, O. 2017. *The benefits of body-worn cameras: new findings from a randomized controlled trial at the Las Vegas Metropolitan Police Department*. CNA Analysis & Solutions. Available at: https://www.ncjrs.gov/pdffiles1/nij/grants/251416.pdf

Braga, A. A., Sousa, W. H., Coldren, J. R., Jr and Rodriguez, D. 2018. The effects of body-worn cameras on police activity and police-citizen encounters: a randomized controlled trial, *Journal of Criminal Law and Criminology*, 108(3), 511–538.

Brustein, J. 2018. The biggest police body cam company is buying its main competitor, *Bloomberg*, May 4, Available at: https://www.bloomberg.com/news/articles/2018-05-04/the-biggest-police-body-cam-company-is-buying-its-main-competitor

Cubitt, T. I., Lesic, R., Myers, G. L. and Corry, R. 2017. Body-worn video: a systematic review of literature. *Australian and New Zealand Journal of Criminology*, 50(3), 379–396.

del Pozo, B. 2017, May 26. There is no such thing as a free body camera, Police Foundation. Available at: https://www.policefoundation.org/there-is-no-such-thing-as-a-free-body-camera/

Farr, S. 2012. Philly police will test attaching video cameras to cops, *The Philadelphia Daily News*, June 15. Available at: https://www.inquirer.com/philly/hp/news_update/20120615_Philly_police_will_test_attaching_video_cameras_to_cops.html

Fox, B. 2015. Rick Smith is on target with cutting-edge taser; innovate: the CEO keeps advancing the police culture, *Investor's Business Daily*, January 16. Available at: https://www.investors.com/news/management/leaders-and-success/rick-smith-builds-a-revolutionary-company-in-taser/

Gelles, D. 2016. Taser International dominates the police body camera market, *New York Times*, July 12. Available at: https://www.nytimes.com/2016/07/13/business/taser-international-dominates-the-police-body-camera-market.html

Goodall, M. 2007. *Guidance for the Police Use of Body-worn Video Devices*, London, Home Office.

Hardy, Q. 2012. Taser's latest police weapon: the tiny camera and the cloud, *The New York Times*, February 21. Available at: https://www.nytimes.com/2012/02/21/technology/tasers-latest-police-weapon-the-tiny-camera-and-the-cloud.html

Henstock, D. and Ariel, B. 2017. Testing the effects of police body-worn cameras on use of force during arrests: a randomised controlled trial in a large British police force, *European Journal of Criminology*, 14(6), 720–750.

Hoium, T. 2018, October 7. Why Axon Enterprise's growth is just the beginning, Motley Fool. Available at: https://www.fool.com/investing/2018/10/07/why-axon-enterprises-growth-is-just-beginning.aspx

Honeycutt, C. and Herring, S. 2009. Beyond microblogging: conversation and collaboration in Twitter [online]. In *Proc. 42nd HICSS*, IEEE Press. Available at: https://www.computer.org/csdl/pds/api/csdl/proceedings/download-article/12OmNBqv2en/pdf

Jany, L. 2018. Minneapolis officials blame growing police records backlog on tech troubles, staffing shortages, *Minneapolis Star Tribune*, September 4. Available at: http://www.startribune.com/officials-blame-growing-records-backlog-on-tech-troubles-staffing-shortages/492445031/

Jennings, W. G., Fridell, L. A., Lynch, M., Jetelina, K. K. and Reingle Gonzalez, J. M. 2017. A quasi-experimental evaluation of the effects of police body-worn cameras (BWCs) on response-to-resistance in a large metropolitan police department, *Deviant Behavior*, 38(11), 1332–1339.

Jennings, W. G., Lynch, M. D. and Fridell, L. A. 2015. Evaluating the impact of police officer body-worn cameras (BWCs) on response-to-resistance and serious external complaints: evidence from the Orlando police department (OPD) experience utilizing a randomized controlled experiment, *Journal of Criminal Justice*, 43(6), 480–486.

Katz, C. M., Choate, D. E., Ready, J. R. and Nuño, L. 2014. *Evaluating the Impact of Officer Worn Body Cameras in the Phoenix Police Department*, Phoenix, AZ, Center for Violence Prevention and Community Safety, Arizona State University.

Koen, M. C., Willis, J. J. and Mastrofski, S. D. 2018. The effects of body-worn cameras on police organisation and practice: a theory-based analysis, *Policing and Society*, 29(8), 968–917. doi: 10.1080/10439463.2018.1467907

Kwak, H., Lee, C., Park, H. and Moon, S. 2010. What is Twitter, a social network or a news media? In *Proceedings of the 42nd Hawaii International Conference on System Sciences – 2009*, IEEE, Kauai, HI. Available at: http://www.computer.org/csdl/proceedings/hicss/2009/3450/00/03-05-05.pdf

Laming, E. 2019. Police use of body worn cameras, *Police Practice and Research*, 20(2), 201–216. doi: 10.1080/15614263.2018.1558586

Manning, P. K. 1978. The police: mandate, strategies, and appearances. Reprinted In *Policing: Key Readings*, Ed. T. Newburn, 2005. Cullompton, Willan Publishing.

Mateescu, A., Rosenblat, A. and Boyd, D. 2016. Dreams of accountability, guaranteed surveillance: the promises and costs of body-worn cameras, *Surveillance and Society*, 14(1), 122–127.

Mesa Police Department. 2013. *On-officer Body Camera System: Program Evaluation and Recommendations*. Mesa, AZ, Mesa Police Department.

Nowacki, J. S. and Willits, D. 2018. Adoption of body cameras by United States police agencies: an organisational analysis, *Policing and Society*, 28(7), 841–853.

ODS Consulting. 2011. *Body Worn Video Projects in Paisley and Aberdeen: Self-Evaluation*. Glasgow, ODS Consulting.

Owens, C. and Finn, W. 2018. Body-worn video through the lens of a cluster randomized controlled trial in london: implications for future research, *Policing: Journal of Policy Practice*, 12(1), 77–82.

Owens, C., Mann, D. and Mckenna, R. 2014. *The Essex Body Worn Video Trial: The Impact of Body Worn Video on Criminal Justice Outcomes of Domestic Abuse Incidents*. Wolsingham, College of Policing.

Peters, S. 2018. Surge in police body cam video brings need for more employees, *Palm Beach Post*, September 10. Available at: https://www.mypalmbeachpost.com/news/local/surge-police-body-cam-video-brings-need-for-more-employees/yROfbDWSGnCtZqN5I2G23M/

Plus Media Solutions. 2016. Louisiana: Louisiana state police to equip troopers with body cameras, *Plus Media Solutions – US Official News*, 26 December. Available at: https://www.knoe.com/content/news/LSP-to-equip-troopers-with-body-cameras-407791455.html

Progressive Media. 2014a. Fresno police department orders taser body-worn cameras, *Progressive Media – Company News*, 13 August. Available at: https://investor.axon.com/press-releases/press-release-details/2014/Fresno-Police-Department-Expands-Body-Worn-Camera-Program-With-Purchase-of-100-Cameras-From-TASER/default.aspx

Progressive Media. 2014b. London Police's front line officers to pilot AXON body-worn cameras, *Progressive Media – Company News*, 2 October. Available at: https://finance.yahoo.com/news/london-met-police-extending-axon-113000689.html

Progressive Media. 2014c. Los Angeles police officers to be equipped with taser's AXON body cameras, *Progressive Media – Company News*, 19 December. Available at: https://investor.axon.com/press-releases/press-release-details/2014/LAPD-Becomes-Largest-US-Police-Department-to-Outfit-Officers-With-AXON-Body-Cameras-and-EVIDENCEcom-by-TASER/default.aspx

Progressive Media. 2015. TASER to supply body cameras to San Antonio police department, *Progressive Media – Company News*, 4 November. Available at: https://www.prnewswire.com/news-releases/taser-receives-largest-body-camera-order-to-date-from-the-san-antonio-police-department-300171046.html

Rayman, G. 2017. No 'cam' do NYPD passes on offer of 'free' body gear, *New York Daily News*, April 6, p. 12.

Ready, J. T. and Young, J. T. 2015. The impact of on-officer video cameras on police–citizen contacts: findings from a controlled experiment in Mesa, AZ, *Journal of Experimental Criminology*, 11(3), 445–458.

The Record. 2017. Taser changing its name, will focus on body cameras, *The Record – Metroland Media Group Ltd*, April 6. Available at: https://www.therecord.com/business/2017/04/06/taser-changing-its-name-will-focus-on-body-cameras.html

Schneider, C. J. 2015. Police image work in an era of social media: YouTube and the 2007 Montebello summit protest. In *Social Media, Politics and the State: Protests, Revolutions, Riots, Crime and Policing in an Age of Facebook, Twitter, and YouTube*, Eds D. Trottier and C. Fuchs, pp. 227–246, New York, Routledge.

Schneider, C. J. 2016. *Policing and Social Media: Social Control in an Era of New Media*, Lanham, MD, Lexington Books | Rowman & Littlefield.

Schneider, C. J. 2018a. Body worn cameras and police image work: news media coverage of the Rialto police department's body worn camera experiment, *Crime, Media, Culture*, 14(3), 449–466.

Schneider, C. J. 2018b. An exploratory study of public perceptions of police conduct depicted in body worn camera footage on YouTube, *Annual Review of Interdisciplinary Justice Research*, 7, 118–148.

Shiffer, J. 2017. Secrecy rules, *Minneapolis Star Tribune*, 30 April, p. 1A.

Smykla, J. O., Crow, M. S., Crichlow, V. J. and Snyder, J. A. 2016. Police body-word cameras: perceptions of law enforcement leadership, *American Journal of Criminal Justice*, 41(3), 424–433.

Sousa, W. H., Coldren, J. R., Jr, Rodriguez, D. and Braga, A. A. 2016. Research on body worn cameras: meeting the challenges of police operations, program implementation, and randomized controlled trial designs, *Police Quarterly*, 19(3), 363–384.

Spivack, M. 2016. Cop videos: public record or not?; Vexing questions linger about privacy, value of police footage, *Dayton Daily News*, December 25, p. Z1.

Stecklein, J. 2012. Forget dashcams, Salt Lake City police chief has faith in eyecams, *The Salt Lake Tribune*, November 16.

Stoughton, S. W. 2018. Police body-worn cameras, *North Carolina Law Review*, 96, 1363–1424.

Wakefield, J. 2017. Edmonton, Calgary police split on body-worn video cameras, *Edmonton Sun*, September 11. Available at: https://edmontonsun.com/2017/09/11/edmonton-calgary-police-split-on-body-worn-video-cameras/wcm/f784da1b-5ccc-4af1-8c07-fa027457b321

Wang, S. 2018. Twitter to predict what you want to see, when it happens, *Bloomberg*, June 13. Available at: https://www.bloomberg.com/news/articles/2018-06-13/twitter-aims-to-predict-what-you-want-to-know-when-it-happens

White, M. D. 2014. *Police Officer Body-Worn Cameras: Assessing the Evidence*, Washington, DC, Office of Community Oriented Policing Services.

White, M. D., Gaub, J. E. and Todak, N. 2017. Exploring the potential for body-worn cameras to reduce violence in police–citizen encounters, *Policing: Journal of Policy Practice*, 11(3), 1–11.

Winston, A. 2015. With Evidence.com, Taser looks to cash in on police brutality debate, *Reveal News*, May 9. Available at: https://www.revealnews.org/article/with-evidence-com-taser-looks-to-cash-in-on-police-brutality-debate/

Yokum, D., Ravishankar, A. and Coppock, A. 2017. *Evaluating the Effects of Police Body-worn Cameras: A Randomized Controlled Trial*. Working paper, The Lab @ DC. Available at: http://bwc.thelab.dc.gov/TheLabDC_MPD_BWC_Working_Paper_10.20.17.pdf

SUBJECTIVITY STRUGGLES: W. E. B. DU BOIS'S CONTRIBUTION TO RADICAL INTERACTIONISM

Gil Richard Musolf

ABSTRACT

The essay explores the profound nature and consequences of subjectivity struggles in everyday life. W. E. B. Du Bois's concept of double consciousness and its constituent concepts of the veil, twoness, and second sight illuminate the process of racialized self-formation. Racialized self-formation contributes to understanding the cultural reproduction of domination and subjugation, the two primary concerns of radical interactionists. Double consciousness, long ignored by symbolic interactionists, cannot be neglected by radical interactionists if they are to articulate a comprehensive account of self-formation in a white-supremacist culture. Reflections on racialization, meritocracy, and subjectivity struggles in contemporary everyday life conclude the essay.

Keywords: Double consciousness; the veil; Du Bois; racialization; subjectivity; superiority delusions

INTRODUCTION

Subjectivity constitutes actors' understanding, interpretation, and lived experience of everyday life. It is a socially and culturally constructed state of consciousness. Subjectivity influences behavior, thoughts, identity, and emotions. Actors' language and conceptual frameworks, and the minded processes they employ, are formative in constructing subjectivity. The two fundamental minded processes actors use, according to symbolic interactionism, are role-taking and defining the situation. Language and conceptual frameworks are internalized through the process of

Radical Interactionism and Critiques of Contemporary Culture
Studies in Symbolic Interaction, Volume 52, 19–33
Copyright © 2021 by Emerald Publishing Limited
All rights of reproduction in any form reserved
ISSN: 0163-2396/doi:10.1108/S0163-239620210000052002

learning from and socialization to culture, subcultures, and significant and reference others. Actors, possessing agency, also contribute to this process, accepting and rejecting aspects of the normative order. Actors make culture, engage in role-making, and contribute to self-formation. Everyone's subjectivity emerges through this dialectical process, an ongoing, lifelong process in which selves and cultures continuously evolve.

Subjectivity or states of consciousness that sociologists find problematic are ones that have been maliciously constructed to produce internalizations of inferiority. Such internalizations arise from role-taking and defining the situation from the ruling class's perspective, incorporating their language and conceptual frameworks. Critical scholars have put forward a number of theoretical constructs to describe this process: ideology, discursive practices, hegemony, ideological state apparatus, epistemological imperialism, false consciousness, symbolic violence, colonization of the mind, racialization, and, in the case I am interested in expounding on here, double consciousness. These concepts explain in various ways how the ruling class induces thinking disorders in the oppressed that result in a subjectivity of inferiority. Language has the power to create reality and dominate consciousness. As the Muses in Hesiod's *Theogony* stated, we "speak many false things as though they were true." And as Socrates revealed about sophists, they have the persuasive power to "make the weaker argument defeat the stronger." Language and representations enchant and enthrall. Oppressors can weaponize words so as to legitimize, justify, and mystify, as is the case in the ideologies of white and male supremacy. In fact, divesting a population of its language is a domination strategy, systematically practiced against Native Americans (Heller and McElhinny 2017, p. 28).

The critical scholars who advanced the above concepts were all seeking to reveal processes by which the ruling class socializes the oppressed to accept "superiority delusions" (Musolf, 2012). Oppressors believe in their representations of superiority, whether self-manufactured or fabricated by merchants as commodities to enhance ruling class domination. Unfortunately, many oppressed also believe in the superiority of their oppressors as well as their oppressors' representations of them as inferior or the other. Thus, oppressor and oppressed may achieve intersubjectivity, a shared understanding of the social world, both accepting the validity of ruling class ideology and representations and both agreeing that the world is a meritocracy and that people receive their just rewards. Many oppressed accept the oppressors' charge that they are exclusively blameworthy for their social status. After all, as the ideology reiterates, the United States is a country of equality of opportunity. Disadvantaged origins are disregarded as mobility barriers and discounted as disabling achievement. One's destination depends solely on the merit and hard work of the individual. Oppressors strut a looking-glass self that emerges from representations of superiority, and the oppressed present a looking-glass self that emerges from representations of inferiority, empowering for the oppressor and debilitating for the oppressed.

Besides unmasking the torment and mythology that superiority delusions foment, what inspires sociologists to attend to such states of mind? Sociologists abhor such mentalities because they believe language and conceptual frameworks manufactured by those with malign intent produce thinking disorders that lead to behaviors that reproduce inequality. Inequality is the major concern of sociologists. Inspired by Antonio Gramsci, Michael Buroway's (1979) pregnant phrase, "the manufacture of consent," gives birth to the social purpose that superiority delusions play in reproducing inequality. White supremacists, male supremacists, and other oppressors find it in their social interest to furnish the language that the oppressed draw on to understand and interpret everyday life. Oppressors achieve this goal by socializing and educating the marginalized to role-take and define situations from the oppressors' perspective, so that the oppressed reproduce their own inequality. A ruling class needs to harvest subservient subjectivities as part of a strategy to maintain legitimation, power, prestige, privilege, domination, and subjugation. A working class that is dependent on ruling class conceptual frameworks and that role-takes and defines situations from an oppressors' ideology is doomed to reproduce its own domination and subjugation. Domination and subjugation in everyday life, and the way they are reconstituted, is radical interactionism's major area of conceptual clarification and research focus (Athens, 2015).

SUBJECTIVITY DISORDERS

Subjectivity struggles emerge from conflict between oppressors and oppressed. All of the concepts brought forth above provide illustrations of how subjectivity is distorted through various processes of representation and language, revealing the effort the ruling class devotes to constructing and reproducing subjectivities that help perpetuate their power. These well-known and extensively studied concepts percolate through the common language of sociology. Ideology is considered the paragon example of a thinking disorder that distorts an oppressed population's understanding and interpretation of the world. Ideology is usually thought of as a conceptual framework that justifies and legitimizes ruling class power. Hegemony has the same goal, only the cultural practices it explores are more extensive and subtle in socializing oppressed populations that the way everyday life is institutionalized is the natural, right, God-given, and immutable way that life should proceed. Ideology, ideological state apparatus, and hegemony maintain power in the hands of the ruling class through conceptual frameworks that legitimize inequality embedded in social structure and culture. False consciousness, symbolic violence, epistemological imperialism, racialization, and colonization of the mind are concepts that illustrate how the ruling class manipulates minded processes to manufacture a subjectivity of inferiority, of constituting the other. Sociologists who write on these concepts usually remark on how actors are unwittingly complicit in their own construction of such a mentality. Actors imprisoned in and afflicted by language and representations that sustain superiority delusions are not likely to oppose oppressive social structure and culture. Superiority delusions are false positives for oppressors and false negatives for the subjugated. For the marginalized, belief in superiority delusions is tantamount to a mobility extinction event. However, the oppressed possess agency and the ability to overcome epistemological imperialism and to achieve epistemological emancipation.

AGENCY

Those who are subjugated need to eliminate language and representations based on the inferiority of class, race, and gender. They should acquire language and representations grounded in the universal concepts of equality and human rights. The oppressed exercise agency when they develop states of consciousness that exemplify Durkheim's notion of moral individualism, that all categories of people, and all individuals, are equal in their human rights, dignity, respect, responsibilities, and opportunities. Human beings are sacred objects. The deconstruction and unmasking of language, conceptual frameworks, and minded processes of negation need to be supplanted with ones that construct humane and life-affirming subjectivities. If this emancipatory process is to grow beyond a personal one, it necessitates solidarity and collective action to ensure that a social structure and a culture exist and are continuously improved upon, so that life-affirming language about and representations of others who share one's social identity are readily available to all from which to role-take and learn. Actors emancipated by language that unmasks superiority delusions are more likely to resist oppressive social structure and culture, not only individually but also in solidarity with others through organizing protest and engaging in collective action to bring about transformation.

STRUCTURE AND AGENCY COMPLEMENTARITY

Good sociology incorporates both nomothetic generalities and idiographic lived experiences, is sensitive to the ecological fallacy and essentialism, and constructs theory that employs both structure and agency. For example, as anomie increases in society, suicide rates escalate. A culture without civil religion – unifying narratives and rituals – diminishes solidarity and creates divisiveness and polarization. But not everyone who confronts such a culture commits suicide; indeed, most do not. To understand the complexity of individuals and their behavior, both the social surround that envelops individuals and their interpretation of and meanings they ascribe to that social surround must be taken into account. It is imperative to understand how individuals enmeshed in a culture riven with moral tribalism and ideological warfare, unregulated desires, and attenuated commitment to rituals at the national, family, and relationship levels define the situation. The same is true for attempts to comprehend the lives of racialized others. Du Bois employs structure and agency in his portrait of the racialized other by underscoring both the structure of racism and the mentality it engenders.

TURNING POINTS: THE PROJECT OF POLITICAL EMANCIPATION

The road to emancipation entails endless transformation. A project of political emancipation began with malformed notions of democracy and human rights in fifth century BC Greece. Those ideals continue to transform the Western world.

Incessant interrogation of self and political systems arose, especially received wisdom: the normative, the sacred, and the established. Aeschylus's themes in his trilogy, *Oresteia*, dramatize the importance of interrogation as a way of political life (Musolf, 2014). Scholars of theoretical rationality since then have worked to universalize conceptualizations of democracy and human rights. The project of political emancipation is an unending journey. New forms of social consciousness, fresh ways to expand human rights and even the rights of other species, and brave new worlds of social justice that we cannot yet imagine await. Social structure and culture are far more egalitarian, and human rights are increasingly more universal, today than they were when the project of political emancipation began. Struggles punctuated by setbacks and turning points define the political landscape. In the United States, the standard bearers of political emancipation – the end of slavery and Jim Crow, the rise of the New Deal and feminism, and the constitutional legalization of same-sex marriage – are turning points. Many other turning points have changed history.

Max Weber argued that ideas are transformative. Durkheim argued that moral individualism, the idea of the individual as a sacred object, has transformed our political system so that constitutional, social, cultural, and behavioral norms have been institutionalized that embody it. Progressives and radicals have advanced the idea that individuals deserve subjectivities and identities free from malicious construction; that desire is far from achieved. W. E. B. Du Bois's social theory has made a contribution toward that potential turning point through his formation of the concept of "double consciousness." This concept enhances our understanding of how subjectivities of inferiority are constituted by domination and subjugation; hence, it contributes to the perspective of radical interactionism.

W. E. B. DU BOIS (1868–1963)

This essay lacks the space to present a biography of Du Bois or to delineate the social context of the times that influenced his writings. It is limited, instead, to exploring Du Bois's concept of double consciousness expounded in *The Souls of Black Folk*, originally published in 1903. Inferences from the concept will allow me to reflect on the repercussions of racialization, meritocracy, and the subjectivity struggles embedded in self-formation, consequences of living life in a social structure and culture in which the color line still dominates.

Lewis (2009, p. 4) has magnificently argued that Du Bois's writings catapulted him to be

> [t]he premier architect of the civil rights movement in the United States ..., the first to grasp the international implications of the struggle for racial justice ... [and the first to discern] that the problem of the twentieth century would be the problem of the color line.

Racist ideologies, bigotry, exploitation, and Jim Crow sucked the lifeblood from the souls of black folk; their blood itself was spilled by beatings, rape, and lynching.

Lemert (1994) has noted the disgraceful history of sociological thought that has ignored the work of Du Bois and his exclusion from the canon of leading sociologists. Sociologists excluded Du Bois since they themselves were infected with the culture of racism. In addition to Lemert, many other scholars, far too numerous to cite, also have worked on establishing Du Bois's richly deserved place in the sociological pantheon. Lemert (1994), Rawls (2000), and Itzigsohn and Brown (2015) have noted Du Bois's neglect by symbolic interactionists, especially disconcerting from those whose aim is the understanding of the process of self-formation. Du Bois's focus on self-formation is illuminated by the fact that he (along with George Herbert Mead) was a student of William James at Harvard University. The above scholars argue that inattention to Du Bois's work on double consciousness impairs social thought on the process of self-formation, the social construction of a subjectivity of inferiority, and the cultural reproduction of domination and subjugation, all concerns crucial to radical interactionists.

RACIALIZATION

Du Bois was interested in the effects racialization had on self-formation. Racialization is the process of constructing an identity of inferiority in African Americans that comes to be accepted by African Americans and whites. It is a process – mutates mutandis – that is applicable to all marginalized or oppressed groups. Racialization is a meaning-making process of arbitrarily singling out observable physical features, phenotypes, and ranking them in terms of moral worthiness (Omi and Winant, 1994). Racialization is the social practice oppressors deploy in a variety of ways to manufacture and merchandise stereotypes, representations, and essentialism – a culture of morally ranked physical differences – and harness them to justify discrimination, scapegoating, displacement, and violence. The racialized are represented as the counternormative other, as a negation of the good, a threat to purity, and of endangering the just and meritorious with contagion. Racialized identities lead oppressors, and many oppressed, to engage in social practices that reproduce inequality. However, racialized subjects possess their own biography and history. Lumping together those who are racialized as experiencing identical lives exemplifies reductionism. Just as there is no archetypal or homogenized woman, there is no archetypal or homogenized racialized other. We all make our own history, even if we share wretched situations. Individuals draw on agency to resist, subvert, overcome, and transform. Reforms, revolts, and revolutions crop up, mostly when oppressors least expect them, as in the case of the Civil Rights movement. African Americans had been defined by sociologists in the 1950s as having come to accept the racist order and the idea that they would perpetually accommodate themselves to that grotesquery (McKee 1993). Even the oppressed have agency and eventually, enough is enough.

DOUBLE CONSCIOUSNESS

As traditionally theorized, "sociology's self-theory" has been "defiantly ahistorical" (Lemert, 1994, p. 390), presenting a "White Universal perspective" (p. 391).

According to Itzigsohn and Brown (2015), the classical theorists of the self – James, Cooley, and Mead – ignored, for the most part, the devastating effects to one's self-formation engendered in a culture that perpetuates racializing as a prevalent social practice.[1] Lemert proposes that by incorporating Du Bois's concept of double consciousness into the canon of self-formation theory, sociologists will have a more comprehensive understanding of self-formation in a racist culture. For radical interactionists, this means that Mead's concepts of role-taking, self-objectification, the generalized other, I and me, and play and game stages, along with Cooley's notion of the looking-glass self need to be grounded in the processes and effects of racialization on self-formation. The same can be said of the process of sexism on women's self-formation. "There is no universal Self. There are only selves" (Lemert, 1994, p. 390). Selves are internally multiple, conflicting, contradictory, and historically and culturally different.

Itzigsohn and Brown (2015, p. 233) argue that what is missing in the work of classical theorists of self-formation is "the limits to communication and to mutual recognition under conditions of racialization." I agree and would add that racialization destroys solidarity, the feeling of community, communion, connection, and togetherness that arises from a unifying national project of inclusive rituals. The racialized cannot feel solidarity with those who dehumanize them. The cultural crime of racializing only abets divisiveness, polarization, and estrangement. Racialization also engenders an identity struggle within the consciousness of African Americans, engendering a double consciousness. Du Bois's classic statement on double consciousness, to which I will refer in the following analysis, is:

> [T]he Negro is a sort of seventh son, born with a veil, and gifted with second-sight in this American world – a world which yields him no true self-consciousness, but only lets him see himself through the revelation of the other world. It is a peculiar sensation, this double consciousness, this sense of always looking at one's self through the eyes of others, of measuring one's soul by the tape of a world that looks on in amused contempt and pity. One ever feels his two-ness – an American, a Negro; two souls, two thoughts, two unreconciled strivings; two warring ideals in one dark body, whose dogged strength alone keeps it from being torn asunder. (Du Bois, 1903, p. 2)

The concept of double consciousness has three component parts: the veil, twoness, and second sight.[2]

The Veil

The veil is a metaphor for the color line separating the social worlds of whites, who racialize, and blacks, who are racialized. The color line is supported by institutional racism and a culture of racist ideologies that socializes individuals to racist beliefs and contributes to discriminatory social practices. Jim Crow and apartheid were the literal illustrations of the color line. Those who have the power to racialize have no need to recognize, or to communicate with, the racialized; the racialized are enslaved, dehumanized, scorned, and ordered about, a source of surplus value, invisible; in general, they are commodities of exploitation. The veil blocks whites from taking the role of African Americans, a fundamental necessity for communication and recognition. Role-taking refusal occurs early. Du Bois recounts an incident from childhood when a white girl refuses him recognition and communication.

> In a wee wooden schoolhouse, something put it into the boys' and girls' heads to buy gorgeous visiting cards – ten cents a package – and exchange. The exchange was merry, till one girl, a tall newcomer, refused my card, refused it peremptorily, with a glance. Then it dawned upon me with a certain suddenness that I was different from the others; or like, mayhap, in heart and life and longing, but shut out from their world by a vast veil. (Du Bois, 1903, p. 2)

Unfortunately, many racialized subjects internalize superiority delusions propagated by a dominant white-supremacist culture. Whites, of course, believe these superiority delusions about African Americans to justify dehumanization. African Americans' acceptance of them constitutes internalized racism, damaging self-esteem. Role-taking from the perspective of the oppressor is offset by role-taking from one's community; nevertheless, it leads to a twoness.[3]

Twoness

Actors role-take from significant others, referent others, and a variety of others in constructing a looking-glass image of themselves. They also role-take from the generalized other. The generalized other is suffused with the ideas of a white-supremacist ruling class; that is to say, a dominant ideology and value system that is racialized. The dominant ideology legitimizes racial subjugation. If African Americans role-take from this racialized generalized other, it contributes to the classical problem of false consciousness. Du Bois clearly recognized that racist incidents, such as the one he experienced with the girl and the visiting cards, can ignite in African Americans a refusal to role-take from the white-supremacist culture, strengthening the veil between whites and African Americans.

> I had thereafter no desire to tear down that veil, to creep through; I held all beyond it in common contempt, and lived above it in a region of blue sky and great wandering shadows. (p. 2)

Du Bois also recognized that all actors, including the oppressed, possess agency. They can defy the dominant ideology and engage in resistance. After the interaction with the girl, Du Bois states that: "That sky was bluest when I could beat my mates at examination time, or beat them at a foot-race, or even beat their stringy heads" (p. 2). Twoness illustrates that role-taking from a racialized generalized other can lead to an identity of inferiority; however, African Americans who role-take from the generalized other of their own communities can acquire nurturance, solidarity, and a looking-glass self that is based on pride rather than mortification. It is this role-taking from diametrically opposed generalized others that leads African Americans to have a double consciousness, two ways of viewing the world and themselves.

Second Sight

Itzigsohn and Brown (2015, p. 236) argue that second sight arises when African Americans refuse to role-take from the white-supremacist culture, thereby "neutralizing" it. After neutralizing a racist culture, second sight or critical consciousness, and identity transformation are possible. Du Bois gives an example of a child transforming its identity through role-taking refusal, of holding the white world in contempt, a process that led to a "self-consciousness, self-realization, self-respect.... He began to have a dim feeling that, to attain his place in the world, he must be himself, and not another" (Du Bois, 1903, p. 5). The "gift" of second sight is a simultaneous process of acquiring a consciousness of oppression and a language of resistance. It is analogous to the process of the working class acquiring class consciousness or feminists engaging in consciousness raising. Second sight is a revelation, a "satori," a coming to see what has always existed but remained invisible because one did not have a language through which to see it. Du Bois describes that process in his story "Of the Coming of John"[4]:

> He had left his ... thought-world and come back to a world of motion and men. He looked now for the first time sharply about him, and wondered how he had seen so little before. He grew slowly to feel almost for the first time the Veil that lay between him and the white world; *he first noticed now the oppression that had not seemed oppression before, differences that erstwhile seemed natural*, restraints and slights that in his boyhood days had gone unnoticed or been greeted with a laugh. (Du Bois, 1903, p. 144; emphasis GRM)

Richard Rorty (1991) in an article titled, "Feminism and Pragmatism," has described this process more eloquently than anyone I know.

> Injustices may not be perceived as injustices, even by those who suffer them, until somebody invents a previously unplayed role. Only if somebody has a dream, and a voice to describe that dream, does what looked like nature begin to look like culture, what looked like fate begin to look like a moral abomination. For until then only the language of the oppressor is available, and most oppressors have had the wit to teach the oppressed a language in which the oppressed will sound crazy – *even to themselves* – if they describe themselves *as* oppressed. (p. 232; emphasis in original)

Anne Forer Pyne invented a previously unplayed role by her coining of the phrase and advocating for the practice of "consciousness raising" so that women could name the unnamed, cultivate solidarity, and launch second-wave feminism (Cowley, 2018). A language of resistance empowers. It includes but is not limited to identity transformation, consciousness raising, counterhegemonic narratives, and deconstructing and reconstructing epistemology, ontology, meaning, and visions of emancipatory progress. If a reconstructed identity and a critical consciousness or language of resistance are connected to solidarity with other African Americans suffering in their community, or in the diaspora around the world, as Du Bois advocated through support for Pan-Africanism, that process has the possibility to engender movements for emancipation. Second sight is revolutionary.

CONCLUSION

The concept of double consciousness and its component parts of the veil, twoness, and second sight is profoundly important to self-formation theory, especially to radical interactionists who address the social and cultural reproduction of domination and subjugation. Understanding the effect of racialization on self-formation improves our hopes for transforming social policy and practice to reduce racialization and inequality.

White-supremacist culture has intentionally concocted supremacy delusions to besiege the lives of African Americans. African Americans role-take from two conflicting looking-glass perspectives. One looking-glass is the viewpoint of superiority delusions that entails internalizing racism. The other looking-glass is the standpoint of the African American community in which members find solace, solidarity, shared humanity, and empathy. These two social mirrors engender a double consciousness in African Americans, two diametrically opposed sources of self-formation. Dehumanized images of African Americans and ideologies of inferiority justify inequality. White supremacy is the seminary of racialization. Oppression and resistance to it are the sources of subjectivity struggles in everyday life.

The oppressed, through role-taking from the perspective of the oppressor, can know what the oppressor thinks; however, they do not have to accept it. Such refusal is the best way to begin the minded process of reconstructing individual and group identity (Musolf 2012). Oppressors refusing to role-take from the point of view of the oppressed walls off oppressors' communication and recognition of the marginalized, fostering dehumanization. Oppressors, however, hardly care if they dehumanize those they subjugate. Emancipation arises when the oppressed refuse to role-take from the perspective of their oppressors – the racialized generalized other, bringing about critical consciousness or second sight, identity transformation, solidarity with other Africans through pan-Africanism, and the possibility to put all of this to good use through resistance and social transformation.

MERITOCRACY, RACIALIZATION, AND SUBJECTIVITY STRUGGLES

The quest to facilitate success in one's children leads to the search for advantages to bestow on them. Advantages become social weapons in class warfare. As Thucydides claimed of all wars, the strong do what they can and the weak suffer what they must. Children of the privileged coddled with financial, social, cultural, and symbolic capital, along with other resources, have enriched life chances. Parents strive to provide their children not equal opportunity but every conceivable advantage.

Time constraint and exhaustion are not easily annulled, making nurturance for single and impoverished parents illusory. For parents with money, de rigueur nurturance entails a methodical search for the best schools, from nursery and kindergarten to boarding and the Ivy League. The desideratum is Harvard Law. Such social superiority embodies in children a habitus to make all the right moves to reproduce their privileges. Imbued through parental nurturance with the values of achievement and excellence, competition and cooperation, and motivation and a work ethic, their socialization is a skein to overcome the labyrinths of life. Perfect SATs, degrees from elite universities, and exclusive skill sets create a commodity of human capital that merits, in the eyes of its possessors, stratospheric rewards. Elite children do not have to game a system that is institutionally gamed. Careers for a generation's brightest and best begin in positions that reward with power and significant compensation. In fact, a remarkable percentage of Ivy League students major in finance and end up on Wall Street (Klein, 2012). Auspicious in prospects and buoyant in confidence, they eventually helm corporations, government agencies, educational institutions, and major NGOs. In all likelihood, they will marry a spouse with similar income, education, and lifestyle, exacerbating inequality (Turner 2009). A long life of elite employment coupled with tax policy that favors low tax rates for the wealthy, minimal capital gains taxes, and no estate taxes reproduces all of the above capital advantages for fortunate children. Such life chances provide a springboard of opportunities and a wish list of ascribed statuses embodied in an exquisite habitus.

A hereditary aristocracy stratified the feudal age, nullifying upward mobility. Thomas Jefferson thought America would yield a "natural aristocracy," so that even those who were born poor would have opportunities to achieve wealth and status. Today, however, as the *Economist* (2015) has argued, a "hereditary meritocracy" describes the current limitations in the opportunity structure. The multiple types of capital required to achieve merit are primarily available to the privileged few. Achieved status is unachievable when the resources to achieve are not accessible to any but the elites. The prerogatives to acquire merit, like royal ones, are now by birth. Inherited advantages result in privileged families having the financial and cultural capital to perpetually assure their children cultivate the human capital to achieve merit, reproducing inequality. Since disadvantages are also inherited, social mobility for children of the working class, whatever their color or gender, is increasingly difficult. Murray (2012), Piketty (2014), and Putnam (2015), three scholars with different disciplinary and political perspectives, have documented that the American Dream is vanishing. In many working class communities, despair now shutters all windows of hope. The working class historically had, at least, dead-end jobs, but increasingly, due to opioid addiction, especially to fentanyl, many just end up dead; fifty-two thousand Americans from drug overdoses in 2015 alone (Caldwell 2017). It's a "winner-take-all society."

Of course, agency is important in any "success sequence" (Reeves et al., 2015). No one can deny the significance of "individual effort and responsibility" of making the right choices that lead to upward mobility. But even when African Americans acquire cultural capital, even when socialized to and actively pursuing the norms of achievement, competition, and excellence, structural disadvantages have a much greater impact on derailing their progress when compared to whites. Patrick Sharkety (2013) has provided empirical evidence that structural factors such as inequality in education and, especially, the disparity in and segregation of neighborhoods, in what he calls "the inheritance of the ghetto," reproduce multigenerational persistent poverty. Mondale (2018) has called residential segregation "a great historical evil" that was structurally maintained by redlining, real estate covenants, and racist practices by real estate agents and bankers. He was the co-author of the 1968 Fair Housing Act that attempted to reverse "systemic segregation." In addition, racial discrimination in the job market and the criminal justice system, in particular, the rise of mass incarceration, destroy opportunity. Many other structures of domination exist. Cultural capital is crucial, but even when acquired, the structure of racism nevertheless restricts the opportunities of African Americans. Norms of aspiration and achievement matter, but, unfortunately, what still matters is the color of your skin. And, as Mondale argues, "research shows even more clearly than in 1968 that where you live matters." Structure matters because

> ...growing up in an integrated community provides children with a better chance to graduate from high school, attend college, get and keep good jobs, earn a higher income and pass on wealth to subsequent generations.

Durable solutions require structural and cultural transformation. Making wise decisions about education, marriage, and children – agency – will be enhanced by such transformation.

Racialization compounds issues of double consciousness and meritocracy. Anderson (2017; emphasis GRM) summarizes empirical research that shows that "for those marginalized by the system – economically, racially, and ethnically – believing the system is fair *puts them in conflict with themselves* and can have negative consequences." Double consciousness can arise between positive images enculturated through family socialization and negative images based on failure to attain what the meritocracy myth tells oppressed youth about the relationship between hard work and success. Research has shown that "marginalized youth" who suffer oppression and believe the system is fair come to blame themselves for a lack of achievement and can fall victim to superiority delusions. My reading of the following quotation is that this is exactly what Du Bois means when he states:

> But the facing of so vast a prejudice could not but bring the inevitable self-questioning, self-disparagement, and lowering of ideals which ever accompany repression and breed in an atmosphere of contempt and hate. (Du Bois, 1903, p. 6)

In addition, the identity conflict of double consciousness, research "show[s,] [leads to] a decline in self-esteem and an increase in risky behaviors," that is, minority youth begin "believing and acting out false and negative claims about their group...." Repression contributes to being "torn asunder." Racialization is a strategy intended to pacify the oppressed. If individuals believe the system to be "just," they might reject political protest. It is only when those among the oppressed recognize that there is no justice that they may demand social change. Perceived justice promotes peace. Consciousness of oppression motivates resistance.

Racialization has been refractory to the medicine of social science. The chronic sickness of the color line persists. Through either intention or an unconscious bias, many Americans endorse policy that promotes a society with a color line and a culture that justifies inequality through superiority delusions. Racialization is a disease of American culture. Treatment for it has the potential to mitigate the virulence of the disease in both the privileged and its victims; that is to say, the ascribed status of the subjugated is not terminal.

Through interrogation, or, as Marx wrote, "unmasking," of superiority delusions or ideologies of inferiority, both the privileged and victims can rid themselves of the infection. Racialization is treatable when the privileged role-take from the perspective of minorities, eliminating dehumanization. In addition, healing occurs when minorities refuse to role-take from the culture of white supremacy, leading to identity transformation. Transformed identities, along with developing critical consciousness and solidarity with others who are oppressed, might spiral participation in collective action that reduces oppression. This process and potential is realizable by all oppressed people. The oppressed may be quiescent at any particular moment but turning points erupt when least expected.

There has always been a kaleidoscope of lenses through which to view the political landscape. Currently, a range of standpoints, from the alt-right to Antifa, exists. Antifa and the alt-right are more radical versions of the traditional left-right spectrum. The many political views expressed in an open society can seem like a labyrinth, but helping citizens find their way through that maze has been the reliable, although not uncontested, contribution of social science; its criterion for truth claims, theory, or conclusions is empirical, preferably probative, evidence. Empirical evidence grounds legitimation. Groups like Black Lives Matter do not articulate querulous charges but present empirical and probative evidence of structural oppression: video recordings of unarmed black men killed by white police officers, for instance. Women from #MeToo, and in other efforts across the globe, are combating male privilege substantiated by countless cases of sexual harassment, the gender wage gap, and glass ceilings. Social change requires institutional transformation, not just punishment for individuals (Faludi, 2017). Lack of support for, and confidence, trust, and consent in, the administration of justice and the equity and fairness of institutions – their exclusions, discrimination, and failure to universalize practices – constitute what Jügen Habermas called a legitimation crisis. The fight against sexist and racist institutions, and overcoming a legitimation crisis, will be harder if traditional notions of empirical evidence and truth evaporate, democratic norms attenuate, and politics deteriorates into a theater of the absurd.

Backlash against women and minorities makes that fight even harder. It is analogous to the response of a hegemonic nation-state to the rising power of an ascendant one. Dominant nation-states fear a redistribution in the balance of power, engendering the Thucydides Trap: war (Allison, 2015). As minorities and women ascend or are perceived to be ascending, eclipsing, or perceived to eclipse, the hegemonic power of whites and males, fear, and backlash arises, a Thucydides Trap of sorts. Race and gender conflict escalate.

Even discussing racism and racial inequality has given rise to a discursive backlash: "white fragility" (DiAngelo, 2011, p. 54),

...a state in which even a minimum amount of racial stress becomes intolerable, triggering a
range of defensive moves ... such as anger, fear, and guilt, and behaviors such as argumentation,
silence, and leaving the stress-inducing situation. These behaviors, in turn, function to reinstate
white racial equilibrium.

Analogously, gainsaying gender inequality can be viewed as constituting male
fragility. Oppressors do not like to be confronted with their privileges, which are
largely invisible to them. It is the height of irony that whites and males who
advance arguments that their prerogatives have long vanished from institutions
do so from a socioeconomic position in which all statistics point to sustained
institutional superiority for both whites and males. What is left for white
nationalists, male chauvinists, and the alt-right is persuasion through the power of
language to concoct superiority delusions and dominate consciousness. Capturing
consciousness – subjectivity struggles – is at the heart of political warfare. White
males, however, cannot be discarded to the dustbin of history if social justice is to
be pursued through party politics (Starr, 2017). Progressives and democrats need
them to win elections. Policies of general social mobility are required. Advancing
inclusive policies while at the same time convincing white males to also commit to
policies of racial and gender equality is the rub (Starr, 2017).

The voyage to liberation is an arduous odyssey. "The Nation has not yet found
peace from its sins; the freedman has not yet found in freedom his promised land"
(Du Bois, 1903, p. 4). Humans shipwreck their humanity for decades, strand
themselves on Circean islands hallucinatory with hatred. No religious visionary,
no social science cartographer, and no charismatic pilot has yet been able to sail
us to the distant shore of universal human emancipation. So far it has been an
undiscoverable country. Our navigation skills have always been but mediocre.
The call to abandon ship is not an option.

ACKNOWLEDGMENT

An ocean of gratitude is due Jill Taft-Kaufman who reviewed this essay and offered
substantive improvements.

NOTES

1. The authors did not explore either Dewey's or Park's writings on self-formation.
2. Separating double consciousness into three component parts – the veil, twoness, and
second sight – has been done by many scholars, including the ones I have and have not cited.
3. Rawls (2000, pp. 244–248) has also summarized Du Bois by noting that African
Americans role-take from two different communities. She also pointed to the importance of
African Americans refusing to role-take from a white-supremacist culture and in finding
solidarity through role-taking from the African American community. Refusing to role-take
from oppressors' perspectives as a form of resistance was taken up in my 2012 article, which
I have applied here. But I am happy that I share this interpretation with a distinguished
scholar.
4. Even though I am quoting Du Bois, the significance of this passage was emphasized by
Itzigsohn and Brown (2015, pp. 241–242) and it is totally to their credit that I am using the
quotation.

REFERENCES

Allison, G. 2015. The Thucydides trap: are the U.S. and China headed for war? *The Atlantic*. Available at: https://www.theatlantic.com/international/archive/2015/09/united-states-china-war-thycydid

Anderson, M. D. 2017. Why the myth of meritocracy hurts kids of color, *The Atlantic*. Available at: www.theatlantic.com/education/archive/2017/07/internalizing-the-myth-of-meritocracy/535035/

Athens, L. 2015. *Domination and Subjugation in Everyday Life*, New York, NY, Routledge.

Burawoy, M. 1979. *The Manufacture of Consent: Changes in the Labor Process under Monopoly Capitalism*, Chicago, IL, University of Chicago Press.

Caldwell, C. 2017. American Carnage: the new landscape of opioid addiction, *First Things*. Available at: https://www.firstthings.com/article/2017/04/american-carnage

Cowley, S. 2018. Anne Forer Pyne, a Feminist who opened eyes, dies at 72. Available at: www.nytimes.com/2018/03/30/obituaries/anne-forer-pyne...dies-at-72

DiAngelo, R. 2011. White fragility, *International Journal of Critical Pedagogy*, 3, 54–70.

Du Bois, W. E. B. 1994[1903]. *The Souls of Black Folk*, New York, NY, Dover Publications.

Economist. 2015. An hereditary meritocracy, *Economist*. Available at: www.economist.com/news/briefing/21640316-children-rich-and-powerful-are-increasingly-well-suited-earning-wealth-and-power

Faludi, S. 2017. The Patriarch is falling. The Patriarch is stronger than ever, *The New York Times*. Available at: https://www.nyti.ms/2pRRWrqu

Heller, M. and McElhinny, B. 2017. *Language, Capitalism, Colonialism*, Tonawanda, New York, NY, University of Toronto Press.

Itzigsohn, J. and Brown, K. 2015. Sociology and the theory of double consciousness, *Du Bois Review*, 12, 231–248.

Klein, E. 2012. Wall street steps in when Ivy league fails, *The Washington Post*. Available at: https://www.washingtonpost.com/business/economy/wall-street-steps

Lemert, C. 1994. A classic from the other side of the veil: Du Bois's Souls of black folk, *The Sociological Quarterly*, 35, 383–396.

Lewis, D. L. 2009. *W. E. B. Du Bois*, New York, NY, Holt.

McKee, J. B. 1993. *Sociology and the Race Problem: The Failure of a Perspective*, Chicago, IL, University of Illinois Press.

Mondale, W. F. 2018. The civil rights law we ignored. Available at: https://www.nytimes.com/2018/04/10/opinion/walter-mondale-fair-housing-act.html?smprod=nytcore-ipad&smid=nytcore-ipad-share

Murray, C. 2012. *Coming Apart: The State of White America, 1960–2010*, New York, NY, Crown Forum.

Musolf, G. R. 2014. The dialectic of domination and democracy in Aeschylus's *Oresteia*: a radical interactionist reading, *Studies in Symbolic Interaction*, 42, 69–107.

Musolf, G. R. 2012. The superiority delusion and critical consciousness: the paradox of role-taking refusal in the microfoundations of dehumanization and resistance, *Studies in Symbolic Interaction*, 39, 70–120.

Omi, M. and Winant, H. 1994. *Racial Formation in the United States: from the 1960s to the 1990s*, New York, NY, Routledge.

Piketty, T. 2014. *Capital in the Twenty-first Century*, Cambridge, MA, The Belknap Press of Harvard University.

Putnam, R. D. 2015. *Our Kids: The American Dream in Crisis*, New York, NY, Simon & Schuster.

Rawls, A. W. 2000. "Race" as an interaction order phenomenon: W. E. B. Du Bois's "double consciousness" thesis revisited, *Sociological Theory*, 18, 241–274.

Reeves, R. V., Rodrigue, E. and Gold, A. 2015. *Following the Success Sequence? Success Is More Likely if You're White*. Brookings Report. Available at: http://www.brookings.edu/research/following-the-success-sequence-success-is-more-likely-if-youre-white/

Rorty, R. 1991. Feminism and pragmatism, *Michigan Quarterly Review*, 30, 231–258.

Sharkety, P. 2013. *Stuck in Place: Urban Neighborhoods and the End of Progress toward Racial Equality*, Chicago, IL, University of Chicago Press.

Starr, P. 2017. An American way for America now, *The American Prospect*. Available at: http://prospect.org/article/american-way-america-now

Turner, J. H. 2009. Toward a general theory of interpersonal processes. In *Within the Social World: Essays in Social Psychology*, Eds J. C. Chin and C. K. Jacobson, pp. 65–95, Boston, MA, Pearson Publications.

G.H. MEAD, MORALITY, AND SOCIALITY: AN INTERACTIONIST READING OF *THE MAN IN THE HIGH CASTLE*

Michael A. Katovich

ABSTRACT

This article combines Mead's notion of sociality with his implicit theory of morality. Specifically, it uses Mead's emphasis on temporality to analyze decisions made by key characters in the cinematic adaptation (Amazon TV) of Philip Dick's novel, The Man in the High Castle. *Using a selective and subversive method to read into this adaptation, I regard Mead's view of morality as complex and as distinguishing between a morality in the specious present and a morality grounded in sociality. The paper links Mead and Mead's pragmatic emphasis to varieties of characters representing immoral foils (e.g., Nazis) and everyday lives to show how morality can emerge from a variety of standpoints, locating Mead's position as distinct from moral absolutism and moral relativity.*

Keywords: Morality; sociality; dominance; awareness; subversion; objective

G.H. Mead did not address, explicitly, the conditions by which social action comprises a universally understood moral behavior, but he did postulate general characteristics comprising what he termed "a community of moral consciousness" (Mead, 1908, p. 313). Such consciousness could not, from Mead's view, encompass an entire monolithic perspective, but rather, required a focus on a plurality of perspectives, derived from the variegated experiences of individuals acting interdependently, in relation to others and their surroundings (Mead, 1934,

Radical Interactionism and Critiques of Contemporary Culture
Studies in Symbolic Interaction, Volume 52, 35–52
Copyright © 2021 by Emerald Publishing Limited
All rights of reproduction in any form reserved
ISSN: 0163-2396/doi:10.1108/S0163-239620210000052003

pp. 387–389). Further, Mead did emphasize the ethical standpoints that self-conscious and self-corrective individuals develop as they relate to others in order to create mutually desirable connections based on empathic understandings (see Pfuetze, 1954, pp. 254–255). Such outcomes, stemming from a commitment to create coordinated and future-directed acts that can provide beneficial results to others, comprise the foundation of a moral consciousness shared among a population of empathetic selves capable of taking the roles of such others. (Mead, 1908, pp. 315–316).

While Mead posited a perspective that emphasized a moral imperative to act in a prosocial way beyond any individual perspective or intention, he did not posit the necessity of demonstrating a seamless connection regarding past, present, and future moral behavior (Mead, 1936, pp. 370–376; Pfuetze, 1954, pp. 251–252). One intriguing aspect of Mead's position involved a transformation regarding individual pursuit of self-interest. Creating patterns of behavior that appear to either contradict or ignore a community of consciousness does not preclude emergent behavior enacted during crucial moments of truth and validating such a community. Moral behavior, from Mead's pragmatic perspective, begins with recognition of a problematic and can emerge from the most unlikely of sources. The enacted histories of others do not necessarily predict the future action such others take. In Mead's world, human beings and the behavior they produce do not create absolute purity or evil (see Douglas, 1966); but human behavior and consequences can create systematic processes of coordination in which people regard moral decision-making as necessary to move forward to presume sociality or creating temporal alignments in the present with mutual reference to a past and mutual orientation to a future (Mead, 1938, pp. 606–613; Stevens, 1967, pp. 615–616).

In the following pages, I draw upon Mead's perspective and view of morality as emergent, coordinated, and empathetic to discuss how characters in a fictional story represent complex constructions of moral activity based upon emergent decision-making (see also Dewey, 1916). In describing this complexity, I discuss Mead's view of a consciousness of morality that rejects moral absolutism (rigid definitions of right and wrong) without resorting to moral relativism (particularistic and idiosyncratic views of right and wrong that serve self-centered purposes). Rather, Mead's approach maintains what Dewey (1929, p. 9) referred to as warranted assertions with an underlying moral premise that disparate others, regardless of past behaviors and present dispositions, can create shared futures and agree on superordinate goals (Sherif, 1958, pp. 349–351). In particular, characters with disparate dispositions can recognize that the potential extinguishing of a consciousness of morality leads to total extinction.

The particular fictional story, *The Man in the High Castle*, focuses on the Amazon TV adaptation of Philip K. Dick's eponymous novel. Both novel and TV series took place in the early 1960s and employ a "what if" method of storytelling; in particular, readers and viewers suspend disbelief to imagine that the attempt to assassinate Franklin D. Roosevelt in 1932 left him too wounded in the aftermath to seek a third term in 1940 (and thus to have no official position during World War II) and, subsequently, that the Axis powers (Nazi

Germany and Imperial Japan) defeated the United States (through the use of a nuclear weaponry). As victors, the Nazi Third Reich and the Japanese Imperial Government have divided the United States into three sectors: the Nazi controlled East Sector with its exacting Germanic law and order, the Japanese Imperialist controlled West Sector with treacherous law combined with civilized Japanese custom, and a "no-person's" Central/Neutral Sector, in which the laws of "self-help" coexist with the laws and customs of East and West (see Black, 1983). The German and Japanese takeover of America creates several systemic oppressive orders including involuntary euthanasia (of the sick and diseased), mortal punishment by law enforcement without trial, organized murder directed toward law-abiding citizens, and impoverished conditions for most non-Nazi and non-Japanese Americans. In this particular context, and focusing on central characters, especially Juliana Crain, the heroine of the story, I wish to show how Mead standpoint regarding morality and an empathic connection to a community of others, emerges amid a dystopian reality that denies a plurality of perspectives and in doing so, a commitment to sociality.

MEAD, MORALITY, AND READING CINEMA TO TEST ASSUMPTIONS

Mead's pragmatic stance dealt with, in part, how disturbing or exaggerated assumptions can nevertheless deserve consideration (1936, pp. 276–279). Mead's commitment to sociality as a potential problematic (in that interactors must work to align past, present, and future so as to proceed with mutually defined coordination) can appear overly sanguine, especially in regard to a belief that dystopian realities represent common ways of structuring interaction in everyday worlds (see Athens, 2002). Even so, entertaining abstract notions of moral action that allow for the possibility of even the least likely people to act for the benefit of others rather than a singular self emphasizes freedom from dogmatism (Mead, 1936, pp. 281–282). Using this particular reading, human interaction of all varieties allows for a possible future of problem solving, temporal alignment, and empathetic moral agreements.

Mead's (1934, 1936, pp. 281–283) view called for examination that human beings in controlled environments (such as the laboratory) create temporal alignment and demonstrate the universality of sociality (see also McPhail, 1979; Couch, 1987). His vision of human coordination in controlled environments presumed flexibility among those attempting to create moralistic behavior, or that which could benefit others as much as it would benefit the self (Pfuetze, 1954). However, such flexibility also would allow researchers to acknowledge that behavior, while patterned and sometimes predictable, also occurred on provocative stages (Katovich, 1994, pp. 52–54) in and out of the laboratory and structured fields. The provocative stages can provide opportunities for observations of crucial decision-making ranging from predictable to sudden and unexpected.

One such provocative stage, emphasizing theatrical moments of predictable and unpredictable acts in scripted media landscapes (including film, TV, and Internet), can allow for an examination of some of the assumptions regarding moral activity advocated by Mead. His communal and future directed view of morality can appear in representative form, depicted in fictional novels, films, or television. Going beyond a laboratory and other structured environments I use a science fiction novel and its television adaptation as opportunities to explore unpredictable transformations. Viewing this adaptation several times can allow for systematic observations and analysis.

Even though Mead did not advocate using his ideas from literary or cinematic sources, narratives from these sources have provided richly textured and imaginary worlds that transcend a strict duality on "real life" as opposed to "a made-up life" (Berger, 1977, pp. 26–30). Both the real and imaginary have consequences defined as real (see Thomas and Thomas, 1928). Audiences show a willingness to engage in "suspension of disbelief" in regard to the imaginary (Wiley, 2003, pp. 172–174). We respond to cinematic and film characters as we respond to friends and loved ones about whom we have invested emotional attachment. Further, examining cinematic representations allows for subversive accounts of imagined existence. Subversive accounts encourage the thinker/writer to explore the thick cultural representations that occur in scripted or unscripted portraits of life understood by audiences who see relevance to their own lives in both depictions (Denzin, 1991, pp. 5–11). A subversive reading of events can also encourage thinkers to expand on and reconsider extant arguments made by prominent intellectuals.

In regard to the above, *The Man in the High Castle* depicts backstage worlds of evil and ordinary machinations; it shows the formation of dominant and subversive relations as they occur in secret societies (Athens, 2007, pp. 141–144). The fictional depiction of *The Man in the High Castle*, in particular, depicts the resistance to oppression that appears in everyday broadcasts of world events, political movements, popular films, television shows, and the news. In effect, what appears in *The Man in the High Castle*, however contrived, resonates to what Mead (1934, pp. 47–48) discussed as the world of significant symbolization, in which even that which is not directly experienced is still recognized, at least on a visceral level.

MEAD AND THE COMPLEXITY OF MORALITY

As mentioned, Mead's view of morality not only avoided the dogmatism of moral absolutism but also attempted to provide a firmer approach than mere moral relativism. His key to such avoidance rested upon two particular notions familiar to interactionists. First, he emphasized the cooperative nature of coordinated social life and the ability to anticipate future consequences as mutually, and even universally, beneficial (Mead, 1932, pp. 45–48). Second, he emphasized the human capacity to become objects to themselves and thus take each other's roles as they engaged in cooperative and coordinated activity (Blumer, 1969). Such a capacity recognizes the other as different from, but fundamentally similar to, the self, especially in regard to future direction and survival of the species.

Mead's notion of sociality and empathy took place in a world of ongoing emergence in which on-the-spot decision-making has consequences for a community of actors and thus to moral consciousness in general. Returning to the usefulness of fictional accounts that represent provocative stages, scripted storylines, while outside of the pragmatic scientist's control, per se, offer dramatic representations of the consciousness of morality that Mead discussed. In our American media landscape, such dramatic representations often involve particular characters "pushing up against" particular foils representing readily apparent contrasts to a community of moral consciousness. Contributing to the interest of the provocative stages in themselves, some characters push against foils in ways that appear to defy their own histories of amoral activity so that moral communities of consciousness can survive.

For instance, the Nazi and any ally of Nazism have become significant foils in that the Nazi and any form of Nazi symbolism presumes immorality (among a majority of people not given to hate induced speech). Unlikely characters representing Mead's emphasis of emergence in regard to moral behavior have appeared in celebrated films such as *Casablanca* and *Stalag 17*. Each of these films depict two self-centered and apparently bitter men contradicting patterns of behavior grounded in their pasts so as to make crucial decisions and sacrifices to triumph over a Third Reich. Even in twenty-first century storylines, acting against a Nazi-like order puts one inside a morally conscious community. For instance, in the recently acclaimed TV series, *Breaking Bad*, the anti-hero, after destroying family and friendships in the pursuit of wealth via production and sales of methamphetamine, redeems himself by giving up his life and saving a friend captured and tortured by neo-Nazis. When one acts in a way that opposes any sort of symbol of brutality, such as Nazi rule, one belongs, however momentarily, in the group advocating a moral program of action.

As Mead's focus on plurality and role taking also calls for understanding of all others, including iconic foils, such foils can engage in behaviors that approach a version of moral action. While such an entrance may seem momentary and perhaps easily reversible (in that one can resume patterns of behavior that do not fit in with a morality of consciousness), the activity incorporates sociality and empathy for the time being (Mead, 1908, pp. 314–315). While advancing a notion that enduring foils have the capacity to engage in sociality and regard others with empathy appears fantastic, the cinematic landscape has provided exemplary scenarios in which people combine allegiance to the apparently immoral and indications of their humanity. American films, such as *The Enemy Below*, and a TV series such as *Combat*, as well as the celebrated German film, *Das Boot*, have depicted those fighting for the Nazi cause as complex and nuanced and, by implication, capable of recognizing how moral action could benefit others beyond one's self-interest. Mead's position advances the idea that even though moral consistency through past empathic behavior and allegiance to communities advancing empathy make future moral action probable, even immediately apparent foils can connect to a moral consciousness. Such an idea can be explored through a media representation that takes viewers into the everyday lives of those we regard as possessing antipathy for a moral way of acting. *The Man in the High Castle* attempts to explore such complexity and in effect depicts Mead's central notions of morality as constructed in the uneven milieus of human coordination.

READING *THE MAN IN THE HIGH CASTLE*

The Man in the High Castle depicts how a particular interactional order of things (Goffman, 1983, pp. 2–3) becomes maintained even against heroic resistance. For the most part, those upholding an interaction order make decisions to sustain noxious and inhumane action as everyday events. The dystopian world depicted is ordered to the point of severe oppression, encompassing inhumane activity as an obdurate reality to which everyday citizens adapt (Blumer, 1969, pp. 8–11). It contrasts with the familiar and idealized non-dystopian America, representing a parallel reality and one familiar to TV viewers through the decades.

The ominous characters in charge of the dystopian world perpetuate and validate the system in efficient and taken-for-granted ways, rendering the frayed background of their plush everyday lives as ordinary (see Garfinkel, 1967, pp. 34–36). These characters move from comfortable and nurturing home routines in the morning to cold blooded decision-making in the afternoon. The working class (non-Nazi drones) do the "dirty work" as a form of routine compliance (see Hughes, 1957, pp. 228–229). The unspoken universe of appearance separates elites from those subservient (Stone, 1962, pp. 88–91). Nazis dress in their gray and black uniforms; the businesslike Imperial Japanese dress in impeccable blue business suits. Once the business of living of dominating (often ruthlessly) concludes, the men return home as daily heroes of their banal business of asymmetrical maintenance (Arendt, 1963, pp. 134–138).

The dystopian reality has its obvious differences with the non-dystopian parallel reality along with a few seemingly trivial popular cultural commonalities. In the dystopian world, the sick and the labeled (mentally unfit or inferior) become chattel. Relations in the dystopian reality also involve a tension between the Axis victors, the Germans and the Japanese. Such tension produces previously unimaginable characterizations. Hitler, the infamous embodiment of evil, becomes portrayed as ailing and, although paranoid, lacks the brutal and violent disposition that defines him. Heinrich Himmler, another historical monster, has become much tamer bureaucrat, resembling the banality of evil (Arendt, 1963). Compounding matters, each guards the status quo – a policy of peaceful cohabitation with the Japanese. As the story develops, viewers learn of a conspiracy within the Reich's elites to murder Hitler and destroy the pact of peaceful coexistence through expansive nuclear holocaust. This conspiracy, making up a secret society of war hawks, involves Martin Heusmann and cronies, who wait for the right time to murder Hitler and blame the Japanese. Heusmann's character has additional significance as the father of another character, Joe Blake, who becomes involved, emotionally, with the aforementioned heroine, Juliana Crain.

The story and its particular arcs (as well as the various characters comprising the arcs) moves in regard to the possibility of an alternate world, representing the non-dystopian reality. The person who apparently knows of such a world, Hawthorn Abendson, has, in the novel, written a book, *The Grasshopper Lies Heavy*. This book recounts history as the viewers and readers know it; Roosevelt remained President until the near end of World War II and the Allied Forces defeated the Axis, culminating in the use of two atomic bombs in Hiroshima and Nagasaki. In the Amazon TV Series, this book becomes represented in an unspecified but large number of documentary-like films, either possessed by individuals scattered across the divided United States or stocked in a warehouse owned by Abendson and in Hitler's Office. The German Reich and the Imperialist Japanese, as well as a group of renegades known as the Resistance (and enemies of the Nazi-Imperialist state), have the common goals to secure as many of the documentaries as possible.

Hitler and Abendson possess many films, but searches continue for others. The documentaries show, in newsreel fashion, the various battles described to viewers in history books. Viewers see the invasion of Normandy, the Japanese surrender, the toppling of the Third Reich, the atomic bombs over Hiroshima and Nagasaki, and importantly, the testing of the hydrogen bomb in the Bikini Islands – which in the Axis-dominated world is considered part of the Japanese Empire. While the novel does not treat the authorship of *The Grasshopper Lies Heavy* as ambiguous, the production of the films in the TV Series has several versions of their origin, creating rumor and speculation. Separate characters make contradictory assumptions about the documentaries, ranging from their creation by Abendson to their appearance via "crossing over" from the dystopian to the non-dystopian worlds. As the viewers learn, some people have the ability to cross over, although such ability seems non-intentional. For instance, another character who becomes important in the series, the Japanese trade minister Nobuske Tagomi, crosses over through meditation. Tagomi's crossover becomes seen as most significant, as he obtains (in the non-dystopian reality) and delivers (to key figures in the dystopian reality) a crucial film that helps avoid nuclear holocaust.

The films represent social objects as Mead (1910, p. 52) defined them in that they have an undeniable existence as things and become transformed into substantial and meaningful commodities with future-oriented value. Viewers become aware of the films as objects when Juliana Crain encounters her half-sister Trudy. Juliana discovers that Trudy has become a member of the Resistance and fears that the Japanese Imperial Government (and, in particular, the Kempeitai – the dominant and ruthless police force) has identified her as a member of the Resistance and put her under surveillance. Under the cover of night, Trudy meets Juliana to pass on one of the contraband films (which is titled *The Grasshopper Lies Heavy*) with instructions to deliver it to a liaison in the Middle Sector so that Abendson can view it. After making the handoff, Juliana witnesses Trudy's death by Kempeitai gunfire.

Shaken, but curious, Juliana watches the film and then shares what she viewed with her lover, Frank Frink, calling its contents, "A better world." Frank recognizes the film as one made either by the man in the high castle or by some anonymous filmmaker with a knack for making the fake look real. Juliana, however, becomes convinced of the film's veracity and decides to pose as Trudy and deliver the film to one of Abendson's contacts in the Middle Sector. Despite Frank's pleas to Juliana to either destroy or get rid of the film, Juliana decides to board a bus that takes her to the destination about which Trudy informed her. Her decision, in the words of the poet Robert Frost, "makes all the difference" or, as Bateson (1972) notes, becomes the difference that makes a difference.

In establishing the importance of the documentaries, the TV Series uses the device of parallel narratives in that many story arcs occur simultaneously. As Juliana makes her decision, Joe Blake, working as a Nazi operative, has managed to gain employment with the Resistance in the Eastern Reich zone. He proceeds to drive a truck to Juliana's destination. The truck, ostensibly delivering coffee pots, also carries another film. Joe's superior, John Smith, the Oberstgruppenführer (or "head honcho") of the Eastern Reich, has devised a plan to lure Abendson into the open. Smith, who first appears as a calm, systematic, and brutal slayer of anyone he suspects as traitorous, becomes a more central and even sympathetic character in the Series. In some key ways, he represents Mead's complex view of an emergent moral consciousness. As Juliana's and Joe's activities develop, another story arc in the parallel narrative, involving Nobuske Tagomi, deals with a system of Government and the Third Reich with personal distaste, despite his position of power. As the series progresses, viewers discover that Tagomi, during one of his crossovers, has procured a film that shows the hydrogen bomb testing in the Bikini Islands. The various arcs merge as significant to the *dénouement* occurring at the end of Season Two.

Obviously, the story arcs and character development in the two TV series of *The Man in the High Castle* provide a surfeit of details and intrigue that goes beyond my intention to fit characters' decisions with Mead's view of morality. All key developments that can set up an analysis, however, revolve around the documentaries. To add further ambiguity, the documentaries do not merely show what American viewers have seen in the newsreels of the day. Some of the documentaries involve characters in the show, involved in particular scenarios, most of which end up in vast nuclear devastation. Unlike Hitler, who watches the documentaries as a horrified viewer, getting all the more paranoid that his world may collapse, Abendson regards the films as providing analytical clues and recognizes a pattern he has seen and memorized (at one point, he burns his entire collection so that the films do not reach Hitler, claiming he has all the pertinent details in his head). From his perspective, one scenario must play out which involves the peace-loving Juliana killing George Dixon, the head of the Resistance in Eastern Reich America. In the documentary, Dixon lays dead in an alley, wearing a Nazi uniform. The story of that documentary represents the only narrative which avoids nuclear disaster.

Juliana, to a degree, resembles the mythological Antigone who traverses various places in all three sectors, transforming from a peace-loving character who has adopted the non-violent traditions of Japanese esthetics (she learns to speak Japanese and has become proficient at Aikido and its philosophy of non-violent self-defense) to one who ends up killing three men, including Dixon (by shooting him in the back). She interacts with all of the main characters and, in one notable twist, has the double identity of Nobuske Tagomi's secretary in the dystopian Nazi-Imperialist dominated reality and of Tagomi's daughter-in-law in modern (early 1960s) non-dystopian America's San Francisco. She also becomes entangled with Joe, after meeting him at the destination to deliver the films. After a series of calamities, she flees to the Eastern Reich where Smith, sensing that she could provide information regarding the Resistance and Abendson, takes her in. Juliana then becomes involved in the Smith family affairs, most notably as the confidant of Smith's son, Thomas, who has a disease that the Nazi's consider treatable only through euthanasia.

The aforementioned notion of superordinate goals that bind the disparate characters revolves around the film that Tagomi has brought into the dystopian world – showing, at least from the perspective of those inhabiting the dystopian world, capabilities of even more vast nuclear destruction that what the Nazi's can infuse. When Heusmann, who has reunited with Joe, now one of the members of the secret society, decides to poison Hitler and blame the Japanese (via an international TV address), Tagomi decides to act. He delivers the film to Chief Inspector Takeshi Kido and instructs Kido to take it to the Eastern Sector and show it to Oberstgruppenführer Smith. Upon receiving the film and discovering that Heusmann plans nuclear destruction, Smith travels to Berlin (one of the substorylines in the series involves the speed and proficiency of world travel – a trip from New York to Berlin comprises less than two hours). Smith convinces a reluctant Blake (the relationship between Smith and Blake has many intricate developments not mentioned here) to show the film to Heusmann, Heusmann's inner circle, and Himmler. Smith also shows Himmler evidence that Heusmann has murdered Hitler and that his plans for nuclear devastation involve control of power rather than revenge against the Japanese. In an alarming and seemingly impossible climax (given our orientations to the evil nature of the Nazi foil), Smith, the efficient and studied sadist, and Himmler, the historical demon, arrest Heusmann and avert the nuclear holocaust that Heusmann had planned.

MEAD'S VIEW OF MORALITY AND THE USEFULNESS OF FICTIONAL REPRESENTATIONS

The narrow focus on developments in the TV Series allows for greater attention of how key characters worked together to avert a nuclear holocaust. The actions of these fictional characters appear relevant to Mead's emphasis on emergence. Past behavioral responses and repertoires cannot, with certainty, predict future outcomes associated with acts and intentions to make acts meaningful (Mead, 1929). Further, in accordance with Mead's perspective that individuals interact with others from a plurality of perspectives, no one perspective serves as a determinate "push toward" inevitable outcomes. Individuals with histories of behaving in untoward ways did not only recognize how particular behaviors could benefit others but also worked to enact such behaviors. Similarly, those who created routine pasts of habitual moral enactments contradicted their behavioral habits and engaged in action that appeared to contradict commitment to a moral community (Mead, 1908, 315–318).

Returning to the apparent odious nature of Nazism, especially as portrayed in American films and TV productions, Mead's view of emergent moral action from a plurality of perspectives that benefits a community of others applies to those devoted to their sadistic tasks. Vile people supporting depraved regimes confront horrors that impel them to act in ways that avert destruction of a community. In effect, Mead's view of morality does not support rigid dualistic thinking regarding right and wrong or good and bad. A position of moral certainty would emphasize how one either joined a Nazi-like movement or fought it consistently, to either get on or off the bus, to borrow from Ken Kesey.

Mead's position between absolutism and relativism appears evident as the storyline continues. Inspector Kido, the man in charge of the Kempeitai and so immersed in his duties that he ordered the deaths of three innocent relatives of Frank Frink, risked his life to make sure that Oberstgruppenführer Smith received the film depicting the hydrogen bomb testing in the Bikini Islands. Smith also risked his stature and even his life by bringing the film to the attention of the Nazi elite. In other instances, Smith deviated from his ruthless agenda to reveal a humane side. He comes across as a devoted husband. He loves his children who reciprocate such love. He also deliberately went against orders from the Nazi elite to destroy Savannah, Georgia, owing to unrest ignited by the Resistance. Despite historical behaviors indicating otherwise, emergent circumstances arise in which unlikely people make immediate decisions that can transcend what appears as an impossible schism between a pluralistic and empathic moral community and an ethos of harm.

Analogously, Juliana and Frank occasionally transform from cooperative, peaceful, and prosocial characters into an activist in an underground, engaging in killing, chicanery, and deception. Juliana shoots a Nazi clad Dixon in the back, on his way to infiltrate Eastern Reich headquarters to use a tape in which Thomas confides to Juliana that he has a terminal disease. Frank murders three Kempeitai guards to save the lives of strangers who happen to be in the Resistance. Juliana's decision to pose as Trudy and take the documentary to the middle sector makes Frank a target of Inspector Kido, who imprisons Frank and demands information pertaining to Juliana's departure, of which Frank knows nothing. The viewers learn that Frank as well as his sister and niece and nephew descend from Jewish origins on his father's side. As Frank cannot reveal any information, his sister, niece, and nephew become detained and gassed to death. Frank himself is sentenced to die by firing squad; seconds before the shooting, Kido discovers that another woman has smuggled films to the middle sector and assumes that she possesses the one that Trudy gave to Juliana. Frank's life is spared, but he lives with the nonhealing scar of his family's death by gassing. In both instances, Juliana has either killed a person who dedicated his life to fight the Nazis or brought attention to vulnerable people who die owing to such attention.

Within a rigid world of purity, immoral activity denies, neglects, or even revels in any sense of harm done to others. Malicious and cold-blooded acts as well as a general pattern of destructive behavior, putting innocent lives in danger (or eradicating innocence) and exterminating those fighting for just causes, qualifies as the antithesis of everyday notions of doing the right things. However, Mead's perspective (1938, pp. 226–228; Mead, 1918, pp. 578–580) diverges from such purity by keying on how empathetic concern for others can sometimes conflict with practical action. Conversely, despite a lack of history in expressing empathetic concern, people can recognize that practical action can protect others' well-being. People cannot be read as racehorses compiling a "track record" on a racing form (see Maines et al., 1983). As such, a moral nature cannot simply be defined as one doing the right thing, consistently. In Mead's terms, moral and immoral behavior (or behavior that has beneficial or detrimental effects to a community of others) can emerge; sustaining a moral course of action across time and space and as a matter of course rather than as a response to emergency becomes Mead's key focus.

MORALITY, SOCIALITY, AND THE SPECIOUS PRESENT

The Man in the High Castle provides a combination of themes and images that link interactors together in regard to a shared future, regardless of past behaviors and animosities. Specifically, *The Man in the High Castle* explores immorality and morality linked to environmental and interactional climates in which a shared consciousness of allegiance in relation with others underlies significant and consequential decision-making. Moral and immoral activities push up against an obdurate reality that pushes back, creating an eternal gray glimmer that hovers over everyday lives of decent and indecent people in a specious present – or a present that appears obvious but that can become altered by and through emergent events.

Rather than key on individual behavior as moral or immoral, Mead seems to suggest that one could dissect regimes that deny multiple perspectives or a plurality of choices. Such denial can create tyrannical or oligarchical control in which choices to create moral consciousness become sacrificed. In this light, Mead's view of the probability of immoral behavior as a pattern of activity has similarities to the iron cages built by adhering to routinization without creativity (Weber, 1958) to how oligarchical organizations emerge from standpoints advocating options (Michels, 1915) and the transformation of horrific evil into banal appearances (Arendt, 1963). However, rather than end at these somber points, Mead regards the capacity to act with attention to the needs of others as possible, even in the most stilted and rigid systems of coordinated behavior. Social structures may possess apparent power, but the capacity to transform, at the individual or organizational levels, provides Mead with his root metaphor of human participation in moral communities.

Almost every main character in the storyline experiences some sort of transformation. Viewers first see Frank as a quiet and unassuming artist, working diligently in a Japanese factory, but who also becomes entangled in the horrific world of political intrigue by becoming a murderer "for a cause." Viewers also first see Nobuske Tagomi as a powerful trade minister working for the Imperial

Japanese (and oppressive) cause. Both become horrified by events that create a consciousness of morality. After joining the Resistance and witnessing how blasé members of the Resistance appear when their acts of violence become matched, tenfold, by the Japanese Imperial regime, Frank expresses outrage. A member of the Resistance chastises Frank for dwelling on his own emotions and his personal involvement and failing to see the "overall plan" associated with the takeover. Nobuske becomes more disturbed by the day regarding the consequences of the oppressive regime to which he contributes through his work. Both Nobuske's and Frank's horror symbolizes the capacity to be shocked by recognition, an underlying element of a moral consciousness linking people to a community of otherness.

The Man in The High Castle cuts across story arcs and the characters involved as they deal with their changing perspectives regarding what would serve the greater good for others unlike themselves and what could allow them to survive. As events in each person's field of awareness become clarified, each of the characters experiences self-transformations that create novel actions (see Strauss, 1959). Returning to Juliana, her accumulation of knowing others inside and outside of the Nazi Reich brings particular insight into what should and what should not occur. Her decision to shoot George Dixon who possesses information that would insure the death of Thomas Smith (and the demise of John Smith for hiding such information) just so happens to create the ending of a particular documentary for which Abendson hoped.

Mead (1932, pp. 9–11) maintained the complexity of lived experience in a specious present, involving the gradual crystallization of a more probable future than the multitude of possible futures prior to the transaction. Mead's notion of perception of a physical thing as an object emphasizes how particular items such as film documentaries become part of a moral community shared by those with highly divergent goals and ideologies. In effect, using the plot devices and symbolism in *The Man in the High Castle* allows for articulation of Mead's complex standpoint regarding morality as recognizable and practical programs of action, shared by those with common and divergent perspectives and histories of action.

That which is made possible in the specious present becomes, pragmatically, impossible as alternative specious presents become defined as irrelevant (Hintz (1975) [2015]). This crystallization of possibility/impossibilities solidifies a connection between an individual's interpretation of phenomena and larger scale (societal) consequences associated with such phenomena (Hintz and Couch, 1975 [2015], p. 35). Juliana's response to Trudy's death and her own orientation to the documentary that Trudy gives to Juliana prior to her death bring the past and future into an emergent focus in regard to Juliana's lived experience. It a much grimmer world, Juliana's new grip of a focus also represents Juliana's transformation from an apolitical adapter into a renegade (from the Nazi and Imperial Japanese perspective) who nevertheless expresses repeated concern for others, regardless of their allegiance.

As mentioned, the documentaries in themselves become emergent objects, the meaning of which changes as Juliana's realization of their content evolves. Consistent with Mead's emphasis on emergence and significant symbolization (or collective recognition and shared responsiveness toward a recognizable object), the trajectory of Juliana's transformation occurs as she moves from one specious present to another (and one transaction to another). Juliana's venture into a world of specious presents contextualized by the politics of evil becomes connected to how the Resistance, the Nazis, and the Japanese interpret and respond to the documentary. Their responses not only represent how the documentaries can represent a "better world" but also how to escape into an actual world that the audience know as historically accurate. The sequence of specious presents in regard to the series also connects Julia to the Resistance. The sequences become turning points for Julia as she begins to see herself as a political dissident in possession of an object that makes mere adaptation to her current world insufficient (Strauss, 1959).

The specious presents become continuous loops in which the past and future, informing and structuring the present, become defined as symbolically reconstructed moments. Seemingly obdurate pasts become altered as negotiable futures, in which people face moments of truth to create significant acts. As seen in *The Man in The High Castle*, specious presents indicate that human beings neither mindlessly react to stimuli (without imagining such stimuli in the context of a past or future) nor simply see the stimuli in pure idiosyncratic terms as it fits into an all-consuming present. In contrast, human beings mindfully locate themselves in reference to the past as they move forward and situate themselves in the future (Miller et al., 1975; Katovich and Couch, 1992).

Mead's view of activating specious presents is relevant to Mills' (1959, pp. 3–5) more global version of a sociological imagination. This imagination links ongoing problematic concerns with broader, historical societal issues. The specious present also puts Mead "at the table" that Zeitlin (1997, pp. 371–372) created when imagining a "debate" between Marx, Durkheim, and Weber in regard to the haunting of social life. On the face of it, Mead's specious present is not haunted by the possibilities of cataclysmic forces, but rather created on the basis of pragmatic outcomes, useful for the time being. However, depending on who controls the dominant narratives of the pasts and future (which the Nazi's do in *The Man in The High Castle*), the commanding and ongoing meaning in the specious present (linked to constructions and reconstructions of the past and future) can fit into narratives associated with Marx, Weber, and Durkheim, especially alienation, routinization (and its "iron cage"), and anomie. The specious present represents a vast area of possibilities in which pasts and futures give structure to the present, but it can become a scripted ordeal that follows the historical forces of those in hostile command.

Even so, Mead went beyond *a morality in the specious present* to discuss the importance of *morality as grounded in sociality* or the convergence of shared pasts and shared futures in a moving and mutable present. Inspector Kido and John Smith acted in accordance with Mead's conception of morality, but their acts occurred in one sequence of specious presents. Kido and Smith acted heroically in a relatively short duration, but have enduring allegiances to oppressive regimes. Juliana, Frank, and Nobuske, however, act with regard to sociality across time and space boundaries. Abendson, in particular, recognizes Juliana's grounding in sociality and her ongoing attitude of empathy after she shoots Dixon, which becomes the *coup de grace* regarding the avoidance of a nuclear holocaust.

When Juliana meets up with Abendson after the events in the particular documentary play out to avoid a nuclear holocaust, Abendson tells Juliana, "The only thing I know is that you, Juliana Crain, were the only hope that any of us had." He explains to her that she represented the link in all the films, appearing in them in varieties of roles and settings, in the background and foreground. Through her, Abendson began his analysis, seeing that all of the characters in the story revolved around her "like an atom." He realized that while these characters changed dispositions and general appearances moment by moment, representing adaptation in the specious present, Juliana remained grounded in empathy (and sociality) despite her surface appearances. Abendson tells Juliana, "you were always you...I got to see a woman who would bet on the best of us, who would bet on people no matter who they were." In effect, Abendson tells Juliana that he saw the one person who exhibited consistent empathy and a morality grounded in sociality rather than in a specious present. As a "happy ending" to the story, Juliana's acts that ensured the reality of one of the documentaries reunites her with Trudy, who due to the events that occurred in the order they occurred, manages to live rather than to die as one murdered by the Kempeitai.

CONCLUSION: MORALITY AS PRAGMATIC ACTION

Exploring the what if or the parallel universes that separate the "better world" (moral) from the world as controlled by the Axis powers (immoral) in *The Man in The High Castle* actually addresses a concern raised by Mead (1929, 1932, 1934, 1938) in a variety of writings. Although Mead avoided rigorous explorations of moral action, per se, he maintained a consistent interest in an obdurate reality that upholds the workable qualities (for the general benefit) of "what is in the present" (1932, pp. 32–35). Mead acknowledged that any person, of course, is free to imagine the world any way he/she wishes. However, simply because one insists on seeing a 2,000-pound truck as nothing more than harmless molecules evaporating into air will not prevent the truck from crushing this person as he/she stands in its way. In effect, in establishing a workable morality that transcends the specious present, Mead emphasized that maintenance of the common good requires the realization of dogged obstacles and plans of action to confront such obstacles in a practical and also empathetic way.

Mead did not wish to fall into a trap that plagued the psychological behaviorists of his day, in particular, his colleague, John Watson. Mead considered the deference that behaviorists seemed to pay to fixed obstacles in the past created a vision of a static future, regardless of any internal intervening process. Mead also viewed the solipsistic psychologists, such as C.H. Cooley, as interior and unable to push back, with any effectiveness, against obdurate constraints. Rather, Mead entertained the "what if" as it exists in the context of sociality. We live in the present, but we do so as people reflecting and reconstructing the past and making hypothetical assumptions regarding the future – the "what is" always entangles itself with "what was" (or apparently was) and "what might be." Aspects of the past that seemed ugly become viewed differently, depending on how present reality becomes constructed. Ominous futures do not simply disappear at will, but must be changed as formulations of the past change. Mead stressed that whatever we call the present or however we study it, careful observers must recognize that such a moment emerges and becomes altered, if necessary pragmatically, as people create programs of moral action in the course of solving problems reflectively, rather than purely reflexively (Mead, 1932; Zavestoski and Weigert, 2017; Puddephatt, 2016). Indeed, confronting the problematic, such as an oppressive system, and entertaining notions of "what if" became a foundation for Mead's view of sociality that allows merging past, present, and future in pragmatic ways (Mead, 1934, pp. 320–322; Miller, 1973).

In the course of implying a morality as grounded in sociality, Mead viewed individual-lived experiences as a process of living in potential multiple "what if" worlds of hypothetical outcomes (see Joas, 1997[1980], pp. 190–191), from comfortable to problematic – which include awareness of hostile phenomenon that threatens the comfortable. Further, in addition to hostile possibilities, the cyclical nature of comfort (or the distinct lack of such comfort and presence of hostility) is not naturally resolvable. From Mead's view, the empirical world is not merely restricted to social facts that have linear beginnings, middles, and ends. Instead, "what if" hypotheses provide continuous information and structure to "what is" reality. Human beings as moral actors provide continuous feedback that, in turn, create additional feedback that form an ongoing sphere of moments (Flaherty and Fine, 2001, pp. 149–150; Mead, 1932, pp. 23–25). This ongoing present becomes filled with temporal processes that self-conscious individuals can observe to use the past and future to inform and structure the present (Mead, 1938, pp. 8–16; Emirbayer and Mische, 1998, pp. 968–970; Maines, 1989, pp. 109–110).

Mead's view of sociality and especially the possibility of moral action as grounded in sociality serves as a basis upon which humans attempt to create a better world, often against the odds. Mead's view fits with the alternative narratives in the documentaries and represents the idealistic possibilities in a world dominated by grim probabilities. Using Meadian thought as a theoretical framework, we can imagine how one version of the past can become more prominent than other versions, even if such versions represent formidable obstacles. In this way, Mead may have imagined a world of traps, cages, and alienation from this world, but he also imagined people as capable of transforming such obstructions.

As implied above, Mead's emphasis on sociality as the "saving grace" of humanity mirrors Abendson's faith in Juliana as the saving grace of the parallel reality in which they live (and from which they may escape). As Abendson implies in his final speech to Juliana, even the most innocuous of acts connect the self, other, and environment (Mead, 1934, pp. 7–8) to intersecting pasts and futures that each actor assumes as "the now." In more complex terms, this "now" becomes connected to other acts, forming a more holistic sense of sequential acts of sociality enlivened by their connection to one another (Flaherty and Fine,

2001, p. 147; Mead, 1932, p 2; Reese and Katovich, 1987, pp. 162–164). All that which people consider as true becomes bound to recognition of emergence. Such emergence can alter the appearance of the factual while maintaining agreement of what becomes defined, consensually, as true for the time being.

Mead's emphasis on the recognition of emergence appears as a *world of being*, emphasizing human coordination and navigation through the spatial-temporal corners and processes of everyday life. This world of being stresses an agreed-to objective and differs from a world *of apparition*, emphasizing a haunting that magnifies human vulnerability to alienation, anomie, and routinization. Such cataclysmic and soulless conditions represent the impact of structural forces and sweeping currents of broad and often cataclysmic transformations on the lived experience of everyday laborers. As Ernest Becker (1968, pp. 140–142) implied, this world of apparition demands an ever-present subtext of forces hostile to the productive and nurturing social bond.

In *The Man in the High Castle*, the world of being becomes defined by sociality and an authentic concern for the fate of others. Such a world is not clean and tidy; as Dixon tells Juliana in regard to New York City prior to the war, the city had a great life to it. It was messy and violent at times, but the people filled it with life through music, creativity, and playing out various lived experiences that the Nazi regime destroyed. The Nazi's, in an effort to "purify" the city, drained the life from it. The key tragedy of such purity is, of course, the inherent flaws of each individual. Such flaws make purity a myth. Thomas, the son of the most powerful Nazi in America, realizes that his flaw (his disease that has no cure) makes him a target of euthanasia. As John Smith, acting in accord with a specious morality and saving the world, for the moment, from nuclear holocaust, Thomas turns himself in to the authorities to be euthanized. Such is Mead's view of morality – filled with flaws, vulnerable to the messy probabilities associated with attempts to coordinate action, and always in process. Yet by committing oneself to a morality grounded in sociality, such imperfection makes for a life worth living.

Mead's view of morality, however unsystematic in its articulation, is complex as it involves acknowledged verification that must be coordinated and constructed by people who transcend their individual imaginations and assume the roles of others. It is also, in particular contexts, laden with the evocative burdens of grief and regret that make closure, in many ways, a myth to which we agree, but from which we never become completely free. We live as pragmatic people on the surface, moving from situation to situation as we accomplish great deeds. But much like Frank and Juliana, we immerse ourselves in such pragmatism as burdened people, never quite shedding ourselves from our pasts and seldom feeling that consummating a future has ended our involvement any particular present.

REFERENCES

Arendt, H. 1963. *Eichmann in Jerusalem: A Report on the Banality of Evil*, New York, NY, Viking Press.

Athens, L. 2002. Domination: the blind spot in Mead's analysis of the social act, *Journal of Classical Sociology*, 2, 25–42.

Athens, L. 2007. Radical interactionism: going beyond Mead, *Journal for the Theory of Social Behavior*, 37, 139–165.

Bateson, G. 1972. *Steps to an Ecology of Mind*, New York, NY, Chandler Publishing Company.

Becker, E. 1968. *The Structure of Evil*, New York, NY, Free Press.

Berger, M. 1977. *Real and Imagined Worlds: The Novel and Social Science*, Cambridge, MA, Harvard University Press.

Black, D. 1983. Crime as social control, *American Sociological Review*, 48, 34–45.

Blumer, H. 1969. *Symbolic Interactionism: Perspective and Method*, Englewood Cliffs, NJ, Prentice-Hall.

Couch, C. 1987. *Researching Social Processes in the Laboratory*, Greenwich, CT, JAI Press.

Dewey, J. 1916. *Democracy and Education*, New York, NY, The McMillian Company.

Dewey, J. 1929. *The Quest for Certainty: A Study of the Relation between Knowledge and Action*, London, Cambridge University Press.

Denzin, N. K. 1991. *Hollywood Shot by Shot: Alcoholism in American Cinema*, New York, NY, Taylor & Francis.

Douglas, M. 1966. *Purity and Danger: An Analysis of Concepts of Pollution and Taboo*, London, Routledge and Keegan Paul.

Emirbayer, M. and Mische, A. 1998. What is Agency? *American Journal of Sociology*, 103, 962–1023.

Flaherty, M. and Fine, G. A. 2001. Present, past, and future: conjugating George Herbert Mead's perspective on time, *Time & Society*, 10, 147–161.

Garfinkel, H. (1967). *Studies in Ethnomethodology*, Englewood Cliffs, NJ, Prentice-Hall.

Goffman, E. 1983. The interaction order, *American Sociological Review*, 48, 1–17.

Hintz, R. A. 1975[2015]. Foundations of social action. In *Constructing Social Life: Readings in Behavioral Sociology from the Iowa School*, Eds C. J. Couch and R. A. Hintz, pp. 59–80, Champaign, IL, Stipes.

Hintz, R. A. and Couch, C. J. 1975[2015]. Time, intention, and social behavior. In *Constructing Social Life: Readings in Behavioral Sociology from the Iowa School*, Eds C. J. Couch and R. A. Hintz, pp. 35–58, Champaign, IL, Stipes.

Hughes, E. 1957. *The Sociological Eye*, Chicago, IL, Aldine-Atherton.

Joas, H. 1997[1980]. *G. H. Mead: A Contemporary Re-examination of His Thought*, (Translated by R. Meyer), Cambridge, MA, MIT Press.

Katovich, M. A. 1994. Symbolic interaction and experimentation: the laboratory as a provocative stage, *Studies in Symbolic Interaction*, 4, 49–67.

Katovich, M. A. and Couch, C. J. 1992. The nature of social pasts and their use as foundations for situated action, *Symbolic Interaction*, 15, 25–47.

Maines, D. R. 1989. Culture and temporality, *Cultural Dynamics*, 2, 107–123.

Maines, D. R., Sugrue, N. and Katovich, M. A. 1983. The sociological import of George Herbert mead's theory of the past, *American Sociological Review*, 48, 161–173.

McPhail, C. 1979. Experimental research is convergent with symbolic interactionism, *Symbolic Interaction*, 2, 89–94.

Mead, G. H. 1908. The philosophical basis for ethics, *International Journal of Ethics*, 18, 311–323.

Mead, G. H. 1910. What social objects must psychology presuppose? *Psychological Bulletin*, 7, 52–53.

Mead, G. H. 1918. The psychology of punitive justice, *American Journal of Sociology*, 23, 577–602.

Mead, G. H. 1929. The nature of the past. In *Essays in Honor of John Dewey*, Ed J. Coss, pp. 235–242, New York, NY, Holt and Company.

Mead, G. H. 1932. *The Philosophy of the Present*, Chicago, IL, University of Chicago Press.

Mead, G. H. 1934. *Mind, Self, and Society*, Chicago, IL, University of Chicago Press.

Mead, G. H. 1936. *Movements of Thought in the Nineteenth Century*, Chicago, IL, University of Chicago Press.

Mead, G. H. 1938. *The Philosophy of the Act*, Chicago, IL, University of Chicago Press.

Michels, R. 1915. *Political Parties: A Sociological Study of the Oligarchical Tendencies of Modern Democracy*, (Translated into English by Edan Paul and Cedar Paul), New York, NY, Free Press. (from the 1911 German source).

Miller, D. E., Hintz, R. and Couch, C. J. 1975. The elements and structure of openings, *The Sociological Quarterly*, 16, 479–499.

Miller, D. L. 1973. *George Herbert Mead: Self, Language, and the World*, Austin, TX, University of Texas Press.

Mills, C. W. 1959. *The Sociological Imagination*, New York, NY, Oxford University Press.

Pfuetze, P. E. 1954. *Self, Society, and Existence: Human Nature and Dialogue in the Thought of George Herbert Mead and Martin Buber*, New York, NY, Harper & Brothers.

Puddephatt, A. 2016. George Herbert Mead: the evolution of mind, self and society through interaction. In *The Interactionist Imagination: Studying Meaning, Situation and Micro-social Order*, Ed M. H. Jacobsen, pp. 95–119, London, Palgrave MacMillan.

Reese, W. A. and Katovich, M. A. 1987. Untimely acts: extending the interactionist conception of deviance, *The Sociological Quarterly*, 30, 159–184.

Sherif, M. 1958. Superordinate goals in the reduction of intergroup conflict, *American Journal of Sociology*, 63, 349–356.

Stevens, E. 1967. Sociality and act in George Herbert Mead, *Social Research*, 34, 613–631.

Stone, G P. 1962. Appearance and the self. In *Human Behavior and the Social Processes: An Interactionist Approach*, Ed A. M. Rose, pp. 86–116, New York, NY, Houghton Mifflin.

Strauss, A. 1959. *Mirrors and Masks: The Search for Identity*, Glencoe, IL, Free Press.

Thomas, W. I. and Thomas, D. S. 1928. *The Child in America: Behavioral Promises and Programs*, New York, NY, Knopf.

Weber, M. 1958. *The Protestant Ethic and the Spirit of Capitalism*, (Translated by Talcott Parsons), New York, NY, Charles Scribner's Sons.

Wiley, N. 2003. Emotion and film theory, *Studies in Symbolic Interaction*, 26, 169–187.

Zavestoki, S. and Weigert, A. 2017. Mead, interactionism and the improbability of ecological selves: toward a meta-environmental microsociological theory. In *Microsociological Theory for Environmental Sociology*, Eds B. H. Bruster and A. Puddephatt, pp. 98–116, London, Routledge.

Zeitlin, I. 1997. *Ideology and the Development of Sociological Theory*, New York, NY, Prentice-Hall.

THE SYMBOLIC INTERACTIONIST AS WRITER*

Joseph A. Kotarba

ABSTRACT

Writing is one of the key features of the life and work of the symbolic interactionist. The foundation of good writing is the establishment of the self and identity of the interactionist qua writer. The best writers are those who write constantly – not necessarily in formal text form but also in term of journals, note-taking, and so forth. Writing does not retrieve our ideas from our minds and memories; it creates them as retrievable gems of our work. My argument is that, as symbolic interactionists, we have the opportunity, if not responsibility, to position the drama of everyday life in our writing because our respondents experience their everyday lives dramatically.

Keywords: Writing; writer; self-identity; symbolic interaction; existential thought; social media; translational science

INTRODUCTION

Like many of you, I have found myself increasingly caught up in the ever-widening web of social media. At the suggestion if not insistence of colleagues, friends, students, and my children, I have surrendered to the temptation to be current – if not hip – by entertaining interest in Facebook, Twitter, Pinterest, TikTok, and so forth. I have also succumbed to the temptation to join occupational or professional sites such as LinkedIn, Academic.edu and Researchgate.net. Being the humble Luddite that I am, I do not trust the large number of

---

*An edited version of a keynote address presented at the Sixth Annual European Symbolic Interactionist meetings, Salford, England July 31, 2015.

Radical Interactionism and Critiques of Contemporary Culture
Studies in Symbolic Interaction, Volume 52, 53–60
Copyright © 2021 by Emerald Publishing Limited
All rights of reproduction in any form reserved
ISSN: 0163-2396/doi:10.1108/S0163-239620210000052004

friends and followers these sites claim I have. Being the crabby old guy that I am too quickly becoming, I do not think I really like as many people and their escapades as Facebook seems to want me to.

What has caught my attention lately are the checklists these services send me to complete in order to construct inventories of my skills and interests. Qualitative research? Problem-solving? Leadership? Team management? Safety regulations? People on LinkedIn seem to be able to do a lot of things. I, on the other hand, like to keep the list of things I do and can do to three or four at most – less chance of screwing up. Of even greater interest to me are the identities I am asked to portray and claim. One does not often see a place to check off sociologist let alone symbolic interactionist on these profiles. Who am I anymore?

THE WRITER

Just who am I at this point in my life and the twenty-first century? The response matrix of course in interactionism is who am I to me – or self – and who am I to others – identity. Lou Zurcher (1979) insightfully told us that we can be different things in different situations, playing out what he called the *mutable self*. In today's society, we need to be different things to different people at different times to survive today's hectic everyday life. In my chosen theoretical perspective, that variety of interactionist thinking known as existential social thought, the sense of self that I ordinarily prefer to project to others as my identity is fluid, constantly evolving as the social and cultural worlds around me rapidly change (Kotarba, 2013a; Melnikov and Kotarba, 2017). And, in the massive world of social media, we are enabled as well as encouraged to change our self-identity at will: what is your Facebook profile today?

The idea of an evolving and complex self is not unique to contemporary social theory. The world of natural and biomedical science increasingly supports the concept of the multidimensional self-identity promoted by social media. I am currently conducting a study of the impact of the translational science movement on health and healthcare delivery. The University of Texas Medical Branch in Galveston receives funding from the National Institutes of Health to change the way biomedical scientists do their work. The traditional scientist worked pretty much alone in their laboratory under the rubric of a unitary self-identity – for example, biologist, gerontologist, and oncologist. Today's translational scientist is expected to work in inter- and cross-disciplinary teams, understand patent law, engage in enterprise fundraising, interact with community stakeholders, and be a jack – and/or jill – of all trades (Kotarba, 2013b, 2014; Kotarba and Wooten, 2017).

I would object to the implied assertion that we as interactionists are simply a collection of skills or specialty areas. The current era of pressure, especially from public and foundation-based sponsors and our universities, to conduct research in interdisciplinary formats have failed to squash our anchors to traditional para-digmatic and intellectual homes. We want to believe that we are more than simply tool boxes, but we also like to believe that we can project the mutable selves of sociologist, symbolic interactionist, ethnographer, etc., as situationally required. What I am proposing is that we pull one tool out of our box that we are generally good at practicing – writing – and actively and self-consciously convert it to an exciting self-identity: writer.

To be and to be known as a writer is somewhat uncommon in the social sciences, although we all write at one time or another. In our common intellectual culture, in both North America and Europe, we think of writers somewhat as humanistic methodologists: the style of their work is sometimes more important, more valuable than the substance of the text. Writers are members of that billowy place known as the humanities. Their stories are commonly derived from if not inspired by their personal experience and biographies (Cooper and White, 2012). Their take on their topics is personal and standpoint. Their writing is stocked amply with metaphors and other varieties of tropes.

Well, that kind of describes us and our work, doesn't it? There are numerous personal and professional rewards for being a writer. The main hook, however, is that writing can bring us great joy and satisfaction as scholars. If we do not enjoy writing, then we are probably poor writers. Being a writer expands the horizon of our co-conspirators and confidants, beyond members of our own discipline. Being a writer can reinvigorate aging careers or ignite new ones.

I fear that we are often too humble to self-identify as writers. Most interactionist attention to date has been placed on discerning, developing, and teaching writing skills, in workmanlike fashion. Howard Becker – of labeling theory and art scenes fame – is one of the leaders in this area. He wrote a book titled *"Writing for Social Scientists"* (1986) and, in proper pragmatist style, subtitled it to the point *"How to Start and Finish your Thesis, Book or Article."* Howard presents all sorts of practical hints and strategies for organizing one's writing, presenting data, and so forth. Howard focuses on what he sees as the major problem faced by social scientists: writer's block or how to get started on your thesis, book, or article. But, his primary directive is: just start writing. This is good advice, except that I feel that we are best served by writing all the time. Cathy Charmaz, in her many detailed works on grounded theory (e.g., Charmaz, 2014), generally says the same thing. In the grounded theory format she champions, the researcher is writing all the time, keeping memos on field observations and interviews, defining and fleshing out concepts that emerge from the data, and so forth. In contrast, I could never really understand how our survey research and demographic brothers and sisters conduct their work in very linear terms. They say,

> Now that we're done with the research, I need to lock myself up in my office, away from all distractions, so I can write. See you in September, as they say.

This account strikes me as the near opposite of the mind frame and work strategy interactionists hold. I would argue that our writing does not help us put our ideas into words as much as it helps us discover our ideas – what Jeff Goins (2014) refers to as "creative writing breakthroughs." Jeff's advice applies to all writers, but perhaps especially to interactionists. To be a writer means you write every day or whenever possible. Writing regularly is much more important than writing a lot. Creative writing comes from being in touch with your research environment. Regular writing during a project is in essence a conversation with your phenomenon. You raise questions you can answer empirically and make observations you can test out and refine in the everyday life of your phenomenon.

We can teach ourselves and our students the mechanics of good writing, but shaping ourselves and them into writers is a bit more of a puzzle. A good strategy for searching for and discovering the essence of the writer is to learn from those who cherish the power of the word.

Robert Nisbet is a good place to start. His thinking was focused on the intersection of the humanities (history) and the social sciences (social thought). Perhaps Professor Nisbet's most relevant work for our discussion is his book on *Sociology as an Art Form* (1976). This was a time of great fervent in our discipline, as witnessed by the powerful critiques of mainstream sociology offered by academic Marxists, the emerging field of ethnomethodology, the energetic stances taken by the existentialist thinkers, and of course the symbolic inter-actionist celebration of everyday life (Adler, Adler, and Fontana, 1987). Nisbet's argument is that the humanist and the social scientist share common under-standings, perceptions, and forms. They both see the world in terms of the common themes of social landscapes (structure and setting); portraits (the individual in terms of roles, statuses and types); the illusion of motion (to describe or portray dynamic strength, motion, or movement – in terms for us such as career and process); and the rust of progress (the costs of social and cultural change). The message for interactionists is clear. Our writing need not always descend to the depths of formulaic tasks such as "technical writing," "report writing," and "writing up the findings." (Although I must confess that I did my share of these technical tasks when I served as Director of the Center for Social Inquiry at Texas State University.) There is something warm and fuzzy about the consideration of an otherwise mundane analytical procedure – the ideal type, for example – as a portrait of some cool feature of everyday life (cf., Pountain and Robins, 2000).

Just how does a symbolic interactionist write as a writer? Let me cite one of my intellectual heroes who, although not a card-carrying social scientist, wrote brilliantly about the human dilemma in words and phrases I find quite conceptual – and concepts, of course, are our great analytical tools as interactionists. Jean Paul Sartre assembled a great story on a foundation of two concepts: freedom and commitment. The story is the *Age of Reason* (1947), the first installment of his trilogy, *Roads to Freedom*. Matthieu was a philosophy teacher in pre-World War II Paris, who found himself facing a number of dilemmas in life. Should he marry his pregnant mistress or borrow money to pay for an abortion? Should he take a side in the Spanish Civil War, and if so, should he side with the fascists or the communists? Sartre's characters are primarily "for-itself beings" who choose to act, but act according to the choices that have molded them. Matthieu sees everyone around him making consequential decisions, but he does not: "All I do, I do for nothing." Matthieu is a modern man going through an existential – or mid-life as we would say today – crisis:

> I'm getting old. Here I am, lounging in a chair and believing in nothing... For 35 years I've been sipping at myself and I'm getting old. I have worked. I have waited, and I have had my desire: Marcelle, Paris, independence: and now it's over. I look for nothing more. This is how

my friends see me: an idle, unresponsive fellow, rather chimerical, but ultimately quite sensible, who has dexterously constructed an undistinguished but solid happiness upon a basis of inertia... Is that what I am? Sartre (1947)

Sartre goes on to say that Mathieu maintains his so-called freedom by doing nothing. In fact, freedom ultimately evolves from the realization that we routinely find ourselves in situations in which we are forced to choose among options provided to us. How does one manage this existential dilemma best? By committing to a project, an idea, or a purpose that gives positive meaning to our choices.

Now, you may be cynically saying that this is the same Sartre who also writes in overly dramatic statements like: "Man is nothing else but what he makes of himself," or who converted to marxism during his mid-life crisis. My argument is that, as symbolic interactionists, we have the opportunity, if not responsibility, to position the drama of everyday life in our writing because our respondents experience everyday life dramatically (cf., Ellis, 2012). As interactionists, we can take the somewhat structuralist term of "agency" and add the vitality of everyday life to it. Let me draw several examples from my two current projects: the social and cultural transformation of the biomedical scientist as I mentioned above and the evolving role of "audience member" in contemporary popular music. The contemporary scientist faces the following somewhat existential dilemmas, that I relay to you in the first person:

- I suddenly find myself expected to be a fairly democratic team member, when my training and career to date posit me as the principal investigator ruling over my laboratory.
- I am a scientist. No one tells me how to do my work. How do I reconcile that fact with the increasing expectation that I also serve as an entrepreneur, community member, and master of legal issues relevant to biomedical research?

Organizational psychologists are most likely to approach these personal issues in terms of rational decision-making. Following Sartre, however, I key my interviews with the scientists in terms of the commitment the scientists must make at this stage of their careers – what kind of scientist I decide to become involves a commitment to what kind of person – self-identity – I want to be. This is an existential dilemma to be addressed, fraught with fear, excitement, possibility, and chance-taking. This is the drama of everyday life we interactionists should capture and document (Kotarba, 2019).

In my research on changing roles and self-identities among contemporary music audiences, I am looking specifically at the relatively new role of "list maker." Until quite recently, the popular music industry provided us with our lists: Top 10 and Top 40 records or songs; Sunday morning radio record countdowns; and MTV top videos. Today, music fans are "forced to be free" – in Sartrean terms – by being strongly encouraged by music sources such a Spotify and ITunes to assemble their own playlists. This phenomenon has spilled over to the increasingly popular practice of assembling one's wedding ceremony and reception or graduation playlist, etc. Assembling and performing a playlist can be extremely dramatic, to the degree that some newlyweds will in fact record their wedding playlists – and actual performances – on DVDs to distribute to guests.

In classic Sartrean terms, I teach the writing of this dramatic production and experience of music to my students through the following exercise. They are to assemble a playlist, consisting of five songs, to be performed or played at their memorial service. At first, they look at me with the blank stare of a deer in headlights – who, me? I'm going to live forever – but quickly come up with fascinating lists. They are required to annotate their songs, in terms of for whom the song is chosen and what reactions they would expect from their survivors. Needless to say, the quality of writing for this assignment is among the best in the semester. Here are two quick excerpts to illustrate my point:

- My second song is *Glycerine* by Bush. I dedicate it to my best friend, Meagan, who held my hand and supported me when I lost my dad and consequently lost my mind. We would sing this song in the car together, but instead of the word glycerine, she would replace it with my name, Grace Elaine.
- I would like them to play *Secret Crowds* by Angels and Airwaves. It represents, to me, purpose. This song sums up the way I feel about life and the way I aspire to love myself and others. This song conveys a sense of beauty in this world, while fighting to make it better because it can be. And living for this is what I want the people in my life to continue doing even after I am gone.

Good writers commonly write about themselves, even in the social sciences, but not necessarily in gross autobiographical terms. Good writers scrupulously but subtly imbed their experiences, thoughts, and interpretations in their work. Data never speak for themselves. There is no such thing as a sociological film or novel, as often portrayed by our colleagues. There are simply portraits of everyday life and its participants for which we have the responsibility to narrate. Our portraits should be richly textured. Our narrations should be crisp and theoretical.

CONCLUSION

Let me conclude by discussing some of the more interesting if practical features of the self-identity of the interactionist as writer. We are what we do, and I am suggesting several practices that encourage us to become writers:

- Book readings: Our writing is very often of great interest to lay and/or nonprofessional readers. Bookstores are generally quite interested in sched- uling readings that bring customers into the store. I conducted readings and signings for my baby boomer rock 'n' fans book (2013a) at the Barnes & Noble stores in Houston and Austin, as well as small, proprietary bookstores and libraries in the Texas Hill Country in Austin, Texas. The crowds were largely comprised of men and women in my age bracket, who let me read the beginning paragraph in my book, but then quickly took over to discuss the "true" meaning of Woodstock, the Who, the Wall, etc. There were also smatterings of young adult music fans who were there to make sure my history of rock 'n' roll was accurate. My point is that readings can help inform us of the readability and practical relevance of our work.

- Building upon Howard Becker (1986), Norman Denzin (2018), and other superb writers in our discipline, the good writer starts writing in order to write constantly. The best writers in interactionism love to write, no question about it. Given the nature of our craft, for example, our heavy use of illustrative tropes, and the nature of our publication outlets, we can write many ways: research reports, essays, blogs, letters to editors, etc.
- Press releases are marvelous media for sharing our work with the real world – universities love them. Isn't that what public sociology is all about?
- I find the white paper format very relevant for translating the applied and policy-relevant work we conducted at my Center for Social Inquiry. For example, we have assembled white papers on the service needs of military veterans, establishing diversity on healthcare boards of trustees, and the value of live music for community development.
- Consider lay book reviews, again, for public sociology purposes and dissemination. Local newspapers are generally on the lookout for the work of local scholars.
- Keeping long-hand notebooks, or journals, is a very elegant way to archive one's ideas as they occur. If you feel that a journal would not allow you to edit, delete, and so forth, that is the point. A journal pays respect to all one's ideas and encourages you to revisit them in the future. As interactionists, we know that ideas are to some degree situational – respect yours.
- Take advantage of the many different outlets available to writers in any field (e.g., blogs and letters to the editor).
- But, do not succumb to the temptation of poor writing à la some of our students – and colleagues – and their 140-character twitters.

When I sit down to write a book, I do not say to myself, 'I am going to produce a work of art.' I write it because there is some lie that I want to expose, some fact to which I want to draw attention, and my initial concern is to get a hearing. —George Orwell (2005).

REFERENCES

Adler, P., Adler, P. and Fontana, A. 1987. Everyday life sociology, *Annual Review of Sociology*, 13, 217–235.

Becker, H. S. 1986. *Writing for Social Scientists*, Chicago, IL, University of Chicago Press.

Charmaz, C. 2014. *Constructing Grounded Theory*, Newbury Park, CA, Sage.

Cooper, K. and White, R. E. 2012. *Qualitative Research in the Postmodern Era*, New York, NY, Springer.

Denzin, N. K. 2018. *Performance Autoethnography: Critical Pedagogy and the Politics of Culture,* 2nd ed., New York, Taylor & Francis.

Ellis, C. 2012. The procrastinating autoethnographer: reflections of self on the blank screen, *The International Review of Qualitative Research*, 5(3), 331–337.

Goins, J. 2014. *So You Are a Writer – Start Acting Like One*, Nashville, TN, Tribe Press.

Kotarba, J. A. 2019. The everyday life intersection of translational science and music, *Qualitative Sociology Review*, 15(2), 44–55.

Kotarba, J. A. 2014. Symbolic interaction and applied research: the case of translational science, *Symbolic Interaction*, 37(3), 412–425. Archived in NIH's PubMed Central.

Kotarba, J. A. 2013a. *Baby Boomer Rock 'n' Roll Fans*, Landam, MD, Rowman & Littlefield.

Kotarba, J. A. 2013b. Translational science and the self-identity of the scientist, *Clinical and Translational Science* 6(2), 157.

Kotarba, J. A. and Wooten, K. C. 2017. The innovation scorecard for continuous improvement applied to translational science, *Journal of Clinical and Translational Science,* 1(5), 296–300. doi:10.1017/cts.2017.297

Melnikov, A. and Kotarba, J. A. 2017. Jack Douglas and the vision of existential sociology. In *The Interactionist Imagination – Studying Meaning, Situation and Micro-Social Order*, Ed. M. H. Jacobsen, pp. 291–314, London, Palgrave Macmillan.

Nisbet, R. 1976. *Sociology as an Art Form*, New York, NY, Oxford University Press.

Orwell, G. 2005. *Why I Write*, New York, NY, Penguin Books.

Pountain, D. and Robins, D. 2000. *Cool Rules*, London, Reaktion Books.

Sartre, J.-P. 1947. *The Age of Reason* [Translated to English by Eric Sutton], New York, NY, Vintage Books.

Zurcher, L. 1979. *The Mutable Self*, Thousand Oaks, CA, Sage.

REFLEXIVITY IN GEORGE HERBERT MEAD

Norbert Wiley

ABSTRACT

Mead's notion of "reflexivity" is one of his key ideas. Our mind "bends" or "flexes" back to itself in this process. Mead argues that universal ideas were first attained reflexively when humans could understand their own communications; for example, when the primate mother could both indicate to her children where food was and also give herself the same message. These two cases, viewed together, constituted the first "universal" (for Mead). This contrasted with the traditional theory of universals, which had the knower abstracting the universal idea, i.e. the "essence," from a group of particulars. Mead's universal is not essentialist but linguistic. It is syntactic and not ontological. This allowed him to sidestep the problem of essences (since no one could find any, anyway). Mead's version shows how reflexivity may have first originated, in the evolutionary process, though he does not actually prove this. I examine reflexivity itself here, singling out several varieties. I look at self-referencing pronouns (especially "I") and show how Cooley's observations of his daughter's use of pronouns clarified this process. I also examine the reflexivity of recognizing one's own face in the mirror. Mead said the body could not be reflexive, but self-recognition in a mirror is a form of bodily reflexivity. And there are several others, for example the varieties of bodily meditation, that Mead missed. Recognizing this reflexivity introduces the body (and, therefore, gender) early in Mead's theory, rather than late, as he has it. This point also opens him to a badly needed infusion of feminist thought, such as that of Nancy Chodorow. The self-recognizing mirror face is, as Lacan points out, "all smiles." This insight also introduces emotion early into Mead. As it is, he has emotion late, as a kind of afterthought. This paper then promotes a badly needed feminization of Mead.

Radical Interactionism and Critiques of Contemporary Culture
Studies in Symbolic Interaction, Volume 52, 61–72
Copyright © 2021 by Emerald Publishing Limited
All rights of reproduction in any form reserved
ISSN: 0163-2396/doi:10.1108/S0163-239620210000052005

Keywords: Reflexivity; Mead; Cooley; symbolic interactionism; emotion; feminist thought

Reflexivity is a "flexing" process of the mind, where a person extends their consciousness in a curvilinear way, bending outward away from themselves, and then back again toward themselves. This is like a U-turn in an automobile. It is also like looking at yourself in a mirror. Macro reflexivity, in contrast, is an organization or institution doing the bending. This paper will be concerned exclusively with the micro variety.

For Mead, reflexivity meant consciousness of one's self. He thought self-awareness was the defining feature of the self. This is one of Kant's views, and Mead may have gotten it from him (Brook, 1994). This property of self-awareness emerged at some (unknown) point in human evolution. Earlier prehumans had only outward awareness. Afterward, they had both outward and inward or reflexive awareness.

The scholarly discussion of consciousness is full of spatial metaphors, such as linearity, shape, and internal compartmentalization. This discussion also leans heavily on self-consciousness. Philosophy is notably precise in its analytic style but also quite loose and analogical in its discovery processes. At times, it lords it over sociology (justifiably) with its conceptual precision, and at other times, it is subject to the same degree of approximation and intuition.

Mead used the term reflexivity in at least five senses: (1) the self, as mentioned, is defined as reflexive, (2) the internal conversation of self-talk is reflexive, (3) action or agency is reflexive, (4) role-taking or taking the perspective of another is reflexive, and (5) communication or interaction with another is reflexive. Actually, all human or semiotic activity is, for Mead, reflexive. But, I have singled out those moments of the self's activity where reflexivity is especially pronounced. Any of these five aspects of human action can be called "reflexivity," just so it is clear it is one among several. To call only one of them reflexivity and act as though this is the only reflexivity is to miss a lot.

In this chapter, I will begin (1) by explaining how Mead thought reflexivity first emerged in human evolution. Then, (2) I will look at the appearance of reflexivity in the infant, doing so from two viewpoints: linguistic reflexivity (especially, the use of the word "I") and the attainment of reflexive self-recognition in the mirror. Both pronominal and specular self-recognition may come only slowly and with trial and error by the child. (3) After looking at the infant's attainment of reflexivity, I will look at objections to Mead's conceptualization of reflexivity.

THE EVOLUTION OF REFLEXIVITY

A problem with Mead's formulation of evolution is that the evidence that humans evolved from primates is weak. His argument has a certain attractiveness and simplicity, but it does not have evolutionary proof or validity. Mead thought that his argument, which is called "phylogenesis," was valid. His other explanation of how human infants, as opposed to the primates, develop selves is called the "ontogenesis" of the self. This argument seems closer to being valid. Mead thought, erroneously, that his phylogenesis and ontogenesis supported each other (that ontogeny more or less recapitulated phylogeny) and that, together, they gave a comprehensive explanation of the self. As such, they would function as philosophical presuppositions for the new discipline of sociology. I might mention that Charles Horton Cooley disagreed with the recapitulation idea (1902, p. 57). This is one of the places Cooley was more valid than Mead.

What Mead actually gave us was (1) a research "program" or plan for explaining the evolutionary origin of the self. This program indicated what Mead thought was a complete explanation, not just a research program, but it is still a useful framework for thinking and hypothesizing about phylogenesis. (2) A theory of ontogenesis, that seems reasonably true and remarkably coherent as it stands. This theory also backs up Mead's theories of how the self functions in humans, from infancy to adulthood. (3) An overall social psychology theory that, despite its limits, is probably the best available for sociology.

I am making a point of criticizing Mead's evolutionary theory of the primate self because it is only a preliminary hypothesis, not a finished product. Crucial steps linking cause (evolution) to effect (primates getting a self) are missing. Several scholars have criticized this theory (De Laguna, 1946; Keen, 1968; Scheffler, 1974). The half dozen or so monographs or textbooks on Mead's theory are extremely useful, and I am not here criticizing them. But, none of them said much about Mead's phylogenesis of the self, for or against.

Before Immanuel Kant, ordinary cognition was considered linear, not reflexive. The knower extended forward toward the object, say a tree, but not backwards again, to the self. Self-awareness for Aristotle, the Scholastics, and the early moderns was implicit in all knowledge. It did not have to be "enacted" in a reflexive curl. But, Mead invented a new approach to the universal, and his approach implied continuous self-reflexivity.

The earlier philosophers explained cognitive universality as attained by an abstraction or a "drawing out" of a common denominator from a series of particulars, say several trees. As I mentioned earlier, Mead rejected abstraction as a theory of universality. He wanted an explanation that would connect to the evolutionary genesis of universality, suggesting how human cognition differs from and builds on that of the animals. Abstraction, as he saw it, jumped over too many problems.

For Mead, the definition of the human centered on reflexivity. Earlier, for centuries, humans were defined as "rational animals." This definition, like the theory of universality from which it derived, was too simplistic for Mead. He wanted to take rationality apart and show how it was constituted. Reflexivity showed, for Mead, the underpinnings of rationality. Rationality derives from reflexivity, and as Mead saw it, reflexivity was the more important idea.

Mead began his explanation of human meaning with animal communication, which he called the language of "gestures," a term he got from Wundt. Gesture is the common denominator for animal and human meanings. The strength of this word is that it supplied a cognitive bridge between animal and human communication.

Before Mead, philosophers had concentrated on the reference of a term. Was it particular or universal? Epistemology was built on this distinction. But, Mead approached this issue in another way; he asked when the speaker's communication had meaning for the speaker as well as for the listener.

Given this approach, there is a sense in which Mead's human not only can communicate with universals *but is a universal.* A universal for Mead is a symbol that has the same meaning for the sender and the receiver. But, the self is both the sender and the receiver of its own communication. This is what Mead's reflexivity means. Therefore, in a somewhat formal sense, Mead's human being seems to be a universal. I will now stop to consider the philosophical implications of this idea.

TWO OBSTACLES FOR REFLEXIVITY: PRONOUNS AND MIRRORS

Children usually learn how to handle reflexivity reasonably well, though there are two difficulties. For one, the learning of reflexive pronouns, such as I, me, and myself, can take a while. A second problem is presented at the mirror. Realizing that the image is a representation of oneself requires that the child attain a more subtle concept of the self. But once these two obstacles are overcome, they lead to a firmer grasp of reflexivity, although they might both also require some trial and error.

Reflexive Pronouns

The problem of reflexive pronouns arose when Cooley was studying the use of self words by his third child, Mary (Cooley, 1908). Mary learned the names of others before she learned her own name. And when she did refer to herself, she tended to see herself as an object rather than as a subject, using the third person rather than the first. She would speak of herself as "Mary" rather than as "me." Cooley's research was repeated by his student, Reid Bain (Bain, 1936), who got essentially the same findings as Cooley. Mead had only one child, and he does not seem to have studied his child, Henry's language acquisition.

Cooley's early findings, then, do not fit well with Mead's idea that the defining feature of the human being is always self-awareness. It takes a child about a year, it appears, to master self-awareness, at least as indicated by their use of language. So, humans are usually, but not always and in all respects, self-aware. Cooley suggested that the child treats itself, for a limited period of time, as though she were other than herself. In particular, although the other people in Cooley's house (Mary's parents and her older sister and brother) could refer to themselves, reflexively as "I," Mary usually referred to herself as "baby," the term her parents used for her.

To put this another way, Mary did not refer to herself as a significant symbol. Subjective words, such as I or myself, would have shown Mary responding to herself as others respond to themselves. Then, we would have had the similarity of response that constitutes Mead's universality. Eventually Mary's self words were the same as those of others, and, therefore, they were (in Mead's sense) significant symbols. But, there was a slow climb to linguistic correctness in her use of these words.

The attainment of truly significant language, then, was uneven for Cooley's children. In particular, the mastering of subjectivity was a slow rite of passage, not finished until Mary was over two years old. Her references to herself without complete linguistic conformity went on for about 12 months. This does not contradict Mead's idea that significant communication entails the same meaning for communicator and communicatee. But, this idea needs to be qualified by the difficulty of mastering words for the self. Reflexivity seems to have been a learned skill for Cooley's daughter, as it evidently is for all of us. Mead never mentions this problem.

He seems to have regarded Cooley as a scholarly rival, and perhaps this is why he missed (or ignored) Cooley's linguistic research. Mead and Cooley were friends at Ann Arbor, in their early years, but they may have had a falling out of some kind, possibly over rivalry for the approval of John Dewey, who was at Michigan with them for several years (Jandy, 1942). In his writings, Mead makes almost no references to Cooley's work. Given that the two scholars were working on the same, highly specialized problems, and were (or had been) personal friends, this would be as though Aristotle did not refer to Plato. In his obituary on Cooley, Mead also seems to be excessively negative, if not a bit reckless (see my appraisal, Wiley, 2011). In other words, Mead seems to have been over-competitive with Cooley at times.

But, I still think Mead's writings were overall superior to those of Cooley. I also think Mead clearly belongs on the list of sociology's founders, along with Karl Marx, Max Weber, and Emile Durkheim. Nevertheless, all four of these founders seem to lean excessively masculine, and the theoretical presence of women is still to be realized in social theory. I do not mean feminism should be sprinkled like a salt shaker. Theoretical feminism needs to be "baked in" at the most profound and theoretical level. Nancy Çhodorow's "Mothering" book (1978) can be understood as a badly needed corrective to Mead's patriarchal tendencies. And I think of her as a fifth founder.

Despite his founding figure status, Mead may have been treated too gently by his intellectual biographers. The philosophical writings, including the PhD theses, on Mead have often been critical of his key ideas. But, the sociological biographers of Mead have mostly ignored Mead's philosophical weaknesses, especially his idea that he discovered the phylogeny of the self. His personality too, especially his critique of the religious soul and his opposition to the moral Puritanism he was subjected to as a youth, need to be looked at more closely. The rivalry with Cooley may be part of this story.

Mirror Self-Recognition

Realizing that it is one's self in the mirror and not another person is an additional problem children have (for a while) with reflexivity. The delay in mirror self-recognition seems to parallel the delay (as with Cooley's daughter) in linguistic self-recognition. In both cases, the child cannot find the curvilinearity or "pivot" of self-awareness. Their consciousness remains linear and, therefore, inaccurate.

Recognizing someone else in a mirror, including other persons in your family, is easy. These recognitions do not entail the curvilinear self-attribution that self-recognition does. If it is your father in the mirror, you just have the two pictures: the one in the mirror and the one standing right next to you. Both are dad, and they look exactly alike.

But in your own case, you do not have two matching pictures. Instead, you have the one in the mirror, and then a second one, based on direct visibility. This one is quite patchy. In particular, you do not have an image of your face, for all you can see of yourself (outside the mirror) is from the eyes on down. The eyes cannot see the face, so the image of one's self is in bits and pieces.

In addition and more challengingly, you have to run a complex reflexive loop to self-recognize, one more complicated than the one in ordinary self-awareness. This seems to take a while.

Ordinary reflexivity is of the self as symbol or idea, not of the self as physical body. The self of premirror self-awareness is both nonvisual and simple. The self of the mirror is visual and full of awkward parts, like ears and limbs. The French psychiatrist, Jacques Lacan, thought the child at the mirror was unable to recognize itself as he or she actually was (Lacan, 1997). He thought we saw a more mature and flattering self than was the case. Lacan thought this "misrecognition" created a kind of imbalance or irregularity in the personality. A lot of his therapy is in correcting this alleged mistake.

I think that, in competition with Freud, Lacan tried too hard to say something new. He had no actual research evidence. It must be admitted, though, Lacan does have a lot of devoted followers. They claim it takes a long time to understand him, and perhaps, I am being excessively dismissive. But as far as I can see, he made a plain, ordinary error.

In contrast, Merleau-Ponty thought the child at the mirror could recognize himself or herself as they actually looked (Merleau-Ponty, 1964, p. 129). He thought the complex reflexive inference could be handled with ordinary common sense, and that infants did exactly that. As Merleau-Ponty put it,

> Why does the specular image of one's own body develop later than that of the other's body? It is because the problem to be solved is much more difficult in the case of one's own body. The child is dealing with two visual experiences of his father: the experience he has from looking at him and that which comes from the mirror. Of his own body, on the other hand, the mirror image is his only complete visual evidence. He can easily look at his feet and his hands but not at his body as a whole. Thus, for him, it is a problem first of understanding that the visual image of his body which he sees over there in the mirror is not himself, and second, he must understand that, not being located there, in the mirror, but rather where he feels himself to be introceptively, he can nonetheless be seen by an external witness at the very place at which he feels himself to be and with the same visual appearance that he has from the mirror. In short, he must displace the mirror image, bringing it back from the apparent or virtual place in the depth of the mirror back to himself, whom he identifies at a distance with his introceptive body. (1964, p. 129)

These two philosophers wrote on this topic several decades ago, and by now, Merleau-Ponty seems to have commanded the most influence. But, in any case, this self-recognition issue stands with the pronominal one as a possible difficulty on the way to smooth reflexivity.

These two obstacles do not disallow reflexivity or make Mead's thesis indefensible. Mead is still, I think, right about reflexivity. But, the two issues I have mentioned show that the attainment of reflexivity is not completely effortless. The child has to work at it. Mead did not recognize the linguistic or mirror-based difficulties of attaining reflexivity. He smoothed things over too much.

At this point, I should mention that obstacles to reflexivity are different from obstacles to finding a satisfactory sense of identity. Self is you, and identity is something about you. Identity is, therefore, different from self. (though this is not the place to treat this complex issue.) I just want to point out how reflexivity and identity are distinct, though closely related, problems in human development.

THREE MISUNDERSTANDINGS ABOUT REFLEXIVITY

To clarify reflexivity, it will be helpful to look at three misunderstandings about this topic. One is John Fichte's idea that reflexivity commits the fallacy of circularity. A second is that nonhuman objects, such as computers and corporate entities, also have reflexivity. A third is that Mead's "generalized other," which operates somewhat like a conscience, determines our behavior, thereby undercutting reflexivity.

Johann Fichte and the Circularity Objection

In Fichte's opinion, the idea that the self can look at itself implies that the self exists before it is brought into existence (Fichte, 1981). This is the fallacy of *circularity*. Fichte's other problem with reflexivity is that he thinks it is a *tautology* because, as he sees it, the predicate is the same as the subject. If we say "this table is this table," we are uttering a tautology. Tautology would make reflexivity meaningless. Fichte thinks if we say "the reflecting self is the reflected self," this is also a tautology. And, if those two selves were exactly the same, he would be correct. But if the two terms were different, which is what I will show, he would be wrong on both counts.

Fichte thought reflexivity was tantamount to Aristotle's principle of identity: that a thing is what it is, or "A = A." Aristotle's identity works when the two terms are the same. If, however, the equivalency were imperfect – in our case, if the "I" is not the same as the "me" – reflexivity would not be identity. And there would be no fallacy. Fichte's error was in not seeing the difference between the I and the me. Both Kant and Mead offer corrections to Fichte. Kant said:

That I am conscious of myself is a thought that already contains a two-fold self, the I as subject and the I as object. How it might be possible for the I that I think to be an object (of intuition) for me, one that enables me to distinguish me from myself, is absolutely impossible for me to explain, even though it is an indubitable fact... Only the I that I think and intuit is a person; the I that belongs to the object that is intuited by me is, similarly to other objects outside me, a thing. (1804/1893, p. 73)

Kant's two selves are clearly not identical. They are also the predecessor to Mead's distinction between the I and the me. Mead's I-me distinction also contradicts Fichte, for the I and the me are not the same. Linguistically, one is in the nominative case, and the other is in the accusative case. Ontologically, the I is the bare actor or person; the me is everything that the actor has made of himself of herself over time. Mead did not explicitly address Fichte on this issue, but he solved both of Fichte's problems. It is clear then that reflexivity is a nonfallacious relation.

Nonhuman Reflexivity

The idea that reflexivity is not exclusive to humans, to go on to the other misunderstanding, is more complex. We need to distinguish two kinds of reflexivity: partial and complete. Complete reflexivity means an entity can reflect on its entire self, including whatever part may be doing the reflecting. A human can assume an outside or meta position and reflect on his or her entire self. A body, with the aid of mirrors, can also engage in complete reflection. In contrast, an organization or corporate person or computer cannot engage in complete reflexivity.

Let us say there is a department in an organization that does the self-examining or reflecting. This department cannot examine itself because it cannot do both things at once. There will be a part doing the examining and a part being examined. If you want to examine the department that is doing the self-examination, you have to allow some other part of the organization to do that. And then who will examine *them*? This creates an infinite regress. In contrast, the self can reflect on or look at its entirety. This is because in reflection it goes meta to, gets outside of, or duplicates itself.

It is now tempting for computer specialists to say computers are humans because they can reflect on themselves just as humans do. This characteristic, which is self-defining for humans, is claimed to be also present in computers. If they have the distinguishing quality of humans, they are humans. But they have only a limited resemblance to humans. Human reflexivity is complete, but computer reflexivity is only partial. Therefore, computers are only machines.

Is Mead's Self Socially Determined or Autonomously Reflexive?

Mead's self is profoundly social, but it is not socially determined, i.e. it is not overdetermined by society. It can make up it own mind. This issue is worth examination.

One of the great innovations of American sociology was the "social self." It replaced the economists' idea of the self-driven solely by self-interest. These social selves usually also embrace values from society. These values entail restraints on how one can deal with others, and goals that are good for society, altruistic goals that are not just good for the self.

The main pragmatists, Peirce, Dewey, James, and Mead, all embraced the social self. They also varied from one to another in exactly how they did this. To understand the pragmatists' composite theory of the self, you have to piece these four thinkers together, as I do in "The Pragmatist's Theory of the Self" (Wiley, 2008) and, in revised form, in chapter 8 of my book on *Inner Speech* (Wiley, 2016).

For the present essay, there is a question about whether Mead was a social (or cultural) determinist. Mead had an element of the self which he called the "generalized other." He is not perfectly clear about this force, but it is more or less the norms or rules or cultural standards of society (Dodds et al., 1997). It is present in, or can be thought to be similar to, the conscience or Freud's superego. Mead treats this factor as our source of what to do about wrong and right. In the inner conversation, Mead often has the "I" talking to the generalized other to get directions for behavior. It looks to me as though he claims we converse with the generalized other for general directions and with the "me" for more specific or particular directions. The generalized other is for strategy, and the me is for tactics. This other will tell us what is the socially approved thing to do under various circumstances. Mead is quit casual about this force, and he makes no attempt to give it a careful analysis, but he seems to regard it as the control over our behavior. We usually do what it tells us to do.

Mead's major concern is the ontogenetic issue of how we can think abstractly in the first place. My account above of why Mead uses reflexivity rather than abstraction connects to his theory of the origin of thought. Whether we also follow a rigid set of rules about how we think and what we choose to do, is of much less interest to him than that we can think at all.

A factor which offsets the generalized other is the "I." Mead's "I" is free and independent. It is a voluntary factor and has some features of free will. It can and does disobey the generalized other quite regularly and easily. The autonomy of the I is a theme that runs throughout Mead's *Mind, Self and Society* lectures (e.g. p. 210). It is clear then that Mead is not a social determinist. To some extent, the generalized other determines behavior, and to some extent, it does not. His generalized other is not the same as Parsons' moral control, usually thought of as determined by value consensus. If Mead's self could be upwardly reduced to values, reflexivity would be ineffective. Instead of being reflexive, we would be reactive in the way we were pushed around by the generalized other.

The "I" function is to some extent that of a free agent, and it can supersede or trump the generalized other. In fact, most people have more than one generalized other. And these regulative systems can contradict each other, giving us con-flicting rules about what to do. I have separate rule systems coming from my various social commitments. These are ethnicity, religion, occupation, politics, and my primary group memberships. These are separate moral streams, to some extent, and I have to choose how to interpret and combine them. This is the nondetermined self, and Mead was thoroughly aware of it.

In addition, the generalized other is not always perfectly up-to-date. New things happen, the generalized other can lag behind the times, and we, as actors, will then have to make up our own minds about how to act. The generalized other will be unavailable. It is true that our morality has a strong social side, just as our cognition (as in the reflexive theory of universals) is thoroughly social, but these social allegiances, including the generalized other, combine with our individual preferences and choices. The generalized other does not have complete control.

Another problem with Mead's generalized other is whether we take the roles of "individual others" as well as that of the generalized other in our moral deliberations. Let me use my marriage as an example. I do scholarly writing all the time, and I find that the only way for me to write successfully is to be obsessive about it.

But to be a good husband, I have to spend a lot of time with my wife as well as with my computer. This is a moral issue, and it looks like it would require a visit to Mead's generalized other to find the solution. But, I do not only want a general rule about how to handle my time. I also want an individual, concrete ruling about how to act in my specific marriage. I want to know what I should do to love Christine, not just to satisfy some general rule.

This means I have to think about the individual traits and needs that Christine has. I have to simultaneously consult Mead's generalized other and the concrete "individual other" of my wife. The two "others" need to be consulted simultaneously, so that I can both follow the general rule and pay attention to the particular qualities of my wife. My wife is as smart as I am (we got the same score on the Miller Analogies test, a kind of I.Q. test). And she wants me to write theory. But not all the time.

It seems to be we are always consulting a "double other": Mead's generalized other (or others) and the individual other we may be interacting with. Mead is simply too general here. This is also an example of the masculine tilt of Mead's thought. Women are more skilled at consulting the concrete other than men are. So, men need to improve their feminine skills to sharpen their moral sense.

CONCLUSION

This essay has been an attempt to clarify Mead's notion of reflexivity. Mead is much more interested in the origin of self than in its use. Accordingly, he is most careful about how he thinks the self could have come about and less careful about how the mature self engages in its activities.

I sense that he felt guilty about becoming an atheist, and for that reason, he went to a great effort to show how the self could have evolved naturally, without God. This evolutionary process, which is called phylogenesis, is described in a cursory way by Mead. His phylogenesis does resemble his ontogenesis, which is a strength. But, his evolutionary theory is too succinct, and it has steps missing.

I also think, regarding Mead's beliefs that any sophisticated theologian could get around his atheism. If there is a God, he is smart, and he could easily have created the Meadian phylogenesis and ontogenesis. If so, Mead would have discovered the detailed and complex way in which God made us, not the way in which evolution (without God) made us. The Mead scheme would have been the divine pathway to the phylogenetic and ontogenetic routes to human nature.

I am a fellow atheist with Mead, so I personally do not believe this theological scheme, but it is a way of bringing Mead, the anxious nonbeliever, back to religion. In other words, sociology is not an irreligious discipline. It is, in a broad sense, "value free," a term with several possible meanings. One introduces one's values as an addition to scientific sociology, not as a substitute for it. So, sociology cannot be religious. But it cannot be irreligious (i.e. opposed to religion) either. Like any other science, it is neutral toward religion.

I also pointed out the limits of Mead's reflexivity theory. He missed the linguistic reflexivity the infant gets when mastering the reflexive pronouns. It would have been better if he had observed his son, Henry, confront the problem of understanding reflexive pronouns. He also should have paid some attention to how the infant learns it is him or her self in the mirror.

Mead also has too simple a moral notion of the generalized others. He did not notice that moral deliberations usually require a double other. We look at the rules and needs of the general human, but we also look at the needs of whatever specific person we are interacting with. I pointed out how this works in a marriage.

On the other hand, Mead can defend reflexivity against various objections. I mention several of these. The result of this essay is a complex overview of the Meadian moral theory. Like all great thinkers, he has both strengths and weaknesses. His strength is that he gave us a powerful theory of how people think and how infants attained the capacity for thinking. He did not explain the evolution of thought as well as he thought he did, but he accomplished so much that this weakness can be ignored. On the other hand, he does not do an adequate job of including the human body, emotions, and the nature of women. In other words, he did a lot, but there is still plenty to continue doing. As mentioned, I think Chodorow (1978) can do much of what Mead did not do.

REFERENCES

Bain, R. 1936. The self-and-other words of a child, *American Journal of Sociology*, 41, 767–775.

Brook, A. 1994. *Kant and the mind*, Cambridge, Cambridge University Press.

Cooley, C. H. 1908. A study of the early use of self words by a child, *Psychological Review*, 15, 339–357.

Cooley, C. H. 1902. *Human Nature and the Social Order*, originally published in 1992. New York, NY, Charles Scribner's Sons.

Chodorow, N. 1978. *The Reproduction of Mothering: Psychoanalysis and the Sociology of Gender*, Berkeley, CA, University of California Press.

De Laguna, G. 1946. Communication, the act and the object with reference to Mead, *Journal of Philosophy*, 43, 225–238.

Dodds, A. E., Lawrence, J. A. and Valsiner, J. 1997. The personal and the social: Mead's theory of the 'generalized other', *Theory & Psychology*, 7, 483–503.

Fichte, J. G. 1981. *The Science of Knowledge*, originally published in 1794–95. Cambridge, Cambridge University Press.

Jandy, E. C. 1942. *Charles Horton Cooley: His Life and His Social Theory*, New York, NY, Octagon Books.

Keen, T. C. 1968. *Mead's social theory of meaning and experience*. PhD dissertation, Columbus, OH, Ohio State University.

Lacan, J. 1997. The mirror stage as formative of the function of the I. In *Ecrits*, originally published in 1949. Ed. J. Lacan, pp. 1–7, New York, NY, W.W. Norton & Company.

Merleau-Ponty, M. 1964. *The primacy of perception*, Evanston, IL, Northwestern University Press.

Scheffler, I. 1974. *Four Pragmatists: Peirce, Mead, James and Dewey*, London, Humanities Press.

Wiley, N. 2016. The pragmatist's theory of the self, 2. In *Inner Speech and the Dialogical Self*, Ed. N. Wiley, pp. 109–133, Philadelphia, PA, Temple University Press.

Wiley, N. 2011. A Mead-Cooley merger, *The American Sociologist*, 42, 168–186.

Wiley, N. 2008. The pragmatist theory of the self, 1, *Studies in Symbolic Interaction*, 31, 7–29.

DISCOVERING THE ROOTS OF AUTOBIOGRAPHY AND AUTOETHNOGRAPHY IN THE *CONFESSIONS* OF JEAN-JACQUES ROUSSEAU: A DIALOGUE

Alina Pop and Marco Marzano

ABSTRACT

This is a two-voice autoethnographic dialogue about Rousseau's Confessions *and their relevance for the contemporary autoethnograpy. The paper examines the possibility that Rousseau was not only the creator of modern autobiography but also a forerunner of autoethnography. Many features of the Rousseau's masterpiece are analyzed and systematically compared to our contemporary autoethnographic sensibility: the purposes which brought him to write an outstandingly detailed description of his life; the fact that he acknowledges autobiography as the only source of true knowledge; his obsession for sincerity and his strong will to disclose all the truth about his own life to his readers (included the dreadful things that he did); the authority that he assigned to the readers in deciding about the truthfulness of his tale; his concern for the ethical issues and the care of the others; and the therapeutic value that he recognized to the practice of writing about themselves. In the end, Jean-Jacques was not only extraordinarily able to use his emotions to analyze human nature, but also he was a radical autobiographer at the limits of intransigence. His considerations on the value of autobiography can help us greatly to legitimize contemporary autoethnographic practice.*

Radical Interactionism and Critiques of Contemporary Culture
Studies in Symbolic Interaction, Volume 52, 73–94
Copyright © 2021 by Emerald Publishing Limited
All rights of reproduction in any form reserved
ISSN: 0163-2396/doi:10.1108/S0163-239620210000052006

Keywords: The confessions; Jean-Jacques Rousseau; autobiography; autoethnography; autoethnograpic dialogue; historical roots of autoethnography

Bucharest (Romania), on an icy and bright January morning, in Alina's living room.

Alina (sitting in front of the computer turned on and taking a glance at the clear, cloudless sky of that corner of Eastern Europe): "Listen Marco, we have to start writing the article on Rousseau for Denzin's journal. We should just follow up on what we have talked about in the last weeks. A few days ago I was reflecting on the fact that this work will be the conclusion of a journey that started for us many months ago, on that spring day spent in Turin, during that walk under the Mole Antonelliana (a spectacular nineteenth-century monument that as a teenage tourist in the city Rousseau did not have the chance to admire) when the idea of working on this topic came to our minds for the first time."

Marco (lying on the sofa holding a book by Tony Judt): "Yes, you're right. We have to start. I believe that the form we have chosen for the paper is the best: a dialogue, we will write a dialogue. We will put down on paper our conversations of these past months on Rousseau, on symbolic interactionism and on the knowledge of the world starting from self-reflection, the autobiographical practice. After all, it is understandable: you are a social psychologist in love with Rousseau's *Confessions*, I am a sociologist very passionate about autoethnography and autobiographical writing, both theoretically and practically. Our goal will be to understand if and to what extent the reading and the study of Rousseau can interest contemporary autoethnographers and which part of the work of this genius is relevant for those who seek to study society in an interactionist and interpretative perspective by resorting to a autoethnographic method. You will see that we will help our readers make some interesting discoveries."

Alina (standing up and walking toward the kitchen): "And then what's more eighteenth-century-like than a dialogue? Rousseau would certainly have appreciated it."

Bergamo (Italy), a few days later, in Marco's living room.

Marco: Well, I would say that we are ready, Alina.

Alina: Yes, we can start.

Marco: You could begin by describing the general features of Rousseau's work.

Alina: I would like to start with a quote I read in an essay by Starobinski, one of his most important exegetists in the twentieth century: "You never come to an end with Rousseau. you always have to start finding him, to reorient or disorient yourself, to forget the formulas and images that made us confident and gave us the reassuring belief that we understood him once and for all. Every generation discovers a new Rousseau, who serves as an example for what the generation wants to be, or also for what it passionately rejects." (1962, p. 379, my translation from German). This is valid surely also for the Confessions, the autobiography of Rousseau on which we will focus.

The *Confessions* form, together with the *Letters to Malesherbes*, the *Dialogues: Rousseau judge, of Jean-Jacques* and the *Reveries of a solitary walker*, what has been subsequently labeled Rousseau's autobiographical work. At the time of their writing (1763–1770), the genre did not yet even have a name, being almost nonexistent; if not quite the inventor of autobiography, Rousseau is considered to have produced a revolution in autobiography, changing completely the psychological, social and literary aspects of this genre (Lejeune, 2009).

Over time, the *Confessions*, which form the hard core of his autobiographical writings, have been interpreted as either a piece of literature or as philosophical work, or both. More recently, the work of Rousseau is considered to be the first deep personal autobiography ever written and, consequently, of great interest for psychologists (Abbs, 2008).

If you agree, I think it would be better if we stated our thesis straight away: Rousseau, who is generally seen as the first secular autobiographer, may be considered a forerunner for autoethnography as well. We interpret key paragraphs from the *Confessions* and the other autobiographical writings, which demonstrate Rousseau's antecedence over and inspiring potential for current autoethnographic research. I would proceed as follows: We start by providing the reader, who may be less familiar with the works that we analyze, with a brief description of them. Then, we show that Rousseau's enterprise to write the story of his life is essentially innovative in that it acknowledges autobiography as the only source of true knowledge. Next, we discuss the continuous challenge felt, and confessed, by Rousseau in making the truth known to the public, while granting the reader the ultimate authority in deciding about the truth. We then turn to discussing the ethics of writing autobiography, attempting to link Rousseau's autobiographical works to more recent autoethnographic approaches. We focus, first, on the practice of full disclosure in autobiography and, second, on the ethical concerns about the effects on the others that appear in the stories that build Rousseau's life. Finally, we look at some of the consequences of writing his autobiography, which we interpret as a form of autotherapy.

ROUSSEAU'S AUTOBIOGRAPHIES

Marco: (handing Alina a steaming cup of forest berries tea and sitting on the sofa next to her): I agree with you on how to proceed. I would therefore start with a general description of Rousseau as inventor of the contemporary autobiography. How did it occur him to tell the story of his life?

Alina: Jean-Jacques Rousseau (b. 1712, Geneva – d. 1778, Ermenonville) started to write about his own life beginning with 1762, and for the rest of his life, he did not undertake any other consistent literary or philosophical project that was not related to autobiography.

The first attempts were the *Letteres à Malesherbes* [Letters to Malesherbes], all four of them dated in January 1762. Some other self-description fragments, collected afterward as *Mon Potrait*, are difficult to date, but may have been written before as a first attempt at self-presentation (MacCannell, 1974). The letters were written just five months before Rousseau's flight from France, which occurred in June 1762, immediately after the publication of *Émile* and the consequent arrest warrant issued for him. In that period, Rousseau lived solitarily at Montmorency, hosted by the marshal of Luxembourg and his wife, and isolated from his friends, "the philosophers," whom he suspected of plotting to delay the publication of the *Social Contract* and of *Émile*. Malesherbes, who was then the director of the "Librairie," actually the chief of state censorship, received four long letters from Rousseau describing some relevant events in his life, but containing mostly a series of justifications for his choice to live in solitude. We should therefore not overlook the instrumental value of the letters, since they were addressed to a powerful person, who could decide the fate of his most important works.

The Letters anticipated his most consistent autobiographical work, the *Confessions*. According to some authors, Rousseau started the project of writing a full account of his life in 1763, when installed at Môtiers, in the canton of Neuchatel (Trousson and Eigeldinger, 2006). The first part of the *Confessions* was completed during the years 1765–1766, when he resided in England, as a guest of David Hume. The six books of the first part cover the first 28 years of his life, between 1712 and 1740. The second part, also divided into six books, was written between 1769 and 1770 and covers the years between 1741 and 1765. Overall, the *Confessions* describe the life of Rousseau until he reached the age of 53 years. Although he announced that the work would be continued, a third part of the *Confessions* was never written. Instead, two other autobiographical works followed, namely the *Dialogues: Rousseau, Judge of Jean-Jacques*, written in 1772–1776, and the *Reveries of a Solitary Walker*, written in 1776–1778. However, these two subsequent works are not accounts of any new period in Rousseau's life; they instead contain some descriptions and interpretations of events already presented in the *Confessions*. This repetitiveness was interpreted by some of Rousseau's analysts as a sign of his pathological mental condition or of a personality flaw like paranoia, narcissism, vanity, and many other "disorders" of which Rousseau was posthumously diagnosed (see MacCannell, 1974, for an inventory). Nevertheless, on looking more carefully at the context in which he wrote the various autobiographies and his self-declared motives, not only can we easily find coherent explanations for the repetitiveness, but also we are able to observe the dynamics of the underlying motives for writing autobiography, which might be valid for all authors that adopt this practice.

Initially titled *The Confessions of J.-J. Rousseau, Containing the Circumstances of the Events of His Life, and of His Secret Feelings in All the Situations in Which He Found Himself*, the most consistent of Rousseau's autobiographies was suggested to him by his publisher, Marc-Michel Rey, who intended to publish it as an introduction to a collection of his writings. Having the project vaguely in mind, as he acknowledged, Rousseau did not devote too much effort to it until 1765–1766, when he wrote most of the first part. It was the publication of a pamphlet, later attributed to Diderot, *The Sentiment of the Citizens*, in which Rousseau was criticized for abandoning his children in an orphanage that gave him true impetus to write about his life. However, besides the desire to defend his public reputation, which was rather good, his conscience enjoined him to justify himself (Guéhenno, 1966). He considered it essential to reveal fully who he was in order to obtain a fair judgment by the public.

The first private readings from the first books of the *Confessions* that Rousseau undertook in 1771 were met with incomprehension and hostility. With the strong desire to be properly understood by his fellows and convinced that his enemies were plotting to denigrate him, Rousseau wrote the *Dialogues: Rousseau, Judge of Jean-Jacques* rather than continuing to write the *Confessions*. These three dialogues, imagined between "Rousseau" and an anonymous Frenchman on the life and work of Jean-Jacques, were intended, again, to show the "true Rousseau" to a public already exposed to the false image constructed by his plotting enemies. In spite of a different literary form, the *Dialogues* were written for the same purpose as the *Confessions*: to reveal his true self in order to be judged correctly by the others.

This motivation changed radically in the last of his autobiographies, the *Reveries of a Solitary Walker*, which he declared to have written only for himself, in a quest for self-knowledge and self-understanding. In the first of the 10 Walks, he explained the shift of interests from the audience to himself and the purpose of the introspection:

> Alone for the rest of my life, since I find consolation, hope, and peace, in myself only, I ought or will not employ my thoughts but on myself. Tis in this state I return to the severe and sincere enquiry I formerly called my Confessions. I consecrate my last days to the study of myself, and to prepare before-hand the account I must soon give of my actions. Let me entirely devote myself to the charms of conversing with my soul, since it is the only thing which I cannot be deprived by man. If, by dint of reflecting on my internal dispositions, I arrive at ordering them better, and correcting the evil which may have lurked there, my meditations will be not entirely useless, and though I am of no value on the earth, I shall not entirely lose my latter days. (*Reveries*, p. 151)

The autobiographer Rousseau switched from self-justification to self-revelation and back again to turn at the end of his life to self-understanding motivated by the desire for self-improvement. It seems that the practice of writing autobiography entails its own dynamics. Rousseau's autobiographies show how a project started as an apology turned into a thorough reflection about the inner self, a veritable exercise of introspection, undertaken more than one century before the invention of psychoanalysis. I believe that the motives explaining contemporary autoethnographic research are somewhat different, aren't they?

Marco: Well, yes, in fact I do not know any sociologist or anthropologist who has declared to have resorted to autobiography to dispel the shadows that had thickened on them, to redeem a reputation which is compromised or at risk. The motivations of autoethnographers – at least the explicit ones – are very different from the one that induced Rousseau to recount his life. And yet, albeit in less clamorous manner than Rousseau who initiated the autobiographical genre, even autoethnographers have challenged the genres and expressive styles of their time (Ellis and Bochner, 2000; Ellis et al., 2011; Holman Jones et al., 2013). In fact, autoethnography is the most explicit and direct attack on the conventions still dominant in scientific writing, according to which social research must be conducted *sine ira et studio*, that is, with objectivity, detachment, and assuming a point of view far from that of the social actors who describe themselves. In mainstream social sciences (including qualitative research), the participation and involvement of the observer must be strictly limited to that minimum amount that allows him/her to understand what is happening before his/her eyes. In any case, it is coldness and the emotional and intellectual distance from the object of study that guarantees the lucidity and richness of its analysis. Autoethnographers completely overturn these assumptions and open the doors of their existences before the readers; they lay themselves bare, renounce all claims to objectivity and neutrality, and include the emotions and subjective feelings in their narratives. Autoethnography is the most important translation of the postmodern turn and of the linguistic turn into the practice of disciplines that study social life, a radical ontological and epistemological challenge to positivism and to the "grand narratives" of sociology and of anthropology combined with the rediscovery of the humanistic and literary aspect of the study of society. In short, concluding on this point, if Rousseau was certainly, and not only regarding autobiography, a huge innovator, the autoethnographers also have many merits. I would now like to deepen the analysis of an element that you have hitherto just mentioned, more precisely why Rousseau considered autobiography to be the only source of true knowledge about human nature.

AUTOBIOGRAPHY – THE ONLY SOURCE OF TRUE KNOWLEDGE

Alina (putting on her glasses and clearing her throat): Rousseau started his *Confessions* by claiming: "I am forming an undertaking which has no precedent, and the execution of which will have no imitator whatsoever" (*Confessions*, p. 5). The statement might correspond to his belief that nobody had and nor will have the same audacity to narrate his/her life as openly as he did. But besides that, the uniqueness of his autobiography is related also to the distinctiveness of the individual who narrates his life. The first modern man, as Nietzsche described Rousseau, was the inventor of the individual, both in thought and in literature. Through his autobiographical project, he set his own self as an object of investigation. He writes: "I wish to show my fellows a man in all the truth of nature; and this man will be myself. Myself alone. I feel my heart and I know men. I am not made like any of the ones I have seen; I dare to believe that I am not made like any that exist." (Confessions, p. 5).

However, even if Rousseau considered himself to be unique, this did not make the story of his life, or rather the "history of his soul," as he preferred to call it, irrelevant for the general study of human nature. On the contrary, in the Neuchâtel Preface (NP) – a first draft of the foreword to his *Confessions* that was eventually replaced with a much shorter version – Rousseau described his autobiography as a first attempt to study of man. The manner and style of such a work, he stated, had less to do with literature and more with philosophy. The method to achieve true knowledge about human beings should be based on comparison, and his account was delivered as a first "item of comparison for the study of the human heart," the only one available at that time. He considered autobiography to be the only authentic source of knowledge, since "No one can write the life of a man except himself. His internal manner of being, his genuine life is known only to him" (*Confessions*, NP, p. 586). Yet many claim to know others very well, but "each hardly knows anyone but himself, if it is even true that anyone knows himself" (*Confessions*, NP, p. 585). The imperfect knowledge that a person has about him/ herself, obtained through solipsistic self-absorption, is then inaccurately used for knowledge about others:

> One makes oneself into the rule of everything, and this is precisely where the double illusion of amour-propre is waiting for us; either by falsely attributing to those we are judging the motives that would have made us act as they do in their place; or – in that same assumption – by deceiving ourselves about our own motives for lack of knowing well enough how to transport ourselves into a different situation from the one in which we are. (Confessions, NP, p. 585)

Marco (apologizing for the interruption): Aren't you exaggerating? If what you say were true then autoethnography wouldn't be possible, since we could talk only about ourselves. Did Rousseau really think so?

Alina (with a sigh): According to Rousseau, comparison is crucial both for the proper understanding of others and the better understanding of oneself. Nobody knows the other if one does not understand oneself. Moreover, nobody knows oneself if one does not know the other. Rousseau wanted to break the vicious circle of imperfect knowledge by offering his own life-story as a starting point for the comparison. He wrote: "(...) I have resolved to cause my readers to make an additional step in the knowledge of men by pulling them away, if possible, from that unique and faulty rule of always judging someone else's heart by means of their own; whereas, on the contrary, even to know one's own it would often be necessary to begin by reading in someone else's. In order for one to learn to evaluate oneself, I want to attempt to provide at least one item for comparison, so that each can know himself and one other, and this other will be myself." (Confessions, NP, p. 585).

Criticisms have been that Rousseau is self-referential while encouraging others always to use the comparison for the study of man but exempts himself from this rigor (Starobinski, 1988). There are, however, scholars who maintain that the comparative approach is indeed present in the *Confessions*, given the fact that Rousseau assiduously studied the nature of man and was familiar with the works of great philosophers and biographers like Plutarch or Montaigne (Storey, 2012).

Besides the knowledge obtained from great texts, Rousseau gained his insights about the nature of man from his direct relations with people belonging to all human estates, "from the lowest up to the highest, except the throne." Born in Geneva as the son of a watchmaker, and without having a social state in France where he lived, Rousseau considered himself to be in "the most advantageous position in which a mortal has ever found himself." This situation enabled him to conduct a far-reaching and comparative study of man, since "The Great do not know anything except the Great, the small do not know anything except the small. The latter see the former only through admiration for their rank and are seen by them only with an unjust scorn. In these too distant relations, the being common to both of them, the man, escapes them equally. As for me, careful to set aside the mask, I have recognized him through everything. I have weighed, I have compared their respective tastes, their pleasures, their prejudices, their maxims. Admitted everywhere as a man without pretensions and without consequence, I examined them at my ease; when they stopped disguising themselves I could compare man to man, and status to status. Being nothing, wanting nothing, I did not trouble or bother anyone; I entered everywhere without holding on to anything, sometimes dining in the morning with Princes and supping in the evening with peasants." (*Confessions, NP*, pp. 586–587).

This privileged position may be today associated with that of the contemporary researcher, don't you think?

Marco: Absolutely yes. Especially ethnographers are, as Rousseau described himself, socially marginal, uprooted people without a very clear social affiliation. And able to descend from fashionable salons to the slums, to be with everyone, to meet anyone, to be intrigued by people of all sorts. In this sense, Rousseau was an excellent ethnographer.

Alina: Anyway, established as the first item for the comparative study of man, Rousseau's autobiography is not intended to take the place of all the others. On the contrary, by claiming that the story of "a man of the people," as he was, deserves all the attention from the readers, Rousseau makes a general call for autobiography, a gesture which is in itself revolutionary (Lejeune, 2009):

> I am writing less the story of these events in themselves than that of the state of my soul as they happened. Now souls are not more or less illustrious except according to whether they have more or less great and noble feelings, more or less sharp and numerous ideas. Here the facts are only precipitating causes. In whatever obscurity I might have lived, if I have thought more and better than Kings, the history of my soul is more interesting than that of theirs. (*Confessions, NP*, p. 586)

By making the subjective experiences of any individual the basis for human knowledge, Rousseau was the real forerunner of the autoethnographic investigations of the twentieth century.

Marco: In short, to summarize what you have said, we can say that, at the bottom of the decision to recount one's life, there is an element that we could call narcissistic, very obvious when Rousseau admits, with a certain naïve candor, that his life deserves to be narrated and known because it is that of an exceptional man. From this point of view, I believe that Rousseau sincerely recognized a great truth underlying all autobiographies (including autoethnographic ones): all those who decide to recount certain episodes or even their entire lives are at least partly narcissistic; they enjoy placing themselves, in one way or the other, at the center of the narrative, and they also implicitly claim the right to be the best interpreters of their own lives. To use a theatrical metaphor, they like to play the parts of both the actors on the stage and those of the critics in the audience. I repeat: I am convinced that a pinch of narcissism is also present in autoethnography, that there is always a factor of exhibitionistic pleasure, so to speak.

That said, however, it seems to me that Rousseau asserted something on which many autoethnographers would agree: namely that the description of oneself in relation to events occurring in one's life is among the best, if not the best, ways to understand human nature. It is true that, at the time of Rousseau, the immense amount of studies on mankind and society available today had not yet been produced, but it is equally unquestionable that autobiography and above all autoethnography are sources of extraordinary knowledge about human nature and the nature of social life, one of the most powerful "humanistic" alternatives, perhaps the most powerful of all, to the positivist and scientist "grand narratives" with their claims of generalizability and impartiality (Denzin and Lincoln, 2017). What, on the contrary, makes an autobiographical or self-narrative narration credible, and therefore to some extent "valid" and "reliable" is the reputation of the narrator, a quality that I believe derives mainly from the credibility of the story, the quantity of details offered to the reader and also from the ability of the storyteller to offer a description so realistic, vivid, and likely that it cannot be false. The goal of an autoethnography is not only to create in the reader the feeling of witnessing, as an invisible presence, the scenes described by the narrator but also to enable him/her to retrospectively understand some of their past experiences similar to those narrated. That is what happened to me when I first read Carolyn Ellis's *Final Negotiations*. Reading that remarkable book reminded me of many events related to the illness and death of my father, which had taken place a year before and then induced me to imitate Carolyn by writing the story of my father's demise (Marzano, 2009). I wonder, in the case of the *Confessions*, how Rousseau built the credibility of his narrative and how he established his reputation as an autobiographical narrator. I would not want us to believe his story only because its author is Rousseau, a genius of philosophy, the author of *Emile or the Social Contract*. What do you think?

THE TRUTH, NOTHING BUT THE TRUTH

Alina (with *Confessions* in her hands): Rousseau believed that: "Among my contemporaries there are few men whose names are more known in Europe and whose person is more unknown" (*Confessions, NP*, p. 587). It was a shortcoming that he decidedly wanted to overcome with the publication of the *Confessions*. He was aware, as you say, about the importance of his works for the future and insisted that posterity should have knowledge about his persona as well. He preferred not to entrust the task to a biographer, fearing that he would receive a fallacious reputation that he would be given virtues of vices that he did not possess. "I prefer to be known with all my flaws and that it be myself, than with spurious qualities, under a character that is alien to me" (*Confession, NP*, p. 588). He encouraged the readers to believe in the truthfulness of his narration because of his honesty and not because of his reputation.

Marco: This is one of the most frequent motivations for subsequent autobiographies of the celebrities and the characters who have attracted the spotlight, drawing the attention of many of their contemporaries and who thought that the right thing for them to do was to offer some elements in order to avoid ambiguity, to reduce misunderstandings, and to reaffirm the truth of what had happened to them in life. Furthermore, Rousseau also rightly believed that he would be remembered by posterity. And this is one more reason for him to try to have the last word on his own life even at the cost of revealing unfortunate and shameful facts. It was the price that he thought he ought to pay for this operation of truth. We will come back to that later? All this is interesting, but it's difficult to link to autoethnography. Don't you think?

Alina: Yes, I think so. Rousseau's gesture of writing his life story, and claiming that nobody else could have done it better, may indeed have been related to his narcissism and exhibitionism, two of the psychological conditions of which he was posthumously diagnosed (de Man, 1979). However, looking more carefully at the attempts to demonstrate the truthfulness of his autobiography and the role ascribed to the readers in deciding upon the truth, his supposed narcissism can be questioned. I will explain.

Convinced that "nobody can write the life of a man except himself" (*Confession, NP*, p. 586), Rousseau proclaimed the truthfulness of his self-narration several times in the text of the *Confessions* and in the sketch for the preface. Moreover, he used various means to demonstrate it. Naming his work *Confessions* is a first proof. Rousseau felt that the label *Memoirs*, a genre more frequently used in those times, would not have the same strength in demonstrating the sincerity of the account, which he presented as an objective description of all the features who built his character and was unleashed by any artistic artifice. He denied his enterprise would be an apology, based on a disguising strategy, and affirmed that he showed himself as he was, not as he wanted to be seen. All features of his character and all his actions, regardless how negative or shameful they were, had to be shown. Designating his enterprise with the name of the religious practice typical for Catholicism, to which he converted after fleeing his protestant country, obviously had the role of proving his sincerity.

Unlike Saint Augustine, who wrote the story of his conversion to Christianity in the form of the Confessions addressed to God, Rousseau confessed to men when narrating his life story. Reference to the "Eternal Being" is made by Rousseau only to assert the authenticity of his account. God, as he stated, already knew him very well and did not need any further details, so He was considered a witness rather than a judge (Lejeune, 2009). The real judge of the Confessions was the earthly public. Rousseau felt a real challenge to convince the readers that all the truth has been told. Telling the most dreadful aspects of his life stood as strong proof of his frankness:

> Few men have acted worse than I have done, and never has a man said about himself what I have to say about myself. There is no vice of character whose admission is not easier to make than that of a black or base action, and one can be assured that whoever dares to admit such actions will admit everything. That is the harsh but certain proof of my sincerity. I will be truthful; I will be so without reserve; I will say everything; the good, the bad, in sum, everything. I will carry out my title rigorously, and never has the most fearful devout woman made a better examination of her conscience than the one for which I am preparing myself; never has she spread out all the innermost recesses of her soul to her confessor more scrupulously than I am going to spread out all of mine to the public. (C, NP, p. 588)

The minute descriptions in the narration of the actions and life events, besides having also other functions (see below), were further proof of the faithfulness of the Confessions. In imaginary dialogues with his readers, Rousseau even apologized for tiring or boring them with seemingly unnecessary information. Nevertheless, for the sake of the truth, he considered no detail useless or negligible. Telling only a part of his life story would have raised suspicion of hiding something, a risk that Rousseau did not want to take:

> In the undertaking I have made of showing myself completely to the public, nothing of me must remain obscure or hidden to him; I must hold myself ceaselessly before his eyes, so that he might follow me in all the aberrations of my heart, in all the recesses of my life; so that he might not lose me from view for a single instant, for fear that, finding the smallest lacuna in my narrative, the smallest gap, and asking himself, what did he do during that time, he might accuse me of not having wanted to say everything. (Confessions, p. 50)

Telling all and in great detail seems to match the current notion of "thick description" in ethnographic research (Geertz, 1973). The details came naturally since the moments of intense feelings, especially positive, were kept more vividly in Rousseau's memory and narrating them procured him pleasure. However, the "method" was used mainly to certify the truthfulness of his stories; the details served more the reader than him. The most surprising thing discovered when I read the *Confessions* was that Rousseau, who wanted to render his "soul transparent to the reader," admitted he had no power in imposing the truth, or his version of the truth, as I would say, on the audience. Instead, he entitled the reader with the ultimate authority in deciding on or constructing his/her own version of the truth. This was the rich description needed to provide the reader the "raw" elements (facts, thoughts, and feelings) that could help him/her make a proper judgment of Jean-Jacques Rousseau. What could be more postmodern than that!?

> I would like to be able to render my soul transparent to the eyes of the reader in some fashion, and to do so I seek to show it to him under all points of view, to clarify it by all lights, to act in such a way that no motion occurs in it that he does not perceive so that he might be able to judge by himself about the principle which produces them. If I took responsibility for the result and I said to him; such is my character, he would be able to believe, if not that I am fooling him, at least that I am fooling myself. But by relating to him in detail with simplicity everything that has happened to me, everything I have done, everything I have thought, everything I have felt, I cannot lead him into error unless I want to, even if I wanted to I would not succeed easily in this fashion. It is up to him to assemble these elements and to define the being made up of them; the result ought to be his work, and if he is deceived then, all the error will be of his making. Now for this end it is not enough for my accounts to be faithful; they must also be exact. It is not up to me to judge the importance of the facts, I ought to tell them all, and leave to him the care of choosing. (*Confessions*, p. 146–147)

Rousseau entrusted the reader to make a right judgment about himself. In the *Dialogues*, the ordinary Frenchman was able to change the false image he had of Jean-Jacques after reading his works and after being given details about his life. The same rationale is to be found in the *Confessions*. Furthermore, he ascribed an additional role to the reader, or at least expressed his hope that the reader could be a better analyst than himself, helping him understand the reasons for which his life had taken such a strange course.

> Thus as I narrate the events that concern me, the treatment I have suffered and everything that has happened to me, I am in no position to go back to the impelling hand and to fix the causes as I state the facts. (…) If any of my readers are generous enough to want to get to the core of these mysteries and to discover the truth, let them reread the three preceding books with care, then let them take the information that will be in their grasp for each fact they will read in the following ones, let them go back from intrigue to intrigue and agent to agent up to the prime movers of everything; I know with certainty at what terminus their research will come to an end, but I get lost in the obscure and tortuous route of the underground passages that will lead them there. (*Confessions*, p. 493).

This may seem to contradict the previous statement that self-knowledge is the only true knowledge available to man. Rousseau's inability to explain what had happened to his life, why he had been so badly treated by his former friends, and why he had been prosecuted made him ask for readers' help. Does the reader have any role in contemporary autoethnographic accounts?

Marco: Of course he has. The reader plays a central role in contemporary autoethnography. He is required to participate in the construction of the meaning that emerges from autoethnographic reports. This is a direct consequence of narrative writing that privileges the description of events over the explanation of the relationships between variables and therefore recognizes the reader's right to construct the meaning of the stories he has read intertwining it with what s/he already knows or with reflection, sometimes induced by reading, on personal events. I would say that in this Rousseau is truly wonderfully postmodern, as you suggest! On this point, his view also shows us all the benefits of the proximity of social research with literature and humanities, the openness to a multiplicity of interpretations, and the respect of readers that come from the humanistic tradition. As you well know, the "scientific" reports drawn up using the style of the "hard sciences" do not assign readers any significant role. The readers simply need to be convinced of the accuracy and precision of the data that are reported in papers or books.

IN THE LABORATORY OF A GENIUS – DISCLOSING EVERYTHING IN THE AUTOBIOGRAPHICAL WRITING

Once again, Bucharest, on an almost spring-like day in March, was strolling through the wonderful Vacaresti, along small paths and amid marshy ponds, and always in the company of our copy of Rousseau's "*Confessions*" which Alina holds in her hands.

Alina (taking care to avoid the small puddles of water formed by the rain of the past few days): I'm satisfied with the work we have done so far. However, we have not yet addressed some terribly important issues. Before referring to the first of these issues, I make a premise: The *Confessions* is a very dense work, which was often described as chaotic, incoherent (Zwerdling, 2017), and even delirious (de Man, 1979). The disorder in the narrative could be explained by, to quote Rousseau himself, the "immense chaos of feelings so diverse, so contradictory, often so low and sometimes so sublime, with which I am ceaselessly agitated" that required the "invention of a language as new as my project" (*Confessions, NP*, p. 588). All the details, however trivial, miserable, revolting, indecent, puerile, or ridiculous they might have seemed for his readers, were considered essential for explaining the secret inclinations of his personality. Therefore, he narrated them without hesitation, producing consequently the first revelation, and celebration, of the atomistic, autonomous self (Gutman, 1988).

The first part of Rousseau's autobiography was written entirely from memory, while for the second part, which concerned his life after gaining a public reputation, he could make use of his correspondence to recall the facts. Rousseau repeatedly expressed his regret for never having kept a diary that could have helped him re-enact his life story. There are differences regarding the style of writing and the content focus between the two parts that could be explained by the availability of auxiliary sources, like the letters, for stimulating the recollection of past events. Psychological research on autobiographical memory has shown that humans generally remember emotionally loaded events from their past. Emotionally loaded events, either negative or positive, are remembered with more vividness than nonemotional ones (Buchanan, 2007). Our memory stores better the history of our emotions and feelings than the history of our actions and thoughts. It is evident that Rousseau had an intuition about this psychological phenomenon when he announced that he offered to the reader the "history of his soul" and knowledge about "men's heart." The emphasis in the *Confessions* on the emotional life may seem strange considering that Rousseau was a philosopher of the Enlightenment, the age of reason (Gutman, 1988). "Feeling comes to fill my soul quicker than lightning, but instead of enlightening me it sets me on fire and dazzles me. I feel everything and I see nothing. I am fiery but stupid: I need to be cool in order to think," wrote Rousseau when explaining the contrast between his heart and his mind (*Confessions*, p. 95). Although he perceived feeling as blocking reasoning, he decided to write in the *Confessions* everything that he felt and almost nothing about his philosophical thoughts. After all, he was an initiator of Romanticism as well (Babbit, 1991)!

Added to the findings in autobiographical memory research, social psychologists have shown that humans are very keen to talk about their emotions. Most of our conversations are about the emotions experienced in the recent or not so recent past. The social sharing of emotions has been recognized as one of the dimensions through which emotion manifests itself (Rimé, 2005). People share positive and negative emotions with the same readiness, and their intensity affects only the length of the period in which they are recounted and not the fact of being shared. There are, however, two emotions about which people are not so eager to talk, that they keep entirely secret or share only with intimates: shame and guilt. Rousseau again proved to have a fine knowledge of human nature when he acknowledged, "It is not what is criminal that costs the most to tell, it is what is ridiculous and shameful" (*Confessions*, p.15). He considered his autobiographical work to be outstanding properly because he succeeded to surpass the embarrassment of admitting and describing publicly the details of such experiences.

Alina: But finally, let's consider the most substantial aspects that we have yet to talk about. Rousseau decided, in the *Confessions*, to narrate all his life, including some really regrettable episodes, quite ignoble actions that he was ashamed of having committed, but which he reported in his autobiography without pretense, without any censorship, and with total honesty. The first odd episode recounted had an ice-breaking effect. Rousseau assured the reader that after making that first painful disclosure, the flow was tuned on: "From now on I am sure of myself, after what I have just dared to say, nothing can stop me any more" (*Confessions*, p. 15). He thus confessed everything, from the most intimate details of his erotic life, which occupy an important part of his autobiography, to the various thins and faults, with variable gravity that he made during his life, like committing criminal acts or neglecting his parental duties or falling in love with the mistress of his friend. Of course, besides that, the good and bad experiences he had in his life, as well as more neutral events he had lived, were all narrated as well.

The first book of the *Confessions* provides a description of Rousseau's first erotic experience, which explains his masochism. It happened when he was about 8 years old and lived as an internal student in the house of his tutor, M. Lambercier. The corporal punishments administered by Miss Lambercier, the sister of his tutor, sexually aroused him. Therefore, to feel the pleasure again, he offended her on purpose. When the fact was discovered, Miss Lambercier stopped the punishment, distanced herself from him, and started treating him as a boy and no longer as a child. This shameful experience was considered crucial for the development of his personality, explaining his inclination for masochistic submission in the relationship with women: "Who would believe that this childhood punishment received at eight years of age from the hand of a woman of thirty determined my tastes, my desires, my passions, myself for the rest of my life, and this, precisely in the opposite sense to the one that ought to follow naturally? At the same time that my senses were inflamed, my desires were so well put off the track, that – being limited to what I had experienced – they did not venture to look for anything else. (...) Tormented for a long time without knowing by what, I devoured beautiful women with an ardent eye; solely to make use of them in my fashion, and to make so many Mlle Lamberciers out of them." (Confessions, p. 14).

Shame is also related to the acts somebody has suffered. Sexual harassment and rape are events that generate feelings of shame for the victims, and this explains why they are more likely to be kept secret (Rimé, 2005). The current #Me too movement shows how much embarrassment victims feel when denouncing sexual attacks or harassment even in liberal societies. Rousseau felt not only embarrassment but also disgust when being himself a victim of homosexual harassment in the Turin convent where he was catechized to become a catholic. A boy who pretended to be Moore and who received religious training as well started to manifest a particular affection for him that was taken for friendship by the naïve Rousseau. The affection turned out to be sexual attraction when the boy pushed him violently to engage in masturbation, a practice "for I did not have the slightest idea what it was all about." Seeing the Moore ejaculating heightened his confusion and made him feel disgusted, since "(...) truly I know nothing more hideous for someone in cold blood to see than that obscene and filthy bearing, and that horrible face inflamed with the most brutal concupiscence. I have never seen another man in such a state; but if we are like this in our raptures around women, their eyes must be very fascinated for them not to be horrified at us." (Confessions, p. 56).

His newly discovered aversion to homosexuals was accompanied by repugnance against the organization, since the monk in charge of his religious training engaged in defending the abuser by minimizing the gravity of the deed and encouraging him to keep silent. Besides helping Rousseau to hurry away from an organization that praised so much docility, this experience made him realize that he was undoubtedly attracted to women, to any women, not just the beautiful ones, and that "for the offenses of my sex I owed them reparation in tenderness of feelings, in the homage of my person, and at the memory of this false African, the ugliest hag became an adorable object to my eyes." (Confessions, p. 58).

He was in the company of women almost all his life, but not every woman received the same consideration from him. For some he had special feelings, for example, Madame de Warens, his "Mamma," the 30-year-old woman he met as a teenager and who became his protector. It was more than love that he felt for her, a feeling however devoid of any need for sexual possession. When "Mamma" decided to initiate him in the art of love, he felt sadness and disappointment, as if the noble feelings had been betrayed. When in Venice, he paid a visit to the Courtesan Zulietta, whom he found charming and deplored her situation. Discovering that she had a physical malformation on one nipple destroyed all the charm, and Zulietta, offended, advised him to forget women and to study mathematics instead. During his journey to Montpellier he met by chance Madame de Larnage, who became his lover for a few days. He felt with this occasion the real pleasure related to the delights of sex, liberated from any constraints and "delirium of the brain" associated with love. He never had physical intercourse with the woman with whom he fell in love in his late adulthood, his greatest love, the Countess of Houdetot. She was actually the mistress of his good friend, Saint-Lambert, who Rousseau admired and toward whom he had guilty feelings.

Rousseau asserts without hesitation that he never felt love for Thérèse Le Vasseur, the women which he eventually married after being his companion for more than 25 years, and that "the needs of the senses which I satisfied with her have been solely sexual, without being at all connected with the individual" (Confessions, p. 348); he was using her just for sex, so to say, in our current language. This woman gave him five children, all of whom he left in front of the foundling hospital as soon as they were born. He often described the act of abandoning his children as fatal, not necessarily because he felt remorse for doing it, but because it made him vulnerable to his enemies, who had therefore the maximum proof of his wickedness. When Thérèse became pregnant, Rousseau thought that his poor and unstable economic situation would not allow him to marry her, so as not to compromise her of course, and to take care properly of the children. The state, he thought, could have done it better and turn them into good citizens. This solution came to his mind after spending much time in the company of ordinary Parisians, who shared their usual stories, among which "clandestine births were the most common texts there, and the one who best peopled the foundling hospital was always the most applauded" (*Confessions*, p. 289). Since decent people resorted to such actions, he found the excuse: this must be the practice of the country, so he could easily follow it.

Against the will of the mother, he took his first new-born child to the foundling hospital and repeated this action four times more, with the feeling that it would have been unjust to keep one child after having abandoned the others. Regret at leaving his children to the orphanage is not very evident even if some reference to the feeling of guilt is made in certain paragraphs. Rousseau did not want to be considered cruel for his gesture, but admitted that he could not feel much attachment to the children with whom he had never lived. He was not insensitive either to the mother's suffering for their loss. He confessed to have preferred many times the "supplement" of masturbating instead of having sexual intercourse with her and risk another pregnancy.

The most dreadful story that he told about himself relates to a crime that he committed in his youth. The remorse that he felt because of it impeded him, as he asserts, from committing other criminal acts for the rest of his life. He then served as secretary of Madame de Vercellis in Turin, who eventually died from breast cancer. Before leaving the house and profiting from the confusion, Rousseau stole an old ribbon. When the object was found in his possession, he falsely accused Marion, a young and pretty servant in the house, of having given it to him. The poor innocent girl was punished and her reputation was considered definitely destroyed: not only was she accused of being a thief but also of using the stolen object to seduce a boy. There is a mix of shame, guilt, and especially remorse that transcends when Rousseau tells this story that he kept secret even to his most intimate friends. Reflecting on his guilt as prosecutor in times when he felt himself to be an innocent victim of others made him recognize, "As long as I lived tranquilly it tormented me less, but in the midst of a stormy life it deprives me of the sweetest consolation of persecuted people who are innocent: it makes me feel very much what I believe I have said in some work, that remorse sleeps during a prosperous fate and grows sour in adversity" (Confessions, p. 72).

Marco: This is, according to me, a point of extraordinary importance. Because from this point of view Rousseau was in my opinion much more courageous than many contemporary autoethnographers believe (and I include myself without doubt on the list). In fact, I have the impression that very seldom autoethnographies, like autobiographies, contain the story of really morally embarrassing episodes for the authors. Autoethnographers sometimes report episodes that show their fragility, their limitations (Ronai, 1995; Ellis, 1998, 2010; Jago, 2002; Tamas, 2016; Pensoneau-Conway et al., 2017), but almost never admit to having committed "immoral" actions such as stealing, abandoning a child, or committing some other crime. And the reason for this is not, I think, the fear of ending up in jail, but rather that, very human and understandable, reason that they do not want to shed bad light on themselves in front on the readers. In the vast majority of autoethnographies, the protagonists are indeed decent people, with a very high morality, in solidarity with their neighbors, altruists, animated by the best intentions, and so on. Even when embarrassing facts are told, they almost always refer to a distant past from which the "repentant narrator" is today light years away. Among the exceptions I am immediately reminded of the extraordinary John Johnson book, *Doing Field Research* (1975), in which the author reveals, among other things, that he had betrayed his wife (without telling her) with one of the people he met in the field. A similar episode, although morally much more acceptable, is also found in *Final Negotiations* by Carolyn Ellis, when the author tells of a fleeting love affair that she had during the long and terribly exhausting illness of her partner. If we want, a small venial sin is also reported by William Foot Whyte in the famous appendix of *Street Corner Society* (1943), when he admits to having voted twice in a local election in Boston to please his North End Italian friends. It seems to me that all these confessions are those of very minor faults, nothing comparable to those reported by Rousseau. I think that Patricia and Peter Adler are right when, following Lofland and Lofland (2006), they write that "It is a maxim in sociology that people only write about the second-worst thing that happens to them" (see also Adler and Adler, 1989).

I think, I tell you sincerely, that we should begin to imitate Rousseau from this point of view and write also, not only of course, autoethnographies that see us play the part of the villain. In short, we should describe and analyze the worst moments of our lives, those in which we have carried out actions of which we are not proud. And we should do it because, and I agree with Rousseau, we would improve our knowledge of how the societies in which we live function and of human nature. Until that happens we will continue to have an extreme need for those fieldworks conducted with the investigative method (Douglas, 1976) and undercover what the IRB actually prevents today in many countries of the world. These researches continue to be crucial in order to find out what people would rather keep secret, in order to bring to light those very important social phenomena that remain shrouded in darkness and lies.

Alina: However, not everybody appreciated Rousseau's determination to narrate unspeakable stories of his life in the same way. For example, Paul de Man (1979), who suspected him of narcissism and exhibitionism, analyzed the Marion episode as a story used as a pretext in order for him to show off, to compel public admiration for his inner self.

Regarding his contemporaries, as Rousseau himself anticipated, the first readers were rather shocked to hear such intimate details about the life of a person. The last paragraph of the *Confessions* describes the reaction of the public to the first reading he gave of it: everyone remained silent when the reading was over, a silence that reveals not only the public's astonishment but also its unpreparedness to hear that kind of stories (Lilti, 2008). After the publication of the first six books, Rousseau was strongly criticized in the periodicals of those times (like *L'Anée Littéraire* or *Correspondance Littéraire*) especially for his insistence on recounting his childhood, a period considered then as completely insignificant. All that "puerile nonsense," like passing water in the neighbor's pot, feeling sexual pleasure when receiving punishment from a woman, or stealing apples when he was an apprentice, were considered trivial and embarrassing for the reader. People could simply not understand how such a big thinker could write about such infamous acts (Trousson, 2014). Such details encouraged the readers to consider the *Confessions* rather a literary text, even if Rousseau did not intend to write it as such. They also allowed critics or even psychiatrists to diagnose him with various mental disorders or character flaws long after he was dead.

TAKING CARE OF OTHERS WHEN
WRITING AUTOBIOGRAPHY

Marco: Another very important question is the one concerning the ethical dimension of ethnographic research and writing. As you know, many ethnographers have repudiated a contractualist or a deontological vision of research ethics and instead embraced a caring or relational perspective (Ellis, 2007; Adams, 2008; Goodson et al., 2017). Attention to care, relationships, and a compassionate approach to the people who study themselves have also become widespread among autoethnographers. The latter, inspired by the seminal works of Carolyn Ellis, has recognized the need to do research and to describe its results in a way that does not damage the reputation or does not hurt the sensitivity of those who are mentioned or even appear as characters in autoethnographic papers. In this way, we autoethnographers implicitly recognize the fact that, even when we talk about stories that happened to us, we are not completely the masters of them and we cannot tell what happened to us without always thinking about the impact on those who appear in our stories and that will read the pages we write. This applies in some way even to those who are no longer there or to those who, for some reason, will never read what we have written. This is also due to the fact that the people mentioned in the autoethnographic stories are obviously easily recognizable, and guaranteeing the anonymity and integrity of the research is very complicated. If, for example, in a self-narration I talk about my brother or my neighbor, it is clear that a person who reads that story and knows me or my brother or my neighbor will immediately recognize the person I'm talking about, coming to know about her some things that would have been better left unsaid.

In short, even autoethnographers have discovered that they have great moral responsibilities, especially toward the weak, the defenseless, and the people who will never have a chance to tell their own story. From this discovery comes the need to treat respectfully the people who populate our narrations, imagining even some kind of collaborative research, in which the traditional roles of the researcher and the subject disappear and the research is done together in some way, and also the results are analyzed together. I imagine that Rousseau did not feel this need. Ultimately, he was a man of the eighteenth century, by force of circumstances very far removed from the feminism and postmodernism that are the foundation of the contemporary ethic of care. But maybe I'm wrong. What's your opinion? How did Rousseau deal with the protagonists of his stories? Did he ever worry about these aspects?

Alina: In the event of their first publication, the *Confessions* created controversy. Rousseau's contemporaries, especially his enemies (real or imagined), feared that their lives would be exposed in an attempt at ultimate revenge by someone who saw enemies and plots everywhere and could invent misleading and dreadful accounts about them. For example, Diderot, who knew about Rousseau's intentions to have his memoirs published posthumously, warned that such a work should not be given much consideration by the public (Trousson, 2014). The fears proved to be unjustified, since the only dreadful stories narrated by Rousseau regarded himself alone.

Moreover, what might again be surprising for an eighteenth century text is the fact that its author reflected about the moral problem raised by exposing, along with his own story, also the lives of other people with whom he interacted throughout his life. He made at least two important references in the text of the *Confessions* and one in the Neuchatel Preface about the responsibility he had not to compromise anyone. Still, the imperative of being sincere in his account required him to "speak as freely about them as about myself" (*Confessions, NP*, p. 589). Two solutions were found in order to avoid any risk of negative exposure. One solution envisaged was the publication of the *Confessions* long after him and all the others were dead, so that the "passage of time makes the facts that it contains inconsequential to everyone" (*Confessions, NP*, p. 589). The manuscript of the book was kept secretly and was entrusted only to "reliable enough hands so that no indiscreet use might ever be made of it" (*Confessions, NP*, p. 589). This safety measure was intended to protect exclusively the others, Rousseau himself having no fears of being despised by the readers or anyway caring little about losing their esteem.

The other solution for protecting the reputation of others relates to how Rousseau depicted them in the stories whose secondary characters they were. His intentions were "...to be just and truthful, to say about someone else as much good as I can, never to say anything but the evil that regards me and only as much as I am forced to." (*Confessions*, p. 335). He could not have done it better, he believed. And, indeed, there is not much criticism of his companions in the book. Except maybe for Friedrich Melchior Grimm, his former friend who he believed had transformed into his most malicious enemy, Rousseau abstained generally from describing in negative terms the traits of character and actions of his peers. But, of course, his concern for protecting the privacy and reputation of others applied only to "certain" others, in general people of high social status or the *philosophers* he frequented. No concerns about exposing the lives of ordinary people or about their weaknesses were expressed. We should not ask from Rousseau more than he could give!

AUTOBIOGRAPHY AS AUTOTHERAPY

Marco: There is a last argument I would like to add to our discussion. As Ellis et al. (2011) have acknowledged, writing personal stories can be therapeutic for their authors. Was it the same for Rousseau?

Alina: Yes, writing his memories had such a therapeutic effect for Rousseau. The handiest example is when he recalls and describes vividly happy moments of his life and discerns "that the reader does not have a great need of knowing all this; but I myself have a need to tell it to him. If only I dared to recount in the same way all the little anecdotes of that happy age, which still make me shiver with joy when I recall them" (*Confessions*, p. 18). Proving a very good knowledge of the human psyche, Rousseau was aware that the recollection of emotions produces their revival, that sharing happy stories from the past procured him the same pleasure again, and that he profited from it, especially since he wrote the

Confessions in periods of solitude and sadness. Writing about unspeakable acts that he had committed during his life had also a therapeutic effect. After recounting the Marion episode, he confessed to finally feel relieved, after keeping the secret for more than 40 years and that: "I can say that the desire to free myself from it in some measure has contributed very much to the resolution I have made to write my confessions" (*Confessions*, p. 72).

But besides the therapeutic effects of remembering emotions, writing his memories had an etiological function (Trousson, 2014). It was a way to make sense about who he was, what he became, and why. Finding explanations for his most dreadful behavior, as well his more noble acts, contributed to self-understanding, but it also helped him maintain, and then project for the others, a good image about himself, so that no one would dare to say *"I was better than that man"* (*Confessions*, p. 5). Autobiography is definitely a form of autotherapy I think.

CLOSING

Bucharest: March 20, 2018.

Alina (looking out of the kitchen windows and observing the thick mantle of snow covering Bucharest in this strange tail-end of winter): I would say that we have completed our work. What do you think?

Marco (replacing the filter of the coffee machine): Yes, I think we've done our best to analyze the work of Rousseau and link it to the contemporary debate on autoethnography. I think we can conclude that reading the *Confessions* is a very useful and profitable exercise also for the autoethnographers of our time and that the autobiographical Rousseau remains a work full of stimuli and suggestions for those who are preparing, more than 200 years from the first publication of the *Confessions*, to look at the world without excluding their own subjectivity and emotions. Many of the problems we face today (some ethical, others methodological, and others of a different nature) were implicitly already present, as you have explained so well, also to Rousseau.

Alina (sitting at the kitchen table and picking up the wonderful old Romanian edition of the *Confessions* with the ochre and brown cover): Here, I would say that our paper can serve, in the best of cases, to shorten the temporal distances, to update Rousseau's autobiographical work on the one hand and make us rediscover the Enlightenment roots of the culture in which we are immersed in the other, and also to suggest new research paths, such as the one concerning the story of the "bad actions" that we have committed in life. Rousseau was a "parrhesiast" a man in love with the truth, convinced that the most noble, most important, most beautiful, and most useful action that each of us can perform is to tell the truth, to tell with absolute sincerity what has happened to us and what we understood about the world and life. In this he is also an heir of classical thought, of the Stoic philosophers of antiquity, and a precursor of the last Foucault, that of the last courses at the Collège de France.

Marco: I would add that our Jean-Jacques was not only extraordinarily able to use his emotions to analyze human nature but also he was, as we said, a radical autobiographer at the limits of intransigence. His epistemological considerations on the value of autobiography can also help us greatly to legitimize contemporary autoethnographic practice.

Alina (smiling): If we could prove at least half of everything we've said, we would have already achieved a great result. I think.

REFERENCES

Abbs, P. 2008. The full revelation of the Self: Jean-Jacques Rousseau and the birth of deep autobiography, *Philosophy now: A Magazine of Ideas*, 68, 17–20.

Adams, T. E. 2008. A review of narrative ethics, *Qualitative Inquiry*, 14(2), 175–194.

Adler, P. A. and Adler, P. 1989. Self-censorship: the politics of presenting ethnographic data, *Arena Review*, 13(1), 37–48.

Babbit, I. 1991. *Rousseau and Romanticism*, New Brunswick, NJ, Transaction Publishers.

Buchanan, T. W. 2007. Retrieval of emotional memories, *Psychological Bulletin*, 133(5), 761–779.

de Man, P. 1979. *Allegories of Reading: Figural Language in Rousseau, Nietzsche, Rilke, and Proust*, New Haven, CT; London, Yale University Press.

Denzin N. K. and Lincoln Y. S. 2017. *The Sage Handbook of Qualitative Research*, 5th ed., Los Angeles, CA, SAGE Publications.

Douglas, J. D. 1976. *Investigative Social Research: Individual and Team Field Research*, Beverly Hills, CA, SAGE Publications.

Ellis, C. 1998. I hate my voice, *The Sociological Quarterly*, 39(4), 517–537.

Ellis, C. 2007. Telling secrets, revealing lives: relational ethics in research with intimate others, *Qualitative Inquiry*, 13(1), 3–29.

Ellis, C. 2010. *Final Negotiations: A Story of Love, and Chronic Illness*, Philadelphia, PA, Temple University Press.

Ellis, C., Adams, T. E. and Bochner, A. P. 2011. Autoethnography: an overview, *Historical Social Research/Historische Sozialforschung*, 12, 273–290.

Ellis, C. and Bochner, A. P. 2000. Autoethnography, personal narrative, reflexivity: researcher as subject. In *Handbook of Qualitative Research*, Eds N. K. Denzin and Y. S. Lincoln, 2nd ed., pp. 733–768, London, SAGE Publications.

Geertz, C. 1973. Thick description: toward an interpretive theory of culture. In *The Interpretation of Cultures: Selected Essays*, Ed C. Geertz, pp. 3–30, New York, NY, Basic Books.

Goodson I., Antikainen A., Sikes P. and Andrews M. 2017. *The Routledge International Handbook on Narrative and Life History*, London, Routledge.

Guehenno, J. 1966. *Jean-Jacques Rousseau, 1712–1778 (2 Volumes)*, (Translated by John and Doreen Weightman), New York, NY, Columbia University Press.

Gutman, H. 1988. Rousseau's confessions: a technology of the self. In *Technologies of the Self: A Seminar with Michel Foucault*, Eds M. Foucault, L. H. Martin, H. Gutman and P. H. Hutton, pp. 99–120, Amherst, MA, University of Massachusetts Press.

Holman Jones, S., Adams, T. and Ellis, C. 2013. *Handbook of Autoethnography*, London, Routledge.

Jago, B. J. 2002. Chronicling an academic depression, *Journal of Contemporary Ethnography*, 31(6), 729–757.

Johnson, J. M. 1975. *Doing Field Research*, New York, NY, Free Press.

Lejeune, P. 2009. Rousseau et la révolution autobiographique. In *Le biographique, la réflexivité et les temporalités. Articuler langues, cultures et formation*, Eds D. Bachelart and G. Pineau, pp. 49–65, Paris, L'Harmattan.

Lilti, A. 2008. The writing of paranoia: Jean-Jacques Rousseau and the paradoxes of celebrity, *Representations*, 103(1), 53–83.

Lofland, J. and Lofland, L. H. 2006. *Analyzing Social Settings*, Belmont, CA, Wadsworth Publishing Company.

MacCannell, J. F. 1974. History and self-portrait in Rousseau's autobiography, *Studies in Romanticism*, 13(4), 279–298.

Marzano, M. 2009. Lies and pain: patients and caregivers in the "conspiracy of silence", *Journal of Loss & Trauma*, 14(1), 57–81.

Pensoneau-Conway, S. L., Adams, T. E. and Bolen, D. M. 2017. *Doing Autoethnography*, Rotterdam, Sense Publishers.

Rimé, B. 2005. *Le partage social des émotions*, Paris, Presses Universitaires de France.

Ronai, C. R. 1995. Multiple reflections of child sex abuse: an argument for a layered account, *Journal of Contemporary Ethnography*, 23(4), 395–426.

Rousseau, J-J. 1995. *The Confessions; and, Correspondence, Including the Letters to Malesherbes*, Eds C. Kelly, R. D. Masters and P. G. Stillman, Translaed by Christopher Kelly, Hanover, PA; London, University Press of New England.

Rousseau, J-J. 2000. *The Reveries of the Solitary Walker, Botanical Writings, and Letter to Franquières, the Collected Writings of Rousseau*, Ed C. Kelly, Trans Charles E. Butterworth, Alexandra Cook and Terence E. Marshall, Hanover, PA, University Press of New England.

Starobinski, J. 1962. Rousseau und die Suche nach dem Ursprung [Rousseau and the search for the origin], *Schweizer Monatshefte: Zeitschrift für Politik, Wirtschaft, Kultur*, 42(4), 379–388.

Starobinski, J. 1988. *Jean-Jacques Rousseau: Transparency and Obstruction*, (Translated by Arthur Goldhammer), Chicago, IL, University of Chicago Press.

Storey, B. 2012. Self-knowledge and sociability in the thought of Rousseau, *Perspectives on Political Science*, 41 (3), 146–154.

Tamas, S. 2016. *Life after Leaving: The Remains of Spousal Abuse*, London, Routledge.

Trousson, R. 2014. Eziologia del ricordo d'infanzia e di giovinezza in J.-J. Rousseau [Etiology of childhood and youth memories in J.-J. Rousseau]. In *Il Pedagogista Rousseau [The Pedagogist Rousseau]*, Ed G. Bertagna, pp. 147–163, Milano, Editrice La Scuola.

Trousson, R. and Eigeldinger, F. S. Eds 2006. *Dictionnaire de Jean-Jacques Rousseau*, Paris, Honoré Champion.

Whyte, W. F. 1943[2012]. *Street Corner Society: The Social Structure of an Italian Slum*, Chicago, IL, University of Chicago Press.

Zwerdling, A. 2017. *The Rise of the Memoir*, Oxford, Oxford University Press.

"SUCK IT UP, BUTTERCUP": STATUS SILENCING AND THE MAINTENANCE OF TOXIC MASCULINITY IN ACADEMIA

John C. Pruit, Amanda G. Pruit and Carol Rambo

ABSTRACT

This autoethnography takes up the matter of toxic masculinity in university settings. We introduce the term "status silencing" as a way to make visible the normalization of toxic masculinity in everyday talk and interaction in university settings among and around colleagues. Status silencing is the process in which the status of a dominant individual becomes a context which renders the story of an individual with a subordinated status untellable or untold. Using strange accounting, we explore active and passive types of status silencing to show how talk and interactions involving toxic masculinity are both internalized and externalized expressions of power and dominance. We argue that while most scholars view toxic masculinity as blatant acts of violence (mass shootings, rape and sexual assault, etc.), it is also a normalized occurrence for feminized others and that toxic masculinity in academic settings is part of an ongoing institutional norm of silence.

Keywords: Toxic masculinity; status silencing; strange accounts; gender inequality; academic culture; autoethnography

"You act like a girl." "Pussy." "Faggot." "Cuckold." "Sissy."

"Are you going to tell your mother?"

"Get over it."

Radical Interactionism and Critiques of Contemporary Culture
Studies in Symbolic Interaction, Volume 52, 95–114
Copyright © 2021 by Emerald Publishing Limited
All rights of reproduction in any form reserved
ISSN: 0163-2396/doi:10.1108/S0163-239620210000052007

"Bitch." "Cunt." "Dyke." "Can't get a man." "Misandrist." "Emotionally unstable, Feminazi, whore."

"Somebody should rape you." "You should kill yourself."

"Butthurt." "Snowflake." "Social Justice Warrior." "Libtard."

"You're being emotional." "Shut the fuck up already."

Based on our online experiences and face-to-face interactions with others, these are some things that *we may expect to hear* as a reaction to writing this. These internalized expectations, built up over time, are based on a "toxically masculine" (Banet-Weiser and Miltner, 2016; Haider, 2016; Hess and Flores, 2018; Kimmel and Wade, 2018; Kupers, 2005) "generalized other" (Mead, 1934). Avoiding this definition of self and fear of loss of access to resources may be enough for some to keep quiet in the face of injustice. We could say "fuck off" in response, but that would only serve to misdirect attention and unmindfully reproduce what we are attempting to discuss, thus missing an opportunity to interrogate a taken-for-granted feature of everyday life for some of us in the academy and beyond.

All three authors are vulnerable. We are perpetrators. We are victims. We are not heroic, or cowards, only ordinary participants in academic culture, complicit in reproducing the culture. To protect ourselves and others in our stories, we will not always say exactly what happened to whom; we might change the time and place of an event, omit information about who we are interacting with, and more. These strategies are employed to craft a "strange account," a form of autoethnographic writing which serves to keep identities, secrets, and meaning "in play" (Rambo, 2016; Rambo and Pruit, 2019) when there is risk involved in the storytelling.

Drawing on Simmel's (1950) concept of "the stranger" to frame the technique/methodology, strange accounting is a form of representation which seeks to find the "sweet spot" between imparting too little and too much information. Too little information creates too much distance between the reader and the topic; it is not salient, there is no relevance or value to what has been written. Too much information can be too close to a situation and can bring harm to those in our stories and/or ourselves. Writing a strange account positions us to observe and report on events while keeping identities and secrets hidden. Often, meanings and identities never settle, they stay in play (Derrida, 1978). A strange account might leave dimensions such as time, rank, race, class, gender, sexual orientation, authorship, characters, place, meaning, and more in play (Rambo and Pruit, 2019). They also "embody an 'ethic of care' which Ellis (2007) advises us requires researchers to act from their hearts and minds, acknowledge interpersonal relationships, and take responsibility for actions and their consequences" (Rambo and Pruit, 2019, p. 236). In this article we explore a phenomenon we have termed *status silencing* and its role in the maintenance of toxic masculinity in academic and other institutional settings.

***

I am on the phone. "I just saw his picture on Facebook," the male social science PhD says, "that haircut, makes him look like an effeminate skinhead." I laugh. In the context of a Trump presidency, the juxta positioning of "effeminate" and "skinhead" feels like an assault on white supremacists, which I initially like, because they would hate it. But it really isn't. It is an assault on my friend; I just laughed at his expense. I also laughed at the male social science PhD's desire to assault my friend in this manner. "What's up with that?" I wonder. I think I know, but I will not say it.

The comment is also an assault on being "feminine." The assumption is if you are a man, being like a woman is derogatory (because hey, back stage, we all know that really, men should not act like women, right?). But that would mean women are intrinsically inferior and we give mere lip service to equality. Our hypothetical skinhead (presumably male) would not like being characterized as similar to a woman (and thus possibly gay, which is also bad, right?). This insult has it all.

I say, "You're homophobic and can't own it."
He says, "No, I'm not, you know my work in that area."
I say, "I should tell him you said it."
He laughs, presumably imagining it, and dares me, "Do it!"
I need to get back to my meeting. I say "Bye" and hang up.

Something in me (what is that?) is compelled to repeat what was said, to see what the response will be. It is a kaon, boring into my brain. It is also shit disturbing, an identity I like. If I am honest, it is an expression of power. I say it in front of more than one group and feed on the attention and laughter all around me. I blame the male social science PhD when in fact he said it to me in private, not to my friend (he never would). I am the one pushing this. Meanwhile, as the haircut slur is repeated, I see the recipient "taking it well." He laughs. There seems to be warmth, collegiality, bonding. I am glad (am I?). We are in on the joke together, we both know the guy who said it; and by not acting "insulted" the owner of the haircut is successfully performing "masculinity" with great ease. He is letting it roll off his back (he should). I comment to the small audience around us that he and the other man "go at each other a lot" so it is "okay" implying that the abuse is equal (when it isn't). He is "being a man about it."

In one fell swoop, I have used sexism, homophobia, and perhaps racism and classism to "be funny" and gain status for myself, bond with a small group, and (re)produce domination and subordination in an academic/institutional setting. But hey, I said it to his face, right? And in reality, the haircut looks sharp, so no harm, no foul, right?

***

I need to look at this again. Did the target of the comment have any choice in the matter except laughter? One high-status person who heard the remark smiled a little, but shook his head and said, "Uh...," indicating that it was not okay. And he also cares about me. He was clearly conflicted. Meanwhile, I can play it off as something my friend said about my other friend. I do not have to take ownership of my comments and their consequences.

***

And as I look at it again, what I see is the first example of status silencing that is the topic of this article. The owner of the haircut was subordinate in status to me and my friend who originally made the comment. Perhaps it bothered him, perhaps it was no big deal. If I were to ask, I am sure he would say it was funny. But what else can he say? Our statuses set the contexts for his options to respond.

***

Which author wrote this story? First, second, or third? Or was it an amalgamation of something that has happened to some or all of us? Was the story teller a man, a woman, or someone who was non-binary? Was the story teller a graduate student working on a PhD, an assistant professor, or a full professor (each of the three authors has one of these ranks)? Does their sexual orientation matter? Their marital status? Did the story happen recently, or a long time ago? These questions will almost always remain deliberately unanswered in an autoethnographic strange account.

***

Any of us who are familiar with work on how the everyday performance of gender is policed (West and Zimmerman, 1987) can handily frame the items in the opening as exemplars of toxic masculinity (Banet-Weiser and Miltner, 2016; Haider, 2016; Hess and Flores, 2018; Kimmel and Wade, 2018; Kupers, 2005). Toxic masculinity is characterized as "always available for men to enact" (Connell and Messerschmidt, 2005, p. 840) and as part of a patriarchal "tool kit" (Swidler, 1986) that men draw upon to defend masculine privilege. In a blog post on *Gender & Society*, Pascoe refers to toxic masculinity as "men's problematic gender practices entailing violence, sexual aggression, emotional repression, and dominance" (Pascoe, 2016). In this article, we conceptualize toxic masculinity as social practices that reify difference, hierarchy, patriarchy, and hegemony through sexual, physical, emotional, political, economic, and symbolic violence and domination directed toward feminized others. It is a process that encompasses behavior and meaning-making. It can be exercised toward others or internalized toward oneself.

There are "residual rules" (Scheff, 1966) regarding toxic masculinity that makes it often "seen but unnoticed" (Garfinkel, 1967, p. 36) until a major violation occurs which rises above what we are willing to take as a normal and everyday occurrence. We are clear it is an instance of toxic masculinity when Alek Minassian identifies as an Incel (Involuntarily Celibate) and deliberately kills 10 people while driving a van down a busy Toronto street or when Elliot Rodger kills 6 and wounds 14 in a Santa Barbara, CA, shooting, because he is angry at women who will not provide him the sex that he feels he is owed. Typically, the violence underpinning most forms of toxic masculinity is unremarked upon because it is ordinary. It does not, seemingly, breach a social norm. For those who may notice it, they may remain silent about it. We explore, through autoethnographic strange accounting, how some of these silences are produced, both passively and actively, and how toxic masculinity is maintained.

"Status silencing" occurs when the status of a dominant individual becomes a context which renders the story of an individual with a subordinated status untellable or untold (silent). It is a tool in the toxic masculinity toolbox, sometimes the result of a tacit assumption, where no action is required. At other times, one participant actively challenges the status quo, while the other silences them by *gaslighting* them and reframing the situation or perhaps through outright *coercion*. Status is the hierarchical position a person occupies in relation to power and prestige within a particular context. Having it "assumed" or "taken for granted" that one has more or less power and control is salient when considering status silencing. At one end of the continuum, status silencing can be passive, where silence is assumed, nothing needs to be said to attain the silence, and the threat of the power difference is enough for the silence to occur. At the other end of the continuum, status silencing can be active, where a lower status person is blocked from telling a story by a higher status person.

Overt, covert, accepted, contested, and/or tolerated practices of masculinized violence and domination are a part of everyday life and occur in the everyday spaces where students, staff, faculty, and administration on university campuses talk and interact (see https://www.chronicle.com/interactives/the-awakening? essay=Pirtle&fbclid=IwAR0-bDOu57uScQSaLyaB3YFbTrrnwlwk8UhPTOHb eUDf2s2fRz0v6-NYz5w). Toxic masculinity emerges during the course of social interaction, although it is typically only recognized by those in lower status positions, such as women or men with contextually devalued masculinities. In university settings, it can also be experienced by undergraduate and graduate students, university staff, instructors, adjunct instructors, untenured assistant professors, and so on. Hence, the question is not "Is masculinity good, bad, absent, or present in educational contexts?" Instead, a more fitting question is, "How is toxic masculinity an uncontested everyday accomplishment in educational contexts?" To address this question, we use strange accounting (Rambo, 2016; Rambo and Pruit, 2019) as a storytelling technique which enables us to give voice to stories that normally remain silenced. To talk about why we have stayed silent in our pasts, we must take risks and breach the norms of silence around toxic masculinity. Those risks can be expensive, the anticipation of which is why status silencing is effective.

***

Masculinities are part of the hidden, if not core, curriculum in education careers. In early childhood education (ECE) and elementary schools, an ongoing argument pits masculinity against femininity. It is referred to as the "dearth of men" argument (Francis and Skelton, 2001; King, 1998, 2009; Sargent, 2000, 2001, 2004; Skelton, 2003) and is part of the growing politics of recuperative masculinity claiming that there is a feminization of education harming young boys (Skelton, 2012). The "harm" is that boys do not have appropriate male role models in schools resulting in the feminization of education (Martino, 2008). This so-called feminization of education is a catch 22. On one hand, there are not enough men in ECE and elementary schools to teach boys how to be "real men" (Sargent, 2000). On the other hand, if men do become ECE and elementary teachers, they are subjected to an undue amount of suspicion about their occupational choice (Pruit, 2014, 2015, 2019).

Masculinity also figures prominently in adolescent boys' school life, especially in relation to identity. Areas of particular interest include school shootings and sexuality. Kimmel and Mahler (2003) and Kalish and Kimmel (2010) point out that masculinity is embedded in the cultural trope of "getting even" (Kalish and Kimmel, 2010) and that it is the single greatest risk factor in school violence (Kimmel and Mahler, 2003). Pascoe (2007) conceptually works to dislodge masculinity from biological determinism by giving attention to how sexuality and masculinity are processes of "confirmation and repudiation" in which high school boys "demonstrate mastery over others" (Pascoe, 2007, p. 14). She found that the "repeated repudiation of the specter of failed masculinity" (2005, p. 5) defined power relations and helped boys achieve a successful high school masculine identity.

Masculinity research in university contexts tends to focus on students' interactions with each other. Archer et al. (2001), for instance, discuss classroom participation strategies as ways of constructing working class masculinity, while Sallee (2011) finds that engineering graduate students are socialized into competitive, hierarchical masculine contexts. A growing segment of masculinity literature also addresses intersections of race, class, and emotions on college campuses. Wilkins (2012) analyzes Black college men's identity work regarding emotional restraint, contending that restraining anger about racism violates masculine expectations. However, Jackson and Wingfield (2013) turn to back-stage contexts in which Black college men in leadership roles display anger to encourage other Black college men to adopt a "respectable" Black masculinity in the front stage to resist the "stereotype threat" (Steele and Aronson, 1995) associated with the "angry Black man." Wilkins' (2012) and Jackson and Wingfield's (2013) upwardly mobile research participants construct dynamic identities in the face of multiple inequalities while interacting in predominantly white university contexts.

Throughout the education career, masculinity is problematized in its absence and/or presence. Masculinities literature focusing on students in university settings, rather than those with higher statuses (faculty, administrators), leads one to believe there is no gender inequality when working at universities (after all, who would dare to ask a fellow faculty member or administrator for an interview about their performances of toxic masculinity?). The absence of higher status others from the literature neatly sidesteps the issue that it is risky to write about toxic masculinity in a critical manner in university settings. This risk causes their lack of representation. Yet, the problem of toxic masculinity in university settings does not begin and end with students. It is normalized through everyday interactions across college campuses between and around university colleagues.

***

Gender both structures and is the product of everyday interactions. West and Zimmerman (1987, p. 127) consider gender a "routine, methodical, and recurring accomplishment" of interaction. In their seminal work, West and Zimmerman argue that doing gender is about "creating differences between girls and boys and women and men, differences that are not natural, essential, or biological" (1987, p. 137); however, the construction of these differences is an unavoidable interactional product (West and Zimmerman, 1987, p. 145). Gender differences, especially identifying "naturalized" and complementary deficits between masculinity and femininity, characterize heterosexual, hierarchical, and hegemonic gender conceptualizations. Much like the opening vignette, where the younger male colleague's haircut is defined as "effeminate," these differences are pervasive and used to construct gender in terms of masculine dominance.

According to Butler (2006), heterosexuality binds men and women in the masculine/feminine binary and in a hierarchical relationship. Heterosexuality, then, is a pretense for the meaning of the relationship between masculinity and femininity and the "basis of the *difference between and complementarity of* femininity and masculinity" (Schippers, 2007, p. 90) [Schippers' emphasis]. The body is central to Butler's gender matrix. Bodies play out in the context of gendered categories and are included or excluded from those categories (Butler, 1993). In this manner, Butler problematizes male/female as a social category based on biological differences.

Connell (1995) and Connell and Messerschmidt (2005) construct a hierarchy involving types of masculinities including hegemonic, complicit, subordinated, and marginalized masculinities. By masculinities, the authors mean "configurations of practice that are accomplished in social action and, therefore, can differ according to the gender relations in a particular social setting" (Connell and Messerschmidt, 2005, p. 836). Hegemonic masculinity refers to a "pattern of practice that allowed men's dominance over women to continue" (Connell and Messerschmidt, 2005, p. 832). While hegemonic masculinity is normative, very few men can actually enact it (Donaldson, 1993). Most men experience a masculinity deficit in the face of hegemonic masculinity. Goffman's (1963) discussion of stigma and physical attractiveness is illustrative. He explains that most American men fall short in one way or another of the ideal. As Goffman put it, "in an important sense there is only one complete and unblushing male in America: a young, married, white, urban, northern heterosexual Protestant father of college education, fully employed, of good complexion, weight and height, and a recent record in sports" (1963, p. 128). Nonhegemonic masculinities are devalued. Connell and Messerschmidt argue that hegemonic masculinity is most powerful in relation to complicit masculinity and heterosexual women. However, their approach has been criticized for being too static (Pascoe, 2005) since researchers tend to identify types of masculinities in association with specific contexts.

Several scholars link toxicity with violent/harmful behavior and hegemonic masculinity (Bridges and Pascoe, 2014; Connell and Messerschmidt, 2005; Creighton and Oliffe, 2010), but fewer focus directly on toxic masculinity (Banet-Weiser and Miltner, 2016; Haider, 2016; Hess and Flores, 2018; Kimmel and Wade, 2018; Kupers, 2005). Hess and Flores (2018) explore online toxic masculine performances as a form of masculinity encouraging men to be "sexually aggressive, to value dominance and control, and to position women as inferior" (Hess and Flores, 2018, p. 1088). Banet-Weiser and Miltner (2016) turn to online "networked misogyny," defining toxic masculinity as a "(heterosexual) masculinity that is threatened by anything associated with femininity (whether that is pink yogurt or emotions)" (2016, p. 171). Banet-Weiser and Miltner contend online violence toward women is not only about gender but also racism, with women of color often being specifically targeted. These trends connect to the broader social world in which

> ...[p]opular misogyny is, at its core, a basic anti-female violent expression that circulates to wide audiences on popular media platforms. This popular circulation helps contribute in heightened ways to a misogynistic political and economic culture, where rape culture is normative, violent threats against women are validated, and rights of the body for women are either under threat or being formally retracted. (Banet-Weiser and Miltner, 2016, p. 172).

Toxic masculinity aligns with hegemonic masculinity in terms of dominating anything relating to femininity. Kupers (2005) addresses toxic masculinity in prison, defining it as a "constellation of socially regressive male traits that serve to foster domination, the devaluation of women, homophobia, and wanton violence" (Kupers, 2005, p. 714). Rather than aligning toxic masculinity with hegemonic masculinity, Kupers distinguishes between positive and negative aspects of hegemonic masculinity; between its socially destructive traits, such as "misogyny, homophobia, greed, and violent domination; and those that are culturally accepted and valued" (Kupers, 2005, p. 716). These negative aspects of hegemonic masculinity are exaggerated and include

> ...extreme competition and greed, insensitivity to or lack of consideration of the experiences and feelings of others, a strong need to dominate and control others, an incapacity to nurture, a dread of dependency, a readiness to resort to violence, and the stigmatization and subjugation of women, gays, and men who exhibit feminine characteristics. (Kupers, 2005, p. 717).

Kuper's distinction between hegemonic and toxic masculinity is problematic. He states, "There's nothing especially toxic in a man's pride in his ability to win at sports, to maintain solidarity with a friend, to succeed at work, or to provide for his family" (2005, p. 716). Interestingly, the examples Kupers uses to illustrate positive aspects of hegemonic masculinity are sports, friendship, work, and family. These are not examples of hegemonic, masculine domains, rather they reflect roles inhabitable by any person. Suggesting that these are positive facets of hegemonic masculinity obscures the expressions of power in which gender dominance manifests. Kupers naturalizes gender in terms of biological difference and patriarchal norms, which undermines his argument and forces a distinction between "good" and "bad" forms of domination (Messner, 2016). Meanwhile, someone is always subordinated for not having certain culturally or situationally valued characteristics.

Rather than distinguishing toxic masculinity from hegemonic masculinity, we consider it to be part of the everyday interactions within patriarchal societies. Because of this, toxic masculinity has a cloak of invisibility in which men expressing it do not appear to recognize it as problematic. Conversely, it is so routinized for feminized others that it becomes an almost unremarkable part of their everyday experience. As such, there is a norm of silence coalescing around it. This silence, status silencing as we have termed it, necessitates a representational strategy that insulates the authors and those they interact with – autoethnographic strange accounting.

***

If gender both structures and is produced in interaction (West and Zimmerman, 1987), then unpacking situations involving status silencing is a way to make the maintenance of toxic masculinity visible as an everyday occurrence. Occupation, education, income, age, sexuality, and context complicate linkages between status silencing and race, class, and gender. Status silencing is likely a common experience among those with (multiple) subordinated statuses (i.e., a Black woman who is also a first-generation college student). An individual's devaluation at a societal level, then, corresponds to the ways in which they are interactionally silenced.

In the following pages, we analyze stories of status silencing and identify two types: *passive status silencing* and *active status silencing*. These types are located on a continuum. On the passive end of the continuum, status silencing is a product of heeding a tacit norm of silence which arises in situ. On the active end, it is the result of an interaction between actors. The first two vignettes illustrate passive status silencing in which self-censorship is an internal, covert response to an uncertain and potentially unsafe definition of the situation. It may arise in confusion over the definition of the situation, such as the case with *conflicted status silencing*, and it is always the case that it arises in response to upholding the understood, everyday, norm of "not causing trouble." The last two vignettes illustrate active status silencing in which censoring is external and occurs as actors overtly attempt to silence protest by reframing the definition of the situation. We discuss two types, *gaslighting status silencing* and *coercive status silencing*. We do not make the claim that these are the only kinds of status silencing which can take place. More than one kind of silencing may be at work in any given situation. Each vignette describes a university context and involves toxic masculinity either in the open or as the subtext of the interactions. We offer each vignette as an exemplar of the types of status silencing we foreground for discussion. In both passive and active status silencing, status enforces a complicit silence which ultimately serves to produce and maintain toxic masculinities.

***

Passive status silencing is a form of status silencing which manifests as self-censorship, no one else is doing "it" to us, and we chose to stay quiet in the situation. When we endure *conflicted status silencing*, a form of passive status silencing, a script does not clearly emerge for the unfolding situation, and we do not know what to say or do. There may be shock, confusion, and/or embarrassment. There is dissonance between our interpretation of what has been said or done and the definition of the situation higher status others are choosing to act on. Hence, in our lower status positions, we remain silent. It is assumed that there is the potential for reprisal.

***

As John, Amanda, and Carol try to take on each other's identities and give each other cover to tell stories, we wondered if we needed to leave this story out – cut and lying on the locker room floor. The two women would have never been there to witness it. While this account has been made strange to protect the guilty and the innocent, the authorship is obvious because of gender. This story we clearly identify as John's.

***

It's June – hot and humid. I am not teaching this summer. I have just finished working out with other university employees. As I enter the locker room, I hear two voices and see three other men who have also just finished their activities. One of the men is getting ready to shower in silence. The other two are engaged in some type of conversation that I willfully ignore as I, too, prepare to shower.

By the time I get into the shower area, all three are already showering. The showers are open with six large metal tubes having four shower heads dispersed throughout the room. As the two White men continue their conversation, their statuses emerge. The listener appears to be a university employee, but not a professor. He briefly speaks about applying to graduate school. He listens to the other White man, a university employee with an unknown position, tell a story about his college days and bar-hopping.

He says, "Oh, man, when I was in grad school, we'd go bar-hopping on the strip. There was this one bar where the chicks were so desperate for attention. You'd go there, and they'd be all lined up. All you had to do was buy them a drink and they'd sleep with you. It was pathetic. Different guy every night. They didn't care. Most of them probably had herpes or worse!"

I look over at the third man, a Hispanic man in his mid-thirties that also works at the university (though I am also unsure of his position). He appears to be doing his best to ignore them.

***

Through their concept of "mobilizing rape," Pascoe and Hollander (2016, p. 69) argue that "sexual assault is not simply an individual incident but a wide-ranging constellation of behaviors, attitudes, beliefs, and talk that work to produce and reproduce gendered dominance in everyday interaction."

***

I am so angry I contemplate a naked shower room brawl. The shampoo in my hair makes me feel like I am held hostage. I do not know his position or importance at the university. He speaks with the type of nonchalant sexist bravado that communicates a higher-ranking status, so I assume he is someone important. Or it could simply be that he is a White, heterosexual man. White heterosexual men often walk around with an unearned sense of entitlement which shields them from apprehending their mediocrity. In any case, my sense is that if I speak out, there could be repercussions for my career. I remain silent.

I quickly finish showering so I can leave. I am stunned that this shit is happening around me at a university. Up to now, I have never heard anyone doing "locker room talk" as Donald Trump terms it. What's more, he works at a university. What if students heard him objectifying and ranting about the predation of intoxicated women? Would he be able to carry on with any sense of dignity? My sense is yes – yes he would continue on as if nothing had ever happened because he does not interpret anything he said as sexist, misogynistic, or perpetuating rape culture. My fear is he will continue objectifying women because I (or we) did not speak up.

***

The speaker's talk revolved around sexism, predation, and dominating those within the vocal landscape. Regardless of who was present, he seemed unconcerned with his audience's potentially negative reaction as he was going to great lengths to demonstrate his masculinity. Looking back, I clearly see how my thoughts and feelings of shock about the situation jumped quickly to physical violence as a solution (the very stuff of toxic masculinity) and then to the reality of protecting my employment status. Toxic masculinity provides very limited resources, namely anger and violence. Anger is an emotional resource and violence (physical, sexual, verbal, symbolic, and so on) is a one-size-fits-all resource expressing power over and through people, places, and things.

***

As my complicity and victimhood overlap and intertwine, I fight the urge to write myself as a flawless character or at the very least a flawed protagonist caught up in unfortunate circumstances – a type of "good guy/bystander" (Messner, 2016; Pascoe and Hollander, 2016). Writing this now, however, I am struck by how I *should* have said something – it is that feeling of falling short and feeling ashamed about it and then feeling ashamed about feeling ashamed – what Ellis (1998) terms "metashame". A tacit assumption associated with toxic masculinity is it is okay to make disgusting speech acts (racist, sexist, classist, and so on) as long as nobody vehemently objects. The other two men were also passive and maybe victims; perhaps having similar thoughts as myself and perhaps not. Even as I felt victimized by his locker room talk and powerless by my own status vis-à-vis my perception of his status, by not speaking out I engaged in an act of complicity (Connell and Messerschmidt, 2005) with toxic masculinity, sexism, and patriarchy.

***

And even as we call out the bar-hopper and his performance of toxic masculinity, we also recognize him as a victim. He needs to elevate himself with other men by discussing "desperate" college women that could be taken advantage of at bars. We suspect he feels like an imposter as a masculine performer with a locker room masculinity deficit (Donaldson, 1993; Goffman, 1963) and thus needs to enact his script with exaggerated vigor to make up for his perceived deficiency.

***

Was the prior vignette a performance of toxic masculinity and contempt on our part? Two "chicks" who have been grad students in bars are weighing in on the story now. Or was it compassion and empathy? Or both? Or none of the above? We will leave this definition of the situation in play.

***

Passive status silencing also occurs when others' silence creates a shared definition of the situation to ignore or disregard toxic masculinity. We experience status silencing in the moment and contend with contextual forces being brought to bear on us. No one speaks up because there is a tacit agreement (Goffman, 1959, p. 238) not to disrupt the shared definition of the situation (Goffman, 1959, p. 77). Similar to the last situation described, there could be any number of individual definitions of the situation. In the meantime, to say something is "troublemaking."

***

I am walking away from a cardio machine in a campus workout facility. Tired, I lean against a wall to drink some water. I open my water bottle and try to tune out the surrounding noise. I pretend to look at something important on my phone, but catch the tail end of a conversation, "...and go sit Indian style. Oh wait, I can't say that because I'm White! I mean sit like a Native American!" The White man cackles at his own so-called joke. The other two men involved in the conversation do not bat an eye. Maybe they did not hear him? Maybe I misheard him? Maybe they think it's okay? I do not want to believe that these men are racist. I want to believe they are too embarrassed or scared to say anything about it and are giving face (Goffman, 1967, p. 9). Maybe they are like Merton's (1949) "fair-weather liberals" who are not prejudiced, but who discriminate because of social pressure to do so. I want to believe they are in a similar situation as me, in a lower, more vulnerable status, which is why they remain silent (why I remain silent).

***

The continued systematic disenfranchisement of indigenous persons, an act of violence in and of itself, masqueraded as White male humor. The intrusion of racism, of White men dominating the vocal landscape and trivializing indigenous peoples and their struggles, imbued the situation with toxic masculinity. What is shocking was the ease with which he did it. It was casual. Toxic masculinity is casual. Passive status silencing requires a tacit agreement that multiple individuals will not point out discriminatory talk, even though they may personally define it as reprehensible. Whatever the men were thinking matters little because the shared definition of the situation, that racist jokes are funny, went unchallenged through a tacit agreement. As a bystander, I felt that it was unsafe for me to confront them.

***

The truth is that I do not know the context of their conversation. Maybe I misunderstood? Maybe they were having a conversation about standing up for indigenous people's rights (yeah right)? I cannot believe I am debating this with myself right now! I feel a lot of doubt in the here and now about submitting this for publication. This level of vulnerability relates to the pile of status I have been able to scrape together over the years. I am worried it will slip away if I admit to doing nothing. I am also worried that it will slip away for saying something. I am so glad I have coauthors.

***

Racism and sexism are often excused as just "locker room talk" or "jokes" opening up space to hierarchize the differences between everyday racism and sexism and extreme racism and sexism. In many ways, Merton's (1949) close-ended continuum of four ideal types of White people in relation to prejudice and discrimination is still with us. Hughey (2014) argues the distinction between "good" and "bad" Whites is problematic to recognizing racism. The same is true for recognizing and speaking out against toxic masculinity (Messner, 2016; Bridges and Pascoe, 2014; Pascoe and Hollander, 2016). Strange accounts of passive status silencing and toxic masculinity show that interactions involving locker room talk or racist jokes are an ordinary, everyday occurrence. The overwhelming frequency of such events gives it an underserved sense of normalcy.

***

As the authors of this story, part of us acknowledges the simplicity of not wanting to be rude, to not be a trouble maker, and to not make problematic the smooth flow of social interaction. If I am a man, I might get into a fight. If I am a woman, I might be called a "bitch" and told to mind my own damn business. As a participant in the academy, we risk being in the line of fire for retribution, later. After all, the academy is a workplace and a place of commerce. Administration may not give a damn whose rights we think we are standing up for. All three of us are the authors of this general story, at different times, with different characters, during numerous parts of our careers.

***

This next vignette is an exemplar of the second form of status silencing, *active status silencing*. During active status silencing, there is no self-censorship, at first. We witness something, we say something, and we are very clear regarding our script. A higher status individual then acts on the situation to attain our silence. They attempt to change our definition of the situation, or they change the subject with threats. For instance, when we endure *gaslight status silencing*, there is an attempt to manipulate and reframe our definition of the situation, trying to convince us that our victimization is of our own making. "Gaslighting" (Abramson, 2014) is a therapeutic term describing a tactic used by individuals seeking to create personal advantages by shifting the victim's subjective reality to the reality of the perpetrator. It originates from Patrick Hamilton's 1938 play *Angel Street*, later developed into the film *Gaslight*, which tells the story of an abusive husband purposefully manipulating his wife to create mental instability by reframing her reality. Gaslight status silencing mutes our lived experience as lower status individuals in favor of the higher status individual's perspective.

***

I am conducting an exit interview with a student about professional challenges during her course of study in our department. She tells me about speaking with a male professor in her field of study (who I know) and about how he convinced her that she caused her own sexual harassment. She said, "I think to me, and this really came from yesterday, too, is that one of the things that I noticed about myself is that I'm very positive. Or at least I come across as very positive, which I don't necessarily think is a bad thing. But it also comes across as overly friendly and I feel like apparently, I've been that way with students, to where some things can be misconstrued. Kind of like that one male student who apparently called me 'hot'. [The social science PhD] said, 'Well, you sort of walked in on that one.' Even if that was not my intention at all."

A wave of disbelief washes over me and I am unsure how to proceed. I know on every level that this student was gaslighted. I do not pursue the discussion for a minute for fear of retaliation from the social science PhD and others. I tell her, "Let's pick that one up later." I feel confusion, disbelief, and I am rocked by a new fear that my "not saying anything" implicates me in being complicit with his victim blaming and toxic masculinity. I am paralyzed by the professional implications from all angles for another second. I finally regain some of my composure and tell her, "The choice to harass belongs to the other individual and the behavior is likely pervasive and unrelated to you."

I later meet with the social science PhD and work the courage up to discuss the situation. He repeats the scenario, summarizing, "The student was too friendly and caused the inappropriate interaction." Angry and scared, I meekly state that the "male student's behavior is indicative of a broader issue and unrelated to the student." I feel vindication for standing up for the woman and also realize this story will never be heard. He half shrugs and moves on to the next topic.

***

The social science PhD's reframing of the female student's experience reinforces gender inequalities by exerting his masculine dominance over her lived reality. The social science PhD used his status as a man, an advisor, and a tenured professor to gaslight the student *and* me. His ability to silence is tethered to toxic masculinity in that each follows broader patriarchal patterns of victim blaming (Scott and Lyman, 1968), a form of violence in its own right. Toxic masculinity, in its many structural and interactional forms, is part of a hidden curricula (Anyon, 1981; Giroux and Purpel, 1983) silencing women and feminized others at all levels of academia. Women's behavior is contested terrain for men. Men's skewed interpretation of women's behavior as flirtatious becomes an invitation for unwanted harassment that is cosigned and defended by other men.

***

We frequently feel intimidated at work, so our interactions with men in academia are a strange mix of functional anxiety and acute awareness of power differentials and gender performances (West and Zimmerman, 1987). It is difficult to discern "normal" interactions with men from their performances of toxic masculinity. Our walls are always up and we are always guarded, while also convincing ourselves we are wrong. We recognize gender inequality is harmful, unjust, and disgusting, while at the same time taken for granted and normalized in academia. Our dissonance signals the structural and interactional compromises of being othered in academia. This is compounded by us gaslight silencing ourselves after this and similar interactions for fear of disbelief and/or reprisal.

***

A short version of this next story has been told elsewhere (Rambo and Pruit, 2019). This vignette serves as an exemplar of another version of active status silencing, *coercive status silencing*. Here too, someone with a higher status is actively manipulating and reframing our definition of the situation. In contrast to gaslight status silencing, no one is trying to convince us that the victimization is of our own making, nor contest the toxicity of the situation. They are simply trying to shut down all discussion of toxic events. They may attempt to redefine the situation, justify it, excuse it, except it, or they may simply tell us not to talk about it. Status and threats are used to obtain our silence in support of the maintenance of toxic masculinity.

***

I have been made aware of a situation a student (could be a fellow student in my distant past, could be one of my students) was suffering. A social science PhD, the student's direct supervisor, required the student to work in his home. At times, the story goes, household tasks were involved. One day he was talking to him/her about his "large" penis, and how injecting medication directly into it made it something special. He had pornographic magazine pictures open on the dining room table as he said these things. He made it known that if the student wanted to cheat on their significant other, that he was available for sex. But he was not pushing (of course).

I discuss this story with higher ups. I am terrified imagining what the student is living through. I am told, "Do you think talking about this is going to help your career advancement? Is that a smart way to get (your degree/tenure)? All you are going to accomplish is being responsible for bringing negative attention to the unit. Is that what you want?"

I hope that the higher ups are scared enough, because so many of us know about it, that they will "take care of it" informally. I hope that the perpetrator will be "scared straight." I work backstage to help the student finish his or her degree, but "help" only serves to assist in the maintenance of toxic masculinity in the entire academic environment.

***

It happens again. I hear about it from a distance. I go to our institution's Equal Employment Opportunity Commission (EEOC). I am told that this is a problem individual they have their eye on, along with "someone else." They laugh out loud about it and say they have both been "slapped on the wrist" several times. I am assured, "It's being handled."

***

And it happens again with the social science PhD. I hear about that from a distance too.

***

Then with the "someone else," another social science PhD. It is openly talked about among the students.

***

And then someone else in another unit, an arts and sciences PhD. The student is intimidated into silence after visiting EEOC. He/she cries with me. I recommend a student activist organization on campus I have been involved with and suggest a lawyer. I go to EEOC on behalf of the student and am told they could not do anything about the individual. It turns out that it has been going on for years with this person too.

***

And then it happens in yet another unit, with a third social science PhD, and this one is "very charged." "We can't let this one get out," I am told. "You know why." They are embattled, their existence is in question, and they have other troubles too. Just because one person is doing this, they should not all have to suffer, right? Much happens behind closed doors. They informally sit down, talk to the perp, and make the person promise not to do it again. I am assured it is taken care of. The student confronts the perp as part of the "deal." As I look at the student, he/she accepts the result, and he/she trusts me (I had suggested he/she ask for this in exchange for the silence), but I am not so sure.

***

Other stories surface. They don't sound good. Students consider dropping out of programs. Rearrangements are made to protect them and procure their silence. They stay.

Oops, the person did it again! There are not enough Brittney Spears lyrics to sing to make this funny, are there? The third social science PhD is allowed to go, quietly. No formal firing, they resign. The student in this case, a rare and brilliant individual, goes out in a pyric blaze of mental health breakdown glory – they had been in love.

The other student who dealt with this perp, the one who got to "confront" the social science PhD, and I run into each other at a party. I almost cannot breathe. There are no words, only sadness, regret, and dysfunction. I can never make this up to him/her or the other students who were harmed; there is no redemption. We manage to connect, regardless, because shitty situations are like that. I should have done more.

***

In some ways, we hate this article because the very mechanics of academic publishing, in our case, embody a form of complicity with status silencing, especially when citing well-known social science PhDs with higher statuses that have been accused of mistreating and silencing persons with less perceived power and control over their situations. Some, including some individuals we cite, remain at the forefront of academic publishing norms. Each time we cite one of them, each time we teach one of their concepts, we are reminded of what they are alleged to have done to others. We are forced to make a distinction between good concepts and toxic people.

***

Through status silencing, toxic masculinity persists as a relatively uncontested practice in everyday university settings. In this article, we analyze the maintenance of gender inequality in university settings by identifying both passive and active status silencing, including conflicted, gaslighting, and coerced status silencing. In each case, status sets the contexts for the options to respond to toxic masculinity. Silence is typically the answer.

Toxic masculinity is not random, remote, or isolated; it is embedded in the interplay of individuals and society. Toxic masculinity can be both unusual (mass shootings, terrorism, rape, and sexual assault) and mundane (everyday interactions involving gender inequality). All of us "riff" off of an internalized, toxically masculine, generalized other, when considering our actions. Status silencing is not an isolated occurrence either; it is a normalized practice between higher and lower status persons. Experiences of toxic masculinity and status silencing are part of everyday life for feminized others.

Typical research on masculinity in university settings has focused primarily on students. Our observations on status silencing open up conversations about faculty and staff relations, across all strata of the academy. The need for the repeated repudiation of the specter of "failed masculinity," which has been documented to shape high school experience, appears to shape university experiences at conferences, in the locker room, the gym, supervising students, and beyond. The lessons learned from interactions in the academy can likely be extrapolated to other institutions and mainstream society. Recuperative masculinity, the argument that the feminization of education is harming young boys, connects to trends in the broader social world including incel subculture, Men Going Their Own Way (MGTOW), White Nationalism, and more. These trends, the Trump presidency, and more signal a need for further examination of the processes involved in the maintenance of toxic masculinity.

Strange accounting creates safety and presents opportunities to undermine existing power structures in academia. Like autoethnography, it is a form of resistance to structural domination and narrow conceptualizations of reliability, generalizability, and validity (Ellis et al., 2011). Strange accounts speak back to the backlash to autoethnography (Delamont, 2009) by illustrating its subversive qualities and strategic usage to tell untellable stories. In resisting status silencing, we tell stories that have been bottled up for days, months, or even years with considerably less risk to ourselves and others. Far from being a cathartic release, here, strange accounts provide a safety net for those that are routinely caught up in the freefall of toxic masculinity; whether they are feminized others and victims, perpetrators, or caught in a complicated snarl of complicity and resistance.

Toxic masculinity is problematic for everyone (including men). Failing to recognize toxic masculinity as an everyday practice perpetuates distinctions between good and bad masculinities (Bridges and Pascoe, 2014; Messner, 2016; Pascoe and Hollander, 2016). When masculinity is normalized in everyday interaction the construction of masculinity and the violence underlying it can be ignored. "Toxic" carries an added connotation of magnifying problematic behavior, such as sexual, physical, and emotional violence. Like masculinity, toxic masculinity flourishes in patriarchal societies in which distinctions between masculinity and toxic masculinity are made using only the most egregious acts of violence as evidence of toxicity. The overarching gender norms dominating acceptable masculine expression are often viewed as unproblematic. This frees up conceptual space for delineating binaries of normal/abnormal types of masculinities, instead of problematizing them. However, toxic masculinity *is* masculinity. Thinking about toxic masculinity as out of the ordinary perpetuates concealment of everyday forms of violence patterned into social structures and social interactions. Practices of distinguishing "good" and "bad" masculinities obscure the harm embedded in gender itself (Butler, 1993, 2006). Emphasizing one form of violence as better or worse than another neglects the fact that all violence is harmful.

Individuals having subordinated statuses are always already available for status silencing by those with overvalued statuses. We have illustrated individual instances of status silencing, group status silencing, institutional level status silencing, and evidence that status silencing is going on at a disciplinary level. Status silencing results in a plethora of untellable stories and has disproportional effects on those that are silenced and those doing the silencing. Those doing the silencing continue dominating the social, political, and economic landscape. This domination includes the power to passively and actively define the situation for themselves and others, even in the face of resistance. They are empowered and emboldened through their achievements, whether they recognize them as domination or the normal order of things. In contrast, those being silenced are disempowered, disenfranchised, and further marginalized. When individuals on social media, for instance, comment about the United States being a white-supremacist culture or rape culture, they are responding to their lived experiences regarding discrimination and violence. These experiences are individual, yet widespread, existing in the shadows of shared silences. Status silencing makes unreasonable demands on victims, rather than offenders. These demands are often in the form of metashame (Ellis, 1998), which revictimizes individuals again and again.

As Bridges and Pascoe (2014) discuss in relation to privilege and patriarchy, it "works best when it goes unrecognized" (Bridges and Pascoe, 2014, p. 256). The idea that certain areas of society, like academia (and especially the social sciences), are exempt from toxic masculinity and status silencing is patently false. Recent stories emerging from the Chronicle of Higher Education, Inside Higher Ed, and social media – #MeTooSociology – indicate that status plays a role in silencing and that these events are not nearly as isolated as previously thought. Prominent scholars (much like our social science PhD in the opening vignette, the social science PhD in the gaslighting vignette, or the numerous social science PhDs in the final vignette) engage in the work of examining the mechanics of inequality and its consequences. This awareness alone does not inoculate them from engaging in exploitative and abusive behavior. This fact directs our attention to other intersecting areas of inequality such as race, class, sexuality, and occupational status, among others. Status silencing serves to maintain these inequalities as well. There is real doubt, fear, anger, shame, and more about being labeled negatively for speaking out in university settings when the accused has a more powerful status (i.e., graduate students versus tenured professors), so many individuals "choose" to remain silent. This choice, however, is about survival. The normalization of toxic masculinity and status silencing within academia is about the power to define toxic masculinity as normal behavior. This is underwritten by assurances that others will remain silent and/or complicit through active and passive threats to well-being.

REFERENCES

Abramson, K. 2014. Turning up the lights on gaslighting, *Philosophical Perspectives*, 28(1), 1–30.

Anyon, J. 1981. Social class and school knowledge, *Curriculum Inquiry*, 11(1), 3–42.

Archer, L., Pratt, S. D. and Pratt, D. 2001. Working-class men's constructions of masculinity and negotiations of (non)participation in higher education, *Gender and Education*, 13(4), 431–449.

Banet-Weiser, S. and Miltner, K. M. 2016. #MasculinitySoFragile: culture, structure, and networked misogyny, *Feminist Media Studies*, 16(1), 171–174.

Bridges, T. and Pascoe, C. J. 2014. Hybrid masculinities: new directions in the sociology of men and masculinities, *Sociology Compass*, 8(3), 246–258.

Butler, J. 1993. *Bodies that Matter*, New York, NY, Routledge.

Butler, J. 2006. *Gender Trouble*, New York, NY, Routledge.

Connell, R. 1995. *Masculinities*, Cambridge, Polity Press.

Connell, R. and Messerschmidt, J. W. 2005. Hegemonic masculinity: rethinking the concept, *Gender & Society*, 19(6), 829–859.

Creighton, G. and Oliffe, J. I. 2010. Theorising masculinities and men's health: a brief history with a view to practice, *Health Sociology Review*, 19(4), 409–418.

Delamont, S. 2009. The only honest thing: autoethnography, reflexivity and small crises in fieldwork, *Ethnography and Education*, 4(1), 51–63.

Derrida, J. 1978. *Writing and Difference*, Chicago, IL, University of Chicago Press.

Donaldson, M. 1993. What is hegemonic masculinity? *Theory and Society*, 22(5), 643–657.

Ellis, C. 1998. "I hate my voice": coming to terms with minor bodily stigmas, *The Sociological Quarterly*, 39(4), 517–537.

Ellis, C. 2007. Telling secrets, revealing lives: relational ethics in research with intimate others, *Qualitative Inquiry*, 13(1), 3–29.

Ellis, C., Adams, T. E. and Bochner, A. P. 2011. Autoethnography: an overview, *Forum: Qualitative Social Research*, 12(1), Art. 10.

Francis, B. and Skelton, C. 2001. Men teachers and the construction of heterosexual masculinity in the classroom, *Sex Education*, 1(1), 9–21.

Garfinkel, H. 1967. *Studies in Ethnomethodology*, Cambridge, Polity.

Giroux, H. and Purpel, H. 1983. *The Hidden Curriculum and Moral Education*, Berkeley, CA, McCutchan.

Goffman, E. 1959. *The Presentation of Self in Everyday Life*, New York, NY, Anchor.

Goffman, E. 1963. *Stigma*, Englewood Cliffs, NJ, Prentice-Hall.

Goffman, E. 1967. *Interaction Ritual*, New York, NY, Pantheon Books.

Haider, S. 2016. The shooting in Orlando, terrorism, or toxic masculinity (or both?), *Men and Masculinities*, 19(5), 555–565.

Hess, A. and Flores, C. 2018. Simply more than swiping left: a critical analysis of toxic masculine performances on Tinder Nightmares, *New Media & Society*, 20(3), 1085–1102.

Hughey, M. W. 2014. Beyond the big, bad racist: shared meanings of white identity and supremacy. In *Color Lines and Racial Angles*, Eds D. Hartmann and C. Uggen, New York, NY, Norton.

Jackson, B. A. and Wingfield, A. H. 2013. Getting angry to get ahead: Black college men, emotional performance, and encouraging respectable masculinity, *Symbolic Interaction*, 36(3), 275–292.

Kalish, R. and Kimmel, M. 2010. Suicide by mass murder: masculinity, aggrieved entitlement, and rampage, *Health Sociology Review*, 19(4), 451–464.

Kimmel, M. S. and Mahler, M. 2003. Adolescent masculinity, homophobia, and violence, *American Behavioral Scientist*, 46(10), 1439–1458.

Kimmel, M. and Wade, L. 2018. Ask a feminist: Michael Kimmel and Lisa Wade discuss toxic masculinity. *Signs: Journal of Women in Culture and Society*, 44(1), 233–254.

King, J. R. 1998. *Uncommon Caring*, New York, NY, Teachers College Press.

King, J. R. 2009. What can he want?: male teachers, young children, and teaching desire. In *The Problem with Boys' Education: Beyond the Backlash*, Eds W. Martino, M. Kehler and M. B. Weaver-Hightower, New York, NY, Teachers' Collee Press.

Kupers, T. A. 2005. Toxic masculinity as a barrier to mental health treatment in prison, *Journal of Clinical Psychology*, 61(6), 713–724.

Martino, W. J. 2008. Male teachers as role models: addressing issues of masculinity, pedagogy and re-masculinization of schooling, *Curriculum Inquiry*, 38(2), 189–223.

Mead, G. H. 1934/1992. *Mind, Self, & Society*, Chicago, IL, University of Chicago Press.

Merton, R. K. 1949. *Discrimination and National Welfare*, New York, NY, Harper & Row.

Messner, M. A. 2016. Bad men, good men, bystanders: who is the rapist? *Gender & Society*, 30(1), 57–66.

Pascoe, C. J. 2005. "Dude, you're a fag": adolescent masculinity and the fag discourse, *Sexualities*, 8(3), 329–346.

Pascoe, C. J. 2007. *Dude, You're a Fag: Masculinity and Sexuality in High School*, Berkeley, CA, University of California.

Pascoe, C. J. 2016. How do we know a toxic masculinity when we see it? Retrieved from https://gendersociety.wordpress.com/2016/10/06/how-do-we-know-a-toxic-masculinity-when-we-see-it/

Pascoe, C. J. and Hollander, J. A. 2016. Good guys don't rape: gender, domination, and mobilizing rape, *Gender & Society*, 30(1), 67–79.

Pruit, J. C. 2014. Preconstructing suspicion and the recasting of masculinity in preschool settings, *Qualitative Research in Education*, 3(3), 320–344.

Pruit, J. C. 2015. Preschool teachers and the discourse of suspicion, *Journal of Contemporary Ethnography*, 44(4), 510–534.

Pruit, J. C. 2019. *Between Teaching and Caring in the Preschool*, New York, NY, Lexington.

Rambo, C. 2016. Strange accounts: applying for the department chair position and writing threats and secrets "in play", *Journal of Contemporary Ethnography*, 45(1), 3–33.

Rambo, C. and Pruit, J. C. 2019. At play in the fields of qualitative research and autoethnography: a strange account, *International Review of Qualitative Research*, 12(3), 219–242.

Sallee, M. W. 2011. Performing masculinity: considering gender in doctoral student socialization, *The Journal of Higher Education*, 82(2), 187–216.

Sargent, P. 2000. Real men or real teachers?: contradictions in the lives of men elementary teachers, *Men and Masculinities*, 2(4), 410–433.

Sargent, P. 2001. *Real Men or Real Teachers*, Harriman, TN, Men's Studies Press.

Sargent, P. 2004. Between and rock and a hard place: men caught in the gender bind of early childhood education, *The Journal of Men's Studies*, 12(3), 173–193.

Scheff, T. 1966. *Being Mentally Ill*, Chicago, IL, Aldine.

Schippers, M. 2007. Recovering the feminine other: masculinity, femininity, and gender hegemony, *Theory and Society*, 36(1), 85–102.

Scott, M. B. and Lyman, S. M. 1968. Accounts, *American Sociological Review*, 33(1), 46–62.

Simmel, G. 1950. *The Sociology of Georg Simmel*, (Translated by K. Wolff), New York, NY, Free Press.

Skelton, C. 2003. Male primary teachers and perceptions of masculinity, *Educational Review*, 55(2), 195–209.

Skelton, C. 2012. Men teachers and the "feminized" primary school: a review of the literature, *Educational Review*, 64(1), 1–19.

Steel, C. M. and Aronson, J. 1995. Stereotype threat and the intellectual test performance of African Americans, *Journal of Personality and Social Psychology*, 69(5), 797–811.

Swidler, A. 1986. Culture in action: symbols and strategies, *American Sociological Review*, 51(2), 273–286.

The Chronicle of Higher Education. 2018. The awakening: women and power in the university. Retrieved from https://www.chronicle.com/interactives/the-awakening?essay=Pirtle&fbclid=IwAR0-bDOu 57uScQSaLyaB3YFbTrrnwlwk8UhPTOHbeUDf2s2fRz0v6-NYz5w

West, C. and Zimmerman, D. H. 1987. Doing gender, *Gender & Society*, 1(2), 125–151.

Wilkins, A. 2012. Not out to start a revolution: race, gender, and emotional restraint among black university men, *Journal of Contemporary Ethnography*, 41(1), 34–65.

MORE LIKE, SONS OF CONFORMITY: MOTORCYCLE CLUBS, MORAL CAREERS, AND NORMALIZATION

Norman Conti[1]

ABSTRACT

This chapter explores that landscape between the imagination and practice of ethnographic research as well as a concomitant transition in a sociologist's felt identity. Specifically, it describes the larger effect of building a persona for fieldwork on the self of the ethnographer. The work begins with an examination of the motives behind a proposed study of a deviant counterculture and the efforts that went into crafting a presentation of self appropriate for the milieu. It offers a detailed analysis of the social foundations of the outlaw motorcycle culture and a phase model of their socialization process.

Keywords: Outlaw motorcycle clubs; ethnography; deviance; honor; degradation; Goffman; anhedonia; elevation

THE PERSONAL IS POLITICAL, OR IN THIS CASE SOCIOLOGICAL

A therapist once told me I was "a wolf." As he explained it:

> You don't subscribe to any particular morality. You create your own, and that is a higher morality. You are a *player*. You're sanguine, *full of blood*. You would make an excellent criminal. You'd be successful on the street and if you had to go *up state*, you'd probably do very well there too. Though, your looks could be a problem. You have to understand that you're aggressive and this is fundamental to your nature. It cannot be changed. You are a wolf.[2]

Radical Interactionism and Critiques of Contemporary Culture
Studies in Symbolic Interaction, Volume 52, 115–132
Copyright © 2021 by Emerald Publishing Limited
All rights of reproduction in any form reserved
ISSN: 0163-2396/doi:10.1108/S0163-239620210000052008

At the time, I couldn't accept his assessment and imagined he was just using a familiar psychological frame to coach me out of debilitating degree of insecurity. So, I protested that this notion of postconventional morality couldn't apply to me because my profound anxiety had led to an assortment of twitches, and my teeth rarely stopped chattering. It should have been obvious that I was no kind of wolf. In rebuttal, he pointed to the correlation between fear and aggression. Further, he noted that my career probably wasn't exciting enough for me anymore and ran down a list of outlets for my *wolfishness* that included everything from volunteer firefighting to a career shift in the direction of politics or business. Finally, he suggested that maybe I could take up something like martial arts or paintball in my free time, of which I had none.

Since most of my anxieties stemmed from the interrelated issues of work, money, and fatherhood, none of these options – *not even paintball* – struck me as particularly realistic solutions, so he brought the focus back to the bigger point:

> You don't need to eliminate your aggressive characteristics; you probably can't. They are what make you who you are. I keep coming back to the same thought about you, Norm is *normal*. You just need to channel your deviant tendencies into something more socially acceptable. Like your work on policing. You go out and tell cops how to be cops. Something like that, only *sexier*. You have to find ways to be a *benign* badass.

Just then I decided that, instead of paintball, maybe I should start looking for a new therapist. Still, his point stuck with me and looking at his notes on the session, it is easy to understand why:

CLIENT NAME: NORMAN CONTI.
DATE OF SERVICE: April 30, 2009
DX 296.25 Major Depressive Disorder, Single, Mild

Client returns for follow-up. He was last seen about a month ago. He reports maintenance of affective gains. He notes continued gains in terms of self-acceptance.

He notes chronic boredom (possibly, depressive anhedonia). A humanistic view of his anhedonia is entertained. Namely, client's desire for excitement is discussed in terms of his baseline temperament and ambition for leadership. Client's leadership-oriented ambitions and excitement-seeking are normalized as legitimate pursuits of wellbeing. Client is given feedback that he appears to have successfully sublimated his "alpha" traits in a variety of socially sanctioned ways (e.g. via education and academic and research pursuits).

Client welcomes this de-pathologizing view of self as yet another new, more self-accepting narrative (to counteract depressogenic, perfectionist self-schema).

Client appears to be progressing well both in terms of inter- and intra-personal dynamics. He schedules to return for a follow-up in a month (in May).

Though I hadn't seen these notes at the time, I understood that shifting focus from my own misery to an interesting research project would undoubtedly have therapeutic value.[3] So, the discovery that my old boxing trainer and longtime family friend was starting a chapter of an outlaw motorcycle club (OMC) known as the Visigoths, presented a great opportunity for both ethnography and psychological relief. [4] Like any idea for a research project, it existed purely as fantasy until I began pursuing it. This chapter explores that landscape between the research imagination and practice as well as a concomitant transition in self.

THOUGH THIS BE MADNESS, THERE IS A *METHOD* [SECTION] IN IT

My plan for entrée into the group hinged upon a decades long friendship between my brother and the leader of the Visigoths – let's call him *Thor*.[5] I expected that my brother would make the initial contact with something along the lines of, "Hey Thor, remember my little brother Norm? Well, he's a professor now and wants to talk to you about the Visigoths." From there, I'd meet with Thor and begin negotiating my way into the club, much as I had done with police academies and correctional facilities.[6] At this point, I was beyond certain that a meaningful family connection would provide entrance into the Visigoths.

As with my previous ethnographies, data would be collected through participant observation over some course of time, maybe a year or so. My plan was to spend as much time with the gang as possible by attending parties and runs.[7] In time, I would undoubtedly strike up friendships with the more sociologically interesting members of the club, and these relationships would yield priceless insights into the backstage world of outlaw bikers. In the end, I would have a stack of notebooks containing a treasure trove of data.

These data would be analyzed from a grounded theory perspective where field notes are coded for emerging processes and themes.[8] Analytic memos would become essential in understanding the structure and function of the group. When the significance of key cultural elements, such as masculinity, solidarity, or whatever, began to emerge, the field notes would be reviewed once more in order to determine how these notions shaped the milieu. Eventually, it would likely become clear that particular narratives and rituals were important mechanisms for illustrating normative orders and facilitating progress through the moral career of the outlaw biker.

Seeing rejection as a distinct improbability, I began to imagine my time with the Visigoths and the tools I would need for the project. First, I would have to blend in, so I started watching Sons of Anarchy, an adaptation of *Hamlet* set within an OMC of the same name. The guys in the club looked as you would expect: long hair, beards, tattoos, jewelry, jeans, and leather jackets. Since I already had a pair of jeans and a goat-tee, the next logical step was to stop getting my haircut. This was no problem and allowed me to reallocate the money I was saving at the barber to other research expenses.

Being tattooed to the point of a distinctive racial categorization is a ubiquitous feature of the outlaw culture and presented a potential problem for me. While I have the great fortune of a popular malt liquor logo forever emblazoned on my left shoulder, I wasn't sure how to work that into my presentation of self without seeming…well, desperate. I could have gotten more visible tattoos, but that would have constituted an expense far beyond my haircut savings. As a compromise, I settled on earrings and adding 40 pounds of muscle to my chest, arms, and back, in order to convey the type of tough guy narcissism expressed in so much body art.[9] Much to my delight, the two-hour sessions in the weight room, as well as innumerable tasty protein shakes, offered endorphin-tastic relief to my major depressive disorder and anhedonia, which lead to a commitment to bodybuilding beyond ethnographic costuming. Later, I discovered that even the creatine supplements, so popular among my weight room "bros," had clinical value for treating depression.

The only other thing I was going to need was a motorcycle. Outlaw clubs are very particular about transportation and anything other than a high-powered Harley Davidson is generally outside of their cultural bounds. Obviously, a vehicle of this class would be an important tool for the project, and more importantly, I would get to ride around on it. On craigslist, these motorcycles tend to range from between five and fifteen thousand dollars. Lacking that sort of personal research budget, I started considering the sorts of internal grants that might fund a chopper.

Yeah, that was going to be me – Pittsburgh's answer to C. Wright Mills – charging down the qualitative highway on a hog paid for by one of the top Catholic universities.[10] There was something about this combination of the sacred and profane that made the image all the more alluring. At the same time, an application to the College of Liberal Arts ethnographic transportation fund would undoubtedly require a lot of paperwork. Not to mention meetings with the Dean, IRB, university counsel, and most likely, a number of my valued colleagues in psychology. Leaving that final methodological issue on the back burner, I began reading everything I could get my hands on related to OMCs.

A STRANGE AND TERRIBLE LITERATURE REVIEW

The scholarly literature on OMC culture is limited to a handful of books and a couple dozen articles with three general themes. First, there is the work that lays out the history of OMCs and discusses the ethos in which their culture is grounded. A decade ago, Baker and Human noted that there were no autobiographies of one-percenters, current or former, that offered any real insight into their experiences.[11] They cite the best-selling autobiography of a former Hells Angels' president as one example of such.[12] However, since 2014, there have been at least a dozen of these sorts of books published. This is easily attributed to the popularity of *Sons of Anarchy*, which started in 2008 with a viewership of 2.21 million that grew consistently to a high of 10.62 million by its final season in 2014. These books were analyzed from the grounded theory perspective described above in order to further develop the theoretical section of this chapter.[13] The one difference is that it was the books themselves, rather than ethnographic field notes that were analyzed.

Second, there is a criminological literature that seeks to say as much about drugs, prostitution, and violence within the world of OMCs as possible. Crime among the outlaw clubs has been divided into four categories based on planning and duration.[14] Research utilizing those categorizations has made it clear that, in addition to the more spontaneous/expressive deviance (i.e., bar fights) or even the planned gang fights traditionally associated with OMCs, there are strains of instrumental deviance that qualify as organized crime. Moreover, within individual clubs, members are categorized as either "radical" or "conservative." As you would expect, conservative bikers join OMCs for the sense of camaraderie that they offer and do not participate in any criminal enterprises, while radicals are deeply committed to criminal careers.[15] The organization of national/international OMCs into local chapters allows some clubs to house small groups of members who are involved in criminal enterprises unbeknownst to – or with the tacit approval of – their conservative membership, while other chapters operate as criminal gangs with no illusions that they are anything but radical.[16]

Finally, there is the more sociological research that addresses mainstream reactions to the OMC phenomenon.[17] Motorcycle clubs are generally classified as either American Motorcycle Association (AMA) sanctioned or deviant. Deviant clubs are mostly homogenous in terms of race, gender, and sexual orientation; within this category of deviant bikers, there is a smaller group known as "one-percenters."[18] This label emerged, after the purported biker takeover of Hollister, California, in 1947, when the president of the AMA claimed that 99 percent of motorcycle enthusiasts were decent law-abiding citizens. His statement drove outlaw clubs toward self-stigmatizing with "1%" patches and tattoos as emblems of elite status within their counterculture. An original Hells Angels describes that seminal moment as follows:

The angels and our friends, rather than being insulted, decided to exploit the glowing tribute. We voted to ally under a "one-percenter" patch. As a supplement to regular colors, it would identify the wearer as a righteous outlaw. The patch also could help avoid counterproductive infighting, because an Angel, Mofo, or any one-percenter would be banded against a common enemy.

Everyone knew the patch was a deliberately provocative gesture, but we wanted to draw deep lines between ourselves and the pretenders and weekenders who only played with motorcycles.

Buoyed by the alliance and wobbly from wine, the outlaws dispersed to all corners of the state to inform their troops and order our patches. Sonny and I mounted our Harleys, zonked yet obsessed with outdoing the rest. A little patch may have been adequate for other one-percenters, but not for us. A trans-bay ride took us to Rich's tattoo parlor in downtown Oakland and after a briefing, Rich's needle made biker history. Although I was too drunk to know until the next morning, Sonny and I had the first of the famous one-percenter tattoos – a symbol that likely will survive as long as outlaw gangs.

Soon our Oakland brothers were lining up for theirs. We were beginning to believe our own mystique. As we stacked a few rules and rituals on the simple foundation of motorcycle riding, we thought we were building a little army. But, in fact, it was a rough blueprint for a secret society.[19]

The development of OMCs was facilitated by the status frustration within the circles from which they draw their membership.[20] Specifically, since the 1960s, lower class white men have faced a growing sense of alienation and anomie.[21] By uniting as bands of outlaws, they were able to establish a counterculture where they could manufacture a sense of supremacy, through hyper-masculine presentations of self. In reaction to their marginalization, the counterculture is grounded in zealous degrees of retreatism, rebellion, and innovation in mixtures that vary across space and time.[22] These groups have been described as secular sects that exist to meet the intense emotional needs of their membership in a fairly cultish manner.[23] Moreover, outrageous characteristics and behavior, frowned upon in mainstream culture, are heralded as indicators of "righteousness" or "true class" among OMCs.[24]

Erikson argued that, "if one wants to understand how any given culture works, one should inquire into the characteristic counterpoints as well as central values."[25] *The Outlaw Creed* is a sort of "values statement" that frequently pops up in both the scholarly and popular literature of OMCs.[26] It defines the OMC world with a stark differentiation between outlaws and citizens, illustrates the importance of the fraternal bond, while also offering a warning about the consequences of betrayal. It reads:

> A one-percenter is the one of a hundred of us who has given up on society and the politician's one-way law. This is why we look repulsive. We are saying we don't want to be like you, so stay out of our face.

> Look at your brother standing next to you and ask yourself if you would give him half of what's in your pocket or half of what you have to eat. If a citizen hits your brother will you be on him without asking why? There is no why. Your brother isn't always right but he's always your brother! It's one in all in. If you don't think this way then walk away because you are a citizen and don't belong with us.

> We are Outlaws and members will follow the Outlaw way or get out. All members are your brothers and your family. You will not steal your brother's possessions, money, women, class or his humor. If you do your brother will do you.[27]

While this passage illustrates core principles within the world of OMCs, its lack of nuance prevents it from offering much in the way of how the culture actually functions.

Hunter S. Thompson's *Hell's Angels: The Strange and Terrible Saga* (1967) was the first of few attempts to seriously understand outlaw culture and as such, conformed to Erikson's edict a decade before it was suggested. Additionally, Thompson discussed the impact of C. Wright Mills upon his work, and the concentration of his sociological imagination is evident in the link between rich ethnographic detail he provides on the counterculture and his dynamic analysis of the mainstream outrage.[28] These factors make it impossible to neglect his work, despite so much already having already been written about it.

Six years prior to the publication of Cohen's (1972) seminal work on moral panics, Thompson chronicled the convergence of media and political interests that facilitated the absurdist framing of OMCs as an ominous threat to the social order.[29] Forty years after the publication of *Hells Angles*, Thompson was remembered as having given America, "a tongue-lashing for creating mythic villains, like motorcycle gangs, which he revealed to be more pathetic than fearsome."[30] In sections like, "The Making of a Menace, 1965," Thompson captures the interplay between self and society as well as illustrating the social construction of reality by documenting how the media and political attempts at demonizing the OMC led to both fear and public outrage as well as fascination. Thompson writes:

> Weird as it seems, as this gang of costumed hoodlums converged on Monterey that morning they were on the verge of "making it big," as the showbiz people say, they would owe most of their success to a curious rape mania that rides the shoulder of American journalism like some jeering, masturbating raven. Nothing grabs an editors attention like a good rape. "We really blew their minds this time," as one of the Angels explained it.[31]

Thompson goes on to explain that the rape case generated a frenzy of media attention that put the Angels on par with Bob Dylan and the Beatles. Further, he offers a detailed accounting of the mechanics of the ensuing moral panic. By documenting the cycle of police/legal intervention, media attention, political reaction, and public sentiment in conjunction with both the positive and negative consequences of their newfound celebrity for the Angels, Thompson offers an almost perfect execution of the sociological imagination.

MORAL CAREERS AND THE OUTLAW ELITE

In his discussion of meaningful contrasts within cultures, Erikson explains that each of the central values and counterpoints exist upon an "axis of variation."[32] Among the mountaineers he studied, Erikson pointed out that while there was a lot of value placed on characteristics like traditionalism, self-assertion, self-centeredness, ability, and independence, everyday behavior was indicative of – or contingent upon – governmental authority, resignation, collectivism, disability, and dependence. Sonny Barger lays out a similar dichotomy for the Hells Angels:

> We Angels live in our own world. We just want to be left alone to be individualists...
>
> Actually we're conformists. To be an Angel, you have to conform to the rules of our society, and the Angels' rules are the toughest anywhere...This stuff [the Nazi insignia and headgear] – that's just to shock people, to let em know we're individualists, to let em know we're Angels...There'd be no trouble if we was left alone. The only violence is when people go after us. Couple of Angels will go into a bar and a few guys gettin drunked up will start a fight, but we get blamed for it. Our two guys will put em down. Any two Angels can take on any other five guys ... You got to want to be an Angel. We don't just take anybody in. We watch em. We got to know they'll stick to our rules...[33]

Above, Barger offers a dialectic that illustrates the ethos of outlaw culture. One-percenters are both individualists and conformists. They "protest too much" with their efforts demonstrating that they are unaffected by public judgments because without that 99%, they have no one to stand out against. In fact, fascist regalia and conformity to a paramilitary culture are the opposite of individualism. Additionally, the potential outlaw must pursue a dialectic of shame and honor in order to gain entrée into the organization. In order to achieve the purported status elevation that accompanies membership, the potential recruit must first accept all of the degradation and subordination that can possibly be associated with the status of conventional citizen. One of the most recent works on the outlaw culture sums this up in the following, "To an extent, All of the East Bay Rats were slaves to their collective: as prospects, they'd beem indentured servants; as rats they'd chained themselves to each other."[34]

The cycles of degradation and elevation, reflecting the larger subcultural dialectics, are observed in the moral career of the outlaw biker. Moral career is defined as "the regular sequence of changes that career entails in the person's self and his framework of imagery for judging himself and others" (Goffman, 1961, p. 128). The consecutive alterations of self within the moral career (i.e. phases) are turning points in worldview marked by particular happenings (i.e., in Goffman's example becoming a mental patient or in this one joining an OMC) that illustrate the link between self and society through which a public event, such as a shift in social category (i.e., from civilian to either inpatient or one-percenter), has a very powerful effect on the self. Thompson begins detailing the framework of the the OMC framework for judging selves and others in the following:

> The outlaws are very respectful of power, even if they have to create their own image of it. Despite the anarchic possibilities of the machines they ride and worship, they insist that their main concern in life is "to be a righteous Angel," which requires a loud obedience to the party line. They are intensely aware of *belonging*, of being able to depend on each other. Because of this, they look down on independents, who usually feel so wretched – once they have adopted the outlaw frame of reference – that they will do almost anything to get in a club.[35]

Members of OMCs generally transition through a moral career made up of three phases: hangaround, prospect, and full-patch member.[36] Currently, the moral career of an outlaw biker is surprisingly bureaucratic and is marked by a series or rituals and artifacts. [37] In the early days of the Hells Angels, induction was a much more relaxed process where, after a few weeks of riding with the club, full-patch members would discuss the personality, riding skill, and motivation of a prospect and then vote on whether to admit him or not. As long as no more than one active member voted against the prospect, he was immediately accepted into the club and issued his patch.[38] However, as the clubs began to attract more attention, and as a result more prospects, loose codes were replaced with strict rules, and their criminality became more organized. In order to ensure a quality membership and keep undercover police from infiltrating their organizations, prospecting became an extended process of demonstrating righteous class through a willingness to suffer degradation and break laws. As one longtime biker put it:

> Being a prospect meant being prepared to hustle drugs at a moment's notice, sometimes multiple times in one day, at different locations across town. It meant standing guard at a post for hours, doing nothing, waiting for something to happen, or running to different shops searching for certain brands of chocolate, beer, or Moon Pie. We understood all else in our lives was secondary, family, kids, dogs, God, country. None of it mattered anymore. Our first priority was the club. If we were tasked with a mission, we were expected to perform even if it meant we might go to prison. If we hesitated or refused, there were consequences. We risked a beating, humiliation, or worse, death. If we wanted to be "outlaws," we had to act like ones. [39]

The transition into outlaw culture begins on the fringes of OMCs as a Hangaround. These friends and family are welcome among the group, but hold no formal status within it. While they rank "one level above women and dogs" within the official club hierarchy, they are not subject to any hazing by members.[40]

In a recent memoir, a former Pagan describes how, as the son of a chapter president, he was essentially born into the outlaw culture. [41] He notes that even at the age of 12, he was bouncing back and forth between the outlaw and civilian worlds, spending days at a time running errands during club parties. He goes on to explain his continued drift toward the club, including the ritual of getting a tattoo that marked him as marginally connected to the club.

> Getting a tattoo didn't change much for me except that I felt branded, marked the way an animal is stamped as part of a herd. But I wasn't *officially* part of anything. At most I was the club's honorary prospect. I wasn't even sure I wanted *that* much responsibility. But I won't lie, I did like the perks. Pretty women smiled at me, impressed that I could mix with one-percenter bikers. Citizens stared at me admiringly, secretly wishing *they* could wear badass. Being with the Pagans and getting my first tattoo had almost the same allure as wearing a uniform, like putting on an alter ego. In the bikers' company I *became* the tough guy they imagined. I understood finally the power of the patch; when bikers put on their vests, they commanded instant respect, recognition and prowess. They could stand in a crowded room and luxuriate in the attention.[42]

In this passage, the author illustrates an important dialectic of both standing out and and fitting in. For him, while more formal connection to the OMC would mean, on the one hand, responsibility and uniformity, it would also generate an outsider status with respect to mainstream society that would, in turn, garner him respect and attention as an individual.

After some period of sustained presence, the hangaround may be asked to join the club. If he accepts, he begins a quasi-apprenticeship sponsored by the inviting member where he assumes the role of prospect. At this point, the prospect has moved beyond the hangaround phase and is officially seeking membership in the gang – wearing a denim or leather vest, like the full members, but devoid of any insignia except for a curved patch on the back displaying the name of the state where the club is located. During this phase, prospects are subject to intensive hazing and background investigations. One of the best descriptions of the prospect phase comes from the memoir of a former National President of the Mongols:

> "Because you are the youngest Mongol prospect, from this point on your new name is Prospect Junior."

> Reaching to the floor beside his easy chair, Fat Man grabbed a paper sack and threw it to Mike. Out of the sack, Mike removed a brand new Levi Jacket with the sleeves cut off, and handed it to me ceremoniously. Unfolding it, I could see the shiny white bottom rocker that read "California."

> Snapping me back to reality, Mike ordered, "Put it on, prospect!"

> With not a second of further hesitation, I put on my what would be known as my colors. All the brothers stood and began to cheer. One at a time, each gave me a hug and what was known as the Mongol handshake. After having been welcomed by the whole crew, each member found his seat and returned to silence.

> Mike spoke up.

> "Prospect Junior, from this time forward you will never shake another brother's hand until you as a full-patched Mongol, unless ordered to do so. Understand?"

> "Yes, Mike I understand."[43]

In this ceremony, the prospect is applauded for his decision to join and honored with a club vest, while also anticipating the degradation that will immediately come with the status (i.e., banned from the most basic of interactions like shaking hands). Junior goes on to explain more of the fundamentals of prospecting.

First of all, a Mongol prospect never has his hands in his pockets unless it is to remove something. A Mongol prospect never lies to a full-patch brother, or he is subject to an ass beating. A full-patched Mongol will never ask a prospect to do something he won't do himself. If the prospect challenges the brother, and in fact the brother does perform the challenged deed, the prospect is subject to an ass beating. A Mongol prospect will not have sex, or [a girlfriend] while prospecting. A Mongol prospect is at the beck and call of any full-patched Mongol 24 hours a day, seven days a week. After you get home from work every night, you will call Fat Man first, then your sponsor. If there are no orders, then you will call each Dago chapter member. You will turn over the pink slip to your bike to the chapter while you are prospecting and, if you quit, you will lose your bike. Your pink slip will be returned once you are a full-patched brother.

"You will not strike or attack a full-patched Mongol, even if you are hit first, and if you do, you are subject to a beating by all surrounding brothers." You will make out a will and have it notarized specifying the Mongols or your family are responsible for your funeral if you are killed.[44]

These rules place the prospect in a status equivalent to a child servant. However, accepting this degradation is a recognition of the honor of full membership and helps to qualify the prospect for that eventual status elevation as well as reifying member status. Additionally, the prospect can demonstrate his superiority to other prospects, especially from other chapters or clubs, as well as to citizens. Another former Mongol National President remembers:

...a prospect Olympics, where they would get four or five prospects and drink until two in the morning and then make them race each other and climb trees – just weird shit. Somebody told me there used to be marshmallow races. They would make the prospects put a marshmallow in the crack of their ass and race from one end of the field to the other. The looser had to eat all the marshmallows. This didn't happen every time with every chapter, but there were cases. They'd make you kneel on top of your bike frame and grab it while they swatted you with a huge paddle until your ass bled; you couldn't move or you'd get beat up even more. [45]

In addition to endurance tests and character contests in which prospects are required to compete against each other in order to bring honor to their chapter, when clubs enter civilian venues, prospects are expected to project an ominous threat while the full members drink and socialize.

Despite all of this formal bureaucratic structure, there are still individuals who are able to use their connections to an OMC, as in the case of the son of a chapter president presented above. This individual was able to vacillate in and out of the prospect role as well as periodically violating the interaction order by failing to show deference to a full-patch member or offering his opinion on matters beyond the scope of a prospect.[46] Another recruit, recognized as the pinnacle of righteousness and nicknamed "Mr Prospect," was able to earn his full-patch membership in less than a month.[47] Finally, Rueben "Doc" Cavazos, perhaps the most controversial of the Mongols, received the unprecedented invitation to avoid prospecting by starting his own chapter of the OMC.[48] As a result, once he ascended to national president, in order to build up the club's enrollment, Cavazos began offering membership to men based upon ethnicity and reputation alone.

Once the prospect has successfully endured sufficient trials, he is then "patched into the club." At this point, he is a full member and receives the remaining club patches for the back of his vest. The OMC literature presents bikers as misfits who join together to form a counterculture, but as that culture is established and maintained, they are conforming to it. They join their clubs because mainstream society has failed to afford them a status that they are content with. Unable to feel strong on their own, the wolves form a pack. However, in an Op-Ed for *The New York Times*, Carl Safina offers an interesting analysis of the expectations for men to channel their "inner wolves" in order to meet the demands of an alpha status.[49] His point in the piece is to debunk the current wolf stereotype in favor of an understanding that will be of far greater value to the males of our species. Based on over 20 years of fieldwork, researchers have learned that, rather than being domineering bullies, the alpha male wolves tend to quietly lead by example and have a calming effect on their pack without needing to act aggressively toward any of its members. These wolves are faithfully devoted to the care and defense of their families while respecting and sharing responsibilities with their alpha female counterparts.

ANY CLUB THAT WOULD HAVE ME AS A MEMBER

As described above, my access to the Visigoths was contingent upon my brother's friendship with Thor, who I was expecting to serve as my key informant. So, I asked my brother to make contact with him and arrange a meeting with me. Unfortunately, my brother extended the invitation via text message. He wrote, "Hey Thor, my brother Norm would like to talk to you about the Visigoths." Thor immediately called my brother and explained that nothing about the Visigoths could ever be put into writing. He went on to explain that due to an unflattering documentary portrayal of the group, by filmmakers granted inside access to the club, the Visigoths were no longer talking about the club to outsiders.

While some may have called it a day with that, a wolf must push on. Some time passed, and I asked my brother to talk to Thor again and see if he could convince him to at least meet with me. Thor was unwilling, but agreed to talk on the phone. The conversation went as follows:

Norm: Hey Thor, thanks so much for calling. I really appreciate that.
Thor: That's okay, no problem.
N: Okay, so my brother explained the situation to me and I wanted to see if there was some way we could work around it.
T: Yeah, but I can't talk to you about the club.
N: Sure, I understand that, but maybe we could meet up then I could talk and you could just listen and see if you could do anything with what I have to say. I understand that the club isn't talking to the media right now, but I'm not the media. Maybe we could come up with something that you could run up the chain of command and see if we could get approved by the national leadership. See, I'd like to write a book about you and I think it could actually be something that's good for the club.

T: No, I can't do that because I can be kicked out of the club for talking to you about the club.

N: Yeah, but you don't have to say anything, just listen.

T: No, I'm sorry but I can't do that.

N: Yeah, but I'm sure we could work something out. I mean, I work with police and in prisons all the time and there's always a way in.

T: See, right there. You work with the police. I mean, someone with police connections is a problem.

N: Yeah, but I'm not a cop, I'm a sociologist.

T: Even still, let's say you're around someone from [an organized crime group] and you ask, "Hey, what's that tattoo mean?" We can't have that. I mean, we're not criminals, but we're a one percenter motorcycle club.

N: Sure, but there's got to be some way to make this happen.

T: Look, I love your family and I don't mean to be a dick, but if you were my own brother I couldn't talk to you about the club. There's just no way.

N: Okay, I don't want to push this any further. I hear what you are saying and I respect your decision.

T: Hey I'm sorry I couldn't help you out here and thanks for thinking of me.

Toward the end of the conversation, Thor was talking a bit faster than he had been. I took this as a sign of stress, so I backed off. At that point, I felt that discussing why he couldn't talk to me was making him think about the potential consequences and what he would lose if kicked out of his club. If that was the case, he could have been experiencing anxiety, as a result of my attempt at negotiating my way into the club, so ethically I had to stop.

A SEA OF TROUBLES… AND ISSUES

When planning this chapter, I decided that returning to the psychologist who origi-nally inspired it would have both research and therapeutic value, but even scheduling the appointment became something of a character contest. In the years since I had been seeing him, I switched healthcare providers, so a therapy session was not covered by my insurance. I informed the Chair of my department about the situation and asked for $150 to cover the session. While agreeing that psychological help was most certainly in order, my Chair informed me that the department could not pay for me to have therapy. Additionally, he informed me that he was on sabbatical, and I should be talking to someone else about this. Later, I contacted the Dean of my college, and he generously covered a $150 consulting fee for a psychologist as a research expense for this chapter.

I scheduled with the therapist, who then canceled, because meeting with me as a consultant would constitute a "dual relationship" and was outside of his ethical boundaries. Having already been rejected by an OMC, I was unwilling to be declined service by a therapist. Pressing on, I asked if he could meet with me solely as a therapeutic client and discuss some of the insights I had gained through my prior sessions with him as well as a paper that I was working on. This definition of the situation fit within his moral universe, so he once again agreed to meet with me – a lone wolf trapped in iron cages of academic and healthcare bureaucracy.

I began experiencing a mild sense of pride thinking about everything that I had accomplished since our last session. In that time, I had been granted tenure, published articles in top journals, and been awarded a major fellowship within my university. More importantly, I had purchased a home for my family, and my children were thriving. His notes on the session indicate that he understood how far I had come.

CLIENT NAME: NORMAN CONTI.
DATE OF SERVICE: JULY 16, 2013
DX 296.25 Major Depressive Disorder, Full Remission

Mr. Conti was last seen a couple of years ago. He has requested a follow-up appointment to discuss his progress. His physical appearance has changed: he lost weight, appeared fitter, has grown his hair long. He does note increased emphasis on physical fitness but also notes maintained gains in terms of mood regulation.

He does, indeed present today in a calm, pleasant manner, with a positive self-view and a positive view of his life since the termination of psychotherapy. He noted increased self-acceptance, a sense of newfound security, stabilization of his family relationships.

In regard to the latter, Mr. Conti notes that he had been able to integrate insights about himself (that he had obtained through the process of therapy) into his academic and writing interests which has subsequently leveraged great job satisfaction.

Summary:

Mr. Conti appears to remain asymptomatic of for depressive or dysthymic symptoms.

Disposition/Plan:

Mr. Conti requests no further assistance at this time. He leaves without any further scheduled follow-up at this time.

However, after I finished describing key moments and changes since our last meeting, he noted a very slight tremor in my voice and asked if I was nervous about meeting with him or if it was something else. I stopped for a minute and then explained that despite my continued improvement over the years, the stress of my life was still overwhelming. He noted that "stress" was just a western notion of fear and asked what I was afraid of. I explained that my greatest fear was failing as a father and the consequences of that for my children.

So, despite all of the gains I had made since we had last met, I was still, to some degree, a prisoner to the fear at the root of my initial depression. Years earlier, I had described it as collapsing under the weight of my life. While I was no longer in such danger of giving way, I still couldn't see any way out of this because I didn't understand how a father could stop worrying. In order to illustrate this point, I asked him, "what if something would happen to one of my kids?"

When he curtly responded, "That would suck," I remembered why it had been so long since our last appointment. Then he went on:

> Let's say the worst thing happened. God forbid, you go home and some tragedy has befallen one of your children. That is the worst pain you could ever imagine, but what do you do? You will find a way to ease your suffering. You could go find a bridge to jump off of, but I don't think so. You are too curious about life; what it's about and how it works. Dealing with that loss would be your real [Visigoth] moment. You run marathons, you bench press 300 pounds. Surviving something like that would be another kind of marathon. It would be like bench pressing 400 pounds. For you it would become an auto-ethnography. You'd be your own [Visigoth]. Maybe you can keep that, like a key, and tuck it away inside yourself, just in case you would ever need it.

Of the *many* therapists I had seen over the years, he was the first to frame suicide as one of *two* possible means for addressing my dysthymia. Still, I took his point and began thinking about a Visigoth spirit and the essential draw of ethnographic work.

Recently, Wozniak has invited us to reconsider the notion and practice of "gonzo sociology."[50] His article was my first introduction to the concept and explained it as one way of doing sociology without the methodological fetishism so prevalent in our discipline.[51] More specifically, it is a valid approach to research where the sociologist steps out of the academic enclave and lives with people, experiencing firsthand their private troubles in order to offer a sociological analysis of the public issues from which they stem. Wozniak bolsters gonzo sociology by highlighting Merton's recognition that observing the strange and unexpected is essential for extending existing, or developing new, theory.[52]

While I am inspired by Wozniak's work on Iraqi police training, as well as the spirit of gonzo journalism, at its core, gonzo sociology is building on something over which basic ethnography has primacy.[53] The anthropological spirit of adventure is a fundamental drive for any ethnographic project. We are so fascinated by something alien to us (i.e., for Wozniak, how police came to be as they are or, in my case, life in an OMC), that we are willing to abandon the order of our everyday lives and physically join the fray with those we do not understand.

Mills described the most general employment of the sociological imagination as being like "traveling at home." Here, he was discussing how bringing history and biography together in order to understand your own most basic experiences in a new light. When you take your sociological imagination out into the field, that rush is exponentially amplified and thrilling on three levels. First, you have to overcome the fear of the unknown that binds you to your ordinary routines. Second, you will be near, if not participating in, things which are new, exciting, or dangerous. These are wonderful experiences; however, they are common to anyone immersing themselves in a new (sub/counter) culture. The third, and most important, kick comes from reflecting upon the experience with your sociological imagination.

NOTES

1. The author is deeply indebted to the men of the SCI Pittsburgh Sequoia Group, and all the *other* disreputables who contributed to his experiences in the normative order and anarchy. Additionally, he would like to thank Dean James Swindal for his financial support of what may, or may not, have been a therapy session.

2. All quotes from therapy sessions come from personal journaling. During this phase of my depression, journaling was suggested as adding value to the therapeutic experience.

3. My therapist provided all session notes used for this project upon my request.

4. "Visigoths" is a pseudonym that I am using for this OMC in order to avoid being murdered – or at the very least severely beaten – in the unlikely event that a Visigoth might come across this chapter. Hunter S. Thompson (1966) made it very clear that being "rat packed" by bikers would not be in my best interest. I mean even *wolves* mark boundaries. Additionally, it has the latent effect of providing anonymity for the club, though I can't see why they should need it in this context.

5. As you may have guessed, his name, in fact, was not Thor. Calling him this helps to protect his identity and, as my therapist would undoubtedly agree, is another of my "legitimate pursuits of well-being."

6. Conti (2001); Conti et al. (2013).

7. "A motorcycle run is a get-together, a moving party. It's a real show of power and solidarity when you're a Hell's Angel. It's being free and getting away from all the bullshit" (Barger, 2001, p. 1). "Runs generally brought out the best and worst in us. Runs were times for both interclub unity and fierce individuality. Times to put women and outsiders in their places. Times to pour down, pop, and smoke a smorgasbord of drugs in mind-burning quantities. Times for getting looser than loose and showing off just what made us Angels... Runs weren't restrained by the clock, the speedometer, the law, or the human body's limits. The first stage was a torturously long motorcycle ride that either could freeze or dehydrate you, depending on weather. We rode in formation, with our provisions and armaments carried by a trailing convoy of cars, trucks, and campers driven by women or disabled members. By whim, we'd fall into single file or fan across all lanes, piling up cars for miles. For a change of pace, we'd split double-line highway divider, well above the speed limit, then thunder past cars, close enough to spit into the windows" (Wethern and Colnett, 2008, p. 130).

8. Glaser and Strauss (1967); Charmaz (1983).

9. Sanders and Vail (2007).

10. Mills road a BMW motorcycle, but I like to think that I would still have been able to channel his sociological imagination.

11. Baker and Human (2009, p. 175).

12. Barger, Zimmerman and Zimmerman (2001).

13. Ball (2011); Ballard (1997); Barber (2012); Boettcher et al. (2004); Burt (2006); Cross and Cross (2013); Danner and Silverman (1986); Davis (2011a); Davis (2011b); Delattre (1990); Droban (2008); Droban et al. (2011); Edwards (2013); Erekson (2010); Fairclough (1993); Fitzpatrick (2011); Hall (2011); Hayes (2005); Hopper and Moore (1990); Male chauvinism (1986); Marech (1999); McDonald-Walker (1998); McDonald-Walker (2000); Montgomery, 1977; Moran (2002); Nichols and Peterson (2007); Nichols and Peterson (2012); Ohle (1983); Queen (2005); Quinn (1987); Rowe (2013); Sarafin (2015); Sawyer and Judd (2012); Sher and Marsden (2004); Toplikar (2012); Vetter (1974); Watson (1980); Wolfe (2008).

14. Quinn and Koch (2003).

15. Wolf (1991).

16. Baker (2007).

17. Katz (2011); Veno and Eynde (2007).

18. Baker (2007).

19. Wethern and Colnett (2008, p. 37).

20. Quinn (2001).

21. Wolf (1991).

22. Quinn (2001).

23. Watson (1982).

24. Montgomery (1976).

25. Erikson (1976, p. 83).

26. Caine (2013).

27. Thompson (2011, p. vii).
28. Despite its sacred status in the gonzo canon, the Penguin Modern Classics edition of *Hell's Angels* classifies it as sociology (Thompson, 2013). Additionally, intellectuals such as Studs Terkel and acclaimed historian Douglas Brinkley refer to the sociological nature of Thompson's work (Summers 2008, p. 6; Brinkley 1999, p. xi).
29. It is worth noting that the "Rockers" from Cohen's *Folk Devils and Moral Panics* were, in fact, bikers.
30. Slackman (2005).
31. Thompson (1967, p. 13).
32. Erikson (1976, p. 83).
33. Thompson (1966, pp. 191–192).
34. Abramovich (2016, p. 175).
35. Thompson (1967, p. 72).
36. This moral career directly parallel the candidate, recruit, and rookie phases observed among police recruits (Conti, 2009).
37. Sher and Marsden (2006, pp. 6–7).
38. Wethern and Colnett (2008, pp. 8–10).
39. Menginie and Droban (2011, p. 193).
40. Falco and Droban (2013, p. 12).
41. Menginie and Droban (2011, p. 32).
42. Menginie and Droban (2011, p. 110).
43. Erekson (2010, p. 68).
44. Erekson (2010, p. 69).
45. Cavazos (2009, p. 78).
46. Menginie and Droban (2011, p. 220).
47. Thompson (2013, p. 156).
48. Cavazos (2009, p. 85).
49. Safina (2015).
50. Wozniak (2014).
51. For more on gonzo sociology, see Sefcovic (1995) as well as Trigger et al. (2012).
52. Merton (1948).
53. Ironically, Altheide's conception of "gonzo justice" as social control through stigmatization in popular media is antithetical to the gonzo varieties of both journalism and sociology (1992).

REFERENCES

Abramovich, A. 2016. *Bullies: A Friendship*, New York, NY, Henry Holt.
Altheide, D. L. 1992. Gonzo justice, *Symbolic Interaction*, 15(1), 69–86.
Baker, T. 2007. *Biker Gangs and Organized Crime*, Cincinnati, OH, Anderson Publishing.
Ball, K. R. 2011. *Terry the Tramp: The Life and Danderous Times of a One Percenter*, Minneapolis, MN, Motorbooks.
Ballard, L. M. 1997. "These youngsters change all these traditions": A perspective on "outlaw" motorcycle clubs in Ireland, *Folklore*, 108, 107–111.
Barber, C. 2012. Fashioning Japanese subcultures, *Times Higher Education Supplement* (2067), 48.
Barger, S. 2001. *The Life and Times of Sonny Bardger and the Hells Angels Motorcycle Club*, New York, NY, William Morrow.
Barger, S., Zimmerman, K. and Zimmerman, K. 2001. *Hell's Angel: The Life and Times of Sonny Barger and the Hell's Angels Motorcycle Club,* New York, William Morrow Paperbacks.
Barker, T. and Human, K. M. 2009. Crimes of the big four motorcycle gangs, *Journal of Criminal Justice*, 37(2), 174.
Boettcher, F., Mummendey, A., Waldzus, S. and Wenzel, M. 2004. Of bikers, teachers and germans: groups' diverging views about their prototypicality, *British Journal of Social Psychology*, 43(3), 385–400.
Brinkley, D. 1999. Introduction. In *Hell's Angles: A Strange and Terrible Saga*, Ed. H. S. Thompon, New York, NY, Random House.

Burt, C. 2006. Motorcycle clubs may help combat violence, *Oakland Tribune*, 2 November.

Caine, A. 2013. *Charlie and the Angels: The Oulaws, the Hells Angels and the Sixty Year War*, New York, NY, Random House.

Cavazos, R. 2009. *Honor Few, Fear None: The Life and Times of a Mongol*, New York, NY, It Books.

Charmaz, K. 1983. The grounded theory method: an explication and interpretation. In *Contemporary Field Research: A Collection of Readings*, Ed. R. M. Emerson, pp. 109–126. Prospect Heights, IL, Waveland.

Cohen, S. 1972. *Folk Devils and Moral Panics: The Creation of the Mods and Rockers*, New York, NY, Routledge.

Conti, N., Morrison, L. and Pantaleo, K. 2013. All the wiser: dialogic space, destigmatization and teacher-activist recruitment, *The Prison Journal*, 93(2), 163–188.

Conti, N. 2001. Ceremonial degradation of a doctoral candidate: an essay on the social situation of graduate student ethnographers and other inmates, *The American Sociologist*, 32(4), 89–97.

Conti, N. 2009. A Visigoth system: shame, honor & police socialization, *Journal of Contemporary Ethnography*, 38(3), 409–432.

Cross, P. and Cross, M. 2013. *Gypsy Joker to Hells Angel*. Minneapolis, MN: Motorbooks.

Danner, T. A., and Silverman, I. J. 1986. Characteristics of incarcerated outlaw bikers as compared to nonbiker inmates, *Journal of Crime and Justice*, 9, 43–70.

Davis, D. C. 2011a. *Out Bad*, Scotts Valley, CA, CreateSpace Independent Publishing Platform.

Davis, D. C. 2011b. *The Aging Rebel: Dispatches from the Motorcycle Outlaw Frontier*. Scotts Valley, CA, CreateSpace Independent Publishing Platform.

Delattre, E. J. 1990, 05. New faces of organized crime, *The American Enterprise*, 1, 38.

Droban, K., Father, P. and Son, P. 2011. *Growing up inside the Dangerous World of the Pagans Motorcycle Club*. New York, NY: Thomas Dunne Books.

Droban, K. 2008. *Running with the Devil: The True Story of the ATF's Infiltration of the Hells Angels*. New York, NY: Lyon's Press.

Edwards, P. 2013. *Unrepentant: The Strange and (Sometimes) Terrible Life of Lorne Campbell, Satan's Choice and Hells Angel Biker*. Toronto, CA: Random House Canada.

Erekson, S. P. 2010. *The Unknown Mongol*, San Diego, CA, Scott Erekson Publishing.

Erikson, K. T. 1976. *Everything in its Path: Destruction of Community in the Buffalo Creek Flood*, New York, Simon & Schuster.

Fairclough, G. 1993. Bangkok's night-riders: tryst with destiny, *Far Eastern Economic Review*, 156(38), 36.

Falco, C. and Droban, K. 2013. *Vagos, Mongols, and Outlaws*, New York, Thomas Dunne Books.

Fitzpatrick, M. 2011. The view from here - Japan. *The Times Educational Supplement*, (4960), 26.

Glaser, B. G. and Strauss, A. L. 1967. *The Discovery of Grounded Theory: Strategies for Qualitative Research*, London, Aldine Transaction.

Goffman, E. 1961. *Asylums: Essays on the Social Situation of Mental Patients and Other Inmates*, New York, Doubleday anchor.

Hall, J. 2011. *Riding the Edge: A Motorcycle Outlaw's Tale*. Minneapolis, MN: Motorbooks.

Hayes, B. 2005. *The Original Wild Ones: Tales of the Boozefighters Motorcycle Club*. Minneapolis, MN: Motorbooks.

Hopper, C. B. and Moore, J. 1990. Women in outlaw motorcycle gangs, *Journal of Contemporary Ethnography*, 18, 363–387.

Katz, K. 2011. The enemy within: the outlaw motorcycle gang moral panic, *American Journal of Criminal Justice*, 36, 231–249.

Male chauvinism sustains motorcycle clubs: Ex-member. 1986. *The Ottawa Citizen*, 21 July.

Marech, R. 1999. BREEZY RIDERS/women savor thrills, power of motorcycle riding in clubs, *San Francisco Chronicle*, 24 September.

McDonald-Walker, S. 1998. Fighting the legacy: British bikers in the 1990s. *Sociology*, 32(2), 379–396.

McDonald-Walker, S. 2000. Driven to action: the british motorcycle lobby in the 1990s, *Sociological Review*, 48(2), 186–202.

Menginie, A. and Droban, K. 2011. *Prodigal Father, Pagan Son: Growing Up Inside the Dangerous World of the Pagans Motorcycle Club*, New York, St. Martin's Griffin.

Merton, R. 1948. The bearing of empirical research upon the development of social theory, *American Sociological Review*, 13(5), 505–515.

Montgomery, R. 1976. The outlaw motorcycle subculture, *Canadian Journal of Criminology*, 332–342.

Montgomery, R. 1977. The outlaw motorcycle subculture II, *Canadian Journal of Criminology*, 356–361.

Moran, N. R. 2002. Motorcycle outlaw clubs going global, *Crime & Justice International*, 18(64), 9–10,

Nichols, D. and Peterson, K. 2007. *One Percenter: The Legenf of the Outlaw Biker*. Minneapolis, MN: Motorbooks.

Nichols, D. and Peterson, K. 2012. *The One Percenter Code: How to Be an Outlaw in a World Gone Soft*. Minneapolis, MN: Motorbooks.

Ohle, K. 1983. Degree of formalization and characteristics of social groups: Exemplified by motorcycle clubs, *Kolner Zeitschrift Fur Soziologie Und Sozialpsychologie, Supplement* 25, 497–509.

Queen, W. 2005. *Under and Alone: The True Story of the Undercover Agent Who Infiltrated America's Most Violent Outlaw Motorcycle Gang*. New York, NY: Random House.

Quinn, J. F., & Koch, D. S. (2003. The nature of criminality within one-percent motorcycle clubs, *Deviant Behavior*, 24(3), 281–305.

Quinn, J. F. 1987. Sex roles and hedonism among members of 'outlaw' motorcycle clubs, *Deviant Behavior*, 8(1), 47–63.

Quinn, J. F. 2001. Angels, bandidos, outlaws, and pagans: the evolution of organized crime among the big four 1% motorcycle clubs, *Deviant Behavior*, 22(4), 379–399.

Rowe, G. 2013. *Gods Od Mischief: My Undercover Vendetta to Take Down the Vagos Outlaw Motorcycle Gang*. New York, NY: Touchstone.

Safina, C. 2015. *Tapping Your Inner Wolf*. New York Times.

Sanders, C. R. and Vail, D. A. 2007. *Customizing the Body: The Art and Culture of Tattooing*. Philadelphia, PA: Temple University Press.

Sarafin, C. 2015, June 5. Tapping your inner wolf, *The New York Times*, A19.

Sawyer, C., & Judd, R. G. 2012. Counselors and bikers collaborate to empower abused children, *Journal of Creativity in Mental Health*, 7(1), 35–48.

Sefcovic, E. M. I. 1995. Toward a conception of "gonzo" ethnography, *Journal of Communication Inquiry*, 19(1), 20–37.

Sher, J. & Marsden, W. 2004. *Road to Hell: How the Biker Gangs Are Conquering Canada*. Toronto: Vintage Canada.

Sher, J. & Marsden, W. 2006. *Angels of Death: Inside the Biker Gang's Crime Empire*. New York, NY: Carroll & Graf Publishers.

Slackman, M. 2005. Hunter S. Thompson's version of the truth, (Wednesday. February 23), *The New York Times*.

Summers, J. H. 2008. New man of power. In *The Politics of Truth: Selected Writings of C. Wright Mills*. New York, NY: Oxford University Press.

Thompson, Hunter S. 1966. *Hell's Angles: A Strange and Terrible Saga*. New York, NY: Random House.

Thompson, H. S. 1967. *Hell's Angels: The Strange and Terrible Saga of the Outlaw Motorcycle Club*, New York, Random House.

Thompson, T. 2011. *Inside the Violent World of Outlaw Biker Gangs*, London, Hodder & Stoughton.

Thompson, T. 2013. *Outlaws: One Man's Rise through the Savage World of Renegade Bikers, Hells Angels and Global Crime*. New York, NY: Penguin Books.

Toplikar, D. 2012, Jun 26. *Local Motorcycle Clubs File Civil Rights Lawsuit against Police*. Chicago, McClatchy - Tribune Business News.

Trigger, D., Forsey, M., & Meurk, C. 2012. Revelatory moments in fieldwork, *Qualitative Research*, 12(5), 513–527.

Veno, A. and Eynde, J. 2007. Moral panic neutralization: a media-based intervention, *Journal of Community and Applied Psychology*, 17(6), 490–506.

Vetter, C. 1974. Playboy interview: Hunter S. Thompson, *Playboy Magazine*, November.

Watson, J. M. 1980. Outlaw Motorcyclists as an outgrowth of lower class values, *Deviant Behavior*, 4, 31–48.

Watson, J. M. 1982. Righteosness on two wheels, *Sociological Spectrum*, 2, 333–349.

Wethern, G. and Colnett, V. 2008. *A Wayward Angel*, New York, NY, Lyons Press.

Wolf, D. R. 1991. *The Rebels: A Brotherhood of Outlaw Bikers*, Toronto, University of Toronto Press.

Wolfe, A. 2008. Gonzo sociology, *New Republic*, 8 October.

Wozniak, J. S. G. 2014. When the going gets weird: an invitation to gonzo sociology, *The American Sociologist*, 45, 453–473.

BECOMING A JOURNALIST: THE CAREER OF YOUNG REPORTERS AND INTERNS IN TWO NEWSROOMS IN ARGENTINA*

Laura Rosenberg

ABSTRACT

This paper analyzes the beginning of the journalistic career of the youngest members of Página/12 *and* Tiempo Argentino *newspapers from Buenos Aires, Argentina. The ethnographic research took place in the newsrooms between 2011 and 2015 to study the socialization process of young reporters and interns in media press. With this goal in mind, it explores how they learn the values and practical rules of the journalistic world, starting with the interactions they engage on with other members of that environment, such as their colleagues and editors, as well as how they deal with the sources. The research was structured in five dimensions of analysis that contributed to explain the socialization process: (1) The channels and strategies to enter the journalistic field, (2) the newcomers' rites de passage, (3) the forms of socialization within the newsrooms, (4) the identification processes, and (5) the strategies that these young people implement in the medium term to stay in the journalistic world.*

*This paper presents the results of a research developed for the doctoral thesis in social sciences, which was financed with a fellowship of the National Council of Scientific and Technical Research (CONICET).

Radical Interactionism and Critiques of Contemporary Culture
Studies in Symbolic Interaction, Volume 52, 133–150
Copyright © 2021 by Emerald Publishing Limited
All rights of reproduction in any form reserved
ISSN: 0163-2396/doi:10.1108/S0163-239620210000052009

Keywords: Journalists; career; newsroom; socialization process; identification; ethnography

INTRODUCTION

This paper presents the results of a comparative study of the socialization process of young journalists of two national newspapers published in the city of Buenos Aires, Argentina: *Página/12* and *Tiempo Argentino*. Regarding their staff dimensions and their sales, within the media field in Argentina, we can say that both are news organizations with an intermediate structure.[1] In both cases, during the period that the research took place, the editorial line tended to be politically close to Cristina Fernández de Kirchner's governments.[2] That is the reason why these newspapers were qualified by its competitors as "officialistic media." The difference between these two media outlets consists of their respective trajectory in the media field. While *Tiempo Argentino* was founded in 2010 during the second Kirchnerist presidency, *Página/12* already had a consolidated position within media world, settled on prestigious investigations that its journalists had developed during the 90s.

By using techniques of ethnographic work – nine months of participant observation in each newsroom and 64 interviews to journalists and members related to the journalistic world – we are going to explain the learning process and the difficulties that young people encounter in the course of the early stages of their journalistic career in these two newspapers, with special emphasis on: (1) The channels and strategies to enter the journalistic field, (2) the newcomers' *rites de passage* (Hughes, 2012), (3) the forms of socialization in the newsrooms, (4) the identification processes, and (5) the strategies that these young journalists implement in the medium term in order to stay in the journalistic world.

Each of these dimensions of analysis focuses on the impact of the bonds that young people establish with other members of the journalistic world, be it their colleagues (interns and other reporters), reporters with more experience, editors and other bosses in the newsrooms, teachers of academic courses that they have attended, members of other journalistic media outlets, and sources during the processes of construction of news. This research has, in this sense, an inter-actionist approach from which it proposes to explain the journalistic work as it is perceived and practiced by the youngest members of the newsrooms.

In relation to our specific field of inquiry, we considered the issues analyzed by newsmaking studies, which intended to understand journalism practices in different national contexts using ethnographic techniques. These studies also inquired about the difficulties that media outlet faced in terms of political, economic, and technological conditions from the 1970s to the present. Among these studies can be highlighted pioneering works such as Altheide (1984), Epstein (2000), Fishman (1988), Gans (2004), Golding and Elliot (1979), Schlesinger (1987), Sigal (1974), Tuchman (1983), Tunstall (1978), as more recent works such as Anderson (2013), Boczkowski (2010), Deuze (2007), Ryfe (2012), Travancas (1992), Usher (2014), among others.

JOURNALISTIC WORLD AND CATEGORIES FOR ITS ANALYSIS

In this section, we present the epistemological perspective and the analytical categories of Symbolic Interactionism that operated as a starting point for our research. We can anticipate that an approach to the cooperation, the senses, and the definitions of the journalistic practice, incorporated in the frame of situations of interaction, is central in the tracing of the trajectories of the youngest journalists of these two media outlets. To apprehend these aspects, it is necessary first to introduce three main concepts that have guided the comprehension of journalistic activity from a Symbolic Interactionist approach: *social world, career,* and *identities.*

We will start with the conception of journalism as a social world. As Robert Merton pointed, the concept of *social world* allows us to explain the Middle-Range Theory, which connects the theoretical abstractions of Symbolic Interaction with its empirical findings (Pereira, 2010). Referring to social world also implies articulating individual aspects with structural factors, analyzing the practices that individuals carry on and the conformation of their identity, and taking into account their roles, social position, and hierarchies. The connection between individual and structural factors becomes possible since the actors participate in a social world, where it is possible to identify rules, conventions, and even conflicts that talk about how individuals cooperate with each other in everyday life.

The concept of *social word* implies the flexibility of its frontiers, where actors with different abilities, roles, or hierarchies can cooperate toward a same objective. For example, in his study about artistic work, Howard Becker (2008) points to the flexibility and amplitude of the frontiers of the space that those individuals related to art share, analyzing how they interact with each other around the artistic activity they have in common. The author brings the notion of *art worlds* to refer to all the people and activities which are necessary for what is defined as art production. The study in terms of social world regards how people coordinate their activities, which conventions organize their practices, and how they cooperate to produce work (Becker, 2008, p. 54).

As in art worlds not everyone that participates in the production can be considered an artist, in the journalistic world not all the participants are journalists. In fact, without the cooperation of the varied kind of sources, it would be hard – and sometimes even impossible – to construct the news. Insofar as it is a space with flexible frontiers, the journalistic world is conceived as a space for interaction among journalists and other actors that are not necessarily tied to the logics of the journalistic world, but whose intervention is of utmost importance in order to complete the daily work done by the media.

The second point regarding interactionist studies focuses on the analysis of labor socialization processes, as we can see in the sociology of work developed by authors like Andrew Abbott (1993), Howard Becker (2009), Becker et al. (1961), Blanche Geer (1972), Everett Hughes (1970, 2012), and Anselm Strauss (Becker & Strauss, 1956). In this aspect, we are going to highlight the conceptualization of *career,* which conceives individuals as active members of their process of socialization. Thus, Hughes (2012) defines *career* according to the subjective point of view; he considers it as the moving perspective from which people perceive their life as a whole, orient themselves to a social order, and interpret the meaning of attributes, actions, and things that happen to them. In this first definition, it is possible to notice that a preponderant place has been assigned to the point of view of the individuals during their work trajectory. Two other relevant elements that are included in the definition of *career* are related to their sequential character and the consideration of the role that others play, so that the *career* can be understood only in terms of a process that is developed in time through a series of stages, where the analysis of situations of social interaction and the participation in networks of cooperation are central to understand work socialization.

For instance, in Becker et al. (1961), the study on the *career* of young physicians was done upon the attention on the dynamics of interactions and the networks of cooperation that were observed within the organization of a medical school. This research exemplified how the symbolic interactionist perspective highlights the more conscious aspects of human behavior by relating them to the individual's participation in group life. Also, here it is possible to comprehend human behavior as a process where the individuals shape and control their behavior considering the expectations of others with whom they interact.

In this paper, we will talk about the *journalistic career,* distinguishing, firstly, the strategies and the channels of entry of young people in both organizations and, secondly, the *rites de passage* that convert the newcomers to journalists with similar abilities that every other reporter in the media has. In this instance of their career, these newcomers reflect on their "*growth*" as journalists, retrospectively observing the difficulties they had during the first months working at the newspaper, as well as the learning that have incorporated thanks to the cooperation of other members of the journalistic world. These themes are going to be developed and explained in sections "Channels and Strategies to Enter the Journalistic Field" and "Rites de Passage" of this paper.

Within the beginning of their career, as well as during the following months working in the media, young reporters and interns incorporated formal and also informal rules which organize everyday news production and the division of labor in the journalistic world. As Becker (2008) pointed out, people do not make decisions each time they need to cooperate toward an objective. If fact, they appeal to previous agreements and conventions that regulate the work in the media. Some of the conventions that rule and give meaning to the daily work are based on formal norms of the organization and/or on laws that regulate the labor market in Argentina and, specifically, the journalistic field. Others consist of informal rules, whose influence should not be underestimated when we try to comprehend situations of interaction within the newsrooms.

All the following sections refer to the conventions and the conflicts that appear related to broken rules, but sections "Forms of Socialization in the Newsrooms" and "Identification Processes in Journalistic World" will attend specially to these various rules that explain not only the internal functioning of these news organizations but also the construction of relationships which shape sociability and conflicts within its members, and contribute to comprehend the labor continuity in these two media outlets. In other terms, we could say that informal rules that organize work in these places also shape the relations between reporters and their bosses, creating senses about the work environment that promote, or not, the desire to continue working in this specific newspaper but not in another. In this study, we find that these facts are also important aspects of the career of young journalists.

The third question that we are going to introduce in this section regards the identification process. Hughes (2012) conceives work as a fundamental component in defining social identity. While individuals relate to other people and play their roles to achieve daily tasks, they acquire a self-conception and develop their personality. Accordingly, Goffman (2009) claims that people play roles constantly, and they get to know each other and themselves while they are executing these roles. This leads us to consider *self-identity* as the subjective sense of each one's own situation, continuity, and character, which someone achieves as a result of a varied social experience that she/he goes through (Goffman, 2006, p. 126).

The analysis of people's different relevant situations allows Goffman to question the idea of biography as a unique story about the experiences and identity of the actors. Instead of that, his conception attends to the existence of a *multiplicity of selves* that are manifested in the different situations that individuals live. This conception will allow us to refer to different identitarian adscriptions for reporters and interns during their career. We will see that the different groups of belonging that young reporters and interns integrate operate as sources of meaning for the processes of identification. And that depends on each situation of interaction, although will see that the category of "workers" prevails over a general conception of "journalists."

In this aspect, it is important to bring up Denis Ruellan's notion of journalism as a *professionnalisme du flou* (Ruellan, 1992), as an ambiguous or "blurred" profession, a notion which questions the essentialist ideas of journalism and defines it as a social practice where the identity of its participants is constantly being transformed. In Argentina, the fluency of the professional identity of journalists is not only related to a labor market that is increasingly expelling workers from the media (SIPREBA, 2017) or to the changes that new technologies have brought to their daily practices (Boczkowski, 2006, 2010). The difficulties to define journalism and its professional identity are also associated to the absence of any institutional requirements for the exercise of the activity. Although many journalists have attended academic courses related to their professional activity, no professional degree is demanded for working in the media.

The perceptions about journalism that our interviewees have are similar to that one presented in "The Professional Journalist Statute" (National Law N° 12.908). In that law, a professional journalist is conceived as someone who works regularly in the media for a monetary retribution. The representations of editors, reporters, and interns from *Página/12* and *Tiempo Argentino* have some points in common with that conception, when they assumed that journalists are closer to any worker – even those from other areas of production – than to the executive directors of the press. As we will see further on in sections "Forms of Socialization in the Newsrooms" and "Identification Processes in Journalistic World", young reporters and interns of these newsrooms internalized this identification between journalists and other workers of the labor market since they participated in the various protests and assemblies that members from the lowest hierarchies of these news organizations carried on to claim for their labor rights.

Other relevant aspects related to identification processes concern the effects of *sociability* and *fight*, as forms of socialization developed in daily work in the newsrooms. As Simmel (2002a, 2002b) defines them, the attention on these forms of socialization helps to explain the union and the conflicts within the members of a community. In the case of these two newsrooms, we relate these forms of socialization to the identification process, and we will add pedagogy as another form, taking into account that young journalists learned how to develop professional practices and incorporate meanings related to that profession when they feel part of a community or a group inside of it. The *struggle* also contributes to show antagonistic positions about the ways work should be done and which professional values are in danger when a reporter, an editor, or even the direction commit mistakes at work or break an informal rule about what is considered a *"good development"* of journalistic practice.

While belonging to a team, a group or an organization is fundamental for the constitution of *self-identity*, so are the oppositions to other groups and organizations of the *social world*, which can be expressed through the distinction between *them* and *us* (Bauman and May 2007). If *us* expresses the group of belonging, whose members share both motivations and the definition of the situation, *them* characterizes the group we do not belong to and we do not even desire to be part of. This opposition, Bauman and May (2007, p. 44) emphasize, produces self-identification. *Them* and *us* are inseparable opposites that we use to understand the world. In this sense, we are going to notice how deontological values emerge from the conflicts between reporters and their bosses and from the criticism to the editorial board that appears in some situations of interaction in the newsrooms. This also reveals the intervention of political and economic logics in the journalistic world that questions the ideal of journalistic autonomy. Besides, as Lemieux (2010) pointed out, the analysis of different situations that journalists face during their work shows the complexity of a profession that cannot be defined as a liberal activity, neither as an activity totally subject to the control of news organization.

The following sections will present the results of the research carried on in *Página/12* and *Tiempo Argentino* newsrooms. The conception and notions that were presented here are going to be recovered in order to explain the socialization process of young journalists from these media outlets. Other concepts that refer to some special stage of their career are going to be introduced in the correspondent sections.

CHANNELS AND STRATEGIES TO ENTER THE JOURNALISTIC FIELD

This first dimension of analysis of the socialization process of journalists in *Página/12* and *Tiempo Argentino* newsrooms inquire about the entrance of young interns and reporters to the journalistic world, attending to their strategies and the channels that the media open for newcomers. Considering that there are no procedures or legislation that regulate the labor insertion of journalists in Argentina, we have focalized on the study of strategies, among which we can highlight three main practices: the insertion in preprofessional spaces of work, the profitability of the network of relations with members of news organizations, and the acquisition of academic degrees in Journalism and/or Social Sciences (especially in Communication).

In this regard, we should point out the first difference between the socialization processes in each newspaper. While *Página/12* used to incorporate interns regularly, it rarely hired new workers during the period that took this study and even the years before 2011. On the contrary, as *Tiempo Argentino* was a new media outlet, it recruited new employers, but during its first years in the media market, it did not incorporate interns. Despite this difference, we have considered that the situation of interns in *Página/12* and that one of the reporters in *Tiempo Argentino* is feasible to be compared because in both cases we are talking about the people from the lowest hierarchies in the newsroom and without much experience or knowledge on the practice of journalism. The difference between them regards their contractual terms with the organizations, which affect work continuity in the case of interns that have worked for *Página/12* for over a year.

The comparison between the cases reveals that interns went through two instances of evaluation for their recruitment: first, in the university, and second, in the newsroom, by editors. This mechanism of recruitment was not reproduced in the case of reporters, whose network of social relations was their main resource to guarantee their access to a steady job in the newspaper. As one reporter pointed out:

> It's really hard to get a steady job in the media. I would say that it is quite impossible for those who don't have a contact with someone who is already working there.

Beyond the strategies that young journalists apply for their entrance, news organizations condition their chances when they limit the channels of access mainly to the previous connections that newcomers have with the journalistic world. As Howard Becker (2009) pointed out, each step of a successful career is a consequence of the building of profitable relationships. However, we could identify some strategies that young journalists apply, not only to increase their chances to access a job but also to learn and improve their daily task in the newsrooms.

We have stated before that the immersion of journalists in the academic world and the obtaining of a degree were not prerequisites for the exercise of the profession. Moreover, one of the most cited conventions during the fieldwork refers to Gabriel García Márquez's words (2015), who said that journalism is a job, which can only be learned as you practice it. Even so, every newcomer, and almost every journalist who works in these newsrooms, has attended academic courses related to journalism and/or social sciences. That is because the academic insertion means a source of knowledge and provides critical points of view to the young journalist. It is usually said that at university they incorporated new ways to question social reality and to perceive relevant social problems. This contributes to explain why many of them choose to attend university, even though academic qualification cannot be converted into resources for their job insertion.

The academic world is also connected to the third strategy that we are going to discuss, that is the possibility of having a preprofessional experience. In fact, as some of them were students at Universidad de Buenos Aires, they were able to run for the internship in *Página/12*. Something similar happened to those students from Universidad Nacional de Lomas de Zamora, who were able to have an unprecedented experience in the first academic news agency of Latin America, which was created by students and professors of the Social Sciences School. Only those students who were part of this news agency could apply for the internship in *Página/12*.

Within these academic spaces, teachers and students found positive results for the objective of reaching an education that conjugated the theory and the practice of journalism. In fact, journalists who went through these experiences developed their work more fluently during the first months in the newsrooms than those who never had such training.

In summary, since the very beginning of their career, the young journalists of *Página/12* and *Tiempo Argentino* have applied three main strategies: the insertion in academic spaces to acquire knowledge and means to interrogate the social reality; the insertion in preprofessional spaces, most of them opened by their academic spaces; and the capitalization of networks of social relations, which provides the most effective guarantee to get a steady job in the media. What we have found at this stage of their career is that the channels that media outlets arrange for the entrance of young journalists prevail over the strategies they use to access a job.

RITES DE PASSAGE

The second dimension of analysis regards the first months working in the newsrooms, and it attends to the practices according to which young people stop perceiving themselves – and are no longer perceived by others – as newcomers, in a space where they already manage the activities related to daily routines. This transition was analyzed in terms of *rites de passage*, intending to answer to the following question: when do newcomers become journalists?

The research inquired about the internalization of the rules of work and the ways how journalists acquire prestige among their colleagues every time they do a *"good job,"* as it is conceived according to the rules of the journalistic world. To this end, we analyzed the difficulties faced by young journalists, whose resolution meant the transition to a new stage of their career, where they handle the tasks related to the news production more easily. The inconveniences that were found responded to the domination of the rhythms of work, to the possibility of "*seeing*" a story and presenting it to the editor, and to the construction of a personal "*list of contacts.*"

Regarding this aspect, journalists pointed out a difference between working with "*their own sources*" and working with secondary sources. Among the latter, resorting to information from news websites and news agency has become more frequent than the opportunities of "*going out the street*" to look for their own material for the news production. In this sense, the Internet is associated to a less valued practice and linked to a standardized mode of news production. For media reporters, writing news on the base of secondhand information while sitting in the newsroom results in a loss of quality of the product. In addition, "*going out the street*" brings possibilities to deal with sources that give new information about the facts that are being investigated by a wide range of media, contributing to produce a *creative work*[3] and distinguishing the journalist positively in a context that tends toward the homogenization of news production (Boczkowski, 2010):

> The best you can do is to try to go to the places and talk to the neighbours, talk to people, talk with someone who can give you particular information ... This is the best you can get, because it makes a difference with the information provided by other media outlet about the same subject. (Young reporter of Tiempo Argentino)

At the very beginning of the research, one of the hypotheses regarded the key role that digital resources would play in the distinction between the work done by young journalists and that one by the other members with more experience in the journalistic world. But, we realized that a traditional way of elaboration of news was privileged in order to get a positive recognition of editors and colleagues. A first indicator of the *rite de passage* is the first news story that appears with the signature of the newcomer, and this reflects the recognition by editors of "*a job of their own production.*" It is rather unusual to get the story signed when the main work has been done with secondhand information from digital sources. In general, the signed stories involved on-site coverage and a direct treatment with the sources, as an intern said:

> ...the signature means a distinction, it is a reward. Your editor asked you on-site coverage, you did it well, so the newspaper publishes the news with your signature on it. As a recognition.

To get this treatment with the sources, networks of cooperation gained prominence in both newspapers. As Woods (1972) realized with students from a Barber College that "learn to learn from peers": "The student who engages in a wide range of interaction acquires more knowledge and practical ability than the 'loner'" (Woods, 1972, p. 24). A central role played by the willingness of colleagues and bosses to give the youngest the access to sources was a proof of that. Youngest journalists were advised on the ways to obtain information or were provided with the channels to obtain the information they needed.

We understand that a second indicator of the *rite de passage* is represented by the instance in which young journalists have their "*own list of contacts,*" of sources to appeal for news production. In this process, ethical factors related to *"care," "respectful treatment," "trust," "seriousness,"* and *"perseverance"* were mentioned by the interviewees, consolidating the bases of a good relation with the sources and guarantying future news coverage. This care for the networks with sources can also demand the suspension of their own professional activity, when it affects the moral integrity of those involved in the facts that are covered. This is also incorporated as part of the repertoire of the *"good practice"* of journalistic work.

FORMS OF SOCIALIZATION IN THE NEWSROOMS

The third dimension of analysis focuses specifically on the forms of socialization in the newsrooms and their implications in the construction of a work environment. Besides the strict workplace relationships, the research identified three other forms of socialization that characterized the bonds within each newspaper: *sociability, struggle,* and pedagogy. Each of them had a specific role in the consolidation of social ties within newsrooms and in the socialization process of the youngest members of each newspaper.

The cooperation of the colleagues with greater work experience meant an essential contribution to understand how to do daily work for the young journalists. Without this counseling or the provision of contacts with the sources, the work done by newcomers would not be possible. Professional keys regarding where to obtain information, who could provide it, and how to use it were the kind of questions that colleagues and bosses could answer young journalists. The interviewees used to establish an analogy between the treatment they received from their bosses and the pedagogical bond that teachers and students have:

> You are learning all the time, your rights as a worker, your obligations as a worker ... what you have to do and what you don't have to do during an interview, for example. It's a matter of trial and error, it's about taking to those who have more experience than you. That helps a lot! Especially during your first months working in the newsroom, it's so important! They are like teachers! (Young reporter of Tiempo Argentino)

In the fieldwork, we could notice this pedagogical form of socialization in both newsrooms from the stage of arrival of the newcomers. In this sense, pedagogy played a central role for newcomers' learning of the profession and for their managing of daily tasks in the newsroom. At the same time, pedagogy consolidated the bond of the youngest members with their bosses and with journalists with greater experience in the journalistic world.

The second form of socialization we are going to refer to is *sociability*, whose treatment in labor studies is rather unusual. It was reflected on the *"good work environment"* in *Tiempo Argentino*, as its own journalists mentioned. Simmel (2002a) defined *sociability* as a ludic form of socialization, where the only interest that people have is to share time with others, leaving apart material motivations. *Sociability* creates the sensation of equality among those who are interacting, and that is the reason why it can be compared to a game where the participants have equal conditions. Simmel argued that this creates a sensation of an artificial world, like a democracy where everyone has the same rights. Hierarchies seem to be suspended in this equal world.

Considering that newsrooms work in the frame of structured organizations with clear distribution of roles and hierarchies, referring to *sociability* as a form of socialization within it could be seen as a contradiction. However, we are not arguing that *Tiempo Argentino* does not have the same hierarchized structure that other media have. In fact, every journalist does his/her work according to the role that has been assigned to him/her. At the same time, we could notice some interactions between reporters and editors, and also between them and the chief editor, that recreates, according to Simmel's conception, that "artificial world" where everyone seems to have the same rights and hierarchy. Social conversations and even jokes gave the sensation of *"being working with friends."* The relevance of this aspect was pointed out by Roy (1959) in his research about the social interaction within a work group of factory machine operatives: "one key source of job satisfaction lies in the informal interaction shared by members of a work group" (p. 166). In our study, many young journalists declared that this sensation made them feel *"happy to go to work every day."*

The affective bonds and the moments of recreation in the newsroom of *Tiempo Argentino* proved to be indicators of the place that *sociability* occupies for the consolidation of the collective workers in the production of this newspaper. In this case study, the analysis developed allows us to affirm that *sociability* centrally fulfills two functions.

The first one is to reinforce the collective character of journalistic work. The attention on the social conversations in the space of the newsroom allowed us to identify the circulation of shared meanings in the decoding of the themes of daily treatment, starting from the group discussion and interpretation of the news. It is in this sense that the collective work of the news product is strengthened. This conclusion contrasts with the young journalists' point of view of their activity, which is usually defined as *"a very individual work."*

But, *sociability* demonstrated not only the collective character of journalistic work but also the bonds of friendship, the subgroups, and the working teams in the newsrooms. This is related to its second function: the guarantee of continuity. Those bonds and networks left a significant mark in the career of the young journalists of *Tiempo Argentino* and made them want to continue working in this media outlet instead of any other. In this sense, it is that *"coming to work happy"* and *"feeling that you are working with friends"* were reasons that lead them to imagine working in this environment beyond the short term.

Sociability, as a relevant form of socialization in *Tiempo Argentino*'s newsroom, established a contrast with the situations of interaction that were possible to characterize in *Página/12*'s work environment. Although journalists of this second newspaper recognize a *"cordial and pleasant"* work environment, they do not assimilate this newsroom to a space where they *"work with friends,"* which turns out to be more of a special characteristic of *Tiempo Argentino*'s newsroom. Besides, in some cases, they identify a more conflictive environment. Therefore, to understand the socialization in this newsroom, we should also incorporate the *struggle* category (Simmel, 2002b), which describes disagreements and conflicts within the newsroom that reinforced the institutionalized division between reporters and editors.

The analysis of the development of the *struggle* demands the attention on the causes that produced such disagreements between the journalists that displayed different roles in the daily work. For example, in the political section, it became rather usual that reporters – and, in some cases, even the interns – confronted their editors when the latter broke informal rules such as *"respecting the story theme that each reporter usually covers and not taking it away from him/her,"* or *"not including the signature of the reporter when their version of the story has been edited too much."*

Even though editors followed formal rules regarding their hierarchical function – they could choose who the reporter that was going to follow a story or another was, and they could introduce changes on reporters' writing as this was what editors were supposed to do – reporters and interns considered that there were some informal conventions of the journalistic world that their editors were breaking, affecting the collective work in the political section. This was revealed, for example, when a reporter said: *"You should have told me that you were going to add so many changes to my story. At least, you should have withdrawn my signature."* Reporters said that this kind of situations impacted negatively in the collective work and reflected an increasing fragmentation within workers who have different roles and hierarchies in the news production. As it is shown in this example, formal and informal conventions are exposed during work routine in the newsroom and are also part of the rules that newcomers internalized during their insertion in the journalistic world.

The last relevant point regarding the forms of socialization in the case of *Página/12* is the internal division between the reporters who were expected to attend daily to the newsroom and those who were not. Within the latter, we can comprehend different roles and hierarchies: from the freelancers, some of which have the worst labor conditions in the journalistic world, to those reporters that have a *"special agreement with their editors"* that allows them to avoid attending to the newsroom every day, up to the columnists, mainly considered as *"figures"* or *"stars"* of the journalistic world. The columnists usually detent privileges regarding their salaries and the frequency in which they are expected to publish in a newspaper like *Página/12* that has been known, since its very beginning, as a *"signatures newspaper."* Paradoxically, these *"signatures"* – who do not attend to the newsroom and do not publish every day – contribute significantly to establish the identity of this newspaper and create identification with its readers.

Thus, the collective that integrated *Página/12* was not only divided according to hierarchic roles but also divided between *"those who make the newspaper every day"* and *"those who do not go to the newsroom."* This speaks about a group of workers that was divided because of the individualization of work conditions, which hindered their union when they wanted to carry on syndical actions.

To summarize, these three forms of socialization – pedagogy, *sociability,* and *struggle* – characterized the labor environment within these newsrooms, and their analysis helps to understand how newcomers learned the journalistic work and its formal and informal rules and conventions. As well as young journalists spent more time in the newsrooms, they explained the *"labor environment"* in relation to those rules and conventions that were involved in daily work and in the conformation of their bonds with other members of this world.

IDENTIFICATION PROCESSES IN JOURNALISTIC WORLD

When we inquired about the fourth dimension of analysis that deals with the processes of identification of young journalists, we based our inquiry on the conceptions about identity that move off the essentialist perspectives that define it as something monolithic and static. On the contrary, the idea of process refers to something that is in continuous construction, which can be reconfigured from a moment to another.

Following this line, the notion of *multiplicity of selves* enable the understanding of the identification as a process that requires the analysis of different situations that people go through, during which they define their identity. We observed the emergence of *multiple identities* in the framework of the process of socialization of the youngest members of the media staff, which were internalized according to the rules that they were supposed to apply in different situations of interaction, in which they participate during their integration into the journalistic world. Regarding Lemieux's perspective, we also consider the existence of different rules in the journalistic world which, in practice, could contradict each other, presenting dilemmatic situations: which rule should be followed? (Lemieux, 2010). The analysis of different situations, and the presentation of the dilemmas that individuals face, will enrich the understanding of journalistic practices and representations even when they seem to fall into contradictions.

Therefore, different situations that journalists go through during daily work were analyzed, which allowed us to find out that they use a set of categories that express a group identity – as well as opposition to others – while they are doing their job. Notions of *us* and *them* (Bauman and May 2007) would change their composition according to the frame of the situations that we are going to present from now on.

(1) Opposition to *"the bosses"* and criticism to editorial line:
    The first situation we are going to refer to is related to the selection of the events for news production. In this aspect, the distribution of roles and the hierarchies – which seemed to be suspended in the analysis of *sociability* in *Tiempo Argentino* – recover their central place in the study of the organization of the work in this newsroom and the division of its workers. Attending to editorial decisions of *"the bosses"* (who were represented by the journalistic directors, the chief editor, and, in the case of *Página/12,* also by editors), those journalists that we define here as *"the critics"* (who comprehend some

reporters, interns, and in the case of *Tiempo Argentino,* include the editors too) offered an alternative point of view of which events should be considered relevant for the construction of the news.

Considering this, the research aimed to demonstrate that the analysis of the criteria for newsworthiness allows us not only to describe the processes of construction of the news but also the construction of the professional identity of the journalists when they discuss about delimitation and hierarchy of news stories. That is why we conceived the criteria for newsworthiness in terms of conventions that organize the work in the newsroom. Although these criteria are shared in the journalistic world, their use is not exempted from conflicts. In fact, we intended to show how their implementation demonstrates an antagonism between journalists who have different roles in the organization, which creates the identification of the group of *"the bosses and their soldiers"* and one of *"the critics."* As regards this opposition, we could notice that what journalists were discussing were the deontological values and the definition of *"good"* and *"bad"* journalism.

Even those criteria for newsworthiness that had greater consensus within the journalistic world – such as "the novelty" of some event or "the geographic and social proximity" of those people who were involved – could be subject to discussion in the newsrooms. As a reporter claimed: *"why do we talk about middle-class housing problems instead of those ones who the lower classes have?"* The conflict between "the critics" and *"the bosses and their soldiers"* increased when they referred to the coverage of political and economic events. In those cases, the relevance of their treatment was not a subject to debate as the editorial line that guided their coverage was. *"This newspaper has become very Kirchnerist!"* were some of the complaints of the journalists of *Página/12.* Critical journalists of *Tiempo Argentino* usually said: *"This newspaper is more Kirchnerist than the government."*

Regarding this first type of identity (the critics), in both newspapers, the disputes around a definition of a professional identity were observed, when journalists claimed that the coverage of the news events should not be conditioned by the political values of the executive directors of the media outlets. What the "critics" were actually claiming was that deontological rules were broken each time that *"the bosses"* seemed to privilege their own values over the journalistic ones.

(2) Opposition between the members of *Tiempo Argentino* and *Clarín:*

The second type of identity refers to the case of *Tiempo Argentino* when it was a recently created media outlet that intended to compete against *Clarín,* the main newspaper in Argentina, which had an editorial line that reflected a critical position toward Kirchner's government. We noticed that the frequent reference to *Clarín* heard in *Tiempo Argentino*'s newsrooms might have had relevant effects on the identification process of the members of its staff. In the frame of those situations where they talked about *Clarín,* the previous opposition between *"bosses"* and "critics" disappeared. *Us* was redefined to include all the members of *Tiempo Argentino,* whose collective represented the opposition to *Clarín's* staff. As its competitor and its political antagonist,

Clarín contributed to join *Tiempo Argentino*'s members together, member who were, in other situations described above, divided according to different conceptions of the professional values that should regulate the journalistic activity.

(3) "Workers" against "Media owners":

The third type of identity was represented in the distinction between *"the owners"* and *"the workers"* of the news organizations. We noticed that this distinction prevailed over the others we have mentioned before, finding that even the interns of *Página/12* – whose status in the newspaper was not formally framed under a work relationship – also conceived themselves as workers.

Leaving out the space of the newsrooms, we could notice the confluence of workers of different media outlet toward syndical actions. In this aspect, it was shown that the identity of journalists was defined not only in terms of the organization where they worked but also beyond its frontiers. Despite the efforts of each owner to distinguish himself from his competitors, all of them were grouped together by *"the workers,"* who became their antagonistic figure. The existence of these two groups of belonging was exemplified in the observation of many syndical actions and protests that expressed *"solidarity"* among journalists that belonged to different media outlets. Journalists of *Clarín* and *Tiempo Argentino* were, in these specific situations, part of the same group.

In this dimension of the analysis, we found that there was not a single meaning for *them* and *us* in the description of the process of identification of journalists of these two news organizations. For example, "the bosses" could become part of *us* in those situations when journalists of *Tiempo Argentino* referred to *Clarín* newspaper; journalists of *Clarín* became part of *us* when reporters were confronting *"the owners"* in contexts of workers' protests. This is not a contradiction, but a characteristic of the process of identification, in which journalists use different categories to construct *self-identity* according to each situation. They interpret the facts and others' actions in line with the roles they are playing in each occasion.

As we have described regarding *sociability*, this approach to the process of identification was also meaningful to the study of the socialization of young journalists. An analysis that tries to cover the different dimensions of socialization of labor should include both the questions about the learning of specific work practices and those questions that inquire about the identity of the actors involved, which refer to the way that labor practices and social relations are lived and felt by the actors.

WORK CONTINUITY

The fifth dimension of analysis inquired about the chances of work continuity of the young journalists that had been working in *Página/12* and *Tiempo Argentino* newspapers. Considering the crisis of the labor market of the Argentinian press, and the fact that the rules that media outlets apply for the recruitment of new workers are not very clear, individual and collective strategies that young journalists have implemented were analyzed to find out how they could continue in the journalistic world.

The cases that were analyzed showed that the chances to access a steady job depended more on the network of relationships that young journalists had established with members of the journalistic world than on their professional skills. This revealed a clear contrast against the case of the interns of *Página/12,* who had entered the newsroom after being evaluated on their academic background and their potential as journalists. Afterward, when they wanted to get a steady job in the media, the profitability of their network of relationships seemed to be the only way to succeed.

Regarding work continuity, it was also questioned why *Página/12* invested in the training of human resources that it did not capitalize later by integrating them to its staff. Many journalists of this media outlet assumed that the organization was *"losing good journalists,"* as it did not hire them once they had finished their internship. In fact, young journalists left the newsroom after their *rites de passage,* just when they felt they were already qualified to develop professionally. The fact was that political and economic context allowed media outlets to resolve daily work appealing to the system of educational internships, which provided human resources avoiding their incorporation as permanent workers.

Continuity in the journalistic world as freelance journalists represented one of the most accessible options for the interns, but their work conditions were signed by flexibility, instability, and work precarity. Besides, working as freelancer did not guarantee permanence in the field in the long term and tended to be conceived as a transitory option while they were looking for a job with greater stability.

FINAL WORDS

The research developed a comparison between the socialization of journalists in two media outlets of intermediate structure (regarding the dimensions of their staff and their average circulation). This characteristic allowed us to compare the situation that interns and young reporters lived in both newsrooms. Besides, both newspapers had a homologous editorial line, politically close to Kirchnerism. At the same time, these media outlets had notable differences regarding their position in the journalistic field; *Tiempo Argentino* was founded when *Página/12* already had recognition and prestige in virtue of its 25 years of presence in the media world. That meant that the comparison of the processes of socialization had to consider the difference between the entrance to a new media outlet and the entrance to a media outlet perceived like *"a signatures' newspaper,"* where many renowned journalists worked in the same place as newcomers did.

Following theoretical and empirical contributions from Symbolic Interactionism, we have designed an analysis model of the socialization process of young journalists that considered the relevance of the construction of networks of relationships for the insertion into the labor market and the learning of rules, values, and practices related to the profession. The journalistic career comprehended five dimensions of analysis that allowed us to explain the socialization of young journalists, contributing to the sociology of journalism in Argentina, where there is a lack of studies regarding both this specific area of work and journalism studies, in general. In this sense, our goal was to provide an analytical tool for the study of journalistic careers in different media outlets, which may also be useful for the understanding of the careers in other areas of the labor market.

The analysis of socialization processes did not circumscribe its findings to individual careers. It aimed to illustrate the internal dynamics of the media outlet too. Regarding this aspect, the research inquired about the strategies that actors applied to their entrance to the journalistic world and which were the channels that the media opened for them. Moreover, this kind of research provides information about the daily work that is done in the media and its internal life, contributing to explain current transformations in the practice of journalism, and the dilemmas that journalists face when they have to deal with political and economic factors while they are working in news production.

NOTES

1. From Monday to Friday, *Tiempo Argentino* and *Página/12* have a circulation of between 10,000 and 13,000 copies. Both media outlets have a staff of nearly 200 workers. While these numbers are well below those of *Clarín* and *La Nación* newspapers – which lead the national press market with 209,000 and 133,000 copies, respectively, from Monday to Sunday – *Tiempo Argentino* and *Página/12* are considered to have an intermediate structure, since both the dimensions of their staff as their average circulation far exceed those of smaller commercial newspapers. Some of the latter have no more than two dozen journalists.

2. Levitsky and Roberts (2011) comprehend Fernández de Kirchner's government in the context of the "Latin American's left turn." Néstor Kirchner, a member of a Peronist fraction, became President of Argentina in 2003, during the worst economic, social, and political crisis that the country has ever gone through. The three Kirchnerist governments (Néstor Kirchner, 2003–2007; Cristina Fernández de Kirchner, 2007–2011 and 2011–2015) shared with other "national-popular" governments in the region the goal of reducing social inequality, by retaking a central place for the State in the economy. Regarding political communication issues, during Cristina Fernández de Kirchner's governments, a new media law was enacted. Its spirit confronted media property concentration and represented a chapter of the struggle between the Kirchnerist government and the mainstream media represented by *Grupo Clarín*.

3. According to Zallo (1988), this concept characterizes the work that is done by cultural industries, which gives their product a unique and irreplaceable character. Here we argue that, in journalistic work, two opposing characteristics coexist: the creative side and the standardized one. The latter is shown here in the frequent use of secondhand information of digital sources, such as the practice of *"cutting"* material provided by news agencies.

REFERENCES

Abbott, A. 1993. The sociology of work and occupations, *Annual Review of Sociology*, 19, 187–209.
Altheide, D. 1984. *Creating Reality: How TV News Distorts Events*, Beverly Hills, CA, SAGE Publications.
Anderson, C. W. 2013. *Rebuilding the News: Metropolitan Journalism in the Digital Age*, Philadelphia, PA, Temple University Press.

Bauman, Z. and May, T. 2007. *Pensando Sociológicamente*, Buenos Aires, Nueva Visión.

Becker, H. 2008. *Los mundos del arte*, Bernal, Universidad Nacional de Quilmes.

Becker, H. 2009. *Outsiders*, Buenos Aires, Siglo XXI.

Becker, H., Geer, B., Hughes, E. and Strauss, A. 1961. *Boys in White: Student Culture in Medical School*, University of Chicago Press.

Becker, H. and Strauss, A. 1956. Careers, personality, and adult socialization, *Chicago: American Journal of Sociology*, 62(3), 253–263.

Boczkowski, P. 2006. *Digitalizar las noticias. Innovación en los diarios online*. Buenos Aires, Manantial.

Boczkowski, P. 2010. *News at Work: Imitation in an Age of Information Abundance*, Chicago, IL, University of Chicago Press.

Deuze, M. 2007. *Media Work*, Cambridge, Polity Press.

Epstein, E. 2000. *News from Nowhere: Television and the News*, Chicago, IL, I.R. Dee.

Fishman, M. 1988. *Manufacturing the News*, Austin, TX, University of Texas Press.

Gans, H. 2004. *Deciding What's News*, Evanston, IL, Northwestern University Press.

García Márquez, G. 2015. Periodismo: el mejor oficio del mundo. In *Yo No Vengo a Decir Un Discurso*, Buenos Aires, Sudamericana.

Geer, B. Eds 1972. *Learning to Work*, Beverly Hills, CA, SAGE Publications.

Goffman, E. 2006. *Estigma*, Buenos Aires, Amorrortu.

Goffman, E. 2009. *La presentación de la persona en la vida cotidiana*, Buenos Aires, Amorrortu.

Golding, P. and Elliott, P. 1979. *Making the News*, New York, NY, Longman.

Hughes, E. 1970. The humble and the proud: the comparative study of occupations, *The Sociological Quarterly*, 11(2), 147–156.

Hughes, E. 2012. *Men and Their Work*, London, Forgotten Books.

Lemieux, C. 2010. Introduction. L'autonomie, nécessité de la practique journalistique. In *La subjectivité Journalistique*, Dir. C. Lemieux, Paris, Éditions de l'École des hautes études en sciences sociales.

Levitsky, S. and Roberts, K. Eds 2011. *The Resurgence of the Latin American Left*, Baltimore, MD, The Johns Hopkins University Press.

Pereira, F. 2010. El mundo de los periodistas: aspectos teóricos y metodológicos, *Guadalajara: Comunicación Y Sociedad*, 13, 101–124.

Ryfe, D. 2012. *Can Journalism Survive? An inside Look at American Newsrooms*, Stafford, John Wiley & Sons.

Roy, D. 1959. Banana time: Job satisfaction and informal interaction, *Human Organization. Society for Applied Anthropology*, 18(4), 158–168.

Ruellan, D. 1992. Le professionnalisme du flou. *In Réseaux*, 10(51), 25–37.

Schlesinger, P. 1987. *Putting "Reality" Together: BBC News*, Londres, Methuen.

Sigal, L. 1974. *Reporters and Officials*, Lexington, KY, Heath and Company.

Simmel, G. 2002a. *Cuestiones fundamentales de Sociología*, Barcelona, Gedisa.

Simmel, G. 2002b. *Sobre la individualidad y las formas sociales*, Bernal, Universidad Nacional de Quilmes.

SIPREBA. 2017, January 13. 2016: un año de despidos, precarización y ajuste salarial en los medios de comunicación. Available at: https://www.sipreba.org/sindicato/2016-un-ano-de-despidos-precarizacion-y-ajuste-salarial-en-los-medios-de-comunicacion/

Travancas, I. 1992. *O Mundo Dos Jornalistas*, São Paulo, Summus.

Tuchman, G. 1983. *La producción de la noticia*, Barcelona, Gustavo Gili.

Tunstall, J. 1978. *Journalists at Work*, Beverly Hills, CA, SAGE Publications.

Usher, N. 2014. *Making News at the New York Times*, Ann Arbor, MI, The University of Michigan Press.

Woods, C. M. 1972. Students without teachers: student culture at a Barber college. In *Learning to Work*, Ed. B. Geer, Beverly Hills, CA, SAGE Publications.

Zallo, R. 1988. *Economía de la comunicación y la cultura*, Madrid, Akal.

CONTEMPLATIVE GROUNDED THEORY: POSSIBILITIES AND LIMITATIONS

Krzysztof T. Konecki

ABSTRACT

The paper will concentrate on the Grounded Theory Methodology (GTM) from the point of view of the contemplative social sciences (CSS). It will analyze how the mind is engaged in the construction of concept and what the role is of the consciousness of the mind's work in creating a theory that is based on the analysis of empirical data. We will review the research and analytical methods that could be inspirations *for Contemplative Grounded Theory (CGT): constructivist grounded theory, classic grounded theory, transformational grounded theory, sociological introspection, holistic ethnography, mindful inquiry and transformational phenomenology, and contemplative qualitative inquiry.*

We can find in many classical books from grounded theory (GT) some seeds of contemplative thinking, and we can reconstruct them (Glaser and Strauss, 1967; Glaser, 1978; Strauss, 1987). We would like to develop the inspirations more and perhaps change the sense of GT after the contemplative turn. We would like to show the possibilities of using CGT in research and also its limitations. Some empirical examples from research and analysis will be given to show how contemplation could be used in GT.

Keywords: Grounded theory methodology; phenomenology; contemplative studies; qualitative research and analysis; mind; sociology

Radical Interactionism and Critiques of Contemporary Culture
Studies in Symbolic Interaction, Volume 52, 151–186
Copyright © 2021 by Emerald Publishing Limited
All rights of reproduction in any form reserved
ISSN: 0163-2396/doi:10.1108/S0163-239620210000052010

INTRODUCTION

The paper will concentrate on the Grounded Theory Methodology (GTM; Glaser and Strauss, 1967; Glaser, 1978; Strauss, 1987; Charmaz, 2006, 2014) from the point of view of the contemplative social sciences (CSS, see Bentz and Giorgino, 2016; Giorgino, 2015). It will analyze how the mind is engaged in the construction of concepts and what the role is of consciousness of the mind's work in creating a theory that is based on the analysis of empirical data. We will review the research and analytical methods that could be *inspirations* for GTM: constructivist grounded theory, classic grounded theory, transformational grounded theory (TGT), sociological introspection, holistic ethnography, mindful inquiry and transformational phenomenology, and contemplative qualitative inquiry. Then, we will use these inspirations to formulate the concept of Contemplative Grounded Theory (CGT) and show examples from our contemplative research and analysis of data (see Appendix 1).

One piece of research was done on experiencing the cemetery space and on self-feelings during All Saints' Day (1st November) and during ordinary weekday visits to a cemetery. The 32 students of sociology that took part in the research were participants of a course that I lectured at the Lodz University in 2017/18: "Contemplative Sociology. Experiencing Self, No-Self, and the Lifeworld." The students were coresearchers. Generally, the visits to the cemetery were difficult experiences for the students. They felt uncomfortable; sometimes, they felt unpleasant emotions, such as fear and distress. The students were prepared to make auto-observation and self-descriptions. They were trained in meditative practices. I tried to teach the students concentration and more discrete and *clean* ways of perceiving the mundane world through meditation and yoga practices. The students wrote contemplative memos on how they felt during the self-observation. They later coded the data according to the methodology of grounded theory (GT), and they also described their feelings, both while coding their own autodescriptions as well as those of others.

The contemplative memos were used as full-value data, and interpretations done not for controlling the objective and distanced point of view of the researchers but to elaborate the research questions (see Appendix 2).

GT is a methodology of research that helps to create theory by analyzing the empirical data. The data are first; the concepts, hypotheses, and interpretations are second. The researchers and analysts try to limit the preconceptualization of the research to be close to the empirical reality and empirical data. The theory comes from the data, not from the concepts that are already in the scientific reservoirs of knowledge.

We can find in many classical books from GT some seeds of contemplative thinking (Glaser and Strauss, 1967; Glaser, 1978; Strauss, 1987). We would like to reconstruct and develop them more, and perhaps change the sense of GT after the contemplative turn. The contemplative turn is the idea connected with research on experience emerging from contemplative practices that overcome the body–mind divide (Giorgino, 2015, pp. 6–7). It is connected with such contemplative practices as mindfulness (Barbezat and Bush, 2014, p. 99; Ergas, 2015,

2017), sitting or walking meditation (Konecki, 2016), and body scan (Giorgino, 2015). It integrates third- and second-person research with the first-person study (Gunnlaugson et al., 2017).[1] We try to develop in this spirit CGT, which we define preliminary at this moment as: *Contemplative Grounded Theory* is a mindful way of developing theory not only through careful observation of the world and analyzing the data but also by including the self-observation and analyses of the work of the mind, emotions, and the body of the researcher, and his or her collaborators while they develop a theory from data and their minds. It is a process of permanent self-observation and conscious analyses of the mind by writing contemplative memos. Contemplative memos should be a part of the data to analyze and should not be treated as a separate "reflexive journal" (see Hansen and Trunk, 2016, p. 14). The researcher/analyst openly shows his/her inner dialog while attempting to limit preconceptualization in the process of coding the data, generating categories and hypotheses, and finally creating interpretations and theory. A very important question here is: Who am I as a researcher? My engagement as a researcher-analyst-human being in the world is crucial here. I would like to quote Norman Denzin (2006, p. 422) when he writes about ethnography for this case:

> Ethnography is not an innocent practice. Our research practices are performative, pedagogical, and political. Through our writing and our talk, we enact the worlds we study. These performances are messy and pedagogical. They instruct our readers about this world and how we see it.

I agree completely with Denzin's statement. GT is also performative and political. The analyst is embedded in reading the analyzed texts as a social practice but also in the actual sociocultural situation of reading and the biographical stage of her his/life. Even seeing letters in a text through the prism of language is a political act. Interviewing and writing are also sociocultural practices and have political meaning (Denzin, 2001), and taking some theoretical filters to see the reality is also a political interpretation (Denzin, 1992). Methodological self-consciousness is needed here (Charmaz, 2016) but so is a deeper insight into the mind and the situation of the researcher.

One of the main principles and issues of GTM is *limited preconceptualization*. We would like to review this principle from the point of view of CGT. We will introduce the procedure of *epoché* from phenomenological research, which could be used in CGT research and help to solve the problem of preconceptualization that must be avoided in GTM.

Another contemplative procedure that could be used in GT is *the deconstruction of the concepts* that come from the literature and everyday life. Individual work on the embodiment of the concepts and work on the mind could be useful here. Meditation and writing contemplative memos could also be implemented here.

An important part of GTM is *the coding procedure*. Coding is the process of choosing a label from a variety of alternative terms that we have at hand (Charmaz, 2014). However, we should remember that the labels also belong to a vernacular language that informs the interpretation of the phenomena from the commonsense point of view (Schutz, 1967, p. 78; Barber, 2016; Eberle, 2012, pp. 282, 289). Coding is sometimes a mechanical activity as we use categories from everyday life to manage the situation we are dealing with. A mindful and careful insight is needed here to have categories that not only fit the data but which also express how it is "fitted" or "unfitted" to the existential position of the researcher-analyst and how it happened that they appeared (Charmaz, 2014). Moreover, the researcher should be aware of the process of fitting the label to the perceived object and of the roots of the theoretical propositions (thesis). We treat here the GT from the first-person perspective to see the situatedness of the theorizing process in a mindful way. So, we introduce here a contemplative inspiration to GT.

Constructing concepts and hypotheses is also connected with the work of the mind. We should remember here the statement by Mead (1934, p. 126): "Mentality is that relationship of the organism to the situation which is mediated by sets of symbols." The symbols are used in the internal conversation in which we describe reality through categories. The consciousness of the analyst and mindful insight are very important to *consciously* create concepts and hypotheses, and to see how the self and the history of the self/ego of the researcher are included in the process (Keane, 2015). Observing self, we can not only be more sensitive to finding the ideas in the data (Corbin and Strauss, 2008, p. 76) but also create the data together with the ideas that interact with the world in our perception of it (Chesney, 2001). Glaser (1978, p. 23) observed the phenomenon of the mind working while generating a GT and called it "preconscious processing." A delayed action by the researcher is observed when, many days after collecting the data or coding, some new ideas come to mind. *Writing memos* is a creative process that comes from anywhere, and Glaser (1998) calls it *the drugless trip.* We should then stop and write a memo to carry out further theoretical sampling or to ask more questions about the researched phenomenon (Holton and Walsh, 2017, pp. 73 and 77; see also *generative questions* by Strauss, 1987, pp. 17 and 22). These ideas are the seeds of CGT that existed in classic grounded theory, and Strauss' writings, in particular, are essential here. However, I think that from the point of view of CGT, we should stop and write a memo about the process of *preconscious processing*, when and where we stopped, and how the thoughts arrived. What conditions/situations generated the new ideas in the mind of the analyst? How did we feel during the processing (emotions, body feelings; the issue of the embodiment of concepts should be considered, Merleau-Ponty, 2005, p. xxiii)? Who generated the new ideas? This is the first-person perspective of the GT.

A very useful *contemplative method for insight could be the exercise of answering the question "Who Am I?"* as a person and social researcher. How do the two roles (as a person with a concrete surname and a researcher with actual achievements) relate to each other? We can make the insight and analysis using the *principle of anamnesis*, recollecting the knowledge that has been forgotten in the stereotypical lifeworld, the knowledge about the *everyday-constant interaction between the "I" and "Me"* in our mind that creates the social world. We are not usually aware of this because we are totally engaged in "Me" and are inclined toward *fast living and thinking* and not a mindful experiencing of the world.

Something else that should be recalled is the *interconnectedness of the all things in the world and the impermanence of the beings and things* (Janesick, 2015). The researcher should be mindful of this knowledge while coding data. The technique of the contemplative method in this aspect is *contemplative memo writing*. It is a memo in which we concentrate on our biography and the self that is situated (the "places" where the person and analyst-researcher stays as well as the social relations), and it refers it to the actual doing (research questions and activities as concrete data gathering in the *here and now*) and data analysis (while constructing categories and their properties and hypotheses in the *here and now*). The analysis is some kind of living experience (see an example of a contemplative memo in Appendix 1). It comes somehow from the mind and is situated here and now. Personal experiences and comparisons with the data can be described in memos, and they are reflective memos (Mills and Francis, 2006), which are one of the practical tools of CGT. However, we also have contemplative memos in CGT that describe something more: how the mind works and how the self is included in it. The process of the embodiment of concepts and other feelings is also described in contemplative memos here if the categories and concepts refer to them.

One useful technique for such contemplation would be meditation. This technique is aimed at concentrating on the here and now without evaluative thinking. The observation of the breath, thoughts, emotions, and feelings of the body could give insight into the flow of the thoughts that often become the codes and memos in our theoretical thinking (Konecki, 2016, 2018).

> Emotions are data too. Observation of emotions includes emotional displays not only in research subjects, but also our own emotional reactions as researchers, both in fieldwork and when analyzing field notes or other text data. (Hansen and Trank, 2016, p. 16)

We should also remember here about *the participants/collaborators of the research*, the ones who give us the information and coproduce the data with us. Their work is indispensable in achieving our research aims. The *anamnesis work* also refers to this aspect of the research into how the mind works and how it refers to the others participating in our analytical endeavor and their categories.

Finally, we should remember to use *the empathy technique* to see how the emotional and experiential level of the situation of the participants, as perceived by us, could be expressed in the naming and defining of categories.[2] Historical empathy of the situation is also needed here (Konecki, 2018, p. 13).

Lastly, we present here the specific and fundamental principles of CGT that we develop in the paper:

(1) Including participants/collaborators of the research in the process of the research and analysis.
(2) Deconstructing the concepts by working with the body, meditating, and memo writing.
(3) Mindful Coding – observing how the mind works by matching the labels to data (contemplative memo writing; see examples in Appendix 1).
(4) *Epoché* plus self-observation and self-reporting what the researcher-analyst brings to the research.

(5) The *anamnesis work* – observing how the mind works through memo writing plus the natural history of the research and analysis.

(6) Using empathy and introspection. Meditation as a preparation technique and historical contemplation/empathy could be useful here to sensitize the researcher before he/she starts writing the theory or interpreting the hypotheses.

We try to show below how the concept of CGT was created based on some inspirations from different kinds of contemplative studies in social and human sciences.

INSPIRATIONS

Constructivist grounded theory (Charmaz, 2006, 2014) is the first inspiration and the most important one that we used in constructing our approach. The constructivist grounded theory was based on the concepts of symbolic interactionism and pragmatism (Charmaz, 2008a; Bryant, 2009, 2017; Strübing, 2004, 2007). From a constructionist point of view, knowledge about the world is not acquired passively, as behaviorists or positivists believe. Knowledge is ach-ieved through our commitment to the world that we study and the meanings we attribute to our perceptions of this world. Meanings are, therefore, determined by ourselves (including researchers); they are not "outside," and we only have to discover them (Mead, 1934, pp. 76–77; Cisneros-Puebla, 2007, p. 5). It is not only a mental faculty but also a result of interacting (Blumer, 1969).

Charmaz's approach assumes that no theory offers either an interpretative portrait of the studied world or its exact image. Hidden meanings of the participants, views based on their own experiences – as well as grounded theories – are the constructs of reality (Charmaz, 2006, p. 10, 2014, p. 3). The researcher is a part of the analyzed situation and its position, privileges, perspectives, and inter-actions that influence the situation itself (Charmaz, 2008, p. 402, 2016, p. 5). It is imperative here to encode the very context of the study and the role of the researcher in it.

The use of well-established theory methods and theorizing alone are social actions that researchers construct together with other participants in the study in specific places and time periods. Therefore, we interact with the data and create theories about them. In addition, we, as researchers and humans, do not come from a social vacuum; we have previously acquired or inherited social assump-tions. The constructivist approach gives precedence to the studied phenomena and accepts both the data and their analyses as products of shared experiences as well as relations/interactions with participants in the studied area.

Constructivists investigate how – and sometimes why – participants construct meanings and actions in specific situations. We should be close to the participants' experiences, but we should also be aware that we cannot replicate these experiences. This approach not only theorizes the interpretive work that the participants perform but also admits that the created theory is an interpretation. The theory depends on the views of the researcher (view); she cannot stand outside these views (Charmaz, 2006, p. 130). Social constructionists study people's constructions and create the sociological constructions (Charmaz, 1990, p. 1161, 2016). Researchers who use GTM construct a theory from the data and, starting with the lived experiences, they can see how the world is constructed (Charmaz, 1990, p. 1162).

Constructivist grounded theorists assume a reflexive position in relation to the research process and its products, and they analyze how their theories have emerged from the data. Both data and analysis are social constructs. However, constructivists try to be aware of their assumptions and understand how they influence their research. They do not claim that the theoretical conclusions from their research are objective nor that they have emerged from the data themselves. The reconstruction of the assumptions and the situations should be very accurate. Our assumptions, interactions, and interpretations influence the social processes of constituting each stage of the research.[3] Reflexivity on the construction of a GT is inherent in GT (Charmaz, 2006, pp. 131, 132, 188, 2014, pp. 13–14, 27, 63, 82, 102, 158, 240, 344 and other pages of the book). It is connected with reflections on the interaction with the participants and also on the self-censorship of the researcher in writing the report (Mruck and Mey 2007; Gentles et al., 2014, p. 5; McGhee, Marland, and Atkinson, 2007; Swartz, 2011). We develop this reflexive stance in our paper through contemplative inspiration.

Classic grounded theory seems to be influential everywhere, thanks to Glaser's ideas regarding the sensitivity of the analysts (Glaser, 1978) and the generative process of theory building. Sensitivity is connected with the thoughtfulness of the researcher-analyst to the situation of the research when he/she generates the categories and hypotheses. The analyst should be mindful of the moments that are appropriate so as to catch new ideas of understanding the situation. Categories and possible hypotheses come to the analyst-researcher's mind, and he/she should catch them and write memos about them. For Glaser, as already mentioned, *preconscious processing* (1978, pp. 23) is important. The researchers are still in the process of analysis even during other life activities, when they rest or do not work. The process is "always on," and the moment of catching the ideas and writing them down belongs to the sensitivity skills of the analysts.

Moreover, a very important part of Classic Grounded Theory is the indication to avoid theoretical preconceptualization (Glaser, 1978, p. 3; see more in the later paragraph *Epoché in GT* in this paper). Theorists also stress here the role of embodied knowledge and the importance of the body–mind connection in theorizing (Holton and Walsh, 2017, p. 95; see also Merleau-Ponty, 2005, p. 61).

Another inspiration for creating CGT is *transformational grounded theory*, which is aimed at uncovering the philosophical background of the approach that is used by the analyst. It identifies the power relation in the research process and also tries to contribute to the transformation of part of the reality under study. TGT has a positive effect on the actions in the researched field. This methodology is inductive and participatory (Redman-MacLaren and Mills, 2015, p. 2). The authors try to establish metatheory for their research and analysis, and establish axiology, ontology, and epistemology for their branch of GT. They disclosed their values (love, social justice, equality), ontology (critical realism – constructivism refers to reality, as it is based on previous experiences and depends on perceptions of it), epistemology (knowledge is culturally and historically situated), and methodology (GT combined with participatory action research and decolonizing methodologies) (Redman-MacLaren and Mills, 2015, p. 3; see also Bainbridge et al., 2013; Bhattacharya, 2013).

It is important in TGT to include the participants in the analysis of the data. Interpretations are obtained in interpretive focus groups:

> By discussing and adapting the developing grounded theory with coresearchers who had experienced the phenomenon being studied, the final grounded theory had greater fit, grab, relevance, and modifiability than if the theory had been generated by the researcher alone. (Redman-MacLaren and Mills 2015, p. 5)

Moreover, we can also find some traces of participation in theoretical sampling by participants of the research and analysis: "In transformational grounded theory, the researcher and coresearchers decide together who will have additional information about the phenomena under study" (Redman-MacLaren and Mills, 2015, pp. 5–6). This kind of practice increases in relation to the authors' theoretical sensitivity,[4] and it also decolonizes the methodology and methodological situation when the participants are treated as equals with the academic researchers, and there is no advantage of power on the side of the academic researchers in relation to the participants. The researchers come back to the participants in the second part of the investigation to discuss the GT that is being developed. The researchers together with the participants decide on the practical recommendations in the researched field, and the participants make decisions about actions.

A significant step in developing the contemplative style of investigation was made by Carolyn Ellis (1991) although she did not use the term contemplation. She developed the concept of *sociological introspection*, which concerns research into emotions. This research technique gives access to private experiences. Introspection for her is a sociological process that "...can generate interpretive materials from self and others useful for understanding the lived experience of emotions" (Ellis, 1991, p. 26). She also introduces "interactive introspection examinations" with research collaborators to reflect together on the subjective part of cognition and experiencing the emotions. Generally, researchers do not want to admit that they have to deal with introspection in the field or while analyzing the empirical materials. Introspection for Ellis is a *covert communicative behavior*. There is an internal dialog that is done with the symbols, while an internal conversation always takes place when we deal with others. The observation of the internal dialog is an important part of introspection (Ellis, 1991, pp. 28–29). What is significant in Ellis' approach is expressed in the following statement: "Sociologists, however, can generate interpretive materials about the lived experience of emotions by studying their own self-dialogue in process" (Ellis, 1991). So, the researcher's internal dialog could be a source of data. The introspection could be materialized, and we could have evidence of the "internal" dialogs:

> In summary, introspection can be accomplished in dialogue with self, and represented in the form of fieldnotes, or narratives; or it can be accomplished in dialogue with others, or by reading and analyzing their journals or free writing, where subjects write non-stop about what they are thinking and feeling and what it means to them. (Ellis, 1991, p. 32)

The techniques of materializing introspection include an "introspective journal," where the authors describe openly and sincerely their internal thoughts and emotions. Introspection is represented as a narrative text (Ellis, 1991, p. 45). What is important in this approach is the intention to observe the real internal process of dealing with emotions without building into it the rational model of human being/researcher. Although theoretical thinking is difficult to include in this kind of approach, we try to do it in CGT (see the next paragraphs).

Holistic ethnography is another inspiration for CGT (Davis and Breede, 2015). The authors compare their approach to the practice of meditation. Holistic ethnography is:

> ...a conscious awareness of experience in which the researcher intentionally and variously focuses her attention on physical sensations, emotions, contemplation, and dialogue to contribute to deep sensemaking and critical examination. (Davis and Breede, 2015, p. 77)

The term holistic refers to multidimensional analysis and suggests a focus on the embodiment of the smell, taste, touch, sound, and sight of the researched phenomena. The approach also uses introspection as a method of understanding and interpretation. Researchers have to immerse themselves in the phenomena subjectively and also to look at it from outside.

> Contemplating with our minds frees us to reflect on the experience and find meaning in it, through sustained contemplation, active visualization of historical positionalities, and intentional and contemplative projection of ourselves across temporal and spatial boundaries. (Davis and Breede, 2015, pp. 79–80; see also Hesse-Biber and Piatelli, 2007)

The method of holistic ethnography consists of four stages of the contemplative process that makes understanding the phenomena deeper and more multidimensional:

(1) Embodied experience: This is achieved by plunging into the field and experiencing it with the senses (Davis and Breede, 2015, p. 81). Researchers take field notes, photographs, and videos of what is around them. After going to the computer, they use the method of introspection to write a narrative using what was written and observed while in the field (see Ellis, 1991).

(2) Emotion/transcendence: In this stage, researchers try to put themselves into the position of the subject (in their case, into the positions of enslaved Africans) and try to feel their emotions as if they were in their situation. Journaling is useful to catch and name the emotions. Some researchers also write poetry on the emotional experiences from the field.

(3) Contemplation/reflection: In this stage, researchers try to understand and catch the meaning of their experiences. Davis and Breede tried to look at the situation from many positions sociologically (different roles), historically, and geographically (different spaces) too (Davis and Breede, 2015, p. 82). Writing, while introspecting about it, was a process of getting these kinds of meanings: "We can't understand fully from the artifacts, but by listening to

their voices, by attempting to feel their emotions, by allowing our body, spirit, and mind to guide us, we can begin to approach empathy. This is an intuitive methodology" (Davis and Breede, 2015, p. 89).

(4) Dialog: This is a way of going from an individual understanding to a communal one. It starts with a dialog with the other researchers and also experts from different fields of investigation. The discussions are related to the research and writings of the researcher. The dialog is also done with the researchers themselves (Davis and Breede, 2015, p. 82). Dialog is about the limitations of the researchers because of where they come from: "But I am simply too privileged to fully wrap my heart around what it was like to be a slave, or even what it is like to be a person of African descent living in the US today…Even my gender is situated in the context of whiteness; my grandparent's poverty is situated in the context of whiteness; my ethnicity, institutionalized faith, and age are situated in the context of whiteness" (Davis and Breede, 2015, p. 90–91).

Through dialog, researchers transcend ethnographic understanding (Davis and Breede, 2015, p. 93).

While turning all their field notes and journals into a narrative about the experience, the investigators write the research report. Narratives make it possible to see the situation holistically. "We suggest that holistic ethnography is necessarily a jointly constructed, sensory, dialogic project with others. Multiple people can play multiple roles, each focusing on the different elements of the process in turn" (Davis and Breede, 2015, p. 95). We can add here one important quote as summarizing the above approach: "Fieldwork is intensely personal; our positionality (i.e., position based on class, sex, ethnicity, race, etc; Bainbridge et al., 2013; Swartz, 2011, pp. 54–56) and who we are as persons (shaped by the socio-economic and political environment) play a fundamental role in the research process, in the field as well as in the final text. Reflexivity must then be a part of our commitment (Denzin, 2006; Garot 2013) and political understanding of the situation of research and our theoretical background (Denzin, 1992). It must become a duty of every researcher to reveal and share these reflexivities, not only for learning purposes but towards enhancing theory building" (Palaganas et al., 2017, p. 428).

Another inspiration which was very important for us was *mindful inquiry and transformative phenomenology*, as elaborated by Valerie Malhotra Bentz (Rehorick and Bentz, 2008; Bentz, 1995). Phenomenology seeks essential features of the phenomena and tries to uncover the meaning of a lived experience in the everyday lifeworld (Bentz, 1995, p. 3). A phenomenological inquiry deepens one's awareness and leads to the process of transforming individuals. While performing research, we can finally see the phenomena and self in a different way. We can more deeply analyze the answers to the question "Who are we?" Phenomenology redirects us to a direct experience as being the basis of our knowledge. "The endpoints of phenomenological work are descriptions of essential structures of experience (following Husserl) and/or rich descriptions of lifeworlds (following Schutz)" (Rehorick and Bentz, 2008, p. 6).

While studying phenomenology and carrying out research, we can transform ourselves. We can say that it is not an applied humanistic science; it is instead an *applied understanding from the point of view of phenomenology*. By finding the foundational feature of the phenomena, we can deepen our understanding of the lifeworld. Rehorick and Bentz offer some basic phenomenological techniques with regard to eidetic phenomenology: bracketing, imaginative variations, and horizontalization.

The so-called *"phenomenological reduction"* (*epoché*), that is, bracketing our assumed conceptual frameworks that structure our perceptions and experiences, is essential in any phenomenological study (Rehorick and Bentz, 2008, pp. 11–12; Christensen and Brumfield, 2010). Thus, it becomes clear that *epoché* allows us to study intentionality instead of causality, while also preventing us from reifying concepts and phenomena (Englander, 2016; Hycner, 1985). It is crucial to elicit the essential characteristics of the phenomenon without using our epistemic and socialized filters. This method was proposed by Edmund Husserl ([1954] 1970). The first level of bracketing is to suspend what we have learned about the phenomenon from scientific studies, accepted theories, and other legitimated sources of knowledge. Next, one must bracket the notions about the phenomenon stemming from one's cultural milieu (Rehorick and Bentz, 2008, p. 12). This knowledge is embedded in the language by typifications and cognitive constructs, which have been internalized and used by ourselves in naming people and objects (Schutz, [1932] 1967, 1970).

Imaginative variation(s) is another technique of phenomenological inquiry, and it is used while scrutinizing the protocols. Here, we seek different meanings by using imagination, various reference frameworks, different perspectives, positions, roles, and functions to fully, and in an all-encompassing manner, describe the structures of our experience as well as its significant attributes. Thanks to using imaginative variations, we are able to distinguish between attributes which are random and those which are necessary for the phenomenon (Rehorick and Bentz, 2008, pp. 14–15; see also Bentz and Shapiro, 1998, p. 99).

The third technique applicable to phenomenological reduction is *horizontalization*. What is essential here is the creation of a context for realizing a phenomenon within a certain experience of the *here and now*.

> *Horizontalization* involves making the elements in a situation equal and putting that situation at a distance to better view it, without assumptions or bias. Normally, we think of some elements as much more important than others. Horizontalization gives each element equal value, opening up possibilities for seeing things differently and changing one's perspective. (Rehorick and Bentz, 2008, p. 16; see also Bentz and Shapiro, 1998, p. 99; Hycner, 1985)

Another stimulus for our concept of CGT is *contemplative qualitative inquiry*, as presented by Valerie Janesick (2015). Janesick is inspired by Zen Buddhism. She accents stillness and silence in research. It means that the practice of meditation and mindfulness is very useful to reach such states of mind to improve insight and concentration while doing research. She sees parallels between Zen and contemplative qualitative inquiry. The main parallel for her is *holism*, followed by *the relationship in the context, body, and mind as instruments of knowing* and *the ethics of no harm and storytelling* (Janesick, 2015, p. 34).

So, how does she define contemplative qualitative research? This practical concept is useful for those of us using qualitative methods to make sense of people's lives; we are connected to our participant/s whether or not we wish to be. I call this approach contemplative qualitative inquiry. The contemplative component has to do with the stillness and silence of thinking with a meditative orientation. It is my intention that this book begins a conversation about these ideas (Janesick, 2015, p. 22). Elsewhere she writes: "I use the term contemplative inquiry to refer to qualitative techniques that place a deep and serious emphasis on thought in every component of a study of the social world" (Janesick, 2015, p. 34). So, the thinking process and the thoughts of the researcher are an important part of qualitative research, and it is important to be aware of how the process is activated. Qualitative research is for understanding not for explaining the causes, according to Janesick. Then, it is essential to get the meaning of the phenomena, not the causes. The phenomenon changes under some conditions, and the causality is conditional and situational, but it could also be questioned.

Research is, for Janesick, a contemplation in action (Janesick, 2015, p. 36). It is very similar to the approach of Rehorick and Bentz (2008) that we mentioned above (compare also Priya, 2010). The interview is a contemplative act for Janesick, where the self of the researcher should *vanish* (Janesick, 2015, see Chapter 3); the interview is also an act of compassion (Janesick, 2015, Chapter 4). We should achieve the state of no-self while interviewing. Being mindful during research is very helpful in describing the situation. Meditation could be used as a tool for increasing the attentiveness in the interview and concentrating on the here and now, and what the interview says to us.

> The act of observation helps students to remove themselves from the observation and become squarely focused on their description of the object, setting, or person. It is the enactment of non-self. (Janesick, 2015, p. 47; see also Giorgino, 2016, pp. 172–175)

It is very helpful in the self-observation to write reflective journals and even poetry. We should also be aware of our emotions and work on the emotions:

> Go to the interview prepared, use all your active listening skills, relax, and enjoy the interview. Put aside any roadblocks obstructing your ability to hear data. Breathe, be calm, and hear the data. (Janesick, 2015, p. 62)

The author should also take into consideration the reaction of the participants to the research report. If we want to keep the research ethical and credible at the same time, we should refer not only to the meanings and definitions of the situation of the participants but also to their interpretation of the meanings that we elaborated and presented to them.

INCLUDING THE PARTICIPANTS/COLLABORATORS OF THE RESEARCH IN THE PROCESS OF THE RESEARCH AND ANALYSIS

We have noticed that many researchers now call the people that they study participants or collaborators, or coresearchers (Charmaz, 2006, 2014, 2016; Redman-MacLaren and Mills, 2015; Janesick, 2015). We can notice the turn toward evaluating the subjectivity of the people that were usually called *respondents*. The research situation is such that the so-called *respondents* are the real participants of the research. The release of the information and talks about their perception of the world and experiences are very important and without which the investigators could not do their research. Participants often become collaborators when we ask them about their opinions on the research data or research results. Sometimes, they provide us with the names of categories that we use in the analyses. The idea of participating in research is more democratic, and paradoxically objective, because we do not create the fiction of being separated from the research and not influencing the results. The same is true for the analysis. Our codes often come from the participants. Very often, we code during the interview or observation. Even if it is not conscious coding, we remember the labels from the field and bring them to our notebooks later. The participants are the authors of the codes and sometimes of the categories. It is fairer and more ethical to name and include the participants in the analysis, or to be frank about their influence or authorship of our codes or interpretations that we express in the memos and later in the theories.

THE DECONSTRUCTION OF CONCEPTS BY WORK ON THE BODY, MEDITATING AND MEMO WRITING

The deconstruction of concepts does not mean refusing their meanings but contextualizing them and coming to a new understanding. By contextualizing phenomena, named in the research by concepts, in the *here and now*, we are offered a different view; the concepts are embodied in the lifeworld, and we are able to construct new meanings (Konecki, 2016).

When a researcher meditates, he becomes able to see beyond the phenomenon of a text or language expressions; he encounters something much more basic to reality; it is in meditative practice that other deconstructive and constructive efforts start. The contemplation practice starts there. Sociologists who meditate know this experience very well. Understanding the experience of meditation practice could change our methodological practice as well.

Dualistic thinking about the self still prevails in social research, operating in the dimension of the self–other duality and even the I–Me duality related to the internal dialog (Immergut and Kaufman, 2014; see also Mead, 1934, pp. 174–175). Charles H. Cooley's (1909) concept of the "looking-glass self" is a good example of how constructivism helped to shape modern sociology. This concept states that self does not exist without others' perceptions and our perceptions of their perceptions. This self is chronically anxious, all the time looking for the evaluations of others and afraid of negative estimations from them (p. 5). In the practice of not thinking, this social conditioning of self disappears because a person is in an "identity vacuum." And that is what is real; the rest is a delusion. This might be one of the directions to pursue in developing anti-essentialist sociology, and GTM, too.

The research on cemeteries was painful for many of my collaborators and for me sometimes, too. Here is an example from my contemplative memos on dealing with the *essential* thinking about the self that was the basis for the fear of death (see also Appendix 2):

Memos on the fear of death.

When I was alone at the cemetery, I felt the fear of death. I felt the same when I coded the data on the others' visits to the cemeteries. I was thinking that nothing will be left of me when I die; that my life and all the efforts I have made are not worth anything. I have witnessed the lack of interest people have in people who are already dead.

Not believing in God and the after-life, I thought about the lack of meaning in suffering, and even helping others here and now. However, in the meantime, I practiced meditation. I ask myself while breathing in: "Who am I"; and I answer while breathing out: "I do not know." Many times, many hours, many days. My feeling of the ego and self deteriorated a little. After that, I performed a thought experiment: what it would be or would happen to me and the others if there was no self? No borders between me and others? And I discovered that everything would be the same, life would be smoother, no defense of ego, less suffering and better relations with others. If "I" die, nobody dies, because I am a small part of others' things and phenomena that are related to each other, and when there is a lack of one element, others come to fill this place and everything goes on as before. No borders, only connections. I am a part of this interdependent world and I, in some sense, co-created it. So, dying is a fiction, nothing really dies. Only the fear of the dead ego fills me with great discomfort, but when the ego disappears, there will be no fear of death, no worries, no suffering.

The world is wonderfully organized; it has a sense, although I do not understand it fully or maybe at all. It does not matter for me now. Nothing specific in me. The self is only a thought. Death is only a thought. No-thought – No-self – No-suffering. Where is the fear of death? (contemplative memo of the author)

Deconstruction is also connected with the contemplation of signlessness. A *sign* is an object of our perception. Signs are the cause of our deceptions, illusions, and often our sufferings. By breaking through the signs, we can touch the reality they are covering:

As long as we are caught by signs – round, square, solid, liquid, gas – we will suffer. Nothing can be described in terms of just one sign. But without signs, we feel anxious. Our fear and attachment come from our being caught in signs. Until we touch the signless nature of things, we will continue to be afraid and to suffer. Before we can touch H_2O, we have to let go of signs like squareness, roundness, hardness, heaviness, lightness, up, and down. Water is, in itself, neither square nor round nor solid. When we free ourselves from signs, we can enter the heart of reality. But until we can see the ocean in the sky, we are still caught by signs. (Nhat, 1999, p. 89)

Nhat (1999) recommends that politicians, economists, and educators should practice signlessness. I think that social scientists should do the same; they can understand that signs, words, and phrases commonly used in everyday life are misleading and deficient.

Below is a fragment from a research report on experiencing the cemetery and of a memo on *bracketing* some signs and etiquette of the phenomenon (fear). The signlessness could be practiced while coding in such a way:

> She wrote that she is afraid of loneliness, death, while I approach it differently. It is known that one day it awaits each of us. I think that it is not worth wasting time on the fear of it, because it is normal.

However, we can understand this reaction more when we know that her father is dead. So the biographical situation of the co-researcher could influence coding and interpreting data.

ON THE CODING PROCEDURE

Coding is not free from our preconceptions. We bring the stock of knowledge at hand from the technical literature that we have read and from our previous experience. The following quotation explains it more:

> So the experienced analyst learns to play the game of believing everything and believing nothing – at this point – leaving himself or herself as open as the coding itself. For all that, the coding is grounded in data on the page as well as on the conjunctive experiential data, including the knowledge of technical literature which the analyst brings into the inquiry. (Strauss, 1987, p. 29)

Conceptualization could be hastened if we were able to leave our field materials and look at the field a little bit from the outside. However, this moment of looking back should be caught in awareness and testified in the memo. Our mind starts to work, and it produces codes and memos too. So, the memos should also be the object of reflection. Writing memos on memos is also a contemplative effort to catch our mind in the production of theoretical codes. Here is an example from my research on the perception of the cemetery space and self-feelings:

> Memo (2) on my memo above, (see memo on the previous page) "On the fear of death."

> I am not sure if my previous memo on the self, ego and the fear of death is not filled with preconceptions connected with refusing the preconceptions. Meditation gives me a feeling of peace, the smooth flow of consciousness and a lessening attachment to ego and fears, including the fear of death. But at the back of my mind, there is still some hesitation about whether I can lose the fear of death, because of my individual feeling and claim of having permanent ego. The thought is coming back. So, not all the fears disappeared... Should I return to mediation? And observe the fear? Or accept it as it is? So, the concept of the fear of death is in suspension. If it is experiential, it never gives the certainty of being real. The experience temporarily gives insight into the phenomenon that exists, but always in suspension. It comes and goes...

> In the previous memos, I wanted to solve the problem of the fear of death once and for all. That was my claim, but it came from the fear of death... The fear of the researcher and the human being at the same time.

The categories and codes could be derived from the existing literature, but they should be coded in terms of conditions and consequences (Strauss, 1987, p. 283). So, they are not taken as they are, they should be fitted to the data and context.

Labeling the data with categories from grand theories (Goffman, Garfinkel, and Marx) to exemplify their ideas should be avoided; "Such labeling is useless and should be avoided like the plague" (Strauss, 1987, p. 283) However, the theories could be used as a sensitizing instrument if they do not block the discovery of new categories. Similarly, reading the technical literature could be helpful in choosing the research topic (Strauss, 1987, p. 273) or in coding data (Strauss, 1987, p. 283), or in sensitizing the researcher in analyzing the data (Thornberg, 2012, p. 255). Strauss even suggests that there is a possibility to generate a theory from another theory if it is grounded. It could be a good springboard to elaborate new categories and theoretical propositions. (Strauss, 1987, p. 283).

The problem of GT very often mentioned in different publications is as follows: how can we avoid preconceptualization if we are researchers that are educated in theories? How can we forget about what we have learned before? How can we avoid our everyday life stereotypes and categorization of objects, actions, and other people? Some researchers state it clearly:

> ...it remains unclear *how* a theoretically sensitive researcher can use previous theoretical knowledge to avoid drowning in the data. If one takes into account the frequent warnings not to force theoretical concepts on the data one gets the impression that a grounded theorist is advised to introduce suitable theoretical concepts ad hoc drawing on implicit theoretical knowledge but should abstain from approaching the empirical data with ex-ante formulated hypotheses. (Kelle, 2005, p. 9)

Could we formulate some rules to solve this difficult problem? Some researchers proposed, for example, group discussions: "The researchers' own questions, their prior understanding and, related to this, their own prejudices concerning the research issue can be worked out by means of brainstorming and group discussions" (Bohm, 2004, p. 270). Working in a group while analyzing the data is often practiced in GT-style research (Strauss, 1987). Some authors try to be very thoughtful concerning the metatheoretical framework that they adapted at the beginning of the research and how it informs them in the research and data analysis as Hoddy (2019) did, adopting the critical realism as a metatheory in the GT style of research.

EPOCHÉ IN GROUNDED THEORY

Limited Preconceptualization

If the theory is *generated* and *discovered*, as the creators of GTM want it to be, it should not be rooted, to a great extent, in existing theories and concepts (Glaser and Strauss, 1967). GT is generated from data and fitted to the data. The method of generating theory deviates from verification rhetoric, so it is not based mainly on logical and deductive reasoning.

Should we read the literature from the research field before doing research? Anselm Strauss strongly inspired by symbolic interactionism and pragmatism (Charmaz, 2008a; Bryant, 2009), answers that question positively – we should read to increase theoretical sensitivity.

> For theoretical sensitivity, wide reading in the literature of one's field and related disciplines is very useful, and probably requisite: not for specific ideas or for a scholarly knowledge, but for authors' perspectives and ways of looking at social phenomena, which can help to sensitize one to theoretical issues. (Strauss, 1987, p. 300)

Classic Grounded Theory, which is represented by Glaser and his school after the split with Strauss and his critics of Constructivist Grounded Theory (Glaser, 1992, 1998, 2002; Holton and Walsh, 2017), accents *emergence* as a pillar of GT. Preconceptualization of the research and analysis is criticized here. The emergence could be stopped by "preconceptions that frequently derail GT intentions" (Holton and Walsh, 2017, p. 32).

The literature review should not be conducted until the core category has emerged. The literature could later be treated as data and analyzed and used in theoretical sampling (Holton and Walsh, 2017, pp. 29 and 33). According to Classic Grounded Theory, theorizing by the researcher is done in rupture with the existing literature; it is not incremental theorizing (theorizing with existing concepts). Rupture theorizing uses new and nascent concepts that were not used before.

Epoché

We can propose here a solution to this tension between emergence and the extant knowledge of the researcher. We draw this solution from the phenomenological concept of *epoché*. We can say that some intuitions of *epoché* are in the works of Glaser (1998), who is fully aware of how the researcher's preconceptions included in his/her worldview could influence the analysis (Holton and Walsh, 2017, p. 47). Therefore, he gave the following advice to researchers:

> The first step in gaining theoretical sensitivity is to enter the research setting with as few predetermined ideas as possible – especially logically deduced, a priori hypotheses ... to remain open to what actually is happening. (Glaser, 1978, p. 3; Holton and Walsh, 2017, p. 48)

Glaser then saw the necessity of limiting preconceptualization and entering the field with an open mind, one that could be the most open when it was free from preconceptions and extant knowledge.

For Classic Grounded Theory (represented by Glaser and his followers, Holton and Walsh (2017), coding is indispensable for the generation of categories and theory:

> A fundamental criterion for coding is a suspension of any preconceived notions about what the data should reveal. Accordingly, a grounded theorist doesn't employ a redefined set of codes assumed to be relevant. (Holton and Walsh, 2017, p. 82)

The suspension could be done using the phenomenological inspiration, as we have written in previous paragraphs. We can list our preconceptions from the scientific world and the lifeworld to see what the influence is of these worlds on our thinking during coding. To what extent are we returning to the ultimate reality of everyday life in our perception of the social and psychological life of the participants?

Especially important here is mindful coding; that is, in the process of coding, the researcher is aware of how the mind works during the analysis of the data. It is connected with a description of the experience GT theorizing. We can find examples of such theoretical memos written by students in the Holton and Walsh book (2017, pp. 89–90). We think, however, that such notes should be written not only by beginners in GT but also by more advanced analysts. They are more strongly influenced by existing theories. We can also see when we write such mindful memos and how we react to our way of working. The contemplative memo is this reaction.

Here is an extract from my research report on the observation of the cemetery by one of the students. Thinking in scientific categories (e.g. social structure) and using commonsense procedures of thinking (comparative thinking, normative thinking) could filter our perception of the reality in front of us:

The observer is aware of his assumptions about the social structure and aesthetics of the cemetery graves. While observing the cemetery and describing it, he thinks as a sociologist. He has had in mind sociological concepts, such as social structure (social stratification, the intelligentsia, the middle class). He testifies to it in the following contemplative memo:

My work is based on the observation of the same cemetery I described on All Saints Day, that it, the so-called "old cemetery" at Ogrodowa street. It is my favorite necropolis in Łódź because it is full of trees, which makes the place nice and friendly, although I am not sure if these words are really good to describe a cemetery. Besides, it is the oldest necropolis in the city, so we can see graves from the end of the 19th century. They are very nice pieces of art. One more thing that seems to be important, and I wrote about it in my first observation, is that we can see at this cemetery social stratification; mainly, the cemetery is devoted to people who belonged to the intelligentsia, the middle classes etc., and even during socialist times, the image of the cemetery did not change too much and the art of the graves was of a higher quality than at other cemeteries, which we can see now visiting these places in Łódź. I think that this general impression influences my reception of this commentary.

Another coresearcher is aware of the normative frame of reference that is connected with the values and convictions about behaving properly in a certain place at a certain time. He also compares his own convictions with those of others (see the extract below from my research report):

Emotions are connected with satisfactory coding (as happiness) and with a normative frame of reference. What is important here is the social norm about "what should we feel at a particular place at a certain moment in time?" The feeling of sadness is also connected with the "normative frame" of All Saint's Day, when we can see improper behavior at the cemetery while coding:

During the open coding, I felt happiness when I read about the habits and some activities which are an important part of the celebration. I felt some kind of approval that I had also taken part in the celebration, so what this person wrote is similar to my description, and we share the same values. But generally, I wondered what the graveyard looked like when she or he was there. I mean, I imagined what this person had described. What this cemetery looked like then, what the tombstones looked like, or if it was was dark then or not, etc. I also felt resignation, because I will also die some day, and some group of students will contemplate their feelings next to my grave. This is unavoidable; nobody can escape from death.

I felt sadness when I was reading about how the holiday is losing importance. I was worried about what it might be like in the future. I also felt anger that people ruin this event with their bad behavior.

For the students that we quote above, imagination and empathy are very important parts of reading and coding the protocol:

> One very important process of the mind is **comparative thinking**. While coding, analysts have in mind the memories of their experiences and a description of them. They refer to them in the description of the feelings during coding. This phenomenon should be taken into account while coding and theorizing. If we would like to suspend our personal knowledge for a moment, we should be attentive to the phenomenon of comparisons. It is difficult to avoid this process of our mind. Intentionality is an arch connecting us with the objects, but also with objects from the past. Past experiences are alive and awaken when we try to understand another person's feelings and thoughts. Our past experiences are the frame to understand them.
>
> While we analyze the feelings and thoughts that appear during the coding, we can notice the strength of **normative thinking** (the second mind's procedure). How important might it be in coding and theorizing? We should take the phenomenon into consideration. The idea of proper behavior always gets into the descriptions of feelings aroused by other behaviors. The feelings are attached to observed behaviors, but they are surrounded by the frame of reference of norms, in this case, what the behaviors of visitors to the cemetery should look like. It is interesting that normative thinking is transferred from the visits and experiences to the cemetery to the coding situation. The participants in both situations refer to the norms regarding how to behave and what to feel during the day at the cemetery.

THE ANAMNESIS WORK

Observing How the Mind Works through Memo Writing Plus the Natural History of Research and Analysis

A fundamental feature of GTM is the awareness of what we are doing at the moment. Anselm Strauss was very aware of it when he wrote on the subject in his very instructive handbook from 1987:

> *Raising awareness and self-awareness.* A very important aspect of teaching grounded theory methods is the raising of students' awareness of analytic operations and their own use of them. It is one thing to utilize those more or less appropriately, and another to have a keen awareness of just which ones are being used, why, how, whether effective or not; but also, when some should be used but aren't being used, and which ones they themselves use well and others not so well.... To supplement this tactic, the instructor may occasionally query: What's going on now? Or the class may be asked to summarize what has been happening during the last ten or twenty or thirty minutes. (Strauss, 1987, p. 297)

This awareness is not only important to beginners but also to more advanced researchers, and this awareness should be extended to include other activities that are apart of research and generating the GT, such as writing.

Writing Is an Activity without Which There Would Be No Theory
How does writing as an activity generate ideas, labels, categories, or concepts? Writing means more than simply describing something; while writing, we are entering a new sphere of existence that allows us to jump off the mundane world. Writing also creates us as well as the theory.[5] The thinking process in writing *draws us in*; writing needs terms/words and relations between the words. So, the style of writing generates the style of theoretical memos and, in consequence, the theory. The fiction that we create is embedded not in the data but in the writing

about the data. The movements of the fingers on the keyboard or movements of the fingers with a pen are embedded theoretical activities. Theorizing is not only thinking (theoretically, abstractly) but also doing it by hand. So, what I can write can become part of the theory. What I cannot write is not included in the theory. Why? What is left behind in my writing? This question is important in our mindful memoing (as I am memoing now). What do I not consider data, or important data, or data that are worth writing about?

We should also think about the cognitive and emotional functions of memo writing for the theorist/writer. Memos increase the cognitive and memory power of the researcher and decrease his/her uncertainty. Very often, we experience wonder when we write and suddenly discover new impressions, connections, and interpretations that we had never thought about writing before. So, would it be possible to generate theory without the physical act of writing? Would it be possible to generate theory while only thinking and memorizing and developing the ideas in the mind? Is the discovering possible by writing about our main experience in theorizing? Are we *planners* in writing or *discoverers* (*planners* have all the ideas in their mind before writing; discoverers can find out the ideas while writing; Chandler, 1992; McEachern, 1984)? If we are planners, how do we discover a new theory? If we are discoverers, the writing is the main activity in discovering GT. Alternatively, maybe we are both planners and discoverers? So, when does the perspective change? What is the main kind of experience in the work of an analyst? Is it a discovery of some truths about self?

Meeting others in our mind is meeting ourselves. Here is a contemplative memo from one of the research participants (conducting research on experiencing the cemetery). By writing, we also discover some truth about ourselves:

> The writing of memos could be a time of **auto-reflection and discovering some truths about the self**. The activity of writing **becomes a tool of self-discovery**. This auto-reflection shows that the subject had not been aware that we have particular qualities; however, while writing, she discovers them and becomes aware of them:

> By coding my work, I concluded that I am saddened by the way I think about people. Both in the first and second work on the visit to the cemetery, I didn't say anything good about them (even in the poem [I wrote] I am sorry for them). And it frightened me. I don't consider myself a bad person, and I even like to meet other people, but ... right? But what? It's bad that the way we write (often without thinking about it) reveals so many things about us - and things that we don't suspect at first glance.

And one final question connected with writing: Does the theorist need a body to create a theory? Why is the body so often forgotten as an agent? Do we have here the phenomenon of an absent body (Leder, 1990)?

Classic GT puts the stress on the *manuality* of theorizing. According to Holton and Walsh (2017, p. 95), we should "do whatever [we] can to stimulate *hand-eye-brain* cognitive and preconscious processing through manual coding, memoing and sorting procedures." They go on to say,

> The physical act of hand sorting memos further facilitates the preconscious processing of matured ideas and guides organization and integration of overall theory. Many researchers use sticky notes to help with their theoretical sorting. (Holton and Walsh, 2017, p. 109)

Manual coding and sorting is needed, so classic grounded theorists also noticed the role of the body (here, it is the hand in manual coding and memo writing) in generating theory.

We need mindful memos to see how the theory is created, not only from the data but also from the situated experience of the writing theorist. The "I" comes to experience after the act, hereafter conceiving the category, property, or hypotheses. The "I" as a reaction is not certain, so some serendipitous potential is included naturally in the situation of analyzing the data (see Mead, 1934, pp. 174–176). The self-observation and reporting of the interaction of "I" and "Me" can show how we are influenced by others in "generating" categories and hypotheses. The mind is a product of social interactions in a concrete environment (Mead, 1934, p. 126; Misheva, 2009, p. 162). We are in some interactions with the real and the imagined others from our Academic World. We follow the rules, and we know what we should avoid (Mead, 1934, p. 121).

What is interesting in Classic GT is that it is serendipitous and systematic:

> Glaser does not view logic and intuition as diametrically opposed but rather as twin foundations for theory generation. The theorizing process in GT operates at both conscious and a preconscious level to process and organize empirically grounded, analytically induced concepts. (Holton and Walsh, 2017, p. 91)

If it is true, we should be very mindful to analyze the relations and how they work for the analyst *here and now* when he/she creates/generates theoretical ideas.

What does it mean when special emotions emerge during coding or memo writing? There could be a passage from the tedious coding to "excitements when the new concepts emerged reigniting my motivation as memos become more full and vibrant with new ideas and connections" (Breckenridge, 2013, quoted in Holton and Walsh, 2017, p. 92). What does this experience mean? If we experience excitement, then it is the moment to capture the ideas of concepts. And the motivation appears which probably connects the excitement's moments with the generation of concepts, which is so vital to GT analysts. We should be aware of this experience and see also the role of the body (writing, manual coding) because it is invaluable to the generation of theory.[6] Touching is important in our life when dealing with other living beings (Konecki, 2008) but also with immaterial things (Konecki, 2011). Touching the paper or other utensils for writing could be a very personal and meaningful experience for GT theorists. In this way, touching becomes some kind of interaction. Martin Heidegger said that our thinking could be mechanized if we use a machine to express the words and refuse to let the hand do it (Chandler, 1992, p. 69).

Contemplative memos can be created by describing the history of our minding and creating the ideas, categories, and hypotheses. Sometimes, field researchers write the natural history of research, which is a very important part of the research report to evaluate, finally, the results of the investigation. However, it would be imperative to include in it the *natural history of analysis*, to present the trajectory of generating the theory and mind-analytical work on it. We could see also how the mind has been working on the trajectory of theorizing. It could also help the evaluators to see how the theory was created and where the ideas come from.

Using Empathy and Introspection

Meditation could be a preparation technique, and historical contemplation could be useful here to sensitize the researcher before he/she starts writing the theory or interpreting hypotheses.

It should be emphasized that we should see our interconnectedness with the world. The observation of self, mind, and body can be useful here. However, what is important here is to observe the reaction of others that are often in us by incorporating their attitudes (Mead, 1934). Observation is possible when we are skillful in the mindful being *here and now*, when we are aware of our body's feelings, thoughts, and emotions without evaluating them. The practice of mindful meditation is associated with concentration and being attentive to the present moment (Kabat-Zinn, 1994; Konecki, 2016). The moments of generating ideas in the GT process could be mindfully observed. We can get to know how they were generated and who their author is. Who is the analyst (Who am I?)? How is he/she connected with the other participants in the research? Here, we have an example from my research on experiencing the cemetery – what a big surprise it was for the research participant when she found big differences between herself and the others and, consequently, when she faced the problem of finding similarities to create the pattern (which is so important in GT):

> Discovering the truth about the self is connected with experiencing emotions and also with comparing the experiences of other visitors with one's own. One of the students discovered that her **experiences are completely different from the others'**:
>
> While coding the work of my colleagues (the first visit to the cemetery), I felt curious, sometimes astonished. Their feelings and views differed from mine, which is why I found it very interesting. While coding, I was wondering if I was interpreting their feelings properly. I also wondered if I could agree with them, but after encoding and analyzing their interpretation, I found that everyone sees the world in a completely different way. I thought that none of those people saw it like I do. It may indicate my sensitivity, or the possibility of looking further, deeper.

During meditation, the *Other* appears in the battle of our thoughts when we want to define and separate the self ("I") from the *Other*. We try to be distinct. However, we can quickly see that it is impossible to be outside of the *Other* completely. Being aware of self becomes *being aware of other* at the same time. I cannot understand the *Other* without understanding the self (and the opposite is also true). The meaning is cocreated in the internal dialog. What we often consider to be "noise," the thoughts that are not connected with our analytical work, could be very important for generating ideas, even if we do not see the connection immediately. But stopping on the *here and now*, and being *in here* not *out there*, could give one the awareness of connections that are not always direct and based on "similarities," but which work on the "opposition rule."

Empathy should also relate to the historical context of our activity as mindful analysts. Historical empathy should take into consideration the following three aspects to see the *Other* and the situation:

- " Historical Contextualization – a temporal sense of difference that includes deep understanding of the social, political, and cultural norms of the time period under investigation as well as knowledge of the events leading up to the historical situation and other relevant events that are happening concurrently.

- Perspective Taking – understanding of another's prior lived experience, principles, positions, attitudes, and beliefs in order to understand how that person might have thought about the situation in question.

- Affective Connection – consideration for how historical figures' lived experiences, situations, or actions may have been influenced by their affective response based on a connection made to one's own similar yet different life experiences" (Endacott, 2013, p. 43; see also Zahavi, 2001).

We can adapt this concept to the analysis of the researcher's immersion in the history. While performing such an analysis, we should refer to our own experiences and how they developed in time. The *historical contextualization* should reflect on our self and how it is related to the concept of community and individuality. Cultural norms and the political immersion of our scientific activities should be contemplated and revealed. How does the bureaucracy of academia (granting the research) influence what I can and cannot do or think as a social researcher? What kind of research is it possible to carry out now and what was possible before? Am I in the historical process of change in the perspectives of research? How does the current journal ranking fetishism (Willmot, 2011) influence my way of writing and revealing research results? How does it influence our possibility to be empathetic toward the research participants (Hansen and Trank, 2016, pp. 1–2)?

We should also take into consideration our *own perspectives* from the past that have changed or are under the process of transformation, and how the current research and analysis change us (see Rehorick and Bentz, 2008, *Transformative phenomenology*; see also Priya, 2010; Swartz, 2011). [7] What did we believe in before and what was our position in the scientific world? Did our courage to proclaim new ideas increase when we became professors? Or is just the opposite happening? Is GTM more accepted now than when I started my scientific career and began using it?

Affectivity should be one of the goals of the metaanalysis. Our emotions and body immersions in a situation influence the taken perspective even if we want to be objective and eliminate our emotional responses (McKinzie, 2017). We are emotional beings not only in the research situation but also in the academic world. We envy other's success; we dislike some kind of researchers and research (sometimes we are angry, or we even hate others). Our motivation is based on the emotional sources that we produced in the past and that we consciously create now. Emotions are in our bodies, carrying us through the twists and turns of research, and we should be mindful of them. Also, the emotional culture of Academia should be considered: what kind of emotions can we express openly and what should be suppressed?

The observation and situating of *Other* in the historical process is very important, as is the situating and observation of the researcher himself/herself. These two aspects of the research situation are difficult to divide. The interconnectedness of both sides is natural and indispensable if we look at the situation from a historical perspective and try to be historically empathetic.

CONCLUSIONS

Although reflexivity is the term that comes to mind here, CGT is not the only reflexive stance in GT. The reflexivity of GT was mentioned in Charmaz's book (2006, pp. 131, 132, 188) and elaborated on further in Bryant and Charmaz (2014; see also Mruck and Mey, 2007; Gentles et al., 2014; Ramalho et al., 2015). We can advise that previous knowledge, such as any literature that has been read, should "lie fallow" (Charmaz, 2006, p. 166; 2014, p. 307) to allow the researcher to be open to the data. The reflexive stance suggests that we should see the researcher's influence on analysis and writing, on choosing the topic of research, on interacting while obtaining data, on choosing the core category and methods, and we should also observe the shifting perspective of the researcher during the study. We should also be aware of how the research changes us (Palaganas et al., 2017, p. 430; Priya, 2010) and what is our positionality (Clarke, 2005; Garot, 2013). Reflexivity is a part of CGT, and we use all the advice and implications from the interactive theoretical base of GT. However, we have something more here in CGT, such as observing how the mind of the researcher-analyst works and produces the data, categories, and interpretations (hypotheses), and how they are self-reported. We have the bracketing procedure used to protect and exploit properly the knowledge that we are aware of and have about the subject.

CGT needs a metatheory that states the principles of seeing and researching the reality. The principles are not assumptions but indications to reflect on how the psychosociocultural reality is perceived, researched, and analyzed. Metatheory is aimed at being mindful of some dimension in which we dwell in the *here and now* while doing research.

General principles to be aware of include the following:

(1) Conditional causality – the actions of the subjects and groups have interconnected causes that change in time, and at some point in time and space, the state of the object could influence the inferred earlier causes. The researcher-analyst is also under these influences, and the situation of research should be attended to and analyzed (see Appendix 2).

(2) The researcher feels emotions. They should be taken into consideration as part of the empirical data and as a research tool. They could be the reaction of "I" to the observed attitudes of others. The act of controlling or the lack of control of emotions should be observed as a process in the context of the investigation, and the researcher should get the meaning of the process for the research and for him personally.

(3) CGT analysts are *open to analyst-researchers' experiences*, and this should be a part of the analysis. Researchers treat the writing of memos as a discovery of not only the so-called external world but also of the self. They are often "discoverers" in writing, not "planners." They freely look for labels in language and try to create metaphors that cover the main concern of the researched area. They connect the discoveries with their own situation and experience of the position in the situation.

The specific and basic principles are as follows:

(1) Including the participants/collaborators of the research in the process of the research and analysis.
(2) Deconstructing concepts by working on the body, meditating, and memo writing.
(3) Mindful Coding – observing how the mind works with matching the labels to the data and creating categories and hypotheses (contemplative memo writing; see Appendix 1).
(4) *Epoché* plus observation and reporting what the researcher-analyst brings to the research.
(5) *The anamnesis work* – observing how the mind works in the internal dialog through memo writing plus the natural history of the research and analysis.
(6) Using empathy (Hansen and Trank, 2016, pp. 7, 9; Priya, 2010) and introspection (Ellis, 1991). Meditation as a preparation technique and historical contemplation could be useful here to sensitize the researcher before he/she starts writing the theory or interpreting hypotheses.

This approach in GTM is connected with the *contemplative turn* that we can observe in social sciences (Giorgino, 2014, 2015; Ergas, 2015; Bentz and Giorgino, 2016; Konecki, 2016, 2017; Varela et al., 1993; Varela and Shear, 2002; Denzin, 2006; Ellis, Adams, and Bochner, 2010; Kacperczyk, 2014). The attention that is applied in each moment of life – here, the working life of the researcher-analyst – is important because the GT analyst constructs the reality, and CGT analyst emphasizes the process. What we see *here and now* is a reality for us, we define the reality; in our case, a definition of reality is a GT. We are in the process that is connected with the attention given to the present. Each moment is experienced by the researcher-analyst. And the time span is filled with thousands of moments. He/she would notice (concentrate on, being attentive) not only the external objects and phenomena but also internal conversations of the researcher. All the observations and codes become part of the lived experience, and the constructed theory is the effect of the attention on the *here and now* and the living experiences of the researcher. The minding of the analyst is not only in abstraction, it is a lived experience. And during this experience, when the analyst is mindful, he/she can ask: Who am I? Mindful attention to this question could reveal many aspects and define the analyst. This refers not only to this person's social role, gender, values, and social position; it is also the ontological immersion in the situation of the research and analysis of the *here and now*. Being in the analysis is being thrown into the world, which is historically and linguistically defined. Coding is laden with history and language.

Understanding the historical context is very important for situating the lived experiences and actions of the individual in addition to feeling the affective experiences which refer to his/her own life experiences. However, we think that this aspect should be considered more carefully. It should be done through the *contemplative autoanalysis* of the analyst-researcher, to show if his/her lived experiences have anything in common with the experiences of the analyzed individuals. It could be done by using memory and the imagination, and the observation of gestures is also needed to get the meaning (Mead, 1934, pp. 300–301). If we do not do this, it is difficult to be empathetic historically. If we do so, we can develop some insights into the personal experiences situated in the historical perspective. Moreover, by *contemplative autoanalysis*, we can see that the past experiences of the Other and our attitudes to them could teach us about today's situation, which we experience in our own life and work as a social scientist (Konecki, 2018). *We should endeavor to theorize without ignoring the mind work in the practice of GT*. GT is impossible without minds being situated and working on – and using a language for – ideas that will become categories and hypotheses.

One of the limitations for developing CGT is the problem of openness on the side of the researcher-analyst. He/she should be open and ready to write self-reports and memos on the assumptions, minding process, body, and emotions. It might often reveal prejudices and personal inclinations, and this could be a difficulty for the writer. The mood coming from the data can influence the coder and analysts, she could feel sad or embarrassed, and it could influence the codes and interpretations of the data (see Appendix 2).

Another limitation is the issue of skills for self-observation. It needs time and patience to learn mindfulness and awareness of the body and self, and to notice internal interactions, how the mind works.

One more limiting factor is the skill for writing about the feelings of the body and self. Empathy also could be a barrier to learning, especially when we investigate a field where we are complete strangers, or we do not agree with the participants' basic assumptions and attitudes to the world (we experience empathy walls; see Hochschild, 2016, pp. 5–8, 56, 121, 131, 233; see also Mead, 1934). Empathy walls can emerge at any moment: "If there is no response, one cannot sympathize with him. That presents the limitation of sympathy as such; it has to occur in a cooperative process" (Mead, 1934, p. 301). Learning empathy and building empathy bridges takes time and effort. Empathy in research is a cooperative process, although sometimes it can be very difficult emotionally for the researcher to break the wall (Hochschild, 2016). However, we can find some approaches and techniques that help in this endeavor (Hansen and Trank, 2016). Empathy could have the humanizing potential that facilitates the healing and self-development of both the researcher and the research participants (Priya, 2010, p. 493).

Another limitation is the analysis of a large amount of additional data from self-reports and contemplative memos. The analyst should take them into consideration in constructing the theory and include them in the main narrative line of the GT. Connecting the contemplative memos with theoretical statements might not only be a technical problem but also be an ethical one. We should think about others included in our self-reports. Learning how to connect the two kinds of empirical protocols can take a lot of time and effort.

FUNDING

This work was supported by the National Science Center in Poland [Opus, grant number 2018/29/B/HS6/00513].

ACKNOWLEDGMENTS

The paper was written as a part of the project that has been financed by National Center of Science, Poland, Opus 15, No Project 2018/29/B/HS6/00513.
The author would like to thank reviewers for inspirations and thoughtful suggestions and revisions. Especially, the author would like to thank Kathy Charmaz for her suggestions and inspirations in writing this paper.

NOTES

1. "Human existence can seem to be disembodied by research in the social sciences, and contemplative knowledge reintroduces us to an intelligent and compassionate body, a body with which humans can live fully in a conscious way" (Giorgino, 2016, p. 164).

2. Here is a short extract from my research on experiencing the cemetery. Even when the researcher/coder denies feeling anything special during coding, he or she tries to be empathetic: "A technical approach was also connected to some coders with empathetic thinking; to code properly is to find herself in the shoes of the auto-reporter: 'There was no special excitement during my encoding. I was more interested in matching good answers. All I did was think and feel just like a writer/visitor and I tried to find myself in his situation'".

3. A similar perspective can be found in situational analysis, which has been somehow added to the grounded theory by Adele Clarke (2003, 2005; see also Kacperczyk, 2007). Clarke is inspired in her concept of situational analysis by the achievements of the philosophy of both pragmatism and postmodernism. She emphasizes that the researcher is not *a tabula rasa* and enters into a study with a certain amount of knowledge that should be revealed, and when it is revealed, it becomes an important argument for the credibility of the research and analysis.

4. The partnership in analyzing the data while using grounded theory we find in more engaged social research as in feminist study (Favero and Health, 2012; Merritt-Grey and Wuest, 1995).

5. "Almost every word we write may place a question mark over the meaning of the thing it expresses. In the experience of writing, words tend to become more dense and ambiguous. Rather than facilitating the conversational nature of human life, they acquire a quality of transparency in a different sense. They open a different realm, a different vista on human existence. The words draw us in. And as words draw us, they seem to open up a space: a temporal dwelling space. We step out of one world, the ordinary world of daylight, and enter another, the world of the text. In writing one develops a special relation to language which disturbs its taken-for-grantedness" (Max Van Manen, http://www.phenomenologyonline.com/inquiry/writing/drawing/).

6. Writers have commented: "Discoverers tend to be more interested in – and identify more with – the generative act of writing... Handwriting (both product and process) is important to discoverers in relation to their sense of self" (Chandler, 1992, pp. 67–68). From the books of classic grounded theory theorists, we can infer that they are discoverers because they prefer manual coding and are generally against using software for coding and theorizing (Holton and Walsh, 2017, pp. 95–97). It would be interesting to perform research to check what kind of writers (planners or discoverers) are GT analysts. Maybe there are differences between the classic and constructivist grounded theorists. How is the body included in the process of theoretical analysis? The answers to these questions need research.

7. "This research experience is changing my life, my critical abilities, and challenging my views on poverty, injustice, and 'goodness'. It has given a human face to poverty and injustice... each story different, each experience and aspiration unique. In spite of their behaviour these youth remain good people – their behaviour toward me has been caring, protective, and honest ... It's been an emotional tour de force (Field notes, Friday 31 December 2004)" (Swartz, 2011, p. 56).

8. The students were asked if they would allow their protocols to be read and coded during the coding session. They agreed. The students agreed also to be quoted in the research report.

REFERENCES

Bainbridge, R., Whiteside, M., and McCalman, J. 2013. Being, knowing and doing: a phronetic approach to constructing grounded theory with aboriginal Australian partners, *Qualitative Health Research*, 23(2), 275–288.

Barber, M. 2016. Alfred Schutz, *The Stanford Encyclopedia of Philosophy*, Ed. E. N. Zalta. Available at: https://plato.stanford.edu/archives/win2016/entries/schutz/

Barbezat, D. and Bush M. 2014. *Contemplative Practices in Higher Education*, San Francisco, CA, Jossey-Bass.

Bentz, V. M. 1995. Husserl, Schutz, "Paul" and me: reflections on writing phenomenology, *Human Studies*, 18(1), 41–62.

Bentz, V. M. and Giorgino V. 2016. *Contemplative Social Research. Caring for Self, Being and Life-world*, Santa Barbara, CA, Fielding University Press.

Bentz, V. M. and Shapiro J. 1998. *Mindful Inquiry in Social Research*, London, Sage.

Bhattacharya, K. 2013. Border crossing: bridging empirical practices with de/colonizing epistemologies. In *Global Dimensions of Qualitative Inquiry*, Eds N. Denzin and M. Giardina, pp. 115–134, Walnut Creek, CA, Left Coast Press.

Blumer, H. 1969. *Symbolic Interactionism*, Englewood Cliffs, NJ, Prentice-Hall.

Bohm, A. 2004. Theoretical coding: text analysis in grounded theory. In *A Companion to Qualitative Research*, Eds U. Flick, E. von Kardoff and I. Steinke, pp. 270–275, London, Sage Publications.

Breckenridge, J. 2013. Doing classic grounded theory: the data analysis process. In *Sage Research Method Cases* [Online Database]. Available at: http://methods.sagepub.com/case/doing-classic-grounded-theory-the-data-analysis-process

Bryant, A. 2009. Grounded theory and pragmatism: the curious case of Anselm Strauss, *Forum Qualitative Sozialforschung/Forum for Qualitative Social Research*, 10(3). Available at: http://nbn-resolving.de/urn:nbn:de:0114-fqs090325

Bryant, A. 2017. *Grounded Theory and Grounded Theorizing*, New York, NY, Oxford University Press.

Bryant, A. and Charmaz, K. 2014. *The Sage Handbook of Grounded Theory*, London, Sage.

Chandler, D. 1992. The phenomenology of writing by hand, *Intelligent Tutoring Media*, 3(2/3), 65–74.

Charmaz, K. 1990. 'Discovering' chronic illness: using grounded theory, *Social Science and Medicine*, 30(11), 1161–1172.

Charmaz, K. 2006. *Constructing Grounded Theory. A Practical Guide through Qualitative Analysis*, London, Sage.

Charmaz, K. 2008. Constructionism and grounded theory method. In *Handbook of Constructionist Research*, Eds J. A. Holstein and J. F. Gubrium, pp. 397–412, New York, NY and London, The Guilford Press.

Charmaz, K. 2008a. The legacy of Anselm Strauss for constructivist grounded theory. In *Studies in Symbolic Interaction*, Ed. N. Denzin (Vol. 32, pp. 127–141), Bingley, Emerald Group.

Charmaz, K. 2014. *Constructing Grounded Theory*, 2nd ed., London, Sage.

Charmaz, K. 2016. The power of grounded theory for critical inquiry, *Qualitative Inquiry Prepublication on-line*, July 26, 2016. doi:10.1177/1077800416657105

Chesney, M. 2001. Dilemmas of self in the method. *Qualitative Health Research*, 11(1), 127–135.

Christensen, T. M. and Brumfield, K. A. 2010. Phenomenological designs: the philosophy of phenomenological research. In *Counseling Research: Quantitative, Qualitative, and Mixed Methods*, Eds C. J. Sheperis, J. S. Young and M. H. Daniels, Upper Saddle River, NJ, Pearson Education, Inc.

Cisneros-Puebla, C. A. 2007. The deconstructive and reconstructive faces of social construction. Kenneth Gergen in conversation with César A. Cisneros-Puebla. With an introduction by Robert B. Faux, *Forum Qualitative Sozialforschung/Forum for Qualitative Social Research*, 9(1). Available at: http://www.qualitative-research.net/fqs-texte/1-08/08-1-20-e.htm

Clarke, A. 2003. Situational analysis: grounded theory mapping after the postmodern turn, *Symbolic Interaction*, 2(4), 553–576.

Clarke, A. 2005. *Situational Analysis: Grounded Theory after the Postmodern Turn*, Thousand Oaks, CA, Sage.

Cooley, C. H. 1909. *Social Organization: Study of Larger Mind*, New York, NY, Shocken.

Corbin, J. and Strauss, A. 2008. *Basics of Qualitative Research: Techniques and Procedures for Developing Grounded Theory*, Thousand Oaks, CA, Sage Publications, Inc.

Davis, C. S. and Breede, D. C. 2015. Holistic ethnography: embodiment, emotion, contemplation, and dialogue in ethnographic fieldwork, *The Journal of Contemplative Inquiry*, 2(1), 77–99. Available at: https://journal.contemplativeinquiry.org/index.php/joci/article/view/34

Denzin, N. K. 1992. *Symbolic Interactionism and Cultural Studies: The Politics of Interpretation*, Oxford and Cambridge, MA, Blackwell.

Denzin, N. K. 2006. Analytic autoethnography, or Déjà Vu all over again, *Journal of Contemporary Ethnography*, 35(4), 419–428. doi:10.1177/0891241606286985

Denzin, N. K. 2001. The reflexive interview and a performative social science, *Qualitative Research*, 1(1), 23–46. doi:10.1177/146879410100100102

Eberle, T. 2012. Phenomenological life-world analysis and ethnomethodology's program, *Human Studies*, 35, 279–304. doi:10.1007/s10746-012-9219-z

Ellis, C., Adams, T. E. and Bochner, A. P. 2010. Autoethnography: an overview, *Forum Qualitative Sozialforschung/Forum for Qualitative Social Research*, 12(1). Available at: http://nbn-resolving.de/urn:nbn:de:0114-fqs1101108

Ellis, C. 1991. Sociological introspection and emotional experience, *Symbolic Interaction*, 14(1), 23–50.

Endacott, J. 2013. An updated theoretical and practical model for promoting historical empathy, *Social Studies Research and Practice*, 8(1), 41–57.

Englander, M. 2016. The phenomenological method in qualitative psychology and psychiatry, *International Journal Qualitative Stud Health Well-being*, 11(1), 30682. doi:10.3402/qhw.v11.30682

Ergas, O. 2015. The deeper teachings of mindfulness-based 'interventions' as a reconstruction of 'education', *Journal of Philosophy of Education*, 49(2), 203–220.

Ergas, O. 2017. Conclusion: the reconstruction of 'education' and the 'contemplative turn'. In *Reconstructing 'Education' through Mindful Attention*, Ed. O. Ergas, London, Palgrave Macmillan.

Favero, L. W. and Heath, R. G. 2012. Generational perspectives in the workplace, *Journal of Business Communication*, 49(4), 332–356. doi:10.1177/0021943612456037

Garot, R. 2013. The psycho-affective echoes of colonialism in fieldwork relations [21 paragraphs], *Forum Qualitative Sozialforschung/Forum for Qualitative Social Research*, 15(1), Art. 12, Available at: http://nbn-resolving.de/urn:nbn:de:0114-fqs1401125

Gentles, S. J., Jack, S. M., Nicholas, D. B. and McKibbon, A. K. 2014. Critical approach to reflexivity in grounded theory, *Qualitative Report*, 19(44), 1–14. Available at: http://nsuworks.nova.edu/tqr/vol19/iss44/3

Giorgino, V. M. B. 2016. Contemplative knowledge and social sciences: close encounters of the enactive kind. In *Contemplative Social Research: Caring for Self, Being, and Lifeworld*, Eds V. M. Bentz and V. M. B. Giorgino, pp. 163–191, Santa Barbara, CA, Fielding University Press.

Giorgino, V. M. B. 2015. Contemplative methods meet social sciences: back to human experience as it is, *Journal for the Theory of Social Behaviour*, 45(4), 461–483. doi: 10.1111/jtsb.12078

Giorgino, V. M. B. 2014. Happiness is an art of living: towards a contemplative perspective on economy as relational work. In *The Pursuit of Happiness and the Traditions of Wisdom*, pp. 51–72, Cham and New York, NY, Springer.

Glaser, B. 1978. *Theoretical Sensitivity*, Mill Valley, CA, The Sociology Press.

Glaser, B. 1992. *Basics of Grounded Theory Analysis*, Mill Valley, CA, The Sociology Press.

Glaser, B. 1998. *Doing Grounded Theory. Issues and Discussions*, Mill Valley, CA, Sociology Press.

Glaser, B. 2002. Constructivist grounded theory? *Forum Qualitative Sozialforschung/Forum for Qualitative Social Research*, 3(3). Available at: http://www.qualitative-research.net/fqs/fqs-eng.htm

Glaser, B. G. and Strauss, A. L. 1967. *Discovery of Grounded Theory: Strategies for Qualitative Research*, Chicago, IL, Aldine.

Gunnlaugson, O., Scott, C., Bay, H. and Sarath, E. W. 2017. *The Intersubjective Turn: Theoretical Approaches to Contemplative Learning and Inquiry across Disciplines*, Albany, NY, State University of New York.

Hansen, H. and Trank, C. 2016. This is going to hurt: compassionate research methods, *Organizational Research Methods*, 19(3), 352–375.

Hesse-Biber, S. N. and Piatelli, D. 2007. Holistic reflexivity. In *Handbook of Feminist Research: Theory and Praxis*, Ed. S. N. Hesse-Biber, pp. 493–514, Thousand Oaks, CA, Sage Publications Inc.

Hochschild, A. R. 2016. *Strangers in Their Own Land: Anger and Mourning on the American Right*, New York, NY, The New Press.

Hoddy, E. 2019. Critical realism in empirical research: employing techniques from grounded theory methodology, *International Journal of Social Research Methodology*, 22(1), 111–124.

Holton, J. and Walsh, I. 2017. *Classic Grounded Theory. Applications with Qualitative and Quantitative Data*, London, Sage.

Hycner, R. H. 1985. Some guidelines for the phenomenological analysis of interview data, *Human Studies*, 8, 279–303.

Immergut, M. and Kaufman, P. 2014. A sociology of no-self: applying buddhist social theory to symbolic interaction, *Symbolic Interaction,* 37(2), 264–282. doi:10.1002/SYMB.90

Janesick, V. J. 2015. *Contemplative Qualitative Inquiry: Practicing the Zen of Research,* Walnut Creek, CA, Left Coast Press.

Kabat-Zinn, J. 1994. *Wherever You Go, There You Are*, New York, NY, Hyperion.

Kacperczyk, A. 2014. Autoetnografia: technika, metoda, nowy paradygmat? O metodologicznym statusie autoetnografii." (Autoethnography: technique, method, or new paradigm? On methodological status of autoethnography), *Przegląd Socjologii Jakościowej*, 10(3), 32–74. Available at: http://qualitativesociologyreview.org/PL/Volume27/PSJ_10_3_Kacperczyk.pdf

Kacperczyk, A. 2007. Badacz i jego poszukiwania w świetle 'Analizy Sytuacyjnej' Adele E. Clarke (The researcher and her search in the "light" of 'Situational Analysis'"Adele E. Clarke), *Przegląd Socjologii Jakościowej*, 3(2), 5–32. Available at: http://www.qualitativesociologyreview.org./PL/archive_pl.php

Keane, E. 2015. Considering the practical implementation of constructivist grounded theory in a study of widening participation in Irish higher education, *International Journal of Social Research Methodology*, 18(4), 415–431. doi:10.1080/13645579.2014.923622

Kelle, U. 2005. "Emergence" vs. "forcing" of empirical data? A crucial problem of "grounded theory" Reconsidered, *Forum Qualitative Sozialforschung/Forum for Qualitative Social Research*, 6(2). Available at: http://nbn-resolving.de/urn:nbn:de:0114-fqs0502275

Konecki, K. T. 2017. Contemplation for economists. Towards a social economy based on empathy and compassion, *Economics and Sociology*, 10(3), 11–24. doi:10.14254/2071-789X.2017/10-3/1

Konecki, K. T. 2011. Zapomniani aktorzy społeczni. Interakcje z przedmiotami, interakcje z naturą, czyli kilka słów o nowym "przedmiocie/podmiocie" analizy socjologicznej (The Forgotten Social Actors. Interaction with Physical Objects, Nature). In *Ludzie I Nieludzie. Perspektywa Socjologiczno – Antropologiczna*, Eds A. Mica and P. Łuczeczko, pp. 115–136, Pszczółki, Wydawnictwo Orbis Exterior.

Konecki, K. T. 2008. Touching and gesture exchange as an element of emotional bond construction. Application of visual sociology in the research on interaction between humans and animals. *Forum Qualitative Sozialforschung/Forum for Qualitative Social Research*, 9(3). Available at: http://nbn-resolving.de/urn:nbn:de:0114-fqs0803337

Konecki, K. T. 2016. Meditation as epistemology: how can social scientists profit from meditation? In *Contemplative Social Research: Caring for Self, Being, and Lifeworld*, Eds V. Bentz and V. Giorgino, pp. 193–238, Santa Barbara, CA, Fielding University Press.

Konecki, K. T. 2018. *Advances in Contemplative Social Research*, Lodz: Wydawnictwo Uniwersytetu Lodzkiego/Krakow: Wydawnictwo Uniwersytetu Jagiellonskiego.

Leder, D. 1990. *The Absent Body*, Chicago, IL, University of Chicago Press.

McEachern, D. 1984. On the phenomenology of writing, *Phenomenology + Pedagogy*, 2(3), 276–286.

McGhee, G., Marland, G. R. and Atkinson, J. 2007. Grounded theory research: literature reviewing and reflexivity, *Journal of Advanced Nursing*, 60(3), 334–342. doi:10.1111/j.1365-2648.2007.04436.x

McKinzie, A. 2017. Scared to death: reflections on panic and anxiety in the field, *Symbolic Interaction*, 40(4), 483–497.

Mead, G. H. 1934. *Mind Self and Society from the Standpoint of a Social Behaviorist*, Ed. C. W. Morris, Chicago, IL, University of Chicago.

Merleau-Ponty, M. 2005. *Phenomenology of Perception*, London, Routledge.

Merritt-Gray, M. and Wuest, J. 1995. Counteracting abuse and breaking free: the process of leaving revealed through women's voices, *Health Care for Women International*, 16(5), 399–412. doi: 10.1080/07399339509516194

Mills, J. B. and Francis, A. K. 2006. Adopting a constructivist approach to grounded theory: implications for research design, *International Journal of Nursing Practice*, 12(1), 8–13.

Misheva, V. 2009. Mead. Sources in sociology, *International Sociology*, 24(2), 159–172.

Mruck, K. and Mey, G. 2007. Grounded theory and reflexivity. In *The Sage Handbook of Grounded Theory*, Eds A. Bryant and K. Charmaz, pp. 515–538, London, Sage.

Nhat Hanh, T. 1999. *The Heart of the Buddha's Teaching,* London, Rider.

Palaganas, E. C., Caricativo, R. D., Sanchez, M. C. and Molintas, M. V. P. 2017. Reflexivity in qualitative research: a journey of learning, *Qualitative Report*, 22(2), 426–438. Available at: http://nsuworks.nova.edu/tqr/vol22/iss2/5

Priya, K. R. 2010. The research relationship as a facilitator of remoralization and self-growth: post-earthquake suffering and healing, *Qualitative Health Research*, 20(4), 479–495.

Ramalho, R., Adams, P., Huggard, P. and Hoare, K. 2015. Literature review and constructivist grounded theory methodology, *Forum Qualitative Sozialforschung/Forum for Qualitative Social Research*, 16(3). Available at: http://nbn-resolving.de/urn:nbn:de:0114-fqs1503199

Redman-MacLaren, M. and Mills, J. 2015. Transformational grounded theory: theory, voice, and action, *International Journal of Qualitative Methods*, 14(3), 1–12.

Rehorick, D. A. and Bentz, V. M. Eds 2008. *Transformative Phenomenology. Changing Ourselves, Lifeworlds, and Professional Practice*, Lanham, MD, Lexington Books.

Thornberg, R. 2012. Informed grounded theory, *Scandinavian Journal of Educational Research*, 56(3), 243–259.

Schutz, A. 1967. *The Phenomenology of Social World*, Evanston, IL, Northwestern University Press.

Swartz, S. 2011. 'Going deep' and 'giving back': strategies for exceeding ethical expectations when researching amongst vulnerable youth, *Qualitative Research*, 11(1), 47–68.

Strauss, A. L. 1987. *Qualitative Analysis for Social Scientists*, Cambridge, Cambridge University Press.

Strübing, J. 2004. *Grounded Theory. Zur sozialtheoretischen und epistemologischen Fundierung des Verfahrens der empirisch begründeten Theoriebildung*, Wiesbaden, VS Verlag für Sozialwissenschaften.

Strübing, J. 2007. *Anselm Strauss*, Konstanz, Uvk Verlags GmbH.

Varela, F. J., Thompson, E. and Rosch, E. 1993. *The Embodied Mind*, Cambridge, MIT Press.

Varela, F. J. and Shear, J. 2002. *The View from within: First-Person Approaches to the Study of Consciousness*, Upton Pyne, Imprint Academic.

Willmott, H. 2011. Journal list fetishism and the perversion of scholarship: reactivity and the ABS list, *Organization*, 18(4), 429–442.

Wojciechowski, J. 1930/1971. *Życiorys Własny Robotnika (Personal Life of the Worker)*, Poznań, Wydawnictwo Poznańskie.

Zahavi, D. 2001. Beyond empathy: phenomenological approaches to intersubjectivity, *Journal of Consciousness Studies*, 8(5–7), 151–167.

APPENDIX 1

AUTOBIOGRAPHICAL CONTEXTS FOR
UNDERSTANDING AND CODING THE DATA

The contemplative memos below represent the effect of analyzing the memoir by Polish worker and writer, Jakub Wojciechowski (1884—1958). The memoir was published under the title: *Personal Life of a Worker* (1930/1971). He was an autodidact writer and received his education only in a German primary school. He worked hard on farms from childhood, including on a forester's farm, and he also excavated trenches. Later, he worked in Germany as a carousel worker and a tram conductor. He was a soldier in the German army during the War in 1914.

He won first prize in a competition for memoirs organized by the Polish Sociological Institute (1922). It was eventually published in 1930. The memoirs describe his hardship, the experiences of misery during childhood (poverty and hard work), and his work in German enterprises.

Contemplative Memo

April 8, 2018.
While reading and coding (open coding) the memoir of Jakub Wojciechowski, memories of my childhood still come to mind. The reminiscences are so strong that sometimes I do not know who wrote this memoir, me or him, or maybe I am here as his incarnation; at other times, he was me, but the structure of his experiences is similar to mine. I am writing about the structure of events as perceived by the external observer. Jakub is the "objective" observer; he even looks like the "pure" positivist. There are no emotions there; if they appear, it happens rarely. But, while reading this memoir, I approach these recollections very emotionally. They move me in every moment; at the beginning, I was very moved, but this emotion was not connected to feeling sympathy toward Jakub, it was compassion for myself – for the Krzysio from my childhood, who took care of cows, he looked after the work there, was helping his parents in the field; I was very tired all the time, and I read books at night, when I had some free time.

I remember my feelings, also carnal work fatigue, but also self-denial. Not letting myself be tired, so as not to show others my weaknesses. Just like Jakub: "And the same with a hay fold, I got so tired that I could no longer catch my breath, but I did not give up."

When I first started reading the diary, I could not distance myself from the text; I still saw myself there or compared myself to Jakub and his life situation: the poverty, threats, the domination of the Church, striving for teachers' recognition in school, home habits, and the naturalistic approach to nature and animals, and also the prevalence of superstitions, etc.

Such a comparison also concerned the conditions of cultivation and farming. For example, even as far back as 1896, the drainage was carried out in a property close to where Jakub lived. In my village, there was no question of this happening, and, in the 1960s, people did not even know what it was (I am a specialist in drainage/irrigation – I learned about it in secondary school, which is why I noticed this fact).

The distance came when I started writing a theoretical memo about the following category: "Personal development in rural conditions at the end of the nineteenth century." I wondered why I had chosen such a core category for my coding. The description of this category, personal development, was probably an attempt to answer a personal and existential question: How was it possible for a person whose structural conditions were not favorable to eventually get out of poverty and a low social position? Was it my question? How could he have done it? What was pushing Jakub to get out of the situation of poverty and humiliation? Where did his motivation come from? It was difficult to find an answer in the fragments of the memoirs I read. The harder it was to find, the harder I looked for it. I searched in the structural and family conditions, with the observation of the diversity of customs in family life from other social classes that he met, etc. And, in this way, I fixed on this category, not necessarily the most important one in the memoir, but, for me, it became the most important one. I was glad that Jakub made it possible for me to try to answer this question.

Sometimes I smiled, and I was happy that something positive had happened to Jakub, for example, when he ate a sausage that he had stolen from the pantry of the host during Lent one year (p. 35).

I often saw in the memoir the code of "recognition" or "seeking recognition." Jakub was looking for recognition not only from teachers but also from some employers (a German employer, cleaning sludge from the canal). Perhaps, it was not really a topic that was so important for Jakub, *but I had read a doctoral thesis on the subject of "recognition" just before, and this category seemed important to me.* I guess it did not come from the data; it was external in relation to them. I had it in my memory, which is why I saw this topic in the data. I think so... Not sure...

When I read about how Jacob was instructed to look into the eyes of other people and speak in an assertive way, I recollected how I behaved and what I got out of my family. I was raised in the same way as Jacob. A lack of self-confidence, a groveling attitude toward others, especially those of a higher social standing. Jakub had to learn from others how to be assertive in his self-presentation; he learned it from the Germans. And me too... ☺

April 12, 2018.

Every time I start reading the memoir of Jakub, I am moved and touched. It is as if I was reading a memory of someone close to me, and sometimes even of myself.

There are many elements similar to life in my village in the 1960s. Conflicts between the peasants, lawsuits, the problem of hygiene, Easter customs (shooting during the Easter Sunday Mass), etc. The analyzed fragment ends before Jakub left his "homeland." I also left my homeland, although, as I have mentioned, I remember well my little homeland. It is difficult to call this remembrance a "sentimental one," but rather a "subjectively recollected objective view," to show the difficulties of living in the countryside and the hard work on the farm.

APPENDIX 2

The descriptions below come from the research report on experiencing the cemetery space and the feelings while being at the cemetery at a special time, 1st November (All Saints' Day) and on an ordinary day (2017).

MOOD, EMOTIONS, AND FEELINGS

The mood of the cemetery created the situation of experiencing the coding of data. The feeling of sadness prevailed. Also, in this mood, *the imagination* could be evoked during coding, e.g., the imagination of parents' death, which is a very depressive experience for the coder:

> After reading the text [for coding], I felt very sad. The described outlook of the cemetery caused me a feeling of nostalgia, not fear; I often go to pray at graves, without my parents. I thought about the loneliness of people whose parents die, about their sadness, because I think that no one can understand a person whose parent has just died... Reading the text, I imagined the death of my parents. It was a terrible feeling. I had never thought about it before and I did not want to think about it. The death of my parents is the worst thing that could happen to me.

The mood is also related to the *fear of death*:

> I thought that I would be afraid to come across a funeral at the cemetery at this moment, like the author of this description. In my mind, I think about how to behave, generally, at a cemetery. I think about the fact that I like going to the cemetery with my grandmother, because I feel safer being with her. Visiting a cemetery alone is very strange. Maybe in our heads we are afraid of death, because in our culture it is a taboo topic. This coding caused this reflective mood in me.

Together with the embarrassment that was felt while coding others' protocols, *the moral aspects of coding* can be discovered.[8] Are we eligible to read and code others' very personal autodescriptions, even if the authors consented? Coding in this situation introduces the private world of the person and family activities that usually are protected from strangers:

> By coding the description of my friend's feelings that accompanied her during the visit to the cemetery, I felt embarrassed. I think that this is due to the fact that this description was very personal. It contained a detailed description of the feelings walking down the road to the cemetery, during the visit to the grandparents' grave and a description of the way back. It also contained numerous reflections on life and death. At times, this description was very moving. Embarrassment accompanied me during the whole coding process. I do not know whether I should, or have the right to speak about other people's personal thoughts, even when they are similar to my own.

Some authors of contemplative memos on coding cannot precisely separate their feelings clearly. *While coding the protocols, they sometimes feel discrepant emotions at the same time.* The author quoted below is full of hesitations about what she feels and also about the correctness of coding ("I don't know"). She has mixed emotions, from amusement to sadness.

The author of the memo also shows that *the coding of "sadness"* that appears in a researcher's description of a visit to the cemetery influences her own feelings. She is also disappointed that she cannot render the atmosphere of the beauty of the day in coding:

> Some Feelings? I don't know. I think it's hard to create the appropriate categories for these statements. I feel tired and unhappy with what I wrote above. I have a sense of ridicule and failure in the work. So, I think it is funny.

> I have the impression that the words used in these statements (like sadness) have influenced my real feelings. That's why I feel so bad, I think. The statements are overwhelming and do not reflect the beauty of All Saint's Day. I'm a little disappointed and tired.

Some of the participants compared emotions and stated that they were similar. Empathetic thinking was aroused during the coding, and we see that *the place creates the basis for similar feelings*. The feelings that are aroused during coding are difficult and not pleasant for the coders. This could also be a subject for further analysis. Why it happens:

> During this coding, I realized that Ania [the name was changed] had similar feelings to me on my second visit to the cemetery.

> Visiting the cemetery is always a weird experience because I feel like death is some kind of a taboo for us. I can understand this because I feel the same emotions as Ania: there is loneliness, emptiness and a little bit of fear.

> I could experience all the feelings Ania had at the cemetery. She was very open about her emotions and described everything with a lot of detail, so I was able to feel like I was there next to her.

> Visiting the graves of family members and walking through the cemetery, as a rule, calls for sorrow and reverie. We mainly feel nostalgia, sadness. As tradition and religion order us, we pray at every grave. Reading about the emotions of the others caused similar feelings and thoughts. I was sad and not comfortable while reading and coding. When I had done the coding, I felt relief - the same as when I left the cemetery. I did not want to think about the fact that everyone is waiting for death. I felt cold, fear and "a void" inside of my body.

We can see in the contemplative memo below that, for the coder, *the differences* of the auto-observations were most important. They can influence how the coder experiences All Saints' Day. What is more important here is that the coder is under the influence of the other texts, and he is going to change his own convictions. His personal and exceptional experiences are going to be changed to make them similar to the other participants' reports:

> My feelings when I coded feelings my college friends are below.

> When I read the feelings of my college friends, I began to see that they were right, and that I didn't look at it as they did. I understood that each of us has a different view of the world on the one hand, so I was satisfied. And on the other, I began to wonder why I did not look at it from this perspective. I was also surprised that my friends pay attention to things completely different to me. I read and coded with interest the descriptions of my classmates. I think I will start to see All Saints' Day in a similar way to them.

The differences could be very deep and associated with a more spiritual attitude. The perception of others experiencing the cemetery space differently is striking to the participants:

> When I coded my colleagues' reports, I could get to know their feelings and thoughts. I wondered what was driving them, and what was driving me. Sometimes I felt the abyss between our senses, seeing how different they were. For a moment, I thought that being there in the cemetery, I was in another dimension, which I did not find in my colleagues' interviews. I realized that I had visited someone's houses, not monuments. They treated it differently; it was mundane. I think they did not feel that way and, in my opinion, each of us feels different, and it is worth talking about.

The interesting experience with coding was connected with repeated coding. Emotions were felt during the first coding. *Comparative thinking* helped the student to code (see the extract below); she felt the empathy and knew what code could be written. However, the emotions vanished when the participant started the second coding of the same text and also when the codes did not easily come to the mind. The experience just happened, and it was a part of the coding process. Emotions seem to be helpful in the thinking process and labeling the text:

> There were two types of coding. One was while reading those stories for the first time. That was when I could feel what they were feeling on All Saints' Day. That's because I had the same experience at the cemetery as they had had. While I was reading that, I could feel like I was with them in those places. I felt the same emotions and I had the same thoughts. I knew how I should code each sentence at that moment. When I finished reading them, something changed. All the emotions were gone. I was empty inside and I felt nothing. It was just me and emptiness. I started to read it again because I thought that all the emotions would come back, but they didn't. I started to feel sadness because I had to code it and I didn't know how. When the emotions disappeared, all the idea for coding went too. That's when I started the second coding but it wasn't the same. I did it automatically, like a robot. With no emotions, no good ideas. When it was over, and all the coding was done, I just hid my pen and my paper and I went home. I have not thought about it until now. That was a weird experience which I don't want to repeat ever again.

RISK, STRUCTURAL STIGMA, AND THE EXERCISE OF POWER: KEYNOTE ADDRESS TO THE 2018 COUCH-STONE SYMPOSIUM AND IX ANNUAL MEETINGS OF THE EUROPEAN SYMBOLIC INTERACTIONISTS

Stacey Hannem

ABSTRACT

Goffman (1963) provided us with an explanation of the operation of stigma in microinteractional contexts. However, his definition and explication of the experiences and processes of stigmatization predate what many consider to be the most major shift in discourse and categorization to develop in the twentieth century – the rise of the language of risk. In this chapter, I discuss the intersections of risk discourse and stigma. Drawing on my empirical research with families affected by incarceration, I illustrate the shift toward structural stigma as an exercise of power and governance. I argue that contemporary "common-sense" understandings and usage of the term stigma emphasize negative individual interactions while ignoring the ways that risk categorizations, even in seemingly benign contexts, create structural disadvantage and serve to "other" stigmatized individuals. Singular focus on stigma at the microinteractional level, particularly in destigmatization campaigns, obscures the pervasive structural stigma couched in the language of risk management that permits systematic marginalization.

Keywords: Stigma; risk; power; structural stigma; prison; ion scanner

Radical Interactionism and Critiques of Contemporary Culture
Studies in Symbolic Interaction, Volume 52, 187–204
Copyright © 2021 by Emerald Publishing Limited
All rights of reproduction in any form reserved
ISSN: 0163-2396/doi:10.1108/S0163-239620210000052011

INTRODUCTION

Were Goffman writing his volumes on *Asylums* and *Stigma* today, rather than in the late 1950s and early 1960s, they would arguably be very different books. The word "risk" appears in *Asylums* only seven times, and in *Stigma* just twice. Only one of these nine mentions is in vague reference to the risk posed by the mental patients to others (Goffman, 1961, p. 159). The others refer to perceived risks to identity. To write an ethnography of a psychiatric hospital today would likely require great exposition on risk scales: clinical and structural sorting based on risk of harm to self and others, risk factors, and their roles in governing the patients. As I have previously argued, the study of stigmatized groups in the late twentieth and twenty-first centuries will always land you in the territory of risk discourse – classifications of people who pose some kind of "risk" or danger, or people who may be constructed as "at risk" or in danger, and in need of assistance (see Hannem, 2012a). Other noted scholars, including, for example, Douglas and Wildavsky (1982), Beck (1992), Giddens (1998), and Garland (2003), have claimed that the rise of risk discourse is one of, if not *the* major shift in language and framing shaping modern life.

In this chapter, I take up the intersections of risk discourse and stigma and illustrate, drawing on some of my empirical work, the need to comprehend structural stigma as an exercise of power and governance that relies on a discourse of risk. In so doing, I argue that common-sense and colloquial understandings and usage of the term stigma emphasize negative individual interactions while ignoring the ways that risk categorizations create structural disadvantage and serve to "other" stigmatized individuals. That is, we cannot take up or combat the application of stigma at the level of the individual without accounting for the structural constraints posed by risk categorizations. In the same way that changing law or policy (legalizing gay marriage, for example) does not eliminate discrimination, bigotry, and stigma at the individual level, promoting individual-level destigmatization does not address the structural and obscures the exercise of power at work in categorizations of risk. Stigma is *both* symbolically realized in individual interactions and structurally embedded in the cultural values, practices, and institutions of society (Hannem, 2012a). In our contemporary society, the discourse of risk is the missing link that is required to make the connection between the interactional and the structural explicit.

To begin, I will first point out the pitfalls of failing to put clear conceptual boundaries around the concept of stigma. I will also discuss the problems with contemporary applications of Goffman's concept of stigma that remain at the microinteractional level and fail to consider structure by exploring what it means to be stigmatized and the role of power in experiences of stigma. I then use my research with families affected by crime and incarceration and their experiences with ion scan technology as an empirical example to illustrate how risk language institutes stigma at the structural level and reinforces symbolic forms of stigma. My intention is to make clear the implications of the failure to conceptualize stigma in this dualistic way, attending to both the symbolic realities of everyday life and the structural constraints of power/knowledge and discourse that shape these realities. I conclude with some reflections on the importance for pragmatist sociology and social justice of explicitly recognizing both the symbolic and structural aspects of stigma.

POWER/KNOWLEDGE AND THE DEFINITION OF THE SITUATION

I begin from the position that the language of risk has become inextricably entwined with social sorting, categorization, and stigma. Contemporary interactionists who attend to discourse and framing cannot engage with the concept of stigma without engaging with the language of risk, and this language of risk implicates the structural in our analyses in very explicit ways. The language of risk prompts us to take up the projects of power/knowledge that underlie the ability to use the construction of risk factors to sort, to classify, to exclude, and to intervene on marginal subjects – in short, the exercise of power that is at the root of all labeling.

Here, and elsewhere, I understand and use the concept of power in the Foucauldian sense, understanding that power is embedded in all interactions and diffused and implicated in discourse, knowledges and "regimes of truth" (Foucault, 1977) – the idea of power/knowledge, of course, suggesting that truth is a function of power in a constant state of flux and negotiation, constituted through the ability to shape discourse and guide social thought and action. In turn, power/knowledge is implicated and enacted in individual (inter)actions, while individual (inter) actions contribute to the social construction of knowledge and symbolic meaning, as identified by Blumer (1969). In this sense, I see the Foucauldian vision of power/ knowledge as wholly compatible with the tradition of symbolic interaction, and I am certainly not the first to make this observation (see Castellani, 1999).

At no point in his volume on *Stigma* does Goffman attempt to explain how it is that certain categories and attributions come to be stigmatized – he takes for granted that "society establishes the means of categorizing persons and the complement of attributes felt to be ordinary and natural for members of each of these categories" (1963, p. 2). In this sense, his book is timeless, asking contemporary sociologists to identify the "means" that society has established for categorizing persons in their own time. We can reasonably assume that these means are transformed over time by discourse, by social structure, and by politics. We can look to Becker, and Berger and Luckman, and the rest of the social constructionists to examine the origins of the construction of social problems – and social problems define deviance and create deviant people, as Howard Becker (1963) wisely noted. Gaylene Becker and Regina Arnold (1986) went on to further unpack stigma as social and cultural constructions that are embedded in sociopolitical and historical contexts.

Understanding that attributes are not stigmatized a priori enables us to ask questions about how and why certain attributes become stigmatized at certain social and political moments, and why others may become destigmatized as social norms and political landscapes change – and why some attributes persist in being stigmatized, despite all efforts at social change. These reflections on the social construction of stigma raise questions about its relationship to power, stereotype, and discrimination. For example, what are the various roles of stereotype and stigma as organizing structures in our complex society?[1] Symbolic interactionists who study stigma must also be attentive to what is at stake in maintaining these hierarchies and power relations – what are the systemic and structural barriers to destigmatization, beyond changing individual minds? I wish to argue that popular and contemporary definitions of stigma that overemphasize symbolic experiences of stigma as a problem of identity, while turning a blind eye to the structural conditions that create inequity, are implicated as a barrier to effective destigmatization.

Over the past decade, stigma has emerged as a contemporary buzzword; there are many "common-sense" ideas about stigma floating around in media, in pop culture, and in pop psychology. My analysis of recent scholarly publications using the concept of stigma shows that even academics are not particularly careful about the definition of stigma and its parameters. There is a sharp distinction between Goffman's definition of stigma and the ways it has been applied by many contemporary sociologists and psychologists. Some applications of the concept appear to suggest that if an attribute or characteristic is "disliked" or described in a less than positive fashion, this is evidence of stigma. For example, a fellow symbolic interactionist shared with me that she read, with some consternation, a paper which attempted to frame family members and social workers describing the terrible negative effects of Alzheimer's disease on patients and their families as evidence that Alzheimer's disease is stigmatized. It is an incorrect use of the concept of stigma to argue that *any* negative characterization of an attribute is necessarily stigma. By saying that a cancer diagnosis is a terrible thing for most people we are not stigmatizing cancer and cancer patients – we are describing an empirical experience that is negative.[2] Similarly, merely noticing or being aware of human differences is also not stigma. We can be aware of physical and other differences between individuals without being stigmatizing of those attributes. The characterization of attention to difference or discussion of negative attributes as stigma must be understood in the context of Goffman's notion of discredited identity.

Current usage, both academic and popular, has moved away from Goffman's original definition of stigma to a more diffuse, less precise, and often muddy understanding. Policing these boundaries is not academic snobbery or dogmatic adherence to our canon. The most important reason to maintain boundaries around the concept of stigma is to prevent a conceptual slippage that would allow stigma to become merely an individualized, existential phenomenon – in which when someone claims that they "feel" stigmatized, they are understood to be so, regardless of the context of their exclusion or experiences, and irrespective of their position in the social structure. By ensuring that the role of power and structure remains an explicit feature of the definition of stigma, we maintain the concept's utility and resonance as a means of describing the experiences of marginalized groups. The concept of stigma and related antistigma campaigns remain strategies for identifying and challenging the phenomena of othering and repression. It is important in this contemporary moment that we not allow conceptual slippage to obscure the exercise of power at the heart of all stigmatization and marginalization.

STIGMA IN INTERACTION VERSUS STIGMA IN STRUCTURE: CLASSIFICATIONS AND SPOILED IDENTITY

Goffman's (1963) discussion of stigma hinges on the idea of what he has termed "spoiled" or "discredited" identity: Goffman described the stigmatized person as "the individual who is disqualified from full social acceptance" (preface). One of the first definitional problems we encounter in defining and understanding stigma is that Goffman didn't tell us what he meant by "full social acceptance" and didn't put any parameters on the kinds of everyday limitations that people encounter in the social world. This has led to broad interpretations of "full social acceptance" that open up the possibility of defining many people as stigmatized in circumstances in which they still have a significant degree of privilege and opportunity.

While Goffman's work does not necessarily clearly delineate the boundaries of what he would conceptualize as stigma and who he would consider to be stigmatized, this does raise questions about the sociological and pragmatic utility of a definition that includes any kind of social exclusion or social sorting. For example, is a teenager stigmatized if she plays in a high school band, isn't athletically inclined, doesn't get invited to the "cool" parties, and remains on the outskirts of the high school social? Does any social sorting, hierarchy, or group adhesion necessitate that those who do not fit in are "stigmatized"? That same teenager gets good grades, is generally well adjusted, has a small group of similarly "uncool" friends, and goes on to become an adult who is relatively successful, both socially and materially – was she stigmatized by her high school peers who didn't invite her to their parties? Is a spoiled identity so easily shed with the passage of time? Goffman's discussion of the status of the ex-convict, ex-addict, and ex-mental patient would suggest otherwise. While he acknowledges that stigma and discredit are contextual and a function of the relationship between attributes and expectations, he immediately goes on to clarify that he wishes to focus on those "important attributes that almost everywhere in our society are discrediting" (Goffman, 1963, p. 4). It is clear that Goffman's concern was primarily with those forms of social exclusion that were less mutable, and not temporally and circumstantially bounded like adolescent cliques. I suggest that we should seek a useful sociological distinction between organic and symbolic social groupings and the kinds of social sorting that are reinforced by structure and the exercise of institutional power.

To make this distinction clear, we can return to Goffman's emphasis on the relationship between attribute and stereotype which defines stigma; informal social sorting may involve *inclusion* on the basis of positively valued attributes (e.g., "coolness"), but it does not necessarily follow that all those who are excluded from that particular group are stigmatized. Were this the case, we would have to concede that virtually *every person* is in one context or another excluded from a social group – and that therefore every person is stigmatized in some particular context. However, I would argue that Goffman's (1963) specific examples of the stigma of tribe and race, of physical deformity, and of moral disrepute do not lend themselves to such a broad interpretation. Stigma and discredited identity are fundamentally about the *application* of a label or marked attribute which is attached to a constellation of negative stereotypes. Conversely, stigma is *not* the absence or lack of a specific positively viewed attribute in a specific social context.

An example of precisely this kind of conceptual misuse appeared in a recent article in *Psychology Today* in which a professor of psychology argued that

> Stigma is an identity element...that disqualifies the individual from playing a particular role. No matter how skilled a doctor she is, no American hospital is going to credit her as one *if she hasn't gone to medical school.* Karson (2018, para. 2, *emphasis added*)

Disqualification from being a doctor due to lack of medical credentials is certainly *not* an example of stigma. The important distinction is that the disqualification does not operate on the basis of a particular ascribed identity marker with associated negative stereotypes (the relationship between attribute and stereotype). Rather, the disqualification is the result of the individual's failure to pursue the necessary credentials to earn the status of "medical doctor."

A definition such as the one put forward by Karson (2018)[3] does a disservice to those individuals who are *perfectly qualified to be doctors, with the necessary credentials,* but who are passed over for hiring, promotions, and the like, because of, for example, the color of their skin, the accent of their speech, their gender expression, sexuality – attributes that are stigmatized and ascribed with negative stereotypes. To maintain the utility and the power of the concept of stigma as a means of highlighting the injustice of negative stereotypes, lost opportunities, and bigotry, it is imperative that we maintain clear boundaries that would proscribe such conceptual slippage.

It is also important at this moment in history that we clearly iterate that a discredited identity is about more than individual criticism or dislike. Millions of people in North America and around the world have criticized Donald J. Trump; they describe him as a buffoon (Donahue, 2017; Zelizer, 2018) and charlatan (Cohen, 2018), question his credentials to be President of the United States, question his judgment and his mental wellness (Glass et al., 2019; Sherman, 2020); they protest him and call him names – but is he stigmatized? Despite all of our individual and collective criticism, Trump remains among the most powerful people in the world. He is a white man with privilege and capital (both physical and symbolic); he can earn money, be hired, qualify for loans, his safety is protected by the state and Secret Service, and he can interact confidently with any person he encounters. His personal and social identities remain very much intact and he does not experience marginality and social discredit. Further, he need not engage identity management techniques, nor hide his identity, to interact effectively in the social world. The labels that have been applied to Trump by political opponents and citizens are deflected and have little effect on his daily life.[4] Furthermore, and most importantly, these labeled attributes are not, as Goffman described, linked to a stereotyped identity construct – they are *individualized* descriptors.

Stigma, then, must be understood not as merely a function of individual dislike or distaste, or even of exclusion from a singular social group, but of systemic, oppressive, categorization, and resulting marginalization from society – in short, *as a function of power.* However, there is a key distinction to be made between stigma which operates at the level of individual interaction (symbolic stigma – the focus of Goffman's work) and stigma which operates at the level of structure or institution, embedded in policy, in law, and in intervention practices (structural stigma) (Hannem, 2012a). I argue that the link between these two forms of stigma is the language of risk.

THE RISE OF RISK DISCOURSE

As I have previously argued, symbolic stigma is commonly experienced by marginalized individuals or groups in their interactions with those who Goffman termed "normals." The entirety of Goffman's volume on *Stigma* is concerned with precisely this form of individualized symbolic stigma and he aptly describes how individuals negotiate these interactions using identity management strategies. These strategies may be more or less successful, but discredited or discreditable individuals go about their daily lives with the understanding that they may be subject to discrimination or negative treatment and the experience of stigma remains primarily an individual emotional or existential concern. In some circumstances, stigmatized individuals come to recognize that there are others like themselves and social consciousness may generate collective resistance to stigmatization that takes the form of political activism or active challenge to the constellation of negative stereotypes that surround a stigmatized identity (see, for example, Husain and Kelly, 2017).

At the individual level, symbolic stigma and the discrimination that may result is troubling; however, like Mills' (1959) distinction between private troubles and public issues, the experience of symbolic stigma becomes a sociological concern when we understand that it is symptomatic of stigma at a structural level that is operationalized as a means of cordoning and controlling a specific group of people:

> Structural stigma is systematically applied by agencies,institutions and individuals to a particular group of people or population as a whole – moving beyond stigma as a perception of an *individual* attribute, to a wider, stereotypical concept of stigma that taints an entire group and pushes them to the margins of society. Increasingly we find that these structural-level identifications of stigmatized attributes are related to the notion of risk, and interventions are justified by the rhetoric of risk-management. (Hannem, 2012a, p. 23)

It is no coincidence that those groups and individuals most at risk of stigmatization exhibit behavior or attributes which are counter to the expectations of dominant society. They are often framed as threatening to social order or to the well-being of the general population and thus are subject to interventions or surveillance designed to minimize this threat. For example, in contemporary society, racialized persons identified as Middle Eastern or as Muslims have been constructed as posing a threat of terrorism and have, as a result, been subject to all manner of surveillance and travel restrictions that we are told (without evidence) function to protect the public from violent attacks. Similarly, many individuals with diagnosed mental disorders are presumed to be a danger to themselves and to others, legitimizing the use of compulsory treatment and coercive confinement when authorities are involved. The well-being and protection of the majority is presumably prioritized over the autonomy and welfare of marginalized individuals like these.

According to Link and Phelan (2001) *structural discrimination* occurs when policy makers and administrators fail to foresee the negative consequences that a policy or practice will have for a specific group of people. Lack of awareness contributes to systematic discrimination, but the blind spots in policies are not deliberately punitive, merely short-sighted. On the other hand,

> ...*structural stigma* arises out of an *awareness* of the problematic attributes of a particular group of people and is based on an intent to manage a population that is perceived, on the basis of the stigmatic attribute, to be "risky" or morally bereft. Here the symbolic meets the structural in a way that causes an inherent disadvantage to a group of people. This stigma is *structural* because the difficulties that arise from it are not so much a product of the attribute itself, or any inherent problems that arise from the condition, but of the institutional and conceptual structures that surround it. Whether or not an individual experiences symbolic and individualized stigma in interactions, he or she is marked and may be subject to a myriad of interventions, regulations, and surveillance, not on the basis of *individual* characteristics, but on the recognition that they belong to a statistically "risky" group. (Hannem, 2012a, p. 24)

Where Link and Phelan's (2001) conceptualization of structural discrimination includes no intent to harm or disgrace, the intent of the intervenor is a hallmark of structural stigma. Structural stigma emerges out of the bureaucratic or institutional intent to manage the risk that a particular population presents – either to themselves, to others, or to an institution. The language of risk and risk management legitimize the imposition of carefully calculated interventions. To clarify, those who create and apply institutional risk management policies do not necessarily intend to *harm* the targeted population; they often frame the intended outcome as one that will help or improve the situation for the individuals on whom they are intervening. For example, the use of coercive treatment and intervention on those who are mentally ill is generally intended to reduce the likelihood that they will harm themselves or others and to return these individuals to a state in which they are able to participate in social life. However, the need for assistance is, in the first place, presented and justified by claims that such individuals are inherently "risky" or "at risk" – that they are "different" from the average person and somehow "tainted" by their differences in way that requires external intervention and management. Stigma, then, emerges as a function of the discourse of those very agencies that provide help.

The concept of structural stigma pushes symbolic interactionists to think beyond Goffman's focus on managing individual experiences of stigmatizing interactions toward an archeology of stigma that would uncover its roots in order to better understand and address stigmatizing discourse and stereotypes. As I have noted, drawing on Mary Douglas'(1966) work on "pollution and taboo," perceptions of risk or danger are often traced to culturally embedded understandings of purity and defilement, whether literal or figurative.[5] For example, in North America and in many western cultures, criminality is highly stigmatized behavior and any association with crime may defile one's identity, extending even to family members and associates (Hannem, 2012b). Crime is considered immoral and is associated with high levels of risk and danger, subject to any number of reactive and pro-active interventions intended to reduce or eliminate harms to innocent victims. In some cases these interventions are exercised on entire groups of people believed to be at high risk of crime (or some other harm), regardless of whether the risk is "real" (actuarially calculable) or merely symbolic (rooted in fear and stereotype). An excellent contemporary example of this is the disproportionate surveillance of and intrusions on persons of visible Middle Eastern descent in North America. As such,

> defining a group of persons as a collective risk in this manner serves to increase stigma at both symbolic and structural levels as individuals negotiate interactions with government and social agencies and other persons. (Hannem, 2012a, p. 25)

Where Goffman focused his attention on better understanding how stigma and identity management play out in individual-level interactions, Foucault's genealogical approach would direct us to more carefully examine the origins of these stigmatizing interactions and how they may be influenced by discourses of power/knowledge that become a part of our corporate understanding and stereotype of marginalized persons. Further, this approach to considering the experience of stigma takes up the idea that structural stigma is applied to individuals in interaction under the guise of risk management, *whether or not there is any evidence of discrimination.*

The experiences of individuals who are subject to structural stigma are under-stood, not as unjust or as rooted in any kind of bias, but as the legitimate outcomes of risk management practices. For example, Rosenhan's (1973) classic work on "being sane in insane places" emphasized how the mere label of mental illness (attached to his perfectly sane "pseudo-patients") legitimized a host of pharma-ceutical and other interventions, despite the absence of symptoms of mental illness and risk. We might understand this phenomenon as the outcome of structural stigma. To further illustrate, I offer a contemporary empirical example of the operation of structural stigma, drawing on my research on families affected by crime and incarceration, to further discuss the link between risk discourse and stigma and its effects on marginalized people.

PRISON FAMILIES, STRUCTURAL STIGMA, AND TECHNOLOGY

My doctoral dissertation research in 2006–2008 focused on the experiences of individuals who had an incarcerated family member; I reprised this research in 2015 in partnership with the Canadian Families and Corrections Network (Hannem and Leonardi, 2015). I was disappointed, though not surprised, to find that very little had changed in the intervening years. Throughout both projects, all of the family members who I interviewed or surveyed had stories of negative social experiences, rejection, condemnation, and avoidance behaviors. They reported the loss of employment, difficulty in finding work, isolation, and lack of support. Friends and extended family often pull away, leaving individuals to deal with the fallout of the incarceration alone. Even children are vulnerable to stigma: I heard stories of school classmates' parents who prohibit their children from playing with the child who has an incarcerated parent. Like many stigmatized individuals, families of prisoners often engage in passing (Goffman, 1963) to conceal and manage their stigmatized identity.

However, situations do arise in which it is difficult or even impossible for the family member of an incarcerated person to pass. A good example of this is the experience of entering the penitentiary as a visitor. Individuals who want to visit an inmate at a Canadian prison must apply for the privilege; they are subject to a criminal background check and their application is linked to the inmate who they want to visit. Family members must inform the staff whom they are there to visit and the correctional service has already documented the nature of their relationship to that individual. There is no way to pass and enter the prison without disclosing one's relationship to an incarcerated person. The vast majority of the family members I interviewed or surveyed reported multiple incidents of rude or demeaning treatment by correctional officers in the visitor center; most reported a general feeling that prisoners' family members were not respected by the corrections staff or treated courteously (Hannem, 2011, 2012b; Hannem and Leonardi, 2015).

Rude and disrespectful treatment of visitors is not consistent with the policies of Correctional Service Canada. Indeed, the institutional mandate includes "respecting the dignity of all persons." However, the seeming prevalence of antagonistic encounters between correctional staff and visitors at penitentiaries across Canada, and at various levels of security, suggests that the phenomenon may be more institutionally pervasive than merely the result of certain individuals' prejudices. It is likely that the attitudes of the correctional officers are reflective of a larger institutionalized stereotype of prisoners and their families as risky individuals who pose a danger to institutional security, and possibly to the public as potential perpetrators of crime. This assumption is enacted in prison security policies, which direct disproportionate scrutiny at visitors and family members while neglecting to inspect the behaviors of staff, volunteers, suppliers, and professionals to the same degree. Family members are keenly aware of this discrepancy and describe a feeling of being targeted and treated "like criminals." The Correctional Service's use of the ion scanner stands out as a key piece of this differentiated security and treatment of prisoners' families.

ION SCANNERS AND STRUCTURAL STIGMA

Ion scanners were introduced to Canadian federal prisons in the early 2000s as an attempt to combat the persistent problem of illicit drugs in prison. Many readers will be familiar with the ion scan technology (even if they don't realize it) and have seen it in use; ion scan is used at airport security around the world to identify trace particles of explosives. The identical technology and machines are used in prisons to search for trace particles of drugs (See Hannem, 2019, for a detailed description of the operation of ion scan technology). However, ion scan is often oversensitive and is plagued by issues of false positives. There are three different ways that false positives occur.

First, contrary to popular belief, the ion mobility spectrum or "plasmagram" that is generated by the ion scanner is *not a unique identifier* for a chemical compound in the same way that a fingerprint or iris scan is a unique identifier for an individual. The ionic particles that make up related chemical compounds may be so similar in weight and size that they produce virtually identical plasmagrams and are indistinguishable at the ionic level. For example, it is well known that the antacid ranitidine (better known by its brand name, Zantac) rings positive as cocaine. The makers of the IONSCAN, Smiths Detection, even helpfully included this information in their patent application. A host of other substances including detergents, perfumes, prescription and over-the-counter medications, and poppy seeds will be detected as various illicit drugs, and Correctional Service Canada admit to keeping a list of known, legal, substances that will ring positive on their machine. A security bulletin to correctional staff issued on October 16, 2017 stated, "CSC is aware that the Ion Scanner can provide false positive results when highly concentrated elements are present (i.e. cleaning agents)." These situations in which other substances are alarming the machine are the best examples of "true" false positives; however, there are other circumstances in which the machine may detect minute quantities of drugs but that alarm does not indicate that the individual is attempting to traffic drugs into the prison – "nuisance positives."[6]

Cross-contamination is a source of nuisance positives. Many individuals who are not drug users come into contact with trace particles of illicit drugs in circumstances in which they are completely unaware. Most paper cash is contaminated with trace particles of cocaine so handling money is a likely source of cross-contamination (Armenta and De la Guardia, 2008), along with any situation in which one comes into contact with surfaces that are handled or touched by a large number of people, any one of whom may be a drug user and transfer trace particles.

Finally, there may be circumstances in which an individual may use illicit drugs recreationally, and trace particles of the drugs may be detected by the ion scanner. However, the presence of trace particles does not indicate that the drug is present in significant quantities nor that the individual is attempting or even likely to attempt to traffic drugs into the prison. This kind of "nuisance positive" is likely to become even more common since although the Canadian government legalized the recreational use of marijuana in late 2018, it remains a contraband (and highly sought-after) substance in Canadian prisons. Recreational users of marijuana who visit family members in prison are likely to alarm the ion scanner due to the presence of trace particles, even if they are not attempting to traffic.

Despite these myriad problems with the accuracy and sensitivity of the ion scanner, noted in Correctional Service Canada's own reports on the subject (see Johnson and Dastouri, 2011), frontline staff insist that the ion scanner works, allowing them to identify "risky individuals" who may carry drugs into the prison and endanger the safety of staff and inmates. William Normington, a correctional officer with 35 years' service, testified to the Parliamentary Standing Committee on Public Safety and Security:

> When the ion scanner is used, there's no doubt in my mind that *the machine doesn't make errors.* We can detect on the individuals who come in, on their wallets or their jewellery or their

clothing, quantities of drugs. We can detain them until the authorities come and arrest them with probable cause, or we can ask them to leave the institution. (House of Commons Parliamentary Standing Committee on Public Safety and National Security, 2011a, p. 9, emphasis added)

CSC policy dictates that a Threat Risk Assessment (TRA) is to follow a positive read on the ion scanner, comprised of a private interview and a search of the individual, before the visit is denied. Family members report that officers do not always conduct TRAs, particularly if visiting rooms are busy. When an officer conducts a TRA, they may still turn away the individual and deny the visit, even if there is no evidence that the individual is carrying any drugs on their person. Some family members have had their visitation privileges and security clearance revoked entirely, such that they have to reapply to visit their family member – a process that can take months. However, other individuals with more cultural and political capital than the families of offenders are offered significantly more latitude when it comes to a positive reading on the ion scanner. For example, Kim Pate, the former executive director of the Canadian Association of Elizabeth Fry societies (a nonprofit prisoner advocacy organization) and now appointed Senator of Canada, testified to the parliamentary committee in 2011:

> Of course, I know the policy, so I'll ask for the risk-threat assessment; I'll ask for all of the appropriate measures. Everybody will agree that they have no concern that after 30 years of coming in [to the prison], I would actually ever introduce drugs to the institution. Yet I've rung off falsely positive, so much so that at one point we went through a whole little charade of what kind of medication I might have touched in the previous two weeks. In the end, it was assessed that a Dimetapp I had given my child two weeks earlier may have caused it. (House of Commons Parliamentary Standing Committee on Public Safety and National Security, 2011b, p. 4)

Most family members entering prisons to visit loved ones do not enjoy Ms. Pate's level of social capital and status and are not offered the benefit of the doubt, which begins with the assumption that she is *not* bringing drugs into the institution.

In the meantime, CSC constructs the ion scanner as an objective and reliable tool. When I filed an access to information request to obtain any data collected on false positives by Correctional Service Canada, I was informed that CSC

> does not possess documentation concerning the reliability factor of the IonScan machines ... CSC staff who have attended training with the manufacturer [Smiths Detect] have been advised that the false alarm rate is below 0.1% as indicated by the manufacturer. (CSC, personal correspondence with the author, June 27, 2016)

Correctional Service Canada have collected no independent data on the efficacy of the IONSCAN machines and accept the claims made by the manufacturer about its reliability (presumably under strictly controlled laboratory conditions and not reflective of "real-world" applications).

CSC also does not record false positives, nor nuisance positives – my 2016 access to information request for data on false positive readings by the ion scanner resulted in this response:

> Considering that such an occurrence rarely occurs, "false positives" are not recorded by any institution within CSC. Therefore, it would be difficult to provide an actual figure. Please note

that the false alarm rate is below 0.1% as indicated by the manufacturer. In the event there is an alarm that appears to be a "false positive" for a controlled substance, CSC consults with the manufacturer to determine if a prescribed medication can cause an alarm. (CSC, personal communication with the author, June 27, 2016)

CSC accepts Smiths Detection's claims that the IONSCAN is objective and reliable, and not subject to false positives, but at the same time acknowledges that they are aware that legal substances may cause the device to alarm *and* that the manufacturer is aware of this issue. This contradiction raises questions about CSC's defense of the technology's effectiveness and its use as a tool for drug interdiction. While they claim the tool is objective and reliable, the tool is applied in an inherently biased way (to visitors and not staff), their policy ultimately falls back on a subjective determination of risk in the form of the TRA which draws on individual negotiations of power and social capital. Thus, the technology and policy masquerade as objective risk management techniques, designed to protect the security of the institution, while effectively reinforcing the symbolic divide between the institutional staff and the prisoners and the families of prisoners.

In an even more blatantly asymmetrical application of the technology, the ion scanner is used to scan visitors to the institution, but *not* correctional staff. This selective use of the technology underscores the symbolic differences between staff and visitors, constructing visitors as inherently more *risky* to the institution, while correctional officers are assumed to be the guardians against such risks. Institutional policy for the use of the IONSCAN ignores evidence that staff members and other individuals who are part of the carceral apparatus may use their trusted status to introduce contraband into prisons. While the construction of the IONSCAN as a neutral tool of risk management obscures the underlying symbolic assumption that it is visitors, *and not staff*, who pose a security risk to the institution, it is understood that high rates of positive hits would make it difficult to use IONSCAN effectively on staff and would highlight the problem of false positives.

The selective application of security technology suggests that its latent function is not as the neutral risk management tool that CSC constructs. The failure to exercise all available forms of interdiction with staff, even in the face of evidence that staff may be implicated in drug trafficking, raises questions about the symbolic value of technology and policy in demarcating risky populations. The former commissioner of corrections, Don Head, acknowledged in his 2011 testimony to parliament that 12 correctional employees had been dismissed and charged with drug trafficking that year (House of Commons Standing Committee on Public Safety and National Security, 2011c). However, it is visitors to the institution (primarily families of inmates) who are singled out as a security risk and subject to increased scrutiny. Identifying a "risky" group in this way also legitimizes and exacerbates symbolic stigma against prisoners' family members who are discredited and treated, as Goffman (1963) phrased it, "as not quite human" (p. 5). Officers feel able to exercise their power in this asymmetrical relationship through interactions that families may experience as disrespectful and dehumanizing (see Hannem, 2011, 2012b).

The ion scanner is one example of the way that institutional policy creates structural stigma, which then further legitimizes the symbolic enactment of stigma through negative individual interactions in power-laden situations. Families report that when they ring positive on the ion scanner – even if it is a false or nuisance positive – they are treated even more poorly by correctional staff and subject to increased suspicion in future visits. This finding suggests that a circular relationship exists between the institutional policy and the symbolic enactment of it. For those of us whose sociology takes a pragmatist approach, the complexity of stigma as both an interactional and structural process raises concerns about how best to address issues of social justice that arise in relation to the construction and management of "risky" populations. I will conclude by turning to this dilemma.

DESTIGMATIZATION AND STRUCTURE

It is contemporaneously fashionable to be "anti-stigma" and to advocate for the destigmatization of various phenomena, experiences, and attributes. A quick Google search for the word "destigmatize" returns thousands of pages with campaigns to destigmatize everything from diverse sexualities and gender expressions, to mental illnesses, depression, addiction, obesity, menstruation, cannabis use, and polyamory. I have argued myself for the destigmatization of families affected by crime and incarceration. The assumption built into each of these campaigns is that by reducing or eliminating stigma we will improve the everyday lives of these marked individuals. That is, if we are kind and accepting of these stigmatized groups, their identities will cease to be spoiled and they will live more fulfilling, comfortable lives than they otherwise would. However, I note that contemporary destigmatization campaigns often focus on the symbolic and relational aspects of stigma without considering the structures, policies, and interventions built up around stigmatized groups that mark them as outsiders – as "risky" or "at risk" and in need of intervention. That is, destigmatization is often understood as something that can be accomplished at an individual, rather than at a structural level.

In contemporary politics and governance, the language of risk serves to obscure mechanisms of stereotype, moral judgment, and discredit; meaningful destigmatization campaigns must address both the symbolic and the structural. For example, despite the fact that Canada instituted marriage equality in 2005, legally destigmatizing gay and lesbian relationships and permitting marriage between partners of the same sex, the stigmatization of same-sex relations persists in other symbolic and institutional forms. The legalization of same-sex marriage was not a panacea for symbolic stigma and bigotry – many LGTBQ+ persons still experience discrimination and have negative interactions with others. Nor did the legalization of marriage eliminate other forms of structural stigma, such as the risk that has been constructed around gay sex. Men who have sex with another man are still not permitted to donate blood in Canada – even if the sex took place with a condom or in the context of a monogamous (legal!) marriage.[7] No such proscriptions are in place for heterosexual women or men who have unprotected sex – even if they have multiple partners. Canadian Blood Services frames this policy as a matter of "risk" of HIV and other blood-borne STIs, and the language of risk and risk management permit this inequitable policy to go unquestioned by the majority of Canadians who are convinced that gay men are vectors of disease and that this policy protects the integrity of the Canadian blood supply. Thus we can see that symbolic and even legal forms of destigmatization do not address the problem of the label of riskiness.

Similarly, the granting of legal rights does not necessarily translate into destigmatization at a symbolic and interpersonal level. For example, although they have been granted legal citizenship rights, Indigenous peoples in North America continue to face stigma and discrimination rooted in powerful stereotypes of "drunken Indians" and "savages." These toxic representations have become entrenched in media and reproduced in government discourse that renders Indigenous peoples as "other." Even when such discourse attempts to address systemic problems by emphasizing, for example, the vulnerability of Indigenous women and children to abuse and harm (as the recent inquiry into murdered and missing Indigenous women in Canada did), the language of risk is implicated and Indigenous people "at risk" are othered and marked for state interventions.

CONCLUSIONS: STIGMA BOUNDARIES AND SOCIAL JUSTICE

All of this discussion of the multilayered symbolic and structural nature of stigma goes to my original point; we must work toward a more clear understanding of the interactional and institutionalized dynamics of stigmatization. This is both a theoretical and a pragmatic argument in the sense that the current uses of the term "stigma" fail to meaningfully distinguish the situation of marginalized groups from other kinds of social sorting. To reiterate, sociologists must think carefully about the meaning of discredited identity and ensure that we give critical thought to the kinds of power/knowledge at work in labeling marginal groups in order to maintain meaningful conceptual boundaries around the concept. When we fail to maintain clear definitional boundaries around the concept of stigma, we open up the possibility that stigma may be reduced to an existential phenomenon that is subject to individual "feelings" of injustice. Such a subjective interpretation would allow individuals in positions of power who feel that they are disliked or challenged to claim that they are "stigmatized" in response to critical or negative interactions with others. In so doing, they erode the potential power of the concept to call out instances of labeling and the practices of subjugation and domination that are exercised over marginal groups. That is, in permitting anyone to claim stigmatization on the basis of a feeling, the concept itself ceases to be sociologically meaningful.

Finally, I would urge scholars of stigma and discreditable identities to be attentive to both the symbolic/micro aspects of stigma, and the structural/institutional policies that mark groups as risky or at risk. If we, like Becker (1967), are concerned with "taking sides" and are invested in the pragmatic application of our research with marginal populations, it is imperative that we understand that meaningful destigmatization must operate at both the symbolic and structural levels to be effective in changing the conditions of existence for marginal people.

ACKNOWLEDGMENT

I would like to thank Thaddeus Muller for his kind invitation to present this address at the 2018 Couch-Stone meetings of the Society for the Study of Symbolic Interaction with the European Symbolic Interaction Meetings at Lancaster, UK. I also gratefully acknowledge that the ideas presented here have benefitted from lengthy conversations and collaborations with my dear colleagues Chris Bruckert and Chris Schneider. This keynote address draws on and extends earlier theoretical and empirical work presented in two previously published edited collections (Hannem and Bruckert, 2012; Hannem et al., 2019). I have updated the published version of this keynote address to reflect the most recent government hearings and findings with respect to the ion scanner.

NOTES

1. In previous work I have argued that a Foucauldian genealogy of stigmatized attributes is in order to unpack the particular circumstances in which social hierarchies and discredit emerge.

2. Rosenhan (1973) also distinguished between the stigma implications for diagnoses of serious physical illness and mental illness, suggesting: "Medical illnesses, while unfortunate, *are not commonly pejorative*. Psychiatric diagnoses, on the contrary, carry with them personal, legal, and social stigmas" (p. 181, *emphasis added*).

3. Indeed, the entire article is full of errors of interpretation with respect to Goffman's understanding of stigma, and it is noteworthy only insofar as it is a publicly available article and may inform use of the term among laypeople, students, and practitioners, who will not ever read the original source document, nor question the author's summary.

4. See Hannem and Schneider (2019), and Schneider and Hannem (2019) for a detailed discussion of the role of power and politicization in deflecting labels. Occurrences following Trump's 2020 failed bid for re-election do raise the possibility that the former president now suffers from a spoiled identity that would impede his ability to engage in social life. This is best exemplified by his removal from social media platforms and the social censure that has been visited on on him and his family members by former allies and friends.

5. Douglas' (1966) work is framed around an anthropological understanding of cultural definitions of "dirt" and defilement that would permit a sociological analysis of how attributions of defilement lead to avoidance and risk-averse behaviors. Douglas' later work with Aaron Wildavsky (1982) further examines and develops the concept of risk as a cultural construct.

6. I am grateful to an anonymous prison officer who attended my talk at the University of New South Wales, Australia, for his helpful provision of this term, used to indicate a situation in which the positive hit is not "false" in the sense that trace particles of drugs are actually present, but in which the positive reading does not indicate the presence of drugs in larger quantities nor present a risk to prison security.

7. In May 2019, as this chapter was under revision, the Canadian government announced that it would reduce the waiting period for men who have had sex with men who wanted to donate blood to three months. This is a reduction from Health Canada's previous requirement of a one-year abstention from sex with other men, which was a reduction from its initial lifetime ban on blood donations from men who have had sex with another man.

REFERENCES

Armenta, S., and de la Guardia, M. 2008. Analytical methods to determine cocaine contamination on banknotes from around the world. *Trends in Analytical Chemistry*, 28(4), 344–351.

Beck, U. 1992. *The Risk Society: Towards a New Modernity*, London, Sage.

Becker, H. 1963. *Outsiders: Studies in the Sociology of Deviance*. New York, NY, Free Press.

Becker, G. and Arnold, R. 1986. Stigma as a social and cultural construct. In *The Dilemma of Difference: A Multidisciplinary View of Stigma*, Eds S. C. Ainlay, G. Becker, and L. M. Coleman, pp. 33–57, New York, NY, Free Press.

Becker, H. 1967. Whose side are we on? *Social Problems* 14(3), 239–247.

Blumer, H. 1969. *Symbolic Interactionism: Perspective and Method*, Berkeley, University of California Press.

Castellani, B. 1999. Michel Foucault and symbolic interactionism: the making of a new theory of interaction, *Studies in Symbolic Interaction*, 22, 247–272.

Cohen, R. 2018, April 13. Tethered to a raging buffoon called Trump, *The New York Times*, Available at: https://www.nytimes.com/2018/04/13/opinion/trump-hitler-europe.html [Accessed 31 January 2020].

Donahue, H. 2017, April 28. How Donald Trump became a buffoon, *Huffpost*, Available at: https://www.huffpost.com/entry/how-trump-became-a-buffoon_b_5902935de4b084f59b49f7bd [Accessed 31 January 2020].

Douglas, M. 1966. *Purity and Danger: An Analysis of Concepts of Pollution and Taboo*, New York, NY, Routledge.

Douglas, M. and Wildavsky, A. 1982. *Risk and Culture: An Essay on the Selection of Technological and Environmental Dangers*, Berkeley, CA, University of California Press.

Foucault, M. 1977. *Discipline and Punish: The Birth of the Prison*, New York, NY, Pantheon Books.

Garland, D. 2003. The rise of risk. In *Risk and Morality*, Eds. A. Doyle and R. Ericson, pp. 48–86, Toronto, ON, University of Toronto Press.

Giddens, A. 1998. Risk society: the context of British politics. In *The Politics of Risk Society*, Ed. J. Franklin, Cambridge, Polity Press.

Glass, L. L., Lee, B. X. and Fisher, E. B. 2019, October 11. Trump is mentally unfit, no exam needed, *New York Times*; letter to the editor, Available at: https://www.nytimes.com/2019/10/11/opinion/letters/trump-mental.html [Accessed 31 January 2020].

Goffman, E. 1961. *Asylums: Essays on the Social Situation of Mental Patients and Other Inmates*, Garden City, NY, Anchor Books.

Goffman, E. 1963. *Stigma: Notes on the Management of Spoiled Identity*, New York, NY, Vintage.

Hannem, S. 2011. Stigma and marginality: gendered experiences of families of male prisoners in Canada. In *Critical Criminology in Canada: New Voices, New Directions*, Eds A. Doyle and D. Moore, pp. 181–217, Vancouver, BC, UBC Press.

Hannem, S. 2012a. Theorizing stigma and the politics of resistance: symbolic and structural stigma in everyday life. In *Stigma Revisited: Implications of the Mark*, Eds S. Hannem and C. Bruckert, pp.10–28, Ottawa, ON, University of Ottawa Press.

Hannem, S. 2012b. The mark of association: transferred stigma and the families of prisoners. In *Stigma Revisited: Implications of the Mark*, Eds S. Hannem and C. Bruckert, pp. 95–117, Ottawa, ON, University of Ottawa Press.

Hannem, S. 2019. The ion mobility spectrometry device and risk management in correctional institutions. In *Security and Risk Technologies in Criminal Justice: Critical Perspectives*, Eds S. Hannem, C. Sanders, C. J. Schneider, A. Doyle and T. Christensen, pp. 87–109, Toronto, ON, Canadian Scholars Press.

Hannem, S. and Bruckert, C. Eds 2012. *Stigma Revisited: Implications of the Mark*. Ottawa, ON, University of Ottawa Press.

Hannem, S. and Leonardi, L. 2015. *Forgotten Victims: The Mental Health and Well-Being of Families Affected by Crime and Incarceration in Canada.* Kingston, ON, Canadian Families and Corrections Network.

Hannem, S. and Schneider, C. J. 2019. Stigma and the "Weinstein effect": a comparative analyses of sexual misconduct allegations against Donald J. Trump and Harvey Weinstein in news media. In *Building Sexual Misconduct Cases against Powerful Men*, Eds S. Chen, J. Chen and N. Allaire, New York, NY, Rowman & Littlefield.

Hannem, S., Sanders, C., Schneider, C. J., Doyle, A. and Christensen, T. Eds. 2019. *Security and Risk Technologies in Criminal Justice: Critical Perspectives*. Toronto, ON, Canadian Scholars Press.

House of Commons Parliamentary Standing Committee on Public Safety and National Security. 2011a. Evidence. Thursday, October 6, 2011. SECU 006, 1st Session, 41st Parliament.

House of Commons Parliamentary Standing Committee on Public Safety and National Security. 2011b. Evidence. Tuesday, October 4, 2011. SECU 005, 1st Session, 41st Parliament.

House of Commons Parliamentary Standing Committee on Public Safety and National Security. 2011c. Evidence. Thursday, September 29, 2011. SECU 004, 1st Session, 41st Parliament.

Husain, J. and Kelly, K. 2017. Stigma rituals as pathways to activism: stigma convergence in a post-abortion recovery group, *Deviant Behavior*, 38(5), 575–592.

Johnson, S. and Dastouri, S. 2011. *Use of Ion Scanners in Correctional Facilities: An International Review*, Ottawa, ON, Correctional Service Canada. Available at: http://www.csc-scc.gc.ca/research/005008-rr11-01-eng.shtml

Karson, M. 2018. Stigma, psychopathology, and President Trump. *Psychology Today blogs*. Available at: https://www.psychologytoday.com/us/blog/feeling-our-way/201801/stigma-psychopathology-and-president-trump?amp

Link, B. G. and Phelan, J. C. 2001. Conceptualizing stigma, *Annual Review of Sociology*, 27, 363–385.

Mills, C. W. 1959. *The Sociological Imagination*, Oxford, Oxford University Press.

Rosenhan, D. L. 1973. On being sane in insane places, *Science*, 179(4070), 250–258.

Schneider, C. J. and Hannem, S. 2019. The politicization of sexual misconduct: an analysis of news media coverage of the 2016 'rape election'. *Sexuality & Culture*, 23, 737–759. doi: 10.1007/s12119-019-09587-6

Sherman, G. 2020, January 28. "The white house knew it and kept it mum": Bolton's revelations set off a three-way GOP impeachment squabble, *Vanity Fair*, Available at: https://www.vanityfair.com/news/2020/01/john-bolton-book-revelations-set-off-three-way-gop-impeachment-squabble [Accessed 31 January 2020].

Zelizer, J. 2018, July 22. Is Trump a danger – or just 'incompetent' and a 'buffoon'? *CNN.com*, Available at: https://www.cnn.com/2018/07/22/opinions/trump-critics-arent-paranoid-opinion-zelizer/index.html [Accessed 31 January 2020].

DIALOGUES AND DRAMAS OF CONVIVIALITY AND CONFRONTATION

Robert Perinbanayagam

Speech is a powerful Lord, which by means of the finest and most invisible body effects the divinest works: it can stop fear and banish grief and create joy and nurture pity, both deem and define all poetry as speech with meter. Fearful shuddering and tearful pity and grievous longing come upon its hearers...through the agency of words the soul is wont to experience a suffering of its own.
– Gorgias

ABSTRACT

Human agents are constantly using "symbols," according to G. H. Mead, or "signs," as C. S. Peirce called them, to engage in what Mikhail Bakhtin has called "dialogues" with each other or with the environment. Such vehicles of communication are not freestanding ones but are drawn from specific and demarcated discursive formations. So drawn, these vehicles are then put to use, as Kenneth Burke has shown in his dramatistic perspective on human social life, as agencies *used by human* agents *to construct* acts, *in defined situations or* scenes – that is social situations and physical locations – *to display given* attitudes, *in order to fulfill one* purpose *or another. Every human move that an individual makes has these Burkean features. Such moves are used to engage in either convivial dramas or confrontational ones.*

Keywords: Dialogue; conviviality; confrontation; identity; emotions; violence

THE DIALOGIC PROCESS

Mikhail Bakhtin, in describing the dialogic process, wrote, "The boundaries of each concrete utterance as a unit of speech communication are determined by a *change of speaking subjects*, that is, a change of speakers" (Bakhtin, 1986, p. 71).

Radical Interactionism and Critiques of Contemporary Culture
Studies in Symbolic Interaction, Volume 52, 205–220
Copyright © 2021 by Emerald Publishing Limited
All rights of reproduction in any form reserved
ISSN: 0163-2396/doi:10.1108/S0163-239620210000052012

To facilitate these processes, agents employ what Bakhtin called *speech genres*. Bakhtin also wrote:

> Language is realized in the form of individual concrete utterances (oral and written) by participants in the various areas of human activity. These utterances reflect the specific conditions and goals of each such area not only through their content (thematic) and linguistic style, that is, the selection of the lexical, phraseological, and grammatical resources of the language, but above all through their compositional structure...These we may call *speech genres*. (Bakhtin, 1986, p. 60)

Addresses using genres of speech, however, are not moves made *ab initio* but are themselves responses to what has been *interpreted a*s either an invitation or a provocation. *Every address is a rejoinder to an earlier address, a rejoinder that takes elements in the address as cues, implicit or explicit, to construct a response. Every rejoinder is an address to an implicit or explicit invitation, resulting in dialogic chains.*

The other may be correct in his or her interpretation of these situations, invitations, or provocations, or there may well have been a misinterpretation, but for all, the other does provide an addressive rejoinder to these addresses. It is in such rejoinders to provocations that a human life is lived, actively responding to the provocations provided by the world in which one finds oneself. Indeed, human agents live dialogically by addressing rejoinders to the provocations that reach them. The dialogue proceeds along these lines in a chain until it is terminated in one way or another – often enough, to restart on other occasions.

The rejoinders can take one of many forms: cordial agreement with the import of the address or an angry rebuttal; witty repartee; abject surrender, if the address was insulting or a return insult; a bantering response to the address; and finally, an indifferent silence. It is, however, not necessary to confine the dialogic process to immediately situated and momentary occasions. An address can be made at one moment and a rejoinder can be forthcoming on a later occasion, insofar as the rejoinder is directed to a particular address.[1]

Semiotics of Dialogue

The speech genres that are used in such dialogues come under the category of what Charles Sanders Peirce called "signs." He wrote:

> A sign, or *representamen,* is something which stands to somebody for something in some respect or capacity. It addresses somebody, that is, it creates in the mind of that person an equivalent sign, or perhaps a more developed sign. That sign which it creates I call the *interpretant* of the first sign. The sign stands for something, its *objec*t. (Peirce, 1955, p. 99)

For Peirce too, these signs are *addressed* in order to *elicit* one interpretant or another. The recipient of these signs that are addressed often provides "a more developed sign." Certainly, but this development can also at times be an under-deployment or an overdevelopment and even a distorted one leading to the emergence of interpretants that are different from the one that the representamen sought to elicit. Indeed, *one may claim that sign-systems emerged in order to promote and facilitate dialogues.* However, to constitute an utterance that has a proper degree of addressivity, so that it is able to elicit a commensurate interpretive rejoinder successfully, it must be framed with proper attention to its rhetoricity.

The signs that are used in such dialogues are fundamentally *rhetorical* devices. Kenneth Burke argued that rhetoric as such is not rooted in any past condition of human society.

> [Rhetoric] is rooted in an essential function of language itself, a function that is wholly realistic, and is continually born anew: the use of language as a symbolic means of inducing cooperation in beings that by nature respond to symbols. (Burke, 1969b, p. 5)

I would add a couple of caveats to this statement by Burke: I would substitute "signs" wherever "language" appears in this excerpt and change "cooperation" to "addressing of a persuasive message." These attitudes are manifested and communicated through the management of *sign-vehicles* – whose concept can subsume verbal, gestural, and material phenomena.

No doubt speech genres as signs are the principal instrumentation of such dialogic processes, but it is not necessary to confine dialogues to only speech. These signs, however, can be *verbal signs* as well as what I will call *material signs*: "I love you to distraction," on the one hand, uses words, and on the other hand, a bouquet of red roses uses material signs to communicate the same idea. We can also consider "Drop dead, you son of a bitch" versus a punch in the face or a move with a knife, club, or gun as examples of the use of verbal and material signs.

Discourse in Dialogue

These Peircean signs or Meadean "significant symbols" that are used to constitute addresses and rejoinders do not stand as isolated entities but are always drawn from larger discourses, and they derive their rhetorical force from being drawn from such discursive formations. In Bakhtin's words:

> An essential (constitutive) marker of the utterance is its quality of being addressed to someone, its *addressivity*. This addressee can be an immediate participant-interlocutor in an everyday dialogue, a differentiated collective of specialists in some particular area of cultural communication, a more or less differentiated public, ethnic group, contemporaries; likeminded people, opponents and enemies, a subordinate, a superior, someone who is lower, higher, familiar, foreign; and so forth. (Bakhtin, 1986, p. 95; italics added)

Once these addresses with certain qualities are delivered, they typically elicit rejoinders that themselves are addresses, to which the original utterer will provide rejoinders of his or her own.

In other words, every articulated speech genre or sign-vehicle is drawn from one or another specific discursive formation from which the participants select one signification with which they construct their particular addresses and rejoinders. A word such as *sin* used in the confession of a Catholic penitent to a priest gets its standing within a particular religious discourse, whereas the same word used in the phrase "sin city" in reference to an area of a town featuring brothels gains its standing in colloquial discourse with a touch of defiant irony attached to it. That is, genres of speech are characterized by what Bakhtin called *heteroglossia*. In Bakhtin's view, language that is used in dialogues codifies one or another voice: "social dialects, characteristic group behavior, professional jargons, generic languages, languages of generations and age groups, tendentious languages, languages of the authorities, of various circles and passing fashions" (1981, pp. 262–263).

He further observed that the use of language "is shot through with intentions and accents" (1981, p. 324). The "language," or specifically the sign-vehicles, that are used in communication are then never isolated units but are part of complex structures of discourse.

Insofar as the language used by human agents is characterized by heteroglossia, it should be extended to include not only verbal modes but all modes of interpersonal communication subsumed by the Peircean concept of the sign. *If there can be heteroglossia, there certainly will be heterosemioticity. Indeed, heteroglossia is really a subset of heterosemioticity insofar as all glossarial entities are signs.* Every sign, then, as it is used in dialogues, acquires its representational status within specific discursive formations and is typically provided with an interpretant within that particular sociohistorical discourse.

If one then expands the dialogic process to include not only verbal sign-vehicles but material signs, we have the following process: human agents address the other by using a variety of sign-vehicles that are replete with varying degrees of addressivity, to which the other makes rejoinders with similar qualities. Such addresses and rejoinders can, for example, be made with words, of course, but also with other vehicles, such as flowers – or clubs, lances, knives, and guns.

Each such sign will then *perforce* be drawn from one discursive formation or another and carry the particular signification – "accents and intentions" – that are relevant to that particular discourse. Once such an address is given using the relevant representamen, the recipient may be able to provide the appropriate interpretant to the extent that he or she is able to envisage its accents and intentions.

Still, there is no guarantee that the signed representamen that the agent uses to address the other will in fact elicit the expected interpretant-rejoinder, since these signs themselves will be characterized by heterosemioticity. A man may proposition a woman, thereby inviting her for an immediate sexual encounter, and she, drawing from another discourse, may take it as a proposal of marriage. In the case of the interactional malady known as *paranoia*, the recipient of addresses from a signifying other produces interpretants that are not commensurate with the "accents and intentions" of the signifying other. A gun, for example, can be an offensive weapon – or an item in a collector's assembly, or just an adornment worn on one's hip to define one's identity. Similarly, a knife can be a weapon, or an implement used on the dining table to cut meat. In the course of a dinner, an altercation between two diners may develop, and the steak knife can become a handy weapon. Such heterosemioticity can, on the one hand, make for confusion in the dialogic moment and a demand for clarificatory addresses and rejoinders and, on the other hand, become a source of confrontations and conflicts. To put it in Peircean terminology, the chosen representamen may not necessarily elicit the rejoining interpretant that the address sought, insofar as it displayed one set of "accents and intentions" while the respondent was operating with a different set.[2]

DIALOGUES AND DRAMAS IN EVERYDAY LIFE

In using "signs" "symbols" and "speech genres" to construct discursive acts human agents are also constituting "dramas," that are addressed to others. Kenneth Burke wrote:

> Where does drama get its materials From the "unending conversation" that is going at the point in history when we are born...It is from this "unending conversation," the vision at the basis of Mead's work... (Burke, 1973, pp. 110–111)

Indeed, then, the stuff and fiber of dramas is conversations couched as dialogic addresses and rejoinders. The essence of dialogism and semiotics becomes fully realized in dramatism. In such dramas of everyday life, and quite distinct from other theories of human conduct, with his theory Burke provides a very comprehensive version, taking into account all the features of human conduct. For Burke, humans are, to begin with, *agents*, performers of their own *acts*, and they use *agencies* that are really sign-vehicles drawn from one discursive formation or another, and with these performances agents announce one *attitude* or another. These acts, Burke argues, are undertaken in defined and delimited scenes, which put their own stamp on the act in question. These acts with their accompanying features are undertaken in order to fulfill one *purpose* or another. The purposes of such acts, indisputably, are to enter into rhetorically wise dialogues, usually with another human agent, and at times with cats and dogs and the physical environment. *In this perspective, however, the central element should be that of agency. Individuals in fact use one sign-vehicle or another to act, thereby establishing themselves as agents and using said vehicles to define scene, display attitudes, and announce purposes.* In fact, every move and moment in the everyday life of every individual is described with these elements of Burke's dramatistic perspective (1969a).[3]

Such dramas are essentially the assertion and presentation of selected identities to which an individual makes claim. Every dramatistic move the individual makes is an enactment of an identity, and typically, the individual will seek opportunities to give it play. A fan of a particular football team, for instance, will display loyalty by means of talk, costuming, attending matches, and shouting himself or herself hoarse in assertions of joy or hatred. Similarly, a deeply religious person will give play to his or her identity by attending the relevant ceremonies and enacting the recommended rituals.

However, one must not define identities as merely aspects of an individual's consciousness but also as claims of membership in larger social formations. One can therefore be an American, a Buddhist, or a Muslim – and a fan of the New

York Yankees. In performing an identity, agents are also automatically relating themselves to larger social formations. As Charles Tilly has forcefully argued:

1 Identities reside in relations with others: you and me and us and them.

2 Strictly speaking, every individual, group, or social site has as many identities as it has relations with other individuals, groups, or social sites.

3 The same individuals, groups, and social sites shift from identity to identity as they shift relations. (Tilly, 2016, p. 8)

Identities, then, are constituted by agents who use one sign-vehicle or another as agencies in particular scenes to address one or another attitude and a purpose to another, which addressed claims may be either validated or rejected. The acts by which identities are claimed are situated within very particulate discursive formations. . In this way "identification becomes the basis of motivation," that is identification with an entity that is larger than oneself as Nelson Foote argued for the development of attitudes and the performance of acts (1969). Such identifications enlarge the self and give it valences and dimensions that it cannot claim as a lonely self.

In the following "representative anecdotes" – to use Burke's concept – one can see that the Burkean hexadic terms are given play, implicitly or explicitly, by the actors as they engage in dialogues of one sort or another to claim and perform their identities and often to take steps to deal with refutations of their asserted identities. Such dramas that human agents find themselves performing in everyday life can be separated into two basic categories: convivial or confrontational dramas, though often there can be mixed dramas too. These procedures are typically infused with certain degrees of emotionality, though some of them have more of the relevant emotions than others. These emotionalities are manifested by the use of verbal signs or material signs though often there are mixtures of both. Indeed it would be impossible for one agent to communicate with another without it bearing some degree of emotionality.

DRAMAS OF CONVIVIALITY

The Discourse of Camaraderie

In such dialogues, there is a deliberate attempt to ensure that the words used present attitudes that are likely to result in moments of conviviality and friendliness. Here is dialogue that is convivial and adopts an almost bantering tone between then-President Nixon and Attorney General Mitchell:

Nixon: Hello, John, how are you?

Mitchell: Mr. President, I'm just great. How are you?

Nixon: You are a big Wall Street lawyer. You do have to admit that you are rich.

Mitchell: Not in front of all these people who collect taxes. I can report that my firm is doing quite well.

Nixon: Are they?

Ehrlichman: There is no reason it shouldn't.

Mitchell: There is no reason why it shouldn't. (*The Washington Post*, 1974, p. 152)

In this short dialogue, President Nixon is greeting Mitchell, the attorney general of the United States, and Mitchell responds by addressing Nixon as "Mr. President." He is giving him the deference due to his office, though Mitchell knew Nixon personally even before he became president, and they were actually friends. Nixon further asks about the success of Mitchell's firm, displaying a friendly interest in Mitchell's life, and Mitchell provides a mocking response: "Not in front of all these people who collect taxes." This dialogue is, in fact, a very convivial exchange, full of friendly interest in the other. The exchange has a slightly bantering tone and displays a certain playfulness.

In another example of conviviality, words are exchanged in a teasing mode between two young brothers. The tone is one of overt humor, punctuated by laughter:

M.J: I bet you a nickel.

G.J: What?

M.J.: Gotta see some money […] bet you a nickel that I am looking sharper than you.

G.J.: No, you wasn't.

M.J.: No, you had your play clothes on (laughs).

G.J.: I ai'nt ha' my play clothes on.

M.J.: You have you Batman socks too.

G.J.: I did (laughs) not.

M.J.: You did (laughs) so. You did so.

G.J.: Ah? Ah?

M.J.: Got something else to say?

G.J.: Wait a minute – let me tell you something. Greg Barber looks better than you. You come in there with your clothes hanging out all the way down to here (laughs).

M.J.: What? (Loman, 1967, p. 1)

Though the brothers seem to be overtly confronting one another, they are in fact engaging in the friendly teasing that often occurs between intimates and siblings.

DRAMAS OF CONFRONTATION
Verbal Signs as Weapons

In ongoing relationships there is often enough a need to enact hostile attitudes and seek to dominate the other and create moments of conflict. To do this effectively, agents need one or more vehicles. One manifestation of the dialogic process is what may be called "quarrels." In the course of ongoing interaction, agents will often find themselves having to disagree with the other and express this to the other verbally. The other will retort, and a quarrel will ensue. In the course of such quarrels, the agents will have to use various instrumentations to assert their respective positions. Such positions will typically consist of.

(1) Fact-based refutation of the other's claims
(2) Insults and recriminations
(3) Sarcasm and irony
(4) Studied silence

In order to construct these discursive acts in the course of dialogic interactions, agents will have to make recourse to the use of one or more sign-vehicles. Consider here an interaction between two young women. I will choose a very simple interaction that shows how a single word can be used to make a refutation and a confrontation.

> Tami: Why were you combing Peggy's hair yesterday?
>
> Heidi: I didn't.
>
> Tami: Yes, you were.
>
> Heidi: I was not.
>
> Tami: You were combing it back.
>
> Heidi: I was not.
>
> Tami: You were *too.*
>
> Heidi: I was *not.* You can go ask Peggy.
>
>   (Peggy walks by)
>
>   Peggy, was I combing your hair?
>
>   (Peggy shakes her head "no")
>
>   See? What did I tell you?
>
> Tami: Whose hair were you combing?
>
> Heidi: I wasn't combing anyone's hair.
>
> Tami: Who was combing Peggy's hair?
>
> Heidi: I don't know. (Eder, 1990, pp. 70–71)

In this case, the dispute between two young females is about one of them having violated the norms of a committed friendship. The wounded young woman is drawing from the discursive formation of committed and loyal friendship. It is eventually settled by the presentation of a credible testimony. However, one can also examine how this conflict was conducted. It begins with an accusatory addressee that is swiftly denied in a rejoinder and proceeds with further accusations and denials. In examining the course of this progression, we can pay attention, at a crucial stage of the interaction, to the emphatic use of the adverb *too*. This is a standard vehicle to indicate both conviction and refutation of the other's claim and is usually accompanied by the necessary tonal emphasis. This is met with another emphatic refutation, a *not*. These vehicles are parsimonious ways of stating one's position as well as indicating a very positive attitude toward one's own claims.

In another form of the quarrel, agents will use sarcasm as the weapon. Here is a good example. In the following text, a patient ("B") had missed an appointment without calling to cancel it and talks with his analyst ("A") about the unexplained absence:

> A: Maybe you felt that the kind of interpretations I was making on Monday were the same thing and you couldn't come yesterday 'cause you were scared of this faggot – who was gonna make a pass at you.
>
> B: It's almost as if I don't want you to get the idea that I am trying to pursue you, and at the same time, I can almost get an indication of whether you're trying to pursue me or not, you know. Like, if I come in here and you were pissed off, you know, I'd be really afraid, you know, I'd say: "Fuck me, man, you know, this guy's really after my ass or something."
>
> A: Oh, you mean if I were pissed off.
>
> B: Yeah.
>
> A: About you're not having come.
>
> B: But as long as, you know, nothing has changed and you just said, "Well, that's the way it goes," you know.
>
> A: That means I don't need you so desperately. I'm not after your ass.
>
> B: Right.
>
> A: I see. So another slight wrinkle that we can add to your not coming yesterday is that you thought Monday I might be too strongly attracted to you.
>
> B: Well, Monday seemed to go real well and I really wondered why, you know.
>
> A: That is what you couldn't stand, isn't it?
>
> B: And – yeah.
>
> A: And then?
>
> B: Oh, I thought: "Jesus, you know, why did I come in here so eagerly or why did I open up so well?" And maybe subconsciously, I thought, you know – all those maybes and shit thrown in, but I am [sigh]. That I may have reacted in a way – well, you are really pushin' today, you know, or you're really in tune with what's happening or you're the one that wants to get back with both feet."
>
> A: Me?
>
> B: Yeah. You've been away for a whole week, you know, and you gotta get back and secure me, you know.
>
> A: Oh yes, I was too eager to recapture your love.
>
> B: Yeah. (Gill and Hoffman, 1982, pp. 102–103)

In this quarrel, a therapist is angry that his client missed an appointment, and the conversation proceeds to establish why the appointment was missed. The therapist makes a number of charges and introduces the sexual theme into the quarrel. The patient was reluctant to come because, according to the therapist, he was afraid that the latter was interested in him sexually. The fundamental strategy that the therapist uses to conduct the quarrel is a sense of sarcastic innuendo.

One sure-fire agency with which confrontational addresses are handled is the use of obscenities drawn from sexual contexts or curses drawn from religious sources. These typically do exhibit neither originality of composition nor subtlety and often the mere use of clichés.

Finally, one may mention studied silence as a method of confronting another. When someone addresses another, then the addressee is obliged to respond, in one way or another, by using a particular sign-vehicle, insofar as the addressor perforce operates in the dialogic world. Such rejoinders can be immediate and pointed, certainly, but a silence, sullen or otherwise, is also a rejoinder. It communicates something to the addressor and may elicit further addresses or a withdrawal from the interaction. Indeed, these silences as rejoinders can often be very powerful. The phenomenon known as "sending someone to Coventry" captures the power of silence as a rejoinder. Here is a brief description of this from *Wikipedia*: "To send someone to Coventry is an English idiom meaning "to deliberately ostracize someone." Typically this is done by not talking to them, avoiding their company, and acting as if they no longer exist. Victims are treated as though they are completely invisible and inaudible. In fact, it has been argued that husbands demean their wives and assert their power and status in interactions by ignoring their addresses and showing that they don't deserve to be taken seriously and thereby essentially erasing their presence by silence (De Francisco,1991).

The Sign of the Gun

Dramas often use material signs called *props* as agencies with which to communicate one signification or another in the course of a play. One prop that is used in constituting dramas in everyday life is the gun, as in some plays on stage – Ibsen's *Hedda Gabler*, for instance, or Chekov's *The Seagull*, though in both cases the gun is used to commit suicide in order to address the agent's significant circles.

The gun, in all its variables, shapes, and strengths, is notable for its power and efficiency as a signifying agency of address, even if it is not actually used. Its mere presence in the hands of an agent is enough to indicate its sign as an agency with which another can, at a minimum, be impressed and told that he or she must take account of its presence, thus making it into an agency in the dialogue process. If that is the case, such dialogues can be conducted, not only with linguistic signs, but all the objects that can be used as sign-vehicles. Guns are in ubiquitous use in modern society. They are used routinely in military combat. In everyday life, they become dialogic vehicles with which agents can present a variety of addresses.

(1) The mere possession of this vehicle will give a sense of importance to the self of the owner. Further, if it is worn on the body of the owner, it becomes an address to whoever beholds the wearer about the wearer's power to assert the self and/or to indicate that the wearer is able and willing to mount a sharp rejoinder if provoked.

(2) The gun as a vehicle can be used in a systematically rational way to subdue a dangerous agent and be presented in a calculating and disciplined manner – for example, by law enforcement.

(3) It can also be used in dialogic interaction to express emotions – anger, resentment, jealousy.

An instrument with such great potential confers on the user a sense that he or she is possessed of powers that are over and beyond those conferred by mere physical attributes. An agent with a gun is an individual with a sense of identity who is endowed with power and authority that can be exercised whenever the agent is called upon to do so – or even when not called upon – because the mere possession and access to the gun will give a powerful valence to identity.

Schools and the Dialogic Quest for Identity

Schools in the United States and elsewhere are not merely places in which young people learn academic subjects. They are the scenes in which the young ones spend most of their waking hours, but they are also places in which these students, in early or later adolescence, undertake to define and present their respective identities, identities that are still in their formative stages. Such processes are, in fact, characterized by doubts and uncertainties for some, and some measure of assurance for others. Nevertheless, for these youngsters – not children anymore, not adults yet – it is a period of flux and process with moments of clarity as well as periods of doubt, caught up in a whirlpool of anxiety.

Identities at this stage of the youngsters' lives are not easily accomplished. Some of them feel challenged (unkindly or unwittingly), rejected, and even ridiculed. These contingencies without a doubt will lead to feelings of resentment, anger, hatred – causative factors that will often lead to certain types of retaliatory acts that will be a payback for the humiliations they have received as well as a move to claim a new identity.

Identity Challenges at Columbine

On April 20, 1999, Eric Harris and Dylan Klebold conducted a series of acts at a high school that they had been attending. They planted bombs in the vicinity of the school in the early hours of the morning and then arrived separately at the school. Here is a real description of their moves from Wikipedia:

> Harris and Klebold armed themselves, using straps and webbing to conceal weapons beneath black dusters. They lugged backpacks and duffel bags that were filled with pipe bombs and ammunition. Harris also had his shotgun in one of the bags.

Wikipedia also noted they provided certain markers of their chosen identities: Harris wore a white T-shirt that read "Natural Selection" in black letters – presumably alluding to the Spenserian axiom about the survival of the fittest as well as certain features of the Darwinian theory – and also a homemade bandolier. Klebold, on the other hand, decided to define himself emotionally: He was filled with "wrath," a claim printed in red on his black T-shirt.

The bombs that they had planted in the school failed to explode. Harris and Klebold then pulled their guns out of their trench coats and went on a killing spree that wounded or killed many of their schoolmates and a teacher. After wandering through the school premises for a while looking for more victims, Harris and Klebold committed suicide. According to Wikipedia,

> Harris sat down with his back to a bookshelf and fired his shotgun through the roof of his mouth; Klebold went down on his knees and shot himself in the left temple with his TEC-9.

Who, then, were these two characters, Eric Harris and Dylan Klebold? It is clear that they had both experienced an extreme degree of humiliation at the hands of their schoolmates. Though the claim that they were "isolates" has been challenged, and they did have a circle of friends, it is clear that they were subject to a great deal of humiliation by their peers at school, as indicated earlier by important crucibles of identity – generation and affirmation. Consider here a Wikipedia report on one of their fellow students, Brown. According to Brown,

> People surrounded them in the commons and squirted ketchup packets all over them, laughing at them, calling them faggots. That happened while teachers watched. They couldn't fight back. They wore the ketchup all day and went home covered with it.

Another student, Laughlin, noted: "I caught the tail end of one really horrible incident, and I know Dylan told his mother that it was the worst day of his life." That incident, according to Laughlin, involved seniors pelting Klebold with "ketchup-covered tampons" in the commons.

The reports from the scene, in fact, described how school life was characterized by bullying of one group or one student by others, with the teachers and administrators doing nothing to confront it. The incident with the ketchup and the tampons is indeed very instructive. Harris and Klebold were subject to humiliation by members of the most admired gang in most high schools – the football team – and called what is a very hurtful term in school, "faggot." Accusations of homosexuality at this stage in life for Harris and Klebold would have been very damaging to their self-esteem and challenging to their process of constituting an identity. The tampon incident too uses a heterosexually charged sign, a "bloody" tampon, challenging Harris' and Klebold's sexual identity once again, though in a subversive way. Klebold also told his father of his hatred of the jocks at Columbine, adding that Harris, in particular, had been victimized. Klebold stated, "They sure gave Harris hell."

Facing this atmosphere in places that are very significant in the lives of young men and women – besides the social interaction in these arenas, they spend most of their daily life there – without a doubt cut them to the quick. After enduring all this, Klebold remarked in a tape he made, "You've been giving us shit for years. You're fucking gonna pay for all the shit!" These, then, were the addresses to which Klebold and Harris felt obliged to construct rejoinders, unusual ones at that.

Facing these issues, Harris and Klebold discovered an agency with which they could obtain a sense of power and control: guns and bombs and knives. These objects become, in fact, extensions of the persona of the individual and provide their owner, if he or she has the capacity to use them, with a sense of invincibility, particularly when the other has no weapons of any kind.

In addition to acquiring lethal – and empowering – agencies, Harris and Klebold acted in various ways to experience this sense of power. In an economics class, when asked to make an advertisement for a business, Harris made a video entitled "Hit Men for Hire," no doubt identifying himself and his buddy Klebold as agents of violent acts. They also went to gun shows and acquired various weapons as a way of feeling powerful.

Harris and Klebold, however, did not stop with the mere ownership of the weapons; they assembled their weaponry and went to the arena where their identities were challenged and represented and ridiculed, and planted the bombs at strategic places, and started shooting. They shot not chosen targets, not the particular people who had tormented them, but anyone they could find on the school premises, though they did grant a reprieve to one friend of theirs by sending him home. Harris and Klebold felt the rage not merely against any particular person but all the members of the school community as representatives of their tormenters. The fellow students of Klebold and Harris understood that the humiliating moves toward the pair were being addressed, but being witnesses or indifferent actors, they also deserve the violent rejoinder that Harris and Klebold directed at them. In the end, 36 young men and women were either killed or wounded, after which Harris and Klebold performed the sacrificial act of killing themselves. Indeed, the two agents responded murderously to the provocations they had endured and did not want to face more such persecutions.

Was the suicide by Harris and Klebold a form of sacrificial martyrdom? Perhaps not, but they certainly decided to kill their tormenters and other representatives to "pay for their shit," and martyring their own selves was a price they were willing to pay for this (Harris and Klebold (n.d.). https://www.google.com/ preferences).

Religion and the Dialogic Quest for Authenticity

Once a specific identity has been formulated by an agent, to use Burkean terminology, an agent would seek to give it play by undertaking various acts in defined scenes and displaying attitudes with the purpose of continuously having his or her identity authenticated. Worshiping at sacred sites, performing rituals, fasting, self-immolation, and even singing and dancing are some of the acts with which believers periodically have their religious identity authenticated. In some religions, killing an animal is a way to assert religious identification. And killing a human agent given a label such as "infidel" – for example, by Islamists or the medieval Crusaders – is yet another, albeit extreme and rare, form of authenticating a religious identity.

The bombing and destruction of the Twin Towers in New York City and its repercussions created an opportunity for several young men to have their identities as faithful and loyal Muslims authenticated. Since this event in 2001, there has been a state of overt conflict between various Islamic groups and the United States. In this case, the United States was using one genre of signs drawn from what one may call the *statist* discourse, whereas the Islamic groups were providing rejoinders drawn from the religious discourse. The perpetrators of the attack claimed to have provided a rejoinder to American undermining of Islamic interests, just as the United States – that is, a *state* – claimed to be responding *specifically* to political and military provocations. Muslims from various quarters of the world became involved in responding to the attack on Iraq by defining it *broadly* as a war, and not a war against Iraq and its leader, Saddam Hussein, but against Islam itself. In other words, the "accents and intentions" of the addressor were, following the implications of heterosemioticity, taken by respondents as representing another set of accents and intentions. Indeed, in practice there is no ready correspondence between a representamen and interpretant, insofar as every human agent has his or her own interpretational universe.

These individual acts by isolated agents did not advance the cause of Islam or the safety of Muslims in any tangible way, and could not possibly have done so. *These acts were, rather, testimonials these agents were making to the authenticity of their own individual identity as Muslims.* A very powerful exponent of this view, one who was raised in the United States and became a very eloquent speaker, emerged in the shape of Anwar al-Awlaki. He spoke in defense of Islam as well as for Muslims everywhere, exhorting them to rise to defend Islam against the United States and its allies. He encouraged individual Muslims to take up arms against the United States in whatever way they could manage. He claimed that after the American invasion of Iraq, he could not live as a Muslim in America. He used the Internet to encourage Muslim young people to take up arms against Americans as individuals and become one of the *mujahideen* – "those who fight the enemies of Islam" – and told them, in countless Internet messages, that Muslim young men had to make one of two choices: to become a *hajji* or a *jihadi* – a pilgrim or a fighter – and to travel to the Muslim homelands and join a movement or become a fighter wherever they found themselves.

Anwar al-Awlaki, in fact, had a powerful – almost indisputable – narrative at his disposal. In the words of Ali Soufan, a Lebanese-American who worked for the FBI, various American moves "fed into the narrative" that al-Awlaki and others were announcing: "The invasion of Iraq; the banning of Muslims; Abu Ghraib; Guantanamo drone strikes against innocent civilians" (Ellwood, 2017). A perfect dialogic structure of conflict has emerged and one that provoked individual adherents of Islam to assert their identity as a Muslim and authenticate it by making the ultimate rejoinder – killing the enemies of Islam or its representatives and sacrificing their own lives.

Among those who responded to the call from Anwar al-Awlaki and his cohorts, one can discuss the San Bernardino incident perpetrated by Syed Rizwan Farook and his wife, Tashfeen Malik. Together they undertook an attack on the Inland Regional Center, a place where Farook, in fact, worked. He was born in the United States, studied in schools and universities there, and used his training to find suitable work. Nevertheless, as a devout Muslim, he became disenchanted with life in America and felt that he was living among his enemies as defined by the various Islamic propaganda screeds available on the Internet. He soon traveled to Saudi Arabia and met a fellow Pakistani, Malik, with whom he had been in contact. They were both committed jihadists and began plotting their rejoinder to what had been presented to them as a war against Islam. According to Wikipedia, the FBI investigation had stated that Farook and Malik had become radicalized over several years prior to the attack, consuming "poison on the Internet" and expressing commitment to jihadism and martyrdom in private messages.

On December 4, 2015, Farook and Malik went to the Inland Regional Center and, after planting some bombs in the entrance, came in well armed with the intent to kill as many of Farook's fellow workers as possible. Farook had interacted with some of them on a friendly basis, and some others had commented on his Muslim identity. They killed 14, and 22 others were seriously injured at what was a Christmas celebration. Farook had, in fact, been at the party in its initial stages, and then went home and returned with Malik and the weapons and started the massacre. He and Malik fled the scene but were cornered and killed by the police in a shoot-out. In one fell swoop, they accomplished their goals: they killed some of the representations of a state that was waging a war against Islam in Iraq and Afghanistan, and attained martyrdom. It was a rather comprehensive rejoinder to what was defined as the hostile and confrontational address that the United States had mounted.

The question arises: why did the perpetrators choose these particular targets to which to direct their emotions? The answer is that they chose the targets that were relevant and integral to their identities: the agents who killed their fellow students were identified against those who rejected or tormented them, and Islamic agents were aligned against those who, even in a remote way, were connected to the powers who were directing the "war against Islam."[4]

ACKNOWLEDGMENTS

The examples of dialogues I use in this essay have appeared in some of my earlier publications, though I am extracting different significations from them here. This no doubt indicates that even the smallest bit of a conversation will present a variety of features for study and analysis.

I have taken the accounts of the shootings from the entries in Wikipedia. This Internet site has very faithfully collected all the accounts of these incidents from a number of sources and made them accessible to all.

I must thank Prof. Doyle McCarthy of Fordham University for reading an earlier version of this article and making helpful suggestions.

NOTES

1. For an examination of the affinity of Bakhtin's work with G. H. Mead's, see Holquist (1990).

2. Wittgenstein (1953) made a similar claim in a pithy sentence: for a large class of cases – though not all in which we employ the word *meaning* – it can be defined thus: "the

meaning of a word is its use in a language game." He claimed that he was using *language game* "to bring into prominence the fact that speaking a language is a form of activity, a form of life" (1953: aphorism 41, p. 18). Games, in fact, are not only structures of activity that are governed by very strict rules, as argued by Wittgenstein, but are inescapably conducted as addresses and rejoinders – that is, they are dialogues between two parties in which each one enforces the rules or hires someone to do so.

3. The concept of drama has been used by many in the description and analysis of social life. However, nearly all of them use either a very truncated definition of drama or claim that in their usage it is only a metaphor. For Burke, however, everyday human life is in fact dramatically organized, and that drama is the ontology of the human species (Burke, 1985). This claim is compatible with the thesis that "dialogicality is the ontology of the human species" insofar as verbal dialogues, the main activity in dramas, are buttressed by other agencies of communication.

4. This claim that there was a war against Islam was reinforced by often using the word *Crusaders* to describe the attackers on Islamic countries by a rhetorical appropriation of the medieval struggle between European Christians and the Middle Eastern Muslim powers to apply it to the current political conflict between some Muslim states and the United States and its allies. The claim was that the attacks on certain Muslim states were nothing but the continuation of the Crusades.

REFERENCES

Bakhtin, M. 1981. *The Dialogic Imagination*, Austin, TX, University of Texas Press.

Bakhtin, M. 1986. *Speech Genres and Other Late Essays*, Austin, TX, University of Texas Press.

Burke, K. 1985. Dramatism as ontology or epistemology: a symposium, *Communication Quarterly*, 33(1), 17–33.

Burke, K. 1969a. *A Grammar of Motives*, Berkeley, CA, University of California Press.

Burke, K. 1969b. *A Rhetoric of Motives*, Berkeley, CA, University of California Press.

Burke, K. 1973. *The Philosophy of Literary Form: Studies in Symbolic Action*, Berkeley, CA, University of California Press.

De Francisco, V. L. 1991. The sounds of silence: how men silence women in marital relations, *Discourse & Society*, 2(4), 413–423.

Eder, D. 1990. Serious and playful disputes: variation in conflict talk among female adolescents. In *Conflict Talk: Sociolinguistic Investigations of Arguments in Conversations*, Ed A. Grimshaw, pp. 67–84, Cambridge, Cambridge University Press.

Ellwood, A. 2017. *American Jihad*. Documentary Film, Four Five Productions Inc.

Nelson, F. 1969. Identification as the basis of motivation. In *Social Psychology through Symbolic Interaction*, Eds G. Stone and H. Farberman, Waltham. MA, Ginn-Blaisdell.

Gill, M. and Hoffman, I. 1982. *Analysis of Transference*, Vol. 2, New York, NY, International Universities Press.

Harris and Klebold (n.d.). Journals of Harris and Klebold. Retrieved from http://www.google.com/preferences

Holquist, M. 1990. *Dialogism: Bakhtin and His World*, London, Routledge.

Loman, B. 1967. *Conversations in a Negro American Dialect*, Washington, DC, Center for Applied Linguistics.

Markova, I. 2003. Dialogicality as an Ontology of Humanity. In *Rethinking Communicative Interaction*, Ed C. Grant, Amsterdam, John Benjamins.

Peirce, C. S. 1955. *Philosophical Writings of Peirce*, Ed J. Buchler, New York, NY, Dover Publications.

The Washington Post. 1974. *The Presidential Transcripts*, New York, NY, Dell.

Tilly, C. 2016. *Identities, Boundaries and Social Ties*, London, Routledge.

Wittgenstein, L. 1953. *Philosophical Investigations*, London, Blackwell Publishing.

RHETORICAL PROCESSES IN THE SALES RELATIONSHIP IN LUXURY RETAIL

Veronica Manlow and Christopher Ferree[1]

ABSTRACT

We examine the work undertaken by salespersons in the menswear department of a well-known department store in New York City that sells specialized "luxury" clothing by using the theoretical perspective developed by Kenneth Burke, the philosopher of language and communication. He has argued that the most comprehensive way to describe human conduct is to examine what was done, what attitude did it manifest, where was it done, who did it, and how was it done. Burke summarized these questions as act, attitude, scene, agent, agency, and purpose. With these terms comprising a "hexad," a great deal of complexity can be captured within an organizational context. Indeed, Burke refers to these terms as "the grammar of motives" – that is, the motives of human conduct (1969a, 1968). In the carefully staged menswear environment we find salesmen who negotiate the goals and purposes of the store as well as their individual motives through implicitly defined sequences of acts on the selling floor.

Keywords: Kenneth Burke; interactional processes; selling; luxury; retail; fashion

INTRODUCTION

In ongoing human interactions and relationships, individuals use one or another symbolic system. Following the work of Kenneth Burke, it is the case that such usages are designed to persuade the other to take one course of action or another. That is, they are in fact *rhetorical* exercises. He wrote: *For rhetoric as such is not*

Radical Interactionism and Critiques of Contemporary Culture
Studies in Symbolic Interaction, Volume 52, 221–235
Copyright © 2021 by Emerald Publishing Limited
All rights of reproduction in any form reserved
ISSN: 0163-2396/doi:10.1108/S0163-239620210000052013

rooted in any past condition of human society. It is rooted in an essential function of language itself, a function that is wholly realistic, and is continually born anew; the use of language as a symbolic means of inducing cooperation in beings that by nature respond to symbols (1969b, p. 43).

Rhetorical exercises are in fact ubiquitous in human interactions and individuals use a variety of strategies to achieve their goals. One such strategy is to use Burke's "grammar of motives" to do this. Burke asked: "What is involved when we say what people are doing and why they are doing it?" and went on to claim that in a "rounded statement about motives you must have some word that names the *act* (names what took place, in thought or deed), and another that names the *scene* (the background of the act, the situation in which it occurred); also you must indicate what person or kind of person (*agent*) performed the act, what means or instruments he or she used (*agency*) and *purpose*" (1969a, p. xv). In a later essay, he added "attitude" to this pentad of terms thus making it a hexad (1968). Such principles are used in rhetorically demanding moments.

These moves are interactional ones in which various acts are addressed to another by an agent, moves facilitated by processes that George Herbert Mead (1934) calls "taking the role of the other" and "taking the attitude of the other." In undertaking these procedures each participant in the interaction will be able to assess the other's intentions and capabilities, indeed his or her more or less complex identity thereby enabling each agent to be rhetorically effective.

A clothing salesman is able to assess the identity of his customer through his appearance alone, which according to Gregory Stone (1969) can be used to come to conclusions about the customer's "value" – that is, his economic and social standing and his "mood" or emotional state which are the features of his presented identity. His interpretation of the customer's presentation of self will help the salesman in articulating an appropriate sales strategy.

Such identities are in Burke's words "affirmed with earnestness precisely because there is a division" (1969b. p. 22). Such relationships are constituted by a process, Burke (1969b, p. 25) avers, of identification and disidentification.

> In pure identification, there would be no strife. Likewise, there would be no strife in absolute separateness, since opponents can join battle only through a mediatory ground that makes their communication possible, thus providing the first condition necessary for the interchange of blows. But put identification and division ambiguously together, so that you cannot know for certain just where one ends and the other begins, and you have the characteristic invitation to rhetoric.

That is in trying to persuade the other to take one line of action rather than another, the agent will seek to entice the other to eschew their separateness and accept an identity of interests – at least for the time being. As Tara Lynn Clapp in a move to unite Burke's grammar and rhetoric of motives into one analytic framework observed,

> A social identity is an interpretive form that is available for rhetorical use, a set of terministic resources that interpret and explain the motives of a potential situation and recommend forms of action in acting-together. (Clapp, 2009, p. 1)

Robert Perinbanayagam too has sought to integrate Burke's theories with George Herbert Mead's work (2000, 2011, 2016) as has Joseph Gusfield (1989).

Burke's theories and the methods which he recommended – which he called dramatism – can be used to analyze the proceedings in various organizational settings. For instance, this perspective on human conduct can be profitably applied in the analyses of the conduct of the salesforce in department stores. In such arenas, agents perform the acts of selling in defined scenes and situations in the course of which they display attitudes with the purpose of persuading the customer to look favorably on an item and purchase it. This is a purpose that is shared by management and the salesforce. Nevertheless the more important of the relevant acts are performed by the salesforce in interactions with customers. In this chapter, we will examine the drama of the interactions in the scene of the menswear division of one department store within which a rich world of intentional acts and attitudes, agencies, and purposes are in play.

Instead of following the Burkean sequence of act, attitude, agent, agency, scene, and purpose, we will begin with purpose – the purposes of the organization that wants to sell merchandise and those of the agents it employs to do the selling – the salesforce. It is the particular purpose for which the organization was established – or its goals – that drives all the agents in the composition of their acts and the attitudes they manifest, and the agencies that they choose to employ in particular scenes.

Interviews of nine salesmen working within the menswear division of a New York department store in various departments, and participant observation, comprise the methodology in this study.

THE PURPOSE OF THE ACTS

Organizations are constituted in order to fulfill certain defined goals. While formal organizations are often described as consisting of structures of power and hierarchy and of roles and statuses they are also delimited arenas of interaction in which agents act and present their selves and constitute identities in order to fulfill both their own purposes and that of the organization. Such purposive acts are undertaken by managing both verbal and visual signs.

Formal organizations are also systems of stratification in which power is unequally distributed and where the interests of various divisions and of individual members may be at odds with those at other levels along the hierarchy. Goals are usually set at the executive level and are passed along to a variety of managers and enacted in face-to-face encounters with customers where they may take on varied forms. Rewards and sanctions are used to gain adherence and "new interests" may emerge (Scott, 1992, p. 314). Lonnie Athens (2015, p. 23) challenges what he sees as the widely held belief that "sociality" is the basis of social order. He implores symbolic interactionists to recognize the importance of conflict and the presence of dominant and submissive attitudes within all interactions within which a "principle of domination" is in operation. Considering this selling relationship in selling relationships allows us to see ways in which power is unequally distributed. While the customer usually is in a dominant position, there are times when the salesman by virtue or his knowledge and expertise holds more power in a sales transaction.

One can define "goals" in Burkean terms as "purpose." For the luxury store in this study, the fundamental purpose of the enterprise and for its management is to have the salesforce sell as many items in the store to visiting customers as possible. The salesforce – *the agents* – has an additional purpose: to secure their continued employment and to make the necessary commission on each sale as well as to enhance their reputation in the firm, and their self-concept as a luxury sales expert. The very success of the organization depends on the energy and perspicacity with which the members of the salesforce function as agents.

CASTING THE AGENT

Henri Peretz in his ethnographic study of luxury sales speaks of the store proposing a "clothing identity program" to customers (1995, p. 22). He explains that this is done through various instrumentations or props such as "window displays and mannequins" but also directly through the salespersons who present "tactical clothing identities" as they sell identity by achieving an identification with their customers, not only through their appearance but also through their attitude which allows them to gain the customer's confidence and act as a role model. In the department store we studied, this meant that salesmen in the tailored clothing department and in furnishings and shoes worked in suits or sports jackets and trousers with ties; pocket squares, watches, and cufflinks were often used to accessorize their ensembles, and proper business shoes were worn. The only way to differentiate the sellers from the customers was the name badge they were required to wear. Salesmen in the designer collections had more freedom to choose what to wear, given the shifting of fashion trends, but still were expected to adhere to a professional dress code that included blazers and trousers and business shoes. More recently as this division began to try to appeal to a younger clientele, denim and sneakers were allowed, and jackets shed in favor of sweaters or bared shirtsleeves. Unless the trend called for it, these salesmen barely wore ties on the sales floor. They wore the same sort of name badge, but were easily differentiated from their customers, who were often dressed in what a salesperson describes as "far more casual or more outrageous ensembles than the sellers were allowed to wear."

In certain professions such as luxury sales, the task of communicating is of paramount importance, in that it is not only considered and planned by salespersons themselves but by a variety of executives, marketers, merchandisers, managers, and supervisors involved in creating specific dramatic forms. Salespersons, in fact, become performers who enact scripts which reflect input from others. And while the salesmen we've observed and interviewed don't have actual words they must say, they follow a series of moves, a set of steps they should take to progress from opening to closing the sale. And in the luxury environment a salesman must perform in a manner that is consistent with the tone of the store, which is described by one salesman as having "an understated, calm masculinity, a sophisticated gentlemanly quality that is neither effete nor priggish but convivial yet restrained." To the best of their ability they have to appraise and then appeal to their customers in as efficient a way as possible to secure a sale: the livelihood of the store, of individual brands, of associated personnel, and indeed their own depends on the success of the selling process. They use the clothing worn by the would-be customer and the ornamentation and demeanor to apprise the customer and then to achieve such an end.

Salespersons are selected by management. The management, merchant teams, and middle or store management who wish to keep up their reputations as purveyors of fine or luxury goods, who need to sell what is on the shelves and racks, need a workforce that is just polished enough to maintain the facade – promising good commission atop a barely livable wage (that is, the promise that with hard work, each seller can attain a better life to afford the goods he or she sells) – a workforce that is just educated or savvy enough to be able to absorb all the product knowledge and repeat it at will to consumers, season after season, year after year. But the sales staff must also be just content enough not to leave because it takes a lot of effort of course to recruit, hire, train, and maintain a competent and sizable enough team to get the work done without having to worry about mass attrition of staff, or at least not have to manage a constantly changing staff of stock, sellers, managers, visual merchandisers, etc. And so then, there is the sales staff. Who are they? How can one describe their backgrounds, education, experiences? How well are they able to relate to this mythical luxury clientele?

There is no one way to describe who works in a luxury store because for every example one could give, there are exceptions. What binds together the disparate group is hard to define, since to use education, class, gender or sexual orientation, religion, ethnicity, age, work history, as examples, would yield a broad aggregate. There is nothing to really bind salespersons into one group. To look more closely at what the work requires, one would list good communication skills, strong sales skills, empathy, a healthy work ethic, robust physical endurance, mental fortitude, emotional maturity, emotional intelligence, a sense of fair play, resilience, self-confidence, a passion and appreciation for material goods, outstandingly good taste (which matches the definition of the brand(s) one sells) discretion, diplomacy, and tact. That would be a wish list, but it perhaps sums up what the job requires at the highest levels, and being a wish list, not every salesperson is going to be endowed equally with the "proper" amount of each, but when management finds someone who at least in the interview hits these marks sufficiently, the candidate becomes the employee, becomes the colleague.

Most sellers of luxury goods do not come from wealth or privilege. In the United States, most come from modest backgrounds, and a good many are transplants to New York City from other parts of the country, or are immigrants or the children of immigrants. Some have higher degrees, some do not. Some speak a language other than English, whether by birth or by choice. For the majority this was not the first choice of career. Some of them found that the in-between job, chosen because they had been laid off from another industry in upheaval and needed to make ends meet, became their sole source of income, while others used it as a way to keep body and soul together until they could break in or return to their desired fields. A lot of retail workers live inside dreams dashed or deferred because they could find no other opportunity that promised them a decent return on their time investment. Very few salesmen thought this would be their lifelong career, and morale often was low, especially when new directives from above interfered with or disrupted their known ways of working with and connecting with customers.

There is a general lack of concern on the part of management in developing new sales staff. There is a hope that some divine magic will hover over and descend on new hires, or perhaps there is a misreading of the collegiality of the floor, not quite understanding that the commissioned-sales environment does not foster any sense of teamwork or generosity of spirit toward coworkers, let alone new hires, who are seen as competitors in the fight for the one big sale that would make the day, week, month, or quarter. Helping coworkers to learn their jobs takes time away from selling, and time is money. Making sales takes precedence over any other tasks, so to stop to help another, was unproductive. Most of the training new hires receive in orientation focused heavily on using the register because it was a given that they could sell, but they had to know how to close the sale operationally or else the effort would be lost. Follow-up training was nonexistent in this regard. The only routine training that salesmen did receive was product knowledge, presented by the account executives of the brands themselves and usually early in the day, before store opening. It would often consist of a brief history of the company and an overview of the current season's offerings using current merchandise as examples. They were usually quite helpful and informative and often invigorated sales for the brands but only temporarily.

ACT AND ATTITUDE

Successful salespersons undertake acts to fulfill the purpose of the organization and communicate with the customer, with varying degrees of precision and insight, on what in fact they should spend their money. Indeed they are tasked with giving the customer an effective and appealing rhetoric of motives. In a typical interaction between a salesman and customer, there will be a lot of verbal and nonverbal communication throughout, as each takes his role, but it is the salesman's responsibility to set the tone of eagerness to assist and to create a sense of trust. Even when the customer is uncooperative, the salesman must complete every step of the process with grace and ease if he wants to earn his living. A typical interaction begins with the customer asking for help. Then the salesman asks what is needed and the customer replies. The salesman presents merchandise to fulfill the need, which the customer either rejects or accepts. The customer may ask for the salesman's assistance. During the presentation of goods, the salesman will offer information about the fit, fabric, finish, and brand of the items he is presenting. He will share ideas about styling or how and when to wear the items. The customer will ask to try them on, and the dialogue continues, the customer now deciding on what he will buy. This interaction can be quick or long, depending on a variety of factors, including unsuitability of the goods or misjudgment by the seller as to what he has offered. They conclude the sale by making any alterations with the expert tailor, and then arranging delivery or pickup before ringing up the purchase. The sale is now effectively closed. At this point, the salesman will offer his business card so that the customer can contact him for future shopping. Furthermore, the seller may ask if he can contact the customer with alerts about new deliveries that would interest him if the customer has not already provided this access. Having finished, they will express mutual gratitude and the customer will depart and the seller will repeat this process with each customer throughout his work shift.

Regarding the knowledge a salesman needs to possess to successfully perform his work, we see that attitude embodies this knowledge and expertise, without which one would lack the self-confidence to form appropriate narratives and to convey knowledge through assertions and gestures of certainty. Especially if one works in luxury or high-end fashion retail, he or she must appreciate the skill of the craftsperson who made the product. He or she should also understand the history of the companies whose merchandise he sells, and how especially at the high end, those companies shape the lifestyles – or have been shaped by the lifestyles – of the consumers for whom they are made. Although he may not actively use everything he knows about a product, a line, a company, if he is selling a particular item, it is beneficial to have a lot of product knowledge at his disposal so he can use those features or benefits, as they're called, and use them at will to enhance the appeal of the item, and to close the sale. And to return to the original question, it is important to appreciate fashion from the current perspective, what's happening now, as well as from a historical one. It is tremendously important to understand how men have dressed in the modern era, since there are so many references to earlier periods in even the most conventional lines. A fashion salesman should know how to dress a man for any occasion. Knowing the rules means he can break them or cheat them when he doesn't have what he needs to build that ensemble, or if the customer wants to subvert the norm by substituting or eschewing the conventional. But then again, there are times when the most conventional or most accepted attire requires every element to be correct. A salesman has to be able to navigate this terrain with his customer, who should not know the rules or expectations better than the one selling. Anyone selling fashion, whether as a freelance image consultant, a retail salesman, or a stylist for a delivery service like Mr. Porter, must have a really good eye and a high taste level. Even if the clothing isn't carrying a high price tag, it is vital that the one selling understands how clothing fits on different body types and how brands vary in their esthetics.

A particular type of attitude is expected of the salesman, one which embodies specialized knowledge and one that displays human skills and the ability to connect well with others. Due to the interpersonal and intimate nature of having conversations about dressing, and assisting in this process, emotions are involved. Customers expect salesmen to be experts about clothing, and experts must understand their subjects – in this case clothing and people – deeply. The consequences of making a wrong choice are significant for the customer. Dressing, and more importantly dressing well, is an emotional endeavor. Even when someone says he doesn't care about how he dresses, he actually does. He just may need some guidance, and that is why he trusts his salesman.

Adeel, a specialist salesman in tailored menswear, speaks of building trusting relationships with customers. He says he has customers for 20 years whose wardrobes he knows in his head. He says that "there is an art to selling" and that you have to use "romance" to sell.

There are various types of customers, and salesmen would concur that the language of selling is much more complex than imagined by management, which reveals in various ways that it is not aware of such complexity. Different types of consumers have different purposes in relation to their shopping and purchasing objectives, and indeed they display corresponding diverse attitudes. These attitudes can be enhanced or suppressed depending on the communication style and disposition of a salesperson. The salesman must ascertain what a customer wants and needs and for what purpose. He must be able to match that information to merchandise that is available and suited to this purpose. A salesman has to get the customer to want and need the merchandise. Even if the customer came in knowing what he wanted, the item has to match his or her vision, his or her conception, or exceed it. The salesman helps that along by knowing as deeply as he can about what he is selling and communicating all that knowledge to his client. And he has to understand his client, both as a type who would shop at his store and as an individual who has unique needs and desires.

Adeel describes his own purpose as "old school." The careful attention he provides comes from the "merchant" approach to selling which he contrasts with the "new school" "banker's" approach.

> Merchants come from sales. They know goods and fabrics. If two customers call they know how to deal with both. It's unfortunate today, they don't teach this. They train salesmen to get immediate satisfaction.

Andrew demonstrates confidence in his level of expertise and selling ability which enables him to communicate a purpose:

> I go to clients' offices and when I tell them what to buy, they buy it. $25,000 in sales. They blindly accept. I deliver accordingly.

In this example we see an instance where a salesman clearly exerts dominance over his client, and takes pride in being able to do so, but where he returns this honor extended to him by providing his client with exceptional service.

THE ACT OF THE SELL AND DISPLAY OF THE ATTITUDE

The salesperson becomes the agent representing luxury in a broad sense, representing the store he works in, and the brands sold in that store. The salesman is charged to address an ideal type clientele, the image of which has been formulated by the store and transmitted to the salesperson. In doing so he creates a rhetorical environment where the objectives of the store, as well as his own goals and interpretations, are put into play in various ways. The environment within which these words and actions take place is symbolically staged in the expectation of eliciting responses from the customer (emotions, reasoning, actions) which culminate in a purchase.

To successfully perform these acts of salesmanship, the agent must display a rhetorically wise attitude. Mary Godwyn points to the emotional labor required by salespersons who must produce "faked smiles" and exaggerated greetings to connect with their customers (2011, p. 503). Certain expressions of empathy, enthusiasm, and excitement convey an attitude that is particular to the luxury selling environment. At the luxury store we are discussing, salesmen are expected to know how to speak to customers. The expectation is that one is seasoned enough to come up with his own discourse. At the Gap, which is not a luxury store, salespersons are provided with a script consisting of four questions which must be posed.

The salesperson–customer relationship is a dialectical one with inherent oppositional elements and unequal power. The vocabularies which emerge and which are employed will reflect these disparities. A certain show of deference and submissive demeanor is required, a recognition that the customer is of higher status which is indeed the case. A salesman should not be "chummy" or overly familiar. Telling an off-colored joke or making a political assertion while not knowing the customer well enough to know what side of the political spectrum he is on would be inappropriate. Speaking in too casual a way would show a lack of necessary deference; for example, one wouldn't use a term like "no problem" in response to a request from the customer. Nevertheless the interaction between the customer and the salesman is characterized by certain contradictions: The customer is definitely of higher status but the salesperson possesses knowledge about the product and both its economic value and social power and will seek to influence or even make demands upon the customer, who may feel vulnerable about his appearance. Such situations call for a certain delicacy in the acts of the salesman and the attitude he may safely display without alienating the customer.

Salesmen spoke of being asked why they were "still working as a salesman" after having been there for a length of time. It was assumed that if one was accomplished he would not stay in this role indefinitely. Certainly he could not have chosen this as a career. If you are only as good as your last sale – which is sadly how most managers in retail think of their staff and most salesman themselves internalize this way of thinking – then what value do salesmen have outside of selling, especially if they are not seen as capable of doing anything else?

Insofar as salesmen embody the brand and stand proxy for consumers, this scenario only works if there exists a trust from the consumer's standpoint that the person standing before them, as a seller and representative of the brand, can achieve this. There is a certain framework in the sales situation and in the conversation that ensues. Within each interaction there is a degree of predictability and yet the possibility for variation. A salesman must put the customer at ease from the first moment. The customer should be made to feel welcomed, appreciated, and important. At no point should he feel pressured to spend his money or that his presence is a burden to the seller. The sale begins with a greeting. This acknowledgment of the customer's presence must happen within a very brief window, almost immediately. Even if the salesman is preoccupied with some other task or another customer, he should make some gesture or show awareness, say something to address the moment and the person. This is not selling, it is service and it is setting up the tone of the sale. A lot of salesmen will greet a customer and step back, giving him time to breathe, to browse, to look around. Customers don't appreciate pushy salesmen, even when they are in a hurry. Since every situation is unique, it is the salesman's responsibility to assess the customer's behavior and body language to determine the immediacy of action. Knowing when to offer assistance and when to give some space to the customer is crucial. If the customer is clearly in a hurry or looking to be assisted, the salesman would step in more readily than if the signals were clear that he is simply looking or needs a moment to settle in before shopping, or is simply browsing. A good salesman keeps his distance but his senses are open, waiting to begin; when the customer is ready he'll signal the salesman, or the salesman will attempt to start the sale, and when the time is right, they will begin. Now that he is ready to shop, here begins the dialogue, the conversation, because the only way a salesman can know what a customer wants is to learn it firsthand. The next step is to ask questions. And to get this information he has to ask open-ended questions, and then listen to the responses, and dig as deep and take as long as he needs, within reason, to get the information he needs. Once he understands the wants and needs of the customer, they can shop together.

This is an example of a common scenario. The salesman is standing in his shop, clearing the merchandise from a previous sale. A man comes in, they greet each other, and make small talk. He seems in a hurry so the salesman asks if this is so. He replies that he is, explaining that he needs a size small navy blue cashmere V neck sweater from a particular label. He's made it easy, giving the salesman everything he needs to know. The salesman responds that he no longer has this item; the customer insists that he saw it in the store last month. Yes, the seller will reply, but we've sold out. Could the seller double-check to be sure. While he knows it is sold out he agrees to check. He returns to say unfortunately the item is truly sold out. Perhaps they discuss it and the customer admits he has been searching for it online and at another store. The customer and seller are facing a dilemma: the customer and the seller do not wish that the customer leave empty-handed. What he does next is to offer an alternative, but he needs to know which of the seven variables that describe the item are negotiable and nonnegotiable: size, color, material, style, type of item, label, and price. Any of them could be substituted or none of them could. But with a can-do spirit and a good working knowledge of the stock he has on hand, the salesman can offer suggestions that might satisfy the customer's request. They go exploring. The seller presents items that may interest the customer and the customer makes his own discoveries until they hit upon the perfect item. It meets enough of the criteria to satisfy his needs (but may be wholly different from what he wanted at the start). The sale is closed. He rings up the item to be gift wrapped and sent, the customer pays, they express mutual gratitude, and say goodbye. Hardly complicated, but a typical interaction. Hopefully, it was a pleasant experience for the customer. The salesman wants repeat business and if he impressed the customer with diligence, honesty, and integrity, he should see him again. Hopefully, this customer will tell people he knows about the experience, bolstering the good reputation of the store and salesman.

There are classes of consumers in a luxury store, but management does not acknowledge this. There are those who spend a lot of their money, sporadically, seasonally, on full-priced goods. They don't return a lot and tend to be fairly loyal to their salesmen, having established a working relationship. These are a minority of customers. There are those who will shop around and wait to see what happens to stick around on the rails until the markdowns – the sales – have begun. They will pester salesmen with the same questions over three to six months, they will visit and try on the coveted items over the course of a season, they will declare their love and need for it, and swear to purchase it the moment the price is reduced. And then ask when the next markdown will be and how much with tax the bill would be. The salesman may never make this sale stick, since the delaying customer may purchase it, only to return it another day, saying it didn't fit or it just wasn't suitable for some other vague reason. He promises to return next season, at which point the seller can only hope that this is also a lie. The single most dreaded question anyone can ask a salesman, especially in a commissioned-sales environment, is what the company return policy is. It gives the salesman, unless he truly is selfless, a very bad feeling that he is working essentially for nothing while at the same time is feeling the pressure to make his numbers, lest he gets fired for lack of productivity, and he can scarcely afford to pay for his lunch, let alone the rent. One can see how this question is unfair to him, and he is obliged to allow for returns, since his company may accept them. This is especially so when selling to stylists who are notorious for returning goods after an event or a photo shoot.

DEFINING SCENES

These agents work in well-constructed scenes which have been arranged to support the claim that this firm is a special, indeed a luxurious one, scenes that enable the agents to fulfill the purposes of the firm. Customers enter a visually refined environment where the tone is quite different from a nonluxury environment. Customers expect undivided attention from salespersons and indeed can use the services of the store's personal shoppers. Tailored clothing can be altered on the premises and purchases delivered. On occasion a salesman may visit someone in his home or office – even abroad; for example, one salesman traveled to Paris to fit a customer for several suits, and then went on to Cannes to fit his son. There are areas where customers can be attended to privately and they can be served a drink or even a meal. There is a restaurant in the store and customers can be provided with a complementary meal. Even a customer buying one item will not find himself or herself standing in line or bustling against other customers. This is due to the conscious arrangement of space and indeed due to the fact that merchandise is of high quality with only a few items of each type displayed on the floor. Customer expectations are high and one-on-one attention of a formal type is provided. It is into this symbolically rich scene that salespersons enter, fitting themselves with expertise in their field as well as a polished appearance, demeanor, and rhetoric, into an organizational structure and culture that bespeaks luxury.

There are some basic assumptions made about who shops and who sells in the luxury retail environment, perhaps driven by the images the brands or retail establishments that purvey these goods wish to create. The brands use marketing to convey images of super wealthy and elite consumers who can afford to buy the merchandise and price the goods in their wholesale and retail outlets so that they are out of reach of the majority of consumers. Further, the items are designed with a set number of body types in mind, hoping to capture this particular segment of the market.

There are also some baseline assumptions about where their customers live, where they vacation, how they live, what they do for a living and in their activities in their leisure time. This is all in aid of creating the impression or illusion, depending on the consumer, that he or she is part of an elite group who lives a refined life.

Like all brands along the spectrum, the manufacturers and stores wish to build a loyal, devoted base of customers to sustain them, and cultivate the next generation of consumers every 10 to 20 years with a radical shift in design or marketing, sloughing off the old in favor of the young. Paradoxically, they will adhere to old modes of dress or maintain the assertion that particular categories, say men's tailored clothing, remain relevant when it has been obvious that most men are no longer, even at the higher echelons, interested in these goods, save for specific occasions, and have foregone this mode in search of a more casual or less formal way of dressing. In response, the luxury brands took on lifestyle marketing, striving to dress the targeted market at any time of day and for any occasion. This has expanded the definition of what luxury is in terms of the range of merchandise offered and for multibrand stores to carry a larger selection of goods to cater to aspirational consumers as well as the elite, wealthy clientele. By adopting a more democratic assortment over the last 15 years, they have tried to enlarge their market share by appealing to those who can afford to shop frequently at full price (but who may opt not to do so) and those who rely on sales or cash in hand to make purchases that give them the appearance of having arrived.

THE AGENCIES OF THE SELL

Salesmen see themselves first and foremost as professionals. Interviews with salesmen revealed a desire by the salesmen to assert a professional identity, and to establish oneself as someone who possesses expertise, a high degree of knowledge about fashion and style, knowledge about brands, about quality and craftsman-ship, a level of taste that required cultivation over time, and a desire to establish the seriousness of the work that they perform and the difficult nature that this type of selling – not comparable to other types of selling at lesser establishments – entail. Andrew referring to this store being at the apex of the luxury continuum explains that: "some people are not cut out for it." He says that one needs a "certain character and personality" to sell luxury at this level. "It's not easy," he explains "to convince men to buy $5,000 suits or $25,000 coats." We see in this statement from Ferree, an assertion of agency: "I'm not mean but I tell men directly. I want the product to sell and to get bonuses and more merchandize. I will pick and choose how I do it."

Ferree reveals another reality which may have made these men feel they had to begin with a strong endorsement of the importance of their profession: a feeling of insecurity. Unlike these salesmen, women who were interviewed in this line of work were not insistent on establishing themselves as professionals at the highest level in a field nor did they tend to argue that the field of selling was not receiving the regard it deserved. They more often began by speaking of an interest in working with people, and an interest in fashion, as the factors leading them to the sales profession. Enjoying their work and finding it challenging and rewarding characterized women's descriptions of luxury sales. Salesmen often connected selling to the work they performed in the corporate world, discussing how their knowledge of finance and marketing related to luxury selling. Adeel explained that he sold complex financial instruments which were more relevant to his current work than working as "a clerk at the Gap" would have been. Some salesmen made a point of drawing parallels between their own backgrounds and accomplishments and their customers'. Adeel says that he too traveled the world and achieved recognition in his corporate career prior to becoming a salesperson. "I speak five languages. It's very easy for me. I use my education, language, management skills, and diplomacy." He continues to say "I am this client. I know it." He says there are only five or six places where one can work at his level and being in this universe requires that one has built networks. Some spoke of earning high salaries while others highlighted cultural knowledge and engagement which put them on par with their customers. Those in men's tailored chose this profession and worked their way up to the level they attained. This did not preclude having an advanced degree that would have allowed one to work in another occupation. There was a resentment toward management for not respecting the work salesmen do as there was for those customers who looked down upon or otherwise dismissed the skills, abilities, and knowledge they possessed.

Some salesmen went further than condemning corporate culture. While speaking out is a form of resistance, there were instances where salesmen defied corporate directives. Paul said that he "fights against" the way corporate demands he does his work. When a selling day was planned without his input he decided to scrap the announcements he was told to send to his customers. He canceled his vacation and decided to create his own announcement which he knew would resonate well with his customers.

> I planned a photo shoot (he proudly shows the photos of the different looks). It took 9 hours to put this together. I did a collage. I went to the basement to get a satellite rack. I was in trouble

for this. But once they saw the numbers they changed their minds. Now they want to take my ideas. We are professionals and we can make critical decisions. They hover over us like a dark cloud.

Paul explains that he feels empowered to actively resist at times because of his sales numbers and because "Mine is the number 1 vendor on the floor so I can say what I want."

CONCLUSION

Selling luxury fashion can be seen as an intentional act by a self-conscious agent, and as such a form of agency. For the agent, this act fulfills a purpose, displays varying attitudes which can be shaped within the interactional context, and reveals social indicators such as status and group membership, whether actual or desired. Before individual customers can use luxury to make claims about their social position, etc., brands and their purveyors, acting as agents, must create and present these systems of meaning to a global audience.

In considering how salespersons present and explain their actions and purposes to others, we must recognize that they operate within motivational frameworks, or particular grammars which are defined in part by the goals of the stores in which they work, and those connected to the brands carried by that store. A sales vocabulary or a grammar is mediated by the acts, agency, and attitudes of customers. Motives take a variety of forms and they are performed in ways which make use of symbols, particular rhetorical strategies and gestures, selected or rejected based on suitability. Management adopts a rhetoric based on profit and makes decisions to enhance this objective, issuing directives from above. We see that certain forms of knowledge and expertise allow for attitudes that are brought about and enhanced by such an experience. A salesperson who lacks a depth of knowledge and who does not possess cultural capital pertaining to his or her domain will execute a less than stellar performance. One who is particularly skilled and successful will at times be able to exert dominant attitudes with his customers and with management. The customer has his or her own perspective and purpose, which might contradict those of the salesperson; for example, customers who are intent on returning merchandise after wearing it. The luxury world is one in which we find complex characters, plots, staging, and indeed an interested and active audience. This research provides some insight into a particular reality and captures some essential points defining the important role that salespersons play within the luxury retail environment in a consumer-oriented society.

NOTE

1. In the recent past Christopher Ferree worked as a salesman for many years in the department store we discuss in this chapter.

REFERENCES

Athens, L. 2015. *Domination and Subjugation in Everyday Life*, New Brunswick, NJ, Transaction.

Burke, K. 1968. Dramatism. In *The International Encyclopedia of the Social Sciences*, Ed. D. L. Sills, pp. 445–452, New York, NY, Macmillan.

Burke, K. 1969a. *A Grammar of Motives*, Berkeley, CA, University of California Press.

Burke, K. 1969b. *A Rhetoric of Motives*, Berkeley, CA, University of California Press.

Clapp, T. L. 2009. Social identity as grammar and rhetoric of motives: citizen housewives and Rachel Carson's Silent Spring, *Kenneth Burke Journal*, 15, Spring. Available at: http://www.kbjournal.org/tara_clapp

Godwyn, M. 2011. Using emotional labor to create and maintain relationships in service interactions, *Symbolic Interaction*, 29(4), 487–506.

Gusfield, J. 1989. The bridge over separated lands: Kenneth Burke's significance for the study of social action. In *The Legacy of Kenneth Burke*, Eds H. Simons and T. Malia, pp. 28–54, Madison, WI, The University of Wisconsin Press.

Mead, G. H. 1934. *Mind, Self, and Society from the Standpoint of a Social Behaviorist*, Chicago, IL, The University of Chicago Press.

Peretz, H. 1995. Negotiating clothing identities on the sales floor, *Symbolic Interaction*, 18(1), 19–37.

Perinbanayagam, R. 2000. *The Presence of Self*, Lanham, MD, Rowman & Littlefield Publishers, Inc.

Perinbanayagam, R. 2011. *Discursive Acts: Language, Signs, and Selves*, 2nd ed., New Brunswick, NJ, Transaction Publishers.

Perinbanayagam, R. 2016. *The Rhetoric of Emotions: A Dramatistic Exploration*, New Brunswick, NJ; London, Transaction Publishers.

Scott, W. R. 1992. *Organizations: Rational, Natural, and Open Systems*, 3rd ed., Englewood Cliffs, NJ, Prentice-Hall.

Stone, G. P. 1969. Appearance and the self. In *Social Psychology through Symbolic Interaction*, Eds G. P. Stone and H. A. Farberman, pp. 394–414, Waltham, MA, Ginn-Blaisdell.

INDEX